1143

SCOTLAND IN MODERN TIMES

By the same author

A HISTORY OF SCOTLAND

Volume I. The Foundations of Scotland:
TO 1286.

Volume II. Robert Bruce King of Scots:
1286-1329.

Volume III. The Rise of the Stewarts: 1329-1513.

Volume IV. The Scotland of Queen Mary
and the Religious Wars: 1513-1638.

Volume V. The Passing of the Stewarts:
1638-1748.

Volume VI. Scotland in Modern Times:
1720-1939.

THE KINGDOM OF SCOTLAND

A Short History.

SCOTLAND IN
MODERN TIMES

1720-1939

BY

AGNES MURE MACKENZIE
M.A., D.Litt.

W. & R. CHAMBERS, LTD.
38 SOHO SQUARE, LONDON, W. 1; AND EDINBURGH
1942

First Published 1941
Reprinted . . 1942

Printed in Great Britain by T. and A. CONSTABLE LTD.
at the University Press, Edinburgh

TO

THE STAFF OF THE BRITISH MUSEUM LIBRARY

AND OF

THE LONDON PUBLIC SERVICES

AND

A LONDON BUTCHER, BAKER, GROCER, GREENGROCER,

MILKMAN, AND COAL MERCHANT

WHO BY CARRYING ON THROUGH OVER FIVE HUNDRED AIR-RAIDS

MADE IT POSSIBLE FOR THE AUTHOR TO WRITE THIS BOOK

IT IS DEDICATED

WITH GRATITUDE AND RESPECT

AND THE HOPE THAT SOME DAY

THEIR GREAT COUNTRY AND OUR OWN

WILL ACHIEVE A RELATION MORE WORTHY OF THEM BOTH

There is an omission of part of modern history which . . . is worse than the omission of the whole. . . . When we observe how history is liable to repeat itself, and that in dealing with Scotsmen we must expect them to be made in the same mould as their predecessors, it seems one of those mistakes which are worse than crimes for a native of Scotland to ignore the history of his country.

> Archibald Philip Primrose, Fifth Earl of Rosebery, in a
> Rectorial Address at Aberdeen University in 1880.

Tradition may be an inspiring thing or a dangerous thing. It is inspiring if it goads as a spur. It is dangerous if it lulls as a soporific. One often hears the comment, ' Oh, the Navy is all right.' The Navy will not be all right unless we make it right and keep it so.

> Geoffrey Shakespeare, Parliamentary Secretary to the Admiralty
> in the House of Commons, 16th March 1939.

It is safe to say that the soundness of politics today will depend on our knowledge of the politics of the past. A statesman who does not know how [Scotland] came to be what she is will have a very bad influence on [Scotland] as she is to be. . . . And we are all statesmen in a small way. If we neglect history we shall choose bad Members of Parliament, and bad Members of Parliaments will choose bad Prime Ministers in bad Cabinets.

> E. E. KELLETT, *Aspects of History*.

PREFACE

WHICH IS ALSO AN EPILOGUE

The chapter on Waterloo . . . fell to my own share. Though I did my best to arrive at exact truth, I cannot conscientiously declare that it would satisfy patriotic Dutch or German readers. In sober fact, it is impossible to write history, save in the most arid form of annals, which will satisfy everyone, whatever his race or creed.

Sir CHARLES OMAN, *On the Writing of History.*

GENERAL histories in several volumes are not uncommon, but the form of this one is rather unusual, and may call for a word of explanation. For several reasons, my publisher and I decided to make each volume self-contained. This decision proved to possess the great advantage that to each of these separate volumes could be given the literary form its contents required. Thus the first volume is a broadly-drawn picture of the origin and shaping of a nation, the second a 'Life and Times,' the third a sequence of these on a smaller scale, while the fourth and the fifth (which are the most closely connected) describe the rise, the progress, and the conclusion of a long-drawn conflict of parties within the nation. This sixth has been forced to a different form again. What form was indeed very difficult to decide, for a reason that is rather interesting. In any narrative writing, the first requirement, when one comes to put the story on to paper, is to choose the stance from which one best may perceive the pattern and significance of the action. For five volumes this position had chosen itself. Without having consciously to think of it, I had naturally looked at my subject-matter from the point of view of the men who governed the nation and were responsible for its safety and welfare. (This does not mean that I always approved of their actions: but it means that I was in the best position to see, and show, the problems they had to face, and the factors involved in their success or failure.) When I came to lay out the plan for this volume, however, I found myself at once in difficulties. As in all the rest, there was perceptible a broad general pattern—in this case revival followed by decay, and at last the first stirrings of revival again: but there was no natural stance from which to see it. I wrestled with the problem for some days before I realised that what was lacking was the thing that had centralised the other volumes and focussed the intricate pattern of their story. That is, there was no national government from whose position I could look at the nation. There was no central point of reference to give unity to the crowding mass of event.

A narrative lacking such a central point is bound to lack organic unity. There was, to be sure, the abstract idea of *Scotland*, which certainly had been (whether she frowned or smiled) behind the concrete figures who came and went in the position of a Government: but though that idea might give unity to the theme, it could not give organic form to the subject. Accordingly, I found myself in the position of having to choose, in method, between two evils. I could handle my tangled and shapeless mass of material by putting down facts in their chronological order, which would certainly be simple for myself, but was likely to be less so for the reader, who would soon lose all that sense of cause and effect which is the neural structure of history: or I could divide it, as it were, by topics, considering one element after another, and tracing its development by itself, at the risk of disturbing the reader's sense of time by the constant returns that the method would involve.

The latter seemed to be the lesser evil. I have tried to minimise it as much as I could by making the major divisions of the book on a chronological basis, at turning dates—1789, 1832, 1914 ; by grouping connected topics as far as I could ; and by relating and comparing them. But no one can be more conscious than myself (since no one but myself has written the book) of the difficulties such a plan involves. I could, of course, have overcome most of them by writing a different kind of history—a generalised survey of 'tendencies.' In the hands of an author capable of wit, such a book would be far more readable than this. But it would be also a great deal less useful in providing a reasonably detailed background for the 'close-up' picture of a specialised study.

There are many such studies concerning this period, and many of them are most thorough and scholarly work. If far too many of those most worth attention have failed to find the public they deserve, it is largely, I think, because the Scottish public possesses no general survey of the period to which the specialised work can be related. The neglect is more than a pity: it is a danger. We have Scotland's future history to shape, and the need to shape it with intelligence has never been more acute than it is today. We cannot shape it unless we know the past. All of our past is relevant to our future, but that part of it which has most immediate bearing is precisely that of which most Scots know least—that is to say, the last two hundred years.

While I have, like all reasonably normal adults, a sense of values in conduct, I have tried in presenting any contest within the nation to let the opposing parties speak for themselves, and as far as possible in their own words. In this volume, the crowding pressure upon space has compelled me to less quotation than in the rest: but I have tried to show the different points of view, whether or not I agree with them myself, and to give their case with at least a certain justice. As my previous work has been variously described as that of a writer Tory, Socialist, Catholic, Episcopalian, Presbyterian, anti- all these, anti-English and pro-English, aggressively Nationalist and anti-Scots, mediaeval and ultra-modern in her outlook, it would seem that I have to some extent succeeded. At least I have written my country's history taking the facts as I found them in my road, seeking neither to gild nor to minimise her shame nor—as is more the fashion of late years—to blacken or to minimise her glories. If the result can serve her, I am content.

I am indebted to Sir Alexander MacEwen and Mr R. E. Muirhead for the kind loan of valuable out-of-print and unpublished material; to Sir John Orr, Sir James Caw, Major Mackay Scobie of the National Naval and Military Museum, and Mr J. J. Davidson of the Health Department for their trouble in answering importunate questions; to Mr John Mackay for the maps and jacket; and as through all this History, to my publishers, without whom the work would never have been begun, and certainly could not have been carried through.

HIGHGATE, *July*, 1941.

CONTENTS

		PAGE
PREFACE - - - - - - - - - -		vii
CHRONOLOGY - - - - - - - - -		xiii

I. SPRING: 1720–89

CHAPTER

I. THE SITUATION - - - - - - -		3
II. THE SITUATION IS FACED: I - - - -		9
III. THE SITUATION IS FACED: II - - - -		27
IV. THE HIGHLAND TRANSITION - - - -		39
V. THE CHURCH STANDS BACK - - - -		47
VI. SLEEPING PARTNERSHIP - - - - -		52
VII. THE DISTANT SCENE - - - - - -		58
VIII. THE RETURN OF POLITICS - - - -		72

II. SUMMER: 1789–1832

IX. SUNSHINE IN PRINCES STREET - - - -		81
X. TOWARDS RELIGIOUS FREEDOM - - -		90
XI. MEN AND MACHINES - - - - - -		96
XII. MACHINES AND MEN - - - - - -		107
XIII. THE RIGHTS OF MAN - - - - - -		116
XIV. BRITAIN AND A DICTATOR - - - -		125
XV. THE VOTE ONCE MORE - - - - -		143

III. AUTUMN: 1832–1914

XVI. PROGRESS: THE SURFACE - - - - -		155
XVII. PROGRESS: THE UNDERSIDE - - - -		170
XVIII. THE CHURCHES - - - - - - -		176

CONTENTS

CHAPTER   PAGE

XIX. THE MIND OF SCOTLAND: I - - - - 187

XX. THE MIND OF SCOTLAND: II - - - - 197

XXI. HOME POLITICS: I—The Framework - - - 212

XXII. HOME POLITICS: II—The Content - - - 243

XXIII. HOME POLITICS: III—The Vacancy - - - 260

XXIV. BEYOND THE MARCHES: I—The Empire - - 269

XXV. BEYOND THE MARCHES: II—Europe - - - 283

IV. WINTER: 1914–39

XXVI. MARTINMAS WIND - - - - - - 303

XXVII. AFTER THE STORM - - - - - - 320

XXVIII. HOME POLITICS - - - - - - - 337

XXIX. NOISES OFF - - - - - - - - 350

XXX. BRAIRD - - - - - - - - - 370

APPENDIX I: The Battle Honours of the Scottish Regiments 394

APPENDIX II: Racialism and Nationalism - - - 397

BIBLIOGRAPHY - - - - - - - - - 399

INDEX - - - - - - - - - - 404

MAPS

NAPOLEON'S EMPIRE - - - - - - - 132

THE SETTLEMENT OF 1815 - - - - - - 284

EUROPE IN 1914 - - - - - - - - 298

THE SETTLEMENT OF 1919 - - - - - - 358-9

CHRONOLOGY

The purpose of this list is less to give a summary of events in Scotland than to fit these into the frame of events in Europe. Dates of British and English events before 1751 are given in Scottish reckoning, counting 1st January as the beginning of the year.

1720. Monroe in Edinburgh. *South Sea Bubble.*

1721. Walpole head of Ministry. *Montesquieu's 'Lettres persanes.'*

1723. Agricultural Society.

1724. 'Tea-table Miscellany.' 'Evergreen.'

1725. Malt Riots. Disarming Act.

1726. Potatoes introduced. Wade's roads begun. 'Winter.'

1727. Death of George I. Accession of George II. War with Austria and Spain. Board of Manufactures. Royal Bank. *Diderot begins 'L'Encyclopédie.'*

1729. Hutcheson in Glasgow. School of St Luke.

1731. Treaty of Vienna.

1734. *Voltaire's 'Lettres anglaises.'*

1736. Porteous Riots. Ramsay's Theatre.

1739. War with Spain. 'Treatise of Human Nature.' Long nan Duine.

1740. *Accession of Frederick II. Invasion of Silesia.* War of Austrian Succession. Secession of Associate Synod. *'Pamela.'*

1741. The Foulises take over Glasgow University Press.

1742. Fall of Walpole.

1743. Dettingen.

1745. Fontenoy. Jacobite Rising. Prestonpans.

1746. Falkirk. Culloden. Cumberland in Highlands. Secretaryship for Scotland abolished. Disarming Act. Act against Highland Dress. Further Penal Laws against Episcopalians.

1747. Abolition of hereditary jurisdictions.

1748. Further Penal Laws against Episcopalians. Treaty of Aix la Chapelle. 'Roderick Random.' 'Enquiry concerning Human Understanding.' *'L'Esprit des lois.'*

1750. *Rousseau's 'Discours sur les lettres.'*

1751. *Reform of English Calendar.* Arcot.

1752. Act for the Improvement of the Highlands.

1754. Death of James Gibbs. Pitt Prime Minister.

1756. Alliance of Britain and Prussia. Seven Years War.

1757. Plassey. Convention of Klosterseven. Death of Allan Ramsay.

1759. Minden. Quiberon Bay. Quebec.

1760. Death of George II. Accession of George III. Carron Ironworks. MacPherson's 'Ossian.'

1761. Pondicherry. Bute Prime Minister.

1762. *Le Contrat social.*

1763. Resignation of Bute. Nor'loch drained. France cedes Canada.

1764. Buxar.

1765. Stamp Act. Watt invents the condenser.

1766. Death of James Francis Edward.

1767. *Invention of spinning jenny.* American Import Duties Act.

1768. *First voyage of Captain Cook.* Dredging of Clyde begun.

1769. Watt's steam-engine. New Edinburgh begun. Fenwick Co-operative Society.

1770. Repeal of American duties, except tea.

1771. Cramond steel-works. 'Man of Feeling.' Birth of Scott.

1773. Boston Tea-Party.

1774. First American Congress. *Death of Louis XV. Accession of Louis XVI.*

1775. American War. Dundas Lord Advocate. Act to relieve bound colliers and salters.

1776. Declaration of American Independence. Death of Hume. 'Wealth of Nations.'

1778. France enters war. *Deaths of Voltaire and Rousseau.* Death of the elder Pitt. *Relief of English Catholics.* Cotton spun at Rothesay.

1779. Spain enters war. Siege of Gibraltar. Anti-Catholic Riots. Rotary steam-engine.

1780. Cape St Vincent. *League of Armed Neutrality.* Holland enters war. Death of Alasdair MacMhaighstir Alasdair.

1781. Surrender of Yorktown.

1782. American independence acknowledged. Les Saintes. Repeal of Act against Highland Dress.

1783. Treaty of Versailles. Glasgow Chamber of Commerce founded. Foundation in Aberdeen of Episcopal Church of America.

1784. Pitt's India Act. Highland Society founded. Royal Burghs demand Reform.

1785. Pitt's Parliamentary Reform Bill.

1786. Commercial Treaty with France.

1787. *Invention of power-loom.*

1788. Death of Charles Edward.

1789. *French Revolution.*

1790. Death of Adam Smith.

1791. *French Constitution.*

1792. *French Invade Belgium.* Friends of the People. Penal Laws against Episcopalians repealed. Death of Robert Adam.

1793. *Execution of Louis XVI. Terror.* France declares war. First Coalition. Trial of Muir. Alexander Mackenzie crosses Canada.

1794. Volunteers. Act against Wrongous Imprisonment suspended.

1795. Capture of Cape and Ceylon. *Directory in France.*

1796. French attack in Ireland. War with Spain. *Bonaparte in Italy.* Death of Burns.

1797. Cape St Vincent. Camperdown. *Treaty of Campo Formio.* Militia Act.

1798. *Bonaparte in Egypt.* Nile. *'Lyrical Ballads.'*

1799. Second Coalition. Acre. *Bonaparte First Consul.*

1800. *Marengo.* Combinations Act.

1801. Union with Ireland. Copenhagen. Alexandria. Population 1,608,000.

1802. Treaty of Amiens. Mahratta War. 'Edinburgh Review.' 'Minstrelsy of the Scottish Border.' S.S. Charlotte Dundas. Peel's Factory Act.

1803. War with France. Assaye.

1804. War with Spain. *Napoleon Emperor.* Threat of invasion.

1805. Third Coalition. Finisterre. Trafalgar. *Austerlitz.*

1806. Death of the younger Pitt, and of Fox. Baird captures Cape. Acquittal of Melville. *Jena.* Berlin Decrees. *End of Holy Roman Empire.*

1807. *Treaty of Tilsit.* Death of Henry Benedict. Fishery Commission.

1808. *Napoleon in Spain.* Vimiero.

1809. Corunna. Talavera. Walcheren. Basque Roads.

1810. Busaco.

1811. Prince of Wales Regent. Fuentes d'Onoro. Albuera.

1812. Cuidad Rodrigo. Badajoz. War with United States. *Napoleon in Russia.* Salamanca. S.S. Comet. Death of Duncan Bàn Macintyre.

1813. Fourth Coalition. Pyrenees. *Leipzig.*

1814. Toulouse. *Abdication of Napoleon. Restoration of Louis XVIII.* Treaty of Paris. Congress of Vienna. 'Waverley.'

1815. Hundred Days. Waterloo. Second Treaty of Paris. New Corn Law. Quadruple Alliance.

1816. *Machine riots in England.*

1819. Death of James Watt. Radical War. Birth of Queen Victoria.

1820. Death of George III. Accession of George IV. Trial of Queen. 'The Provost.'

1823. *Monroe Doctrine.* Death of Raeburn.

1824. Repeal of Combinations Acts.

1825. Attack on pound note. *Stockton-Darlington Railway.* First Factory Act.

1826. Monkland-Kirkintilloch Railway. '*Poems by Two Brothers.*'

1828. Hot-blast furnace.

1829. Catholic Emancipation. Religious freedom in Scotland.

1830. *Revolution in France, Belgium, and Poland.* Death of George IV. Accession of William III and IV. *Louis Philippe King of French.*

1831. Edinburgh-Dalkeith Railway. *Belgium independent.*

1832. First Reform Act. Death of Scott.

1833. Municipal Reform Act. Abolition of slavery. '*Pauline.*'

1834. *English Poor Law Act.* General Assembly's Veto Act.

1835. *English Municipal Reform Act.*

1836. State Grant for Education. '*Sketches by Boz.*'

1837. Death of William III. Accession of Victoria. Hanover separated from Britain. Highland Famine.

1838. Afghan War. Chartist movement. Anti-Corn-Law League. First Scots steamer to cross Atlantic.

1839. First Chinese War.

1840. Marriage of Queen. Penny Post. War in Syria.

1841. Livingstone in Africa.

1842. Glasgow-Edinburgh Railway.

1843. Disruption. Scinde War.

1844. 'Vestiges of Creation.' *Trial of Daniel O'Connell.*

1845. Poor Law Act. First Sikh War. *First iron screw steamer. Irish famine.*

1846. Highland Famine. Repeal of Corn Laws.

1847. Russell's Factory Act. Bank crisis. Anaesthetics. Lord Elgin in Canada.

1848. *Revolution in France, Bohemia, Hungary, and Prussia.* Chartist rising. Second Sikh War. Lord Dalhousie in India.

1849. *Repeal of English Navigation Laws.*

1851. *First submarine cable.* Population 2,888,000.

1852. *Second Empire in France.* Second Burmese War.

1854. Crimean War. Alma. Balaclava. Inkerman.

1855. Sebastopol taken.

1856. Second Chinese War.

1857. Indian Mutiny. Bank crisis. War with Persia.

1858. Universities Commission.

1859. Volunteers. Third Chinese War.

1860. Fusion of Universities of Aberdeen. Antiseptic surgery.

1861. *American Civil War. Italy a kingdom.* Death of Prince Albert Education Department.

1864. *Prusso-Danish War.*

1866. *Austro-Prussian War.*

1867. Commission on Trade Unions. *Das Kapital.* Beginning of federation of Canada.

1868. Second Reform Act. *Queen of Spain expelled.*

1869. Women received municipal franchise.

1870. *Franco-Prussian War.* First Women's Suffrage Bill.

1871. Trade Union Act. *Creation of German Empire.*

1872. Ballot Act. Education Act. School Boards.

1874. *Monarchy restored in Spain.* Ashanti War. First Labour M.P. 'City of Dreadful Night.'

1875. Purchase of Suez Shares.

1876. Graham Bell's telephone.

1878. Factory Act. Congress of Berlin. Bank crisis. 'An Inland Voyage.'

1879. First steel ship on Clyde. Death of Sir James Clerk Maxwell. *Dual Alliance of Austria and Germany.*

1880. University College, Dundee.

1881. *Italy added to Dual Alliance.* Death of Carlyle. Lord Fife demands Scottish Office.

1882. *Serbia a kingdom.* Crofter agitation.

1883. *Death of Karl Marx.* Agricultural Holdings Act.

1884. *Dreikaiserbund.* Third Reform Act.

1885. Redistribution Act. Scottish Office.

2

CHRONOLOGY

1886. Crofters' Holdings Act. Home Rule Association.

1887. First Imperial Conference. Entente with Italy.

1888. *Wilhelm II Kaiser.* Scottish Labour Party. Leaving Certificate.

1889. First (Scottish) Home Rule Debate in Parliament. Universities Commission. County Councils.

1890. *Dismissal of Bismarck.*

1891. *Alliance of France and Russia.* Society of Scottish Artists.

1893. Education free up to fifteen.

1894. *Accession of Czar Nicholas II.* Local Government Act.

1896. Jameson Raid.

1897. *Germany bidding for naval power.* Congested Districts Board.

1898. *Spanish-American War.* Omdurman.

1899. South African War. *Wireless Message across English Channel.* Boxer War in China. Private Legislation Procedure Act.

1900. Australian Commonwealth Act. Union of Free and United Presbyterian Churches. Death of Ruskin.

1901. Death of Victoria. Accession of Edward I and VII. Federation of Australian colonies. Carnegie Trust. Population 4,420,000.

1902. Alliance with Japan.

1903. *First power-driven aeroplane.*

1904. *Russo-Japanese War.* Entente Cordiale. Lords' Decision on Free Church.

1905. *Tangier Incident.* Education Department takes over Normal Colleges.

1906. Conference of Algeciras. Trades Disputes Act. Workmen's Compensation Act.

1907. Treaty with Russia. Income-tax reaches 1s.

1908. Eight-hour day for miners. Old Age Pensions.

1910. Death of Edward I. Accession of George V. *Portugal a republic.*

1911. Parliament Act. Health Insurance Act.

1912. *Balkan War.*

1914. German War. Mons. Marne. First Ypres. Turkey enters war.

1915. Second Ypres. Festubert. Loos. Gallipoli. Italy and Bulgaria enter war.

1916. *Verdun.* Somme. Military Service Act. Jutland. W.R.I. founded.

1917. *Russian Revolution.* America enters war. Vimy. Messines. Third Ypres. Cambrai. Jerusalem.

1918. Fourth Reform Act. *Treaty of Brest-Litovsk.* German offensive. Allied victory. New Home Rule Association.

1919. Peace Treaty. League of Nations. Treaty of Triple Guarantee.
First Atlantic Flight. First Woman M.P. Rowett Institute.

1920. *Germans in Ruhr.* Spa Conference. Government of Ireland
(Partition) Act. Cost of living 135 per cent. of pre-war. Torry
Marine Laboratory.

1921. Cost of living 233 per cent. of pre-war. British Taxation £17
per head: (*German £2, 11s. per head*). *Fascist riots in Florence.*
Trade agreement with Russia. Ultimatum to Germany. Irish
Free State created.

1922. Peace with Ireland. Cost of living 182 per cent. of pre-war.
March on Rome. Lausanne Conference. Railway Act.

1923. *Hitler leader of National Socialists.* Cost of living 169 per cent.
Last Peace Treaty (Turkey). *Mark 19,000 million to £. Munich
putsch.*

1924. *Death of Lenin. France guarantees Czechs. Italo-Jugo-Slav alliance.* Great Britain recognises U.S.S.R. First Labour
Government. National Convention.

1925. Resumption of gold standard. *France at war in Morocco.* Locarno
Conference. Navy reduced.

1926. *German-Soviet Treaty.* General Strike. Seven-month Coal Strike.
Germany enters League.

1927. Army and Air Force reduced. World Economic Conference at
Geneva. Naval Limitation Conference. *Germany repudiates
responsibility for War. Millionth house built in England and
Wales since War.*

1928. *Italo-Turkish Non-aggression Pact. Bolshevik Government buying
foreign wheat.* Kellogg Pact. *Greco-Italian Pact of Friendship.*
National Party of Scotland founded.

1929. Second Labour Government. *New York financial crisis:* 434
banks fail. Re-union of U.F. Church with Establishment.
Local Government Act.

1930. 1326 *U.S. banks fail.* Young Plan. London Naval Conference.
Last allied soldiers off German soil. Macaulay Institute.

1931. *Laval Prime Minister of France. Spain a republic. Deutschland
launched. German economic crisis.* National Government.
Britain off gold. Statute of Westminster. Dundee School of
Economics.

1932. *Russo-Finnish Non-aggression Pact. Oslo Agreement—Scandinavia,
Holland, Belgium, Luxembourg.* Disarmament Conference.
Lausanne Conference. *Nazi majority in Reichstag.*

1933. *Hitler Chancellor of Germany. Japan attacks China. Reichstag
Fire.* 1400 *U.S. banks re-open. Hitler's Peace speech. Austria
bans Nazis. Four-power Pact. Germany leaves League.*

1934. *Germany and Poland sign ten years peace. Riots in Paris.* Work recommenced on S.S. Queen Mary. *Hitler in Venice. Murder of Dollfuss. Hitler Führer.* Agreement on German debts.

1935. *Saar returned to Germany. France lengthens Army service. German Air Force announced. Abyssinia appeals to League.* Stresa Conference. *Germany declares Christianity a danger. Franco-Soviet Pact. German laws against Jews. Italy attacks Abyssinia.* Hoare-Laval Plan.

1936. Death of George V. Accession of Edward II and VIII. *'Guns or butter.' Hitler in Rhineland.* London Naval Treaty. *Spanish Civil War. U.S.S.R., Germany, and Italy promise non-intervention. Berlin-Rome Axis. Anti-Comintern Pact.* Television in Britain. Abdication of Edward II. Accession of George VI. Saltire Society.

1937. *Mussolini attacks democracy. Mussolini appoints himself Protector of Islam. Italian Pact with Yugo-Slavia.* Naval agreements with Germany and Russia. *Sino-Japanese War. Italy leaves League.*

1938. Singapore base opened. *Hitler in Austria. German conscription of workers.* Italian agreement with Britain. First Scottish Folk-School. Glasgow Exhibition. *Hitler in Czecho-Slovakia.* Munich.

1939. *Hitler annexes Czecho-Slovakia. Mussolini annexes Albania.* Scottish Office moved to Edinburgh. Highland Committee Report. *Hitler attacks Poland.* Second German War.

I
SPRING
SIXTY-NINE YEARS: 1720–89

'The frost of the Scottish people melts like a snow-wreath, and the dissolving torrent carries dam and dyke before it.'

Sir WALTER SCOTT, *Guy Mannering*.

I

THE SITUATION

c. 1720

To prevent farder mischieves, whereof there hath been enough.
            Sir WALTER SCOTT, *The Heart of Midlothian.*

IT has long been the custom to end a History of Scotland with
either the 'Forty-five or the Disruption. Yet two centuries have
passed since the former event, and one since the latter. Our
history in that time has not stood still. Nor is it standing still at
the present moment.

The Scotland that we know is the creation of two thousand years
of recorded history, not to speak of long millennia before that; and
every century, every year of that time, has left a print which is
traceable today: but the story of modern Scotland can be said to
date from the 1st of May 1707, when the third of the three Scottish
Revolutions reached its climax by accomplishing the transfer of the
seat of Scottish government to London. There followed a curious
pattern of event, so like in essence to the course of a year that it
is not, perhaps, unduly fanciful to give to the four divisions in which
it falls the names of the seasons. There is spring at first, a gradual
breaking forth of new quickening growth from an apparent hopeless barrenness; then a rich summer of prosperous strong life; an
autumn fruitful indeed, but increasingly with the sense of chilling
sap and shortening light; and then with a violent storm the death
of winter, the smothering of life again in cold and darkness . . .
till suddenly, on a February day, one sees that the bare trees are
flushing with rising sap. And though the harsh lamb-storms the
Border shepherd dreads come after that, and are upon us now, the
year goes on and the fields may be green again, to bring a more
lasting harvest than our fathers'.

Only, there is a condition to that hope. Our fathers' failures
were grave, all but disastrous. Their successes were splendid, and
most honourable. We need to forget neither failure nor success,

3

but to consider the causes of both alike, and to shape our conduct according to that knowledge: for history is not a scholar's game, but the record of what has been done by men and women; and what those who have gone before us have done in the past, we can do, or avoid, for this country of ours today, who has need of all the service that we can give her.

Looking back on history, one can see a pattern of movements that have their beginning and their end. The beginning of one and the end of that before it, however, very rarely coincide. Nearly always they overlap. Such overlapping is very marked in our beginning here. Our 'eighteenth century' begins with the Union: but the age of the long and fierce religious wars which had marked the sixteenth and seventeenth centuries was not truly concluded till 1746 had ended the series of efforts to overthrow the Whig dominance gained in 1689, and the curtain had fallen on the religious conflict with the Penal Laws of 1748.

The story of that long struggle has been told in two earlier volumes of this History. We must concern ourselves now with another, whose first action was lost seven years before the Union, but whose full beginning does not come till after the Jacobite Rising of 1715.

The Presbyterian Establishment secured by William of Orange in 1690 and the subsequent suspension, in 1707, of Scotland's independent political life, were to determine, until the present day, the country's religious and political framework, and strongly to affect many aspects of life. With them came also that change in preoccupations which is marked in all Europe round about 1700. An era of religious wars was passing. In Scotland, most men were deeply weary of it. They stood back from the struggle to contemplate its results, and were, reasonably, appalled by what they saw.

Trade, farming, scholarship, the arts, were a desert. The total amount of money in the country, *before* the Darien crash lost a third of it, is reckoned at fifteen shillings sterling a head. After Darien and the dreadful years of famine that brought farming to ruin round about 1700, one in five of the population was a beggar, dependent on the charity of others who were merely poor without being destitute, but whose poverty in fact was acute and bitter. The thriving, well-governed land of the Alexanders, the kingdom which had won the Three Hundred Years War and recovered from it to a vigorous national life, a conspicuous place in the affairs of Europe, was a derelict province, bled almost to death.

It is not wonderful that some despaired. The men who, against the general will of Scotland, made possible the Treaty of 1707, were not all merely venal, it is clear. Some indeed sold their country for thirty pieces of silver, or as much more, in the way of place and advantage, as they could succeed in drawing to themselves: but others supported them, with more excuse, for a mess of pottage to feed a starving nation—for a share in English transatlantic trade.

Indeed, economic motives were present on both sides. England, of course, had for her central aim (as indeed she avowed very frankly at the time) to secure that political domination of Scotland for which, in the previous nine hundred years, she had poured out a constant stream of blood, gold, and ink: but even in her case there were commercial reasons. Scots trade was chiefly with Holland and with France. England was trying to destroy the trade of France, and she feared lest the Dutch and Scots might succeed in breaking her immensely rich monopolies overseas.

In Scotland the Dutch trade had been gravely injured by the Anglo-Dutch wars of the last two generations: and earlier, the Thirty Years War had ruined the old trade with the Germanies and the Baltic. The only Scots ventures westward had been in Ulster, cut off by the English domination in Ireland, and in Nova Scotia and later Darien, both strangled deliberately to serve England's interests. What England had done, she would certainly do again, nor had Scotland the slightest chance of preventing it. The remainder of trade, with France, was in grave danger, since England was even then going about to wreck it. In the country's helpless and poverty-logged condition, it seemed to the Scottish merchants that the sole course was to identify their interests with England's and thus find a door to the markets of the New World.

There was an ample scope there for both countries. The English colonies, by 1700, were of course no more than a very little fraction of the British Empire as it stands today.[1] Yet still they were of much actual importance, and their potential importance was far greater. At the time of the Union of Crowns,

---

[1] Far their greater part, incidentally, was to be lost within a lifetime of the Treaty of Union, and practically the whole of the present Empire has come into British hands since 1707.

in 1603, England laid claim, if not always very surely, to Newfoundland, Virginia, and New Albion (California), while the newly
established East India Company was beginning to challenge Portugal
in the East. Since then she had founded eleven colonies on the
North American coast of the Atlantic, between the Bay of Fundy
and the Savannah; and though any sort of effective occupation did
not run more than at most two hundred miles inland (about the
distance between Wick and Glasgow), they had an enormous hinterland beyond. She also held certain of the West Indian islands and
small colonies on the Caribbean coast, while also some trading
stations had been established on the Atlantic coast of Africa (whence
the slave trade was very profitable) and in India, that fabulous source
of enormous wealth. And to none of these might any vessel sail,
even from a port in England with English goods, unless at least
two-thirds of her crew were English. Yet the riches of the Indies
were a proverb, the American hinterland inconceivably vast. Thus
a share in these potentialities seemed to the merchants who supported
Union the only possible means of recovering Scotland, since it
appeared to be the only direction where England was certain not to
do again what she had done to the Darien colony.

Union, admittedly, was a desperate remedy: but it seemed to
them the only remedy for an increasingly desperate situation, which
(after all, in the manner of many moderns) they could see only in
economic terms. So they fell in behind Queensberry and Seafield.
The birthright was sacrificed for the mess of pottage: and the
porridge-basin, when it was handed over, was discovered to contain
remarkably little, and that with less meal than became the amount
of salt.

The last of the old European markets had been surrendered.
To reach the new ones hoped for overseas Scots merchants must
join the English companies, who had no intention of offering them
a welcome. Even internal trade had been badly damaged by the
loss not only of Court but of Parliament, which removed those few
who had any great spending power from the capital to one far
outside the March. And all those stipulations in the Treaty which
happened to be of benefit to Scotland were regarded by England
as merely being favours which might be withdrawn whenever it
should please a Parliament in the hands of the English merchants,
in which the few Scottish delegates were helpless.

Concrete examples soon drove home the lesson. The taxes

rose, and a duty upon salt gave the final stroke to the dying fisheries. It was indicated to the Government that the plentiful timber beyond the Highland Line would benefit both the Government and the Highlands if the country could be opened up by roads. The roads were refused, and the supply of timber continued to come, at great cost but in English ships, across the Atlantic. Again, a bill was brought forward exempting from duty coal shipped from the West of England ports to Ireland. Ayr had a coal-trade with the Irish ports, and the Scottish members claimed accordingly that the bill should be amended to 'West of Britain.' This was done, but only for the first two readings: in the third, 'England' was quietly restored again, and in that form the bill passed through the Lords.

The staple Scottish manufacture was linen, which in England occupied a minor position. In 1711 Parliament proposed to clap on it a heavy export duty. The Scots members pointed out that linen in Scotland held an analogous place to wool in England, and demanded equal treatment for the two. Said the Lord Treasurer indignantly, 'Have we not bought the Scots, and a right to tax them?' Lockhart of Carnwath then explained to him that the Fourteenth Clause in the four-year-old Treaty of Union supported the Scots: but the bill was passed none the less, the only concession being that, as the Scots 'piece' was only a quarter the length of the English one, the tax should be applied not by the piece, as in the original draft, but by the yard.

Linen proved, indeed, a disillusioning fabric. The Crown gave £10,000 as subsidy to the Irish trade, in which England had an interest. It was considered that this trade would be helped by the exportation of Scottish yarn to Ireland. Such export, being a handicap to Scots weaving (that is, to the main industry of the country), had been prohibited by Scottish law. The Scottish members said so, and were told 'Whatever are or may be the laws of Scotland, yet now she is subject to the sovereignty of England, she must be governed by English maxims and laws.' The Scots, led by Lockhart, appealed as before to the Treaty, in virtue of whose provisions they were present; and the House had to admit that they were right. None the less, the Lords refused to sacrifice an opportunity of helping Ulster for what, as Lord Sunderland was pleased to remark, 'must now be reckoned as a county of Britain'; and to teach the recalcitrant 'county' a useful lesson, not only did they insist upon the export, but they removed the duty from Irish linen: and the Speaker informed the House with satisfaction that 'they had catcht Scotland and would keep her fast,' while the London pamphleteers agreed with him, and were paid by the Government for doing so.

There were men who sought a way out of the situation, a cancellation of the disastrous Treaty, by restoring once more the old Dynastic Union. It meant restoring the old dynasty, for the House of Hanover was in the hands of the Whigs, whose power would be threatened did the Treaty fall. Such restoration could only come by arms: and a series of attempts at it were made—in 1708, directly after the Treaty, on a formidable scale in 1715, and again in 1719. Had James avoided measles in 1708, had the Jacobite leader in 1715, instead of Mar, been, not Bruce or Montrose, but Graham of Claverhouse or even Borlum, James VIII might well have found himself King of Scots. But men who saw beyond that saw ahead, to a King who with excellent qualities as a man had little that was inspiring in a leader, and whose accession was certain to reopen the double conflict which had ruined Scotland, the generations of civil wars of religion, and beside them the grim Three Hundred Years War itself, to which artillery and the growing effect of economic factors upon war were only too likely to give a different issue. The country, too, was sick and weary of war. For over five centuries, and on her soil, war, or the threat of war, had been incessant. By 1720 she had been fought to a standstill—sick, starved, humiliated, hopeless, helpless, in as evil case as she had been in 1305. There seemed to be nothing for it but despair.

Yet, as in 1305, there were men and women who refused to make that surrender to despair. The odds against these were as long as in 1305: yet they faced these odds, and though less spectacularly, with no less real gallantry than their fathers in the desperate struggle under Robert Bruce. There was no Bruce now, not even a Thomas Randolph or Black James Douglas. No single man stands out above the rest as leader in a united national movement. The parallel is less with Bruce's War than with the equally desperate resistance when Scotland seemed crushed again under David II. Writing of that, I have said 'Men fought where they stood.' So it was now. One man and then another looked round about him, and very precisely as their fathers had done when the Border beacons lighted among the hills, they tackled the dangers pressing at their doors with good cold iron—but the ploughshare, not the spear.

II

THE SITUATION IS FACED: I

SIXTY-SIX YEARS: 1723–89

Any state is better than despair. Let us at least make one effort, and if we must fall, let us fall like men.

The last speech of William Pitt, Earl of Chatham.

FIRST, and most urgent, the people had to be fed: and since there was not the money to pay for imports, the food had to be produced from Scottish earth. Now Scotland, in spite of the efforts of her Kings to protect *the pure folk laboraris of the grund*, had never been a notable farming country, and the only districts naturally rich had been open to constant devastating invasion: in the last great burst of the Three Hundred Years War, the terrible assaults of Henry VIII, one raid alone had looted ten thousand cattle, twelve thousand sheep, while the crops had again and again been fired in the fields. There had been some recovery under James VI, but the long civil wars had borne with disastrous effect on precisely the districts best adapted to farming, and, with military age sixteen to sixty, had caused a long and widespread diversion of man-power. The comparative peace that followed the Restoration (for the Covenant risings, large as they bulk in tradition, were not in fact very extensive, and were confined to a seventh of the country's area) had not produced the benefit it should, owing to Lauderdale's long misgovernment. And the Seven Ill Years of appalling weather, from 1696 to 1703, when people were forced to eat the weeds of the kirkyards, and in Lothian, the granary of Scotland, three hundred died out of nine hundred in one parish, had sent a good deal of land out of cultivation.[1]

---

[1] One has to remember—it is often forgotten—that though about the time of the Treaty of Union a general malnutrition was the rule, the earlier standard had clearly been much higher. There is grim evidence to that effect in English remarks on the physique of Scots corpses, so late as the early sixteenth century ; and more in the country's long amazing resistance to centuries of almost constant aggression by an enemy with five times her population. Starving men sometimes fight extraordinarily well, but they cannot hold out through three hundred years war against odds.

Where the land was worked, the methods were painfully backward. Weeds stifled the soil, which was overcropped and starved: there were sometimes twenty crops without manuring. Four seeds for one was thought a noble harvest, and when the ground had been cropped to nakedness, the only remedy was seven years fallow. For lack of drainage the rich alluvial land lay sour and barren: the poor high ground was worked with either the foot-plough[1] or a most cumbersome eight- to twelve-ox plough, that needed three or four men to handle it, and then took them a day to plough half an acre. The cattle were almost always housed in winter, on a starvation mess of mashed whins and straw, and by spring had been reduced to such a condition that they had to be carried bodily from the byre.

Where men might perhaps have attempted better methods, they were shackled by the vicious system of tenure. Much ground was worked collectively, as run-rig, with each man changing his portion every year; and the larger one-man farms were on yearly leases, which gave the tenant no security. The lairds themselves had commonly little more than 'a pickle land, a mickle debt, a doo-cot, and a lawsuit,' and there was no ready money for improvements, since rents were paid largely in kind or in services, and loans could only be raised by wadsets on land, which would go if the money laid out were not recovered.

It was very clear that something had to be done. To most it seemed equally clear that it could not be done. Certain men resolved to attempt it, none the less—Adam Cockburn of Ormiston in Lothian, his son John, and the Earl of Haddington, and two conspicuous anti-Union stalwarts, Andrew Fletcher of Saltoun and John, Lord Belhaven. They spurred on others—lairds, ministers, peers, and lawyers: by 1723 (the year after the last witch was burnt in Scotland) there were three hundred to constitute themselves, by a modernised version of the familiar *band*, the Honourable the Society of Improvers in the Knowledge of Agriculture in Scotland, to investigate modern methods in other countries, and provide the best advice, free, to inquirers.

Of course the young Society made mistakes. Of course it was sneered at heavily by those who would not take the risk of joining a new thing. Of course it was hampered by apathy and despair in

---

[1] The *cas chròm*, however, has come in for some rather indiscriminate abuse. For patches of good ground in difficult positions, such as are often found in upland crofts, it seems to have genuine advantages : and it eats nothing.

those whom it set out to benefit. In 1727 an English traveller remarks on the general lack of enterprise:

the people are not only poor, but look poor; they appear dejected and discouraged, as if they had given up all hope of ever being otherwise than as they are

. . . and he was by no means an unfriendly observer, for (making the patriotic exception of London) he is warm in praise of pretty little Glasgow as 'the cleanest and beautifullest city in Britain.'

Yet Ormiston and the rest carried on their white war. Dr Johnson later, in 1773, gives an example of what was their spirit:

We met with Mr Donald Maclean, a young gentleman, the eldest son of the laird of Col, heir to a very great extent of land, and so desirous of improving his inheritance that he spent a considerable time among the farmers of Hertfordshire and Hampshire, to learn their practice. He worked with his own hands at the principal operations of agriculture, that he might not deceive himself by a false opinion of skill.

Men slowly woke to the fact that farms here and there were producing better crops and better bestial. Hope stirred—the thing the country needed most—as men of all classes pooled experience, borrowed new tackle, then bought it, and tried new crops. Turnips had been introduced in 1716, but at first only for the table: in time their use revolutionised cattle-breeding, and so provided manure for arable. They forced, too, rotation of crops and enclosure of fields. Lime began to be used, and Lord Haddington introduced artificial grasses. In 1726 Ormiston grew potatoes in his garden, but not for several years were they grown in fields, when they brought a cheap and valuable foodstuff. Local societies for study were founded: few at first, in a lifetime they spread all over the country. New tools came in. So early as 1710 Saltoun had made experiments with a new mill, and with winnowing fans— which the ministers denounced as 'the devil's wind.' John Small of Dalkeith invented, in 1750, the two-horse swing-plough, and Andrew Meikle, in 1787, perfected a thrashing-mill to replace the flail.

The range of these dates suggests the slow pace of progress, as it seemed to men who were living at the time. Even so late as 1773, a prosperous farmer of East Lothian could say

the bulk of our farmers are creeping in the beaten track of miserable husbandry, without knowing better or wishing to know better.

It was not, perhaps, till after the failure of crops in 1782 that the movement really caught the tenant-farmer, as distinct from the actual owner of the land. Indeed, there were set-backs. Some uncritically used French or English methods, without adapting them to local conditions, and disheartened not only themselves but their neighbours also. Others were in too great a hurry for money, and tried to enforce unpayably high rents, or caused a violent and justified sense of grievance by enclosing and breaking up what was common pasture. (In Galloway in 1724 the people turned out and levelled the new fences.) Yet looking at the period as a whole, the threescore and ten years that followed 1720 reveal a steady and surprising progress. As more money came in, it was laid out in further improvements, which made more again. Better wages increased the national purchasing power, and made more work, not only on the land. New villages grew, and housing began to improve. The Merse and the Lothians set the pace at first: it was not till after the mid-century that the new movements really spread west and north.

Before the 1760's had gone by, farming and planting were fashionable crazes. The Dukes of Argyle and Gordon, the Marquis of Tweeddale, the Earls of Eglinton,[1] Loudon, Rothes, and Findlater, and the famous lawyer and man of letters Lord Kames succeeded Saltoun and Ormiston as leaders. The forests began to spread now with the fields. Their effect was apparent not only in landscape beauty or in the trade in timber, for well-judged planting is an invaluable help to farming; and in spite of various mediaeval laws, the Low Country had been almost stripped of trees. Dr Johnson remarked in 1773

I had now travelled over two hundred miles in Scotland, and seen only one tree not younger than myself.

New kinds came in—the larch and beech, the chestnut, walnut, laburnum. The greater lairds planted literally in millions. Clerk of Penicuik planted three million in thirty years, the Duke of Athol reafforested 16,000 acres: and even the small men were 'aye stickin' in a tree—it'll grow while ye're sleepin'.'

Gardens too became their pride. Before 1730 one or two great men had brought in Switzer to new-lay their grounds. In 1754

---

[1] Lord Eglinton introduced the famous Ayrshire cattle. Argyle's interest is part of the faithful portrait in *The Heart of Midlothian*.

James Justice of Crichton published *The Scots Gardener's Director*, and by the last third of the century, Scots gardeners were in demand all over Europe: even in 1760 their English brethren were protesting, in a pamphlet called *Adam Armed*, against the favour shown to imported Scots.[1] The movement spread outward from the great country houses, and the cottar folk took a new interest in their kailyards, which made for more varied diet and better health . . . and for the sense of creating, effecting, something which is essential to healthy human life.

By the end of the century the once starving country could export, to England alone, some 100,000 head of cattle yearly: a few years later the export figures for grain were 116,000 quarters: and the rural population of the Lowlands were better fed and housed than they long had been. Perhaps the best measure of what had been effected was the rise in the value of land within a lifetime. In the Merse it rose from one and sixpence an acre to a guinea; in Perthshire from five shillings to forty-five; and in the Carse of Gowrie from six and eightpence to six pounds an acre. Yet by the second half of the century many farmers all over the Lowlands were buying their farms, and the wages of the labourers had doubled. It is true that mistakes, and grave ones, had been made, which were in time to exact as grave a payment. Of that we shall need to speak later: but in this place we may rather consider the greatness of the achievement that a few gallant men had initiated when Scotland lay derelict and in despair.

Throughout the eighteenth century agriculture was still the country's main economic basis.[2] Yet the new life which was stirring in the farm woke also in the counting-house and the shipyard. It was needed no less. The Union had brought more taxes and less trade: the customs dropped, the revenue did not balance expenditure. Actual coin was so scarce that foreign currency had to circulate, and even then it was often impossible to get silver

---

[1] The Royal Botanic Gardens at Kew, near London, were the work of William Aiton, appointed in 1759. William Forsyth (*ex quo* forsythia) was later Superintendent of the Royal Gardens of St James's and Kensington; and Thomas Blaikie was gardener to the Duc de Chartres at the Revolution, and kept an interesting diary.

[2] The fisheries, its natural complement, did not share in its revival, for the Salt Tax imposed by the Westminster Parliament had dealt them what seemed to be the final blow. In 1750 the Dutch had 150 vessels off the Scots coast, which they called their gold-mine : the Scots themselves had two.

change to cover a pound note. Any sort of enterprise was further checked by the mere difficulty of movement and transport. So late as 1740 it took Lord Lovat no less than eleven days from Inverness, the capital of the Highlands, to Edinburgh, the capital of the kingdom—a distance of under a hundred and ninety miles. When nine years later the public coach from Edinburgh to Glasgow began to run regularly twice a week, taking no more than twelve hours to forty-five miles, it was a brilliant improvement on earlier conditions: the previous running time was thirty-six hours. Until so late as 1754 the only means by which all but the very few wealthy could travel from the country's capital to what was now the seat of government was a monthly coach which might take sixteen days on a distance of slightly under four hundred miles: letters went faster, taking only six, but so remote were the capitals from each other that on at least one occasion the London post-boy arrived with a single letter in his bag. One can guess from these facts what the transport of goods was like. Even in the South, when in 1753 Lord Cathcart offered free carts to his Ayrshire tenants, the roads were so bad they had to refuse the gift.

In all the first quarter of the century, there was very little trade outside the country. Glasgow, however, provided a growing exception. The little city (12,500 inhabitants at the Union—not quite so many as present-day Galashiels) really did receive some benefit from the Treaty, as did Greenock, which immediately built a harbour. Even they, however, were slow enough in realising their hope, since it was not till eleven years after the Union that the first ship sailed to America from the Clyde.

Glasgow was fortunate in concentrating on a new trade which was quickly and steadily growing. Tobacco was now becoming a staple commodity, and the English colonies in America were its main producers. In 1724 (the year after the Agricultural Society was founded) the town managed to import four million pounds, of which three-quarters were exported again. The Bristol merchants found Glasgow becoming a rival, and contrived to secure new customs legislation, which handicapped the young trade; but the town persevered, and in 1775, on the eve of war with the overseas colonies, the four million pounds had risen to forty-six—more than half the total import of Great Britain—and the Glasgow Tobacco Lords, with their gold-headed canes and scarlet cloaks, held the

crown of the causeway in the growing city.[1] The trade was of
course no more than an entrepôt one, but even so it had the useful
effect of bringing in more money to the country, and of helping
ship-building and allied crafts, although the great days of Clyde
shipping did not begin until tobacco had come to a sudden end.

Glasgow, however, was a lucky exception. Twenty years after
the Union, Scots manufactures were in as evil case as agriculture,
and seemed even less likely to undergo revival. Their problems,
however, were tackled in the same spirit, although the difficulties
were even greater: an improving laird had at least the land to begin
with, while his younger brother the merchant had no assets, except
what he carried underneath his wig. In Scotland, as earlier in
Italy, a man of family might turn his hand to trade without doing
any damage to his blazon: and poverty and the effect of the Penal
Laws on the careers of Episcopalian gentry set many to commerce,
even to handicrafts, some of them on a very humble scale: a son
of Wemyss of Wemyss Hall managed a lint-mill, a son of Macleod
of Geanies, with a pedigree running to Odin, was a joiner. These
men, with their wider background and their inherited turn for
leadership, brought new blood and new vision: for often, in spite
of their great poverty, they were men of a certain education and
culture. (No doubt Dumbiedykes was a fairly common figure,
even as common, perhaps, as Squire Western in England: but the
impression left by foreign accounts both of travels in Scotland and
of the Scot abroad suggests there were many men of a different
type.) Such followed the work that Saltoun and Ormiston were
doing for farming, and began to study the general problems of
trade and initiate a new, direct attack. It is notable that the two
who stand out as leaders were both of them men of comparative
wealth for the time, who worked for the country as well as for
themselves: they were Duncan Forbes of Culloden, Lord President,
and Patrick Lindesay, Lord Provost of Edinburgh.

As 1723 marks the turn in agriculture, so does 1727 in industry.
The country's major manufacture was linen. It was, in fact, her
main exportable product, and poor as the trade was, it had at least
the advantage that linen was one of the domestic staples. It was
used not only for napery and bedding but universally for under-
garments, and was also a very common dress material, as the only

[1] In 1755, Glasgow's population was 23,546, in 1785, 45,889. Tobacco, however, was by no means the only cause of the increase : see below.

alternative to wool and silk. Home consumption alone was thus considerable: but it was largely supplied by domestic work, the housewife spinning her own, which was then woven by the 'customer webster' to her private order. The finer makes were imported, and very dear. That made for export was coarse and inferior, and the craft lacked capital and organisation. The thread was spun by women, working at home, in the country districts where the lint was grown: the weaving was done by men, chiefly in towns, working also at home, but in whole-time occupation. To organise the contact of spinner and weaver, supply the lint and bleach the finer goods (a process which took something like eight months, and could only be done where there was suitable water) and market the goods on a commercial scale required men with a certain amount of capital: and of all the things needed, there was least of that.

Now as offset to the higher Union taxes, some part of the Equivalent [1] was meant, under an article of the Treaty of Union, to encourage fisheries and manufactures. Twenty years had now gone by since the Treaty was signed, and the promised money had never been forthcoming. The Convention of Royal Burghs dunned for it dourly: and at last, after much remonstrance and many snubs, an act was passed and £20,000 was granted to encourage the linen trade. A Board of Trustees for Manufactures was set up, to collect and diffuse information as to technique: it offered premiums to encourage output, set up schools for spinning and weaving, brought in skilled workers from the 'fine weaving' towns of Picardy. Nor did it neglect that very important matter, the due encouragement of the consumer. Great ladies were invited to set the fashion, and even so early as 1731 we hear of a ball at which all the guests were pledged to appear in materials of Scottish manufacture: the Misses Mure of Caldwell went to it in 'striped linen with heads and ruffles of Paisley muslings.'

Behind the triple attack upon the farms, on the entrepôt trade in tobacco, and on the looms, a new artillery took its place in support. The banking system fell in behind the leaders as an organised source of supply to their followers. A Bank of Scotland, indeed, had been founded already, so long ago as 1695, in the course of that first

[1] The Equivalent was the sum of £398,085, 10s. to be paid by England in terms of the Treaty of Union as compensation to Scotland for her assumption of a share in a National Debt eleven and a quarter times her own, incurred in a war to which she was not party.

impulse to revival which had been checked by the luckless Darien Scheme. It had been granted a monopoly for twenty-one years, but in spite of this advantage, its career by the 1720's had been chequered: and its work was confined to the discounting of bills: it took no deposits and gave no cash credits. It did issue notes, for £12 Scots—that is, at the then exchange, for £1 sterling: these *ticquets* it was obliged to cash in specie, and in 1704 and 1715 bad runs had gravely threatened its existence.

Now, less than half of the Equivalent had been paid in the sorely needed specie. The rest had come in paper, and caused much trouble. Debenture holders could get no interest: none was paid, in fact, till twelve years after the Union. A number of English speculators, therefore, bought up the bonds from discontented holders, and formed a society to deal with the interest, which now that the bonds were passing to English hands, had some chance of being paid. Certain long-headed Scots saw what was happening, and did likewise: and in 1727, when the Bank of Scotland's monopoly expired, the two groups joined forces as the Royal Bank.

It was frankly a rival to the Bank of Scotland, and since the latter was thought to be Jacobite, while the Royal had many English shareholders, the Government gave the Royal the whole of its business. There was war between the Banks, and some intricate and rather shady practice, which nearly caused the ruin of the old Bank; but the Royal, none the less, did useful service when it established, in 1728, the peculiarly Scottish system of cash credits, thus greatly helping both the 'improving' lairds and the men who sought to develop industry. The Bank of Scotland followed two years later, and also began to take in cash deposits, an arrangement which made very much easier the passage of money through the veins of trade.[1]

The effects of these labours took time to show themselves. Looking back, it is easy and exhilarating to see how new life was stirring in the 'twenties. Men living at the time would perceive it less. Even so late as the year 1730—seven years after the founding of the Agricultural Society and three-and-twenty after the Treaty

---

[1] Private banking houses were also being established. In 1723 John Coutts, Lord Provost of Edinburgh, founded one which worked up a great connection abroad. The famous London banking firm of Coutts developed from one of the branches of this business : Queen Victoria's friend, the Baroness Burdett-Coutts, was a great-granddaughter of the original John.

of Union—the country seemed indeed to be fairly bankrupt. The revenue was but £30,000, and falling. Even the salaries of high law officials had dropped as much as twelve months in arrears: and naturally, many men declared that the situation was completely hopeless, that the Board of Manufactures could do nothing, that the Improvers in Agriculture were gowks, and that the Bank loans were a wild expedient. But in the counting-house as on the land the clearer-headed, more courageous men 'fought where they stood,' undeterred by their slow progress. Those who were Whigs had a further spur to aid them, for the general poverty and discontent were a strong stimulus to Jacobite feeling: if the 'Forty-five could have come in 1730, much more than the Highlands would have supported it.

One can see the double motive in Lord Provost Lindesay, whose *Interests of Scotland Considered* comes in 1733, and *Reasons for encouraging the linnen manufacture* two years later. He is very careful to assure the country of 'the care and tenderness of the British Parliament': but his main point is that one should not depend on it. Scotland has the nucleus of a trade in linen, and Acts of Parliament will do less for that than a higher grade of flax, prepared with care, the training of skilled craftsmen in better technique, and the careful preparation of new markets.

His views carried weight, and the work of the Board was making itself felt now. The linen trade grew, in quantity first, in quality more slowly, although the agricultural revival began to provide it with better raw material. For a good many years, till the mid-century, the competition of German and Austrian goods sorely hindered the small export trade: the chief overseas market was the colonies, and the Westminster Parliament helped the Teutons there because their goods went out in English ships. The Board and the Convention of Royal Burghs protested, as did every Scots town concerned, from Paisley to Aberdeen; but without result till in 1742 the Government were induced to allow a bounty to encourage the export of British and Irish linen, while four years later the British Linen Bank was founded to 'rationalise' the trade's finances and deal with the general problems of marketing.[1]

---

[1] 1753 brought an unsuccessful experiment, which wasted a good deal of money. From the revenues of the Forfeited Estates £3,000 yearly for nine years was assigned to establish a linen industry in the Highlands. Flax, however, would not grow there : and as with so many later Highland schemes, the plan foundered on the slowness and cost of transport.

By the 1760's quality had improved to the point where fine Scots materials were growing famous. The Paisley websters, the leaders of their craft, had turned their skill to making delicate gauzes and to the handling of imported silk: the Paisley merchants opened their shops in Paris, and with success. The Edinburgh damasks won high repute. And quantity had increased with quality. In 1732, when Lindesay was writing, the output had been four and a half million yards. By 1748 it was already seven and a third: by the end of the century this last figure was trebled, and still had such possibilities of expansion that in less than a century after the Board's foundation the annual output had multiplied by eight, in spite of the competition of newer crafts, and the annual value by a great deal more, for Scots weavers by then were among the best in the world.

Through the third quarter of the century, linen was still the major manufacture. Other textiles, however, were growing up as well, as increasing success made men look for further openings. Even so early as 1725, Christian Shaw of Bargarran had founded, on a small scale, what was to become the thread industry of Paisley. (It is worth note, as an index to the change in preoccupations, that in 1697 the same lady was the heroine of a famous, and horrible, witch-case.) Paisley silk came to rival even the famous gauzes: by 1760 the town had 5,000 silk-looms, whose work was worth £350,000 a year. Aberdeenshire had a stocking industry: the stockings, knit by the women in their homes, were so fine that some fetched as much as five guineas a pair, and a couple of guineas was a common price. They went mostly to the Continental market, but the French Revolution and the resultant wars put an end to a delicate and flourishing craft that brought in £120,000 a year. The great rival of linen, whose place it was to take, was none of these, however, but a new product, dependent on imports for its raw material.

It was born of what seemed disaster to the revival. By the 'sixties, progress had become so marked that those who in the past had refused to believe that any progress at all was possible were now pressing forward with unconsidered haste. The banks multiplied too fast, and too recklessly: in 1772 the collapse of the house of Douglas, Heron, and Co. brought down many of the smaller private firms. It paid its creditors fully in the end, but its promoters (among them an earl and two dukes) lost something like £660,000. That crisis was barely weathered when there followed the war with the American colonies. It cut the very foundations from under Glasgow. Her tobacco imports in 1775 had been 46 million pounds: two years later they were only a hundred-and-fiftieth of that amount. The Colonists had also repudiated a debt to the town of about a million sterling; while the war also struck a blow at the linen trade, for the colonies were the chief market for heavy stuffs.

Of the two main commodities of Scottish trade, one had crashed with a spectacular completeness, and the other had been seriously hurt . . . and it was yet no more than half a lifetime since the prosperity now overthrown had even so much as begun to come to being. Glasgow, however, the town most gravely affected, refused to stay in ruins, and faced the problem. The Scots entrepreneurs, who were used by now to thinking principally in terms of linen, turned to develop the making of other textiles. There was already the nucleus of a cloth-trade, going back indeed as far as the Middle Ages: and in 1778 a Fife sea-captain and merchant, David Loch, published essays on its possibilities. But the native wool was still unfit for fine weaves, and the main interest was in a newer fabric, whose raw material came from the West Indies.

For centuries, cotton stuffs had come from the East. By this time Europe had turned to making them, and already the skilled gauze-workers of Paisley had tried to use cotton in their delicate webs. It was a raw material that paid for working. A pound of raw cotton cost about five shillings: spun ready to weave, its value was something like twice as many pounds. It therefore appealed to men with more technical skill than ready money at their immediate disposal. It was more difficult than flax to handle, but in England new devices for dealing with it were coming into use, increasingly. The spinning jenny and the water-frame, about 1770, greatly multiplied output, and the latter could be worked by water-power; while in 1775 the mule was devised, making possible an almost invisible thread.

The successful working of cotton requires a damp climate: and in 1778 an English firm sought, and no doubt found, a suitable one in Rothesay. The Glasgow men, scrambling for recovery, saw the new thing, and many men took it up, including one benefactor to the race, the Mackintosh who later invented waterproofing.

The results were rapid. Even so early as 1783, the Glasgow Chamber of Commerce, the first in Britain, was being founded to cope with the recovering trade. In that year too a Scotsman, Thomas Bell, invented a process of machine-printing fabrics, and brought a new and valuable side-line, for English calicoes were sent north to print.

The new trade was to lead to many changes, but these fall to be discussed in a later chapter. In the meantime, while linen and cotton alike developed, their expansion, and the increasing wealth of the country, made possible growth in various other directions; and a number of new 'light' industries sprang up. The improvement of roads, and of lairds' bank-balances, caused in Edinburgh a considerable trade, both home and export, in leather and coach-building: the town also made glass, furniture, and silver, though the latter was less fine than earlier work. Glasgow's first pottery had come in 1748, and from 1765 Greenock began to take an interest in West Indian sugar.

The most notable of the new small trades, however, was that of the manufacture of fine books. Paper was made so early as 1709, though on a small scale. In 1727 (the year when the Board of Manufactures was founded) there was still a complaint that

the far greater pairt of the books taught in our Schools and Colledges are Imported from fforaigne places into this Country.

In Glasgow, the University Press, established in the previous century, had been allowed to lapse in the general débâcle. There were unsuccessful attempts at its revival: about 1720 the Duncan brothers were printing in Greek, Hebrew, and Chaldee type. Its great days began when in 1741 Robert and Andrew Foulis took it in hand, and before long it was famed all over Europe for magnificent editions of the classics, which are still among the treasures of connoisseurs. In Edinburgh the firm of Hamilton and Balfour—now Neill and Co.—was founded in 1749, and many more followed, some of them still surviving. The present firm of Oliver and Boyd was established there in 1778; and by the end of the century Edinburgh had become the major centre of British printing, especially the finer, more scholarly grades.

The printing trade links the industrial revival to the intellectual which was growing beside it. It was not, however, the only link between them. One result of the intellectual revival was the 'heavy' industries which in course of time were to grow so preponderant as to oust the rest. One has to remember that all these threads, traced here in separation, were in actual working closely intertwined. As more money circulated, more goods were demanded, and there were both means and scope for new enterprises: as science grew, so did new possibilities; for Scotland, who had for a generation been an eager learner from many other countries, began to appear as a teacher in her turn: and what she taught revolutionised the world. The marriage of coal and iron, modern sea-transport, two vital elements in land-transport also, and the use of 'power' as the servant of man's labour all derive from that re-awakening of ruined Scotland. This present age of mechanised civilisation was born, for good and ill, on Glasgow Green.

Before the engines, there had to be metal for them. Coal had been used for six centuries at least: its importance as fuel was early recognised: in the sixteenth century its export was forbidden. Little iron, however, had been smelted in Scotland. As elsewhere, the furnaces were fired with charcoal, and the works were therefore mainly in the Highlands. In 1727 there were such works at Invergarry, Taynuilt, and Inveraray, the first being carried on by an English firm. The problem of transport handicapped them sorely. Invergarry gave up in 1736, though Taynuilt carried on till as late as 1806.

In the seventeenth century, Dud Dudley, an Englishman, discovered a method of smelting iron by coal: but he kept it secret, and it died with him. In 1709 Abraham Darby, an Englishman, rediscovered it. In time, it was put to active use in Scotland. An English medical student, by name John Roebuck, had been drawn north by the fame of the great Scots professor, Joseph Black. He specialised in Black's science, chemistry, and he turned to its industrial application. In 1749, at Prestonpans, he established a firm for making sulphuric acid, then in demand for a new way of bleaching linen: this firm is the germ of the Scottish chemical trade. Later, in partnership with a Cockenzie merchant called Cadell, and a Birmingham man, Garbett, he began to consider the production of iron. At Carron, near Falkirk, they established a foundry, whose first furnace was blown on the first day of 1760. They began by the customary use of charcoal, but Roebuck knew of Darby's rediscovery, and very soon was seeking to employ it.

After a time, his experiments succeeded, and he discovered a practicable process. He was hampered by difficulties in mining coal, and at one time, indeed, appeared to have failed completely: but the great engineer James Watt came to his help, the problems were successfully overcome, and the firm's sound policy, of producing only the highest class of goods, made the Carron Ironworks famous all over Europe. They made all kinds of goods, from stoves to munitions of war (the Seven Years War was in progress when they opened), and their *carronades* were the best guns of the day.

In spite of Roebuck's evident success, the new industries developed rather slowly: until so late as 1781 there was only one other coal-using casting works, and it was managed by a Swedish firm, though others were using coal in the making of wrought-iron, and a steel-works was founded at Cramond in 1771. Right up to the end of the century, in fact, 'Scottish industries' meant, predominantly, textiles.

That Scotland should have played so huge a part in the development of modern transport seems almost fantastic when one recollects what her communications had been like. They had in fact direly hampered her growing trade, and their ill effects were early recognised. Even so early as 1714 a Turnpike Act imposed a tax on Midlothian vehicles for the improvement of the local roads. It was followed by more: but the vehicles were few and the roads a nightmare, and nothing more effective had been done till the Government grew nervous about the Highlands and decided to open them to the passage of troops. A fine system of military roads was constructed by the extremely efficient General Wade; 250 miles, with 40 bridges, were built between 1726 and 1737, and enlarged to 800 after the 'Forty-five. They did the Royal Engineers much credit, for they were the best roads in the United Kingdom: but as an adjuvant to Scottish industry, their value was less conspicuous than their merit.

The sheer vileness of the roadways farther south led however to the use of a supplement which was to develop in a way then unguessed at—a track of iron rails, along which trucks were propelled so easily that one horse could draw well over four tons of coal. Its history is impossible to trace, but there was one such near the field of Prestonpans at the time of the battle in 1745: so does the old world brush against the new.

In the period covered by this chapter, however, the major improvements were in water transport—almost entirely, in fact, in transport by sea. A Forth and Clyde Canal had long been talked of, but nothing was done until 1762, when Lord Napier had it surveyed at his own cost. Much muddle and waste of money followed thereafter, and though the Canal was eventually built, it was not opened until 1790.

Sea-transport met with very much greater success, in spite of the fact that it started almost from scratch. Thirteenth-century Scotland had built ships for French magnates, fifteenth-century Scotland possessed, and had built herself, what was the greatest warship of her day. But the tradition had practically vanished, and at the beginning of the trade revival, Scots goods were carried mostly in Dutch bottoms. On the eve of the Union, less than a hundred ships flew St Andrew's Cross, their united tonnage being something under 6,000.[1]

The demand for ships grew swiftly as trade expanded, and men of enterprise set to work to fulfil it: by 1760 there were a thousand Scots ships, and by 1770 half as many again, with a total tonnage of nearly 90,000 and employment at sea for some 15,000 men, without counting the shore trades which depended on them.

The main ports had always been on the East Coast, but the opening of trade across the Western Ocean shifted the centre of gravity to the Clyde. In spite of its long sheltered stretch of water, it was, however, a poor natural harbour: only the smallest ships could get up to Glasgow. Just after the Restoration had seemed to end the Civil War, she had built herself a port further down river: but in 1736 the Clyde ports together had no more than sixty-seven small ships between them.

A short lifetime later there were over five hundred. Few people even in Glasgow realise that twelve miles of one of the world's great water-ways were *made*, by resolute and clear-sighted men. It was a task to daunt the most audacious: in the stretch alone from Glasgow Bridge to Renfrew there were twelve shoals, of which five had but two feet of water at low tide. In 1755 a plan was projected, and Smeaton, the great English engineer, was called in to survey the river. The results were so discouraging, however,

---

[1] The average small coastwise passenger ship or cross-Channel packet of to-day runs from a quarter to a third of this tonnage. Three times its amount would be small for a modern liner, and Scotland now builds ships of 80,000 tons and more apiece.

that the scheme was laid aside as impossible. None the less, there were men who refused to abandon it, and in 1768 another Englishman, Golbourne, was asked to survey once more. He suggested piers to control the river scour, so that the stream would work to clear itself; and in 1770 they were begun. Eleven years later he reported proudly that the channels he had dredged to seven feet had successfully scoured to twice and thrice that depth; and the grateful city, with true Glasgow warmth, not only presented him with a piece of plate and a trifling tip of £100 for his son, but raised his contract fee of £2,300 by another £1,500 in free gift.

By the time when a well-fed and slightly unsteady Golbourne drove, nursing his plate, from a Town Council Dinner, that had happened for which his dredged channel now was ready. The end of the seventeen-seventies, in fact, is a turning-point in the history of the world. The motive power of all men's mechanisms had been, from time out of mind, his own bodily strength, that of the various beasts whom he could tame, the uncertain wind and the more certain but highly localised water. He could multiply the effect of any of these by the use of various forms of the lever and pulley: but such multiplication, however ingenious, was, from our standpoint, very limited. As direct result of the Scots Revival, however, one Sunday afternoon on Glasgow Green an idea flashed into the head of a young man walking: and mankind had won control of the power of steam.

A century and three-quarters—so new it is. Yet its roots go back for some two thousand years. Hero of Alexandria first discovered that the thrust of expanding steam had power in it. Not till the seventeenth century, however, did the Frenchman Denis Papin go on to find that steam would push a piston up a cylinder— the foundation principle of the steam-engine. Two Englishmen, Thomas Savory (d. 1715) and Thomas Newcomen (d. 1729), carried on his experiments, and Newcomen tried to put them to practical use. He invented a steam-pump which in 1712 was actually used to pump water from mines. It was very little more than a scientist's toy. It could pump, but it could not be used to drive a machine, and even as pump it was hardly a success, since it needed an enormous amount of fuel.

During the year 1754, however, when John Roebuck already was working at Prestonpans, a young Greenock scientist, by name James

Watt, came up to Glasgow. His great interest was in experimental physics, though he was sorely hampered by lack of funds. The University staff were kind to him, especially two already distinguished professors, Adam Smith of the Chair of Moral Philosophy, and Joseph Black, who held that of Chemistry and who had already been the teacher of Roebuck . . . and had just made the interesting if abstruse discovery of the possibilities of latent heat. They gave him working space, and encouraged him. One day he was asked to repair a damaged model of Newcomen's pump. The clumsy little engine set him dreaming. It was little use, but suppose it could be used? Suppose one could lower its fantastic consumption of fuel?

For long the problem baffled him completely: but he had been thinking of Black's discovery also, and one Sunday afternoon on Glasgow Green in the early summer of 1765 the two lines of thought crossed suddenly in his mind, and he had conceived the idea of the condenser. The problem of economic use of fuel was, in principle, solved. It took years of work to perfect yet. Indeed, it was not till 1768 that he made an effective condenser: but it was done.

Now at this time Roebuck of the Carron Ironworks was much troubled by the flooding of new coal-pits, which threatened to wreck his enterprise altogether. In desperation, he tried Newcomen's pump. It failed. His old teacher Black came to the rescue, and suggested calling in Watt. Watt saved the mine, and thenceforth Roebuck backed his experiments, as did Roebuck's friend, Matthew Boulton, of Birmingham. Progress was slow, but by 1779 Watt had devised a method of transmission which successfully used the principle of the crank to convert the reciprocating action of the engine to a rotary one which might drive a working machine. According to his English biographer, the idea of the fly-wheel, on which success depended, was 'given away' by the chatter of a workman, so that the first full-size engine of this pattern was made by one Matthew Wasborough, of Bristol, whose employer, Pickard, patented the device, ahead of Watt, in August 1780.

Economic, industrial, and social life were all to be revolutionised to their bases. The working size of the world itself was to shrink. Since he first used iron, man had found no such servant: and the Scripture curse on a servant when he reigneth was not to occur to him for some time to come.

III

THE SITUATION IS FACED: II

SIXTY YEARS: 1729–89

It would almost seem as if the educated class in Scotland consciously set themselves to endow their country with an independent life in the domains of philosophy, literature, science, and art.

WILLIAM HUNT, in *The Cambridge History of English Literature.*

In his *History of Civilisation in England* Henry Buckle became so lost in admiration at the intellectual achievements of the Edinburgh of Mackenzie's day that he forgot to say anything about England.

HAROLD WILLIAM THOMPSON [of Harvard],
A Scottish Man of Feeling : *Henry Mackenzie.*

THE dead exhaustion consequent on long war which marks the first quarter of the century was not shown only in poverty and starvation. With these, and linked with them in a vicious circle, went a corresponding deadness of the mind. Yet once a few men had broken the black ring, the circle became benevolent instead; the lifetime that witnessed material revival saw an equal quickening in things of the intellect, till in the year of Watt's perfected engine— that is to say, in 1781—a Hungarian man of letters could write from Paris,

Toutes les fois que les Anglais m'ont parlé de Scotchmen avec un ton de mépris qu'ils affectent quelques fois, je leur ai conseillé d'aller à Edimbourg pour apprendre à vivre et à être hommes. . . . Pour les sciences exactes, Edimbourg vaut mieux qu'Oxford et Cambridge ensemble.[1]

And that was the general opinion of cultured Europe.

There was far to go before that point was reached: but the growth of the country's wealth soon improved the funds of the starved and moribund universities, endowed research, gave the arts effective patrons: the scholars and the scientists in turn brought trained minds to bear upon the nation's problems— economic and industrial, at least. Low as the level of scholarship

---

[1] ' Every time English people have talked to me of Scotchmen with a tone of scorn which they at times affect, I have advised them to go to Edinburgh to learn the art of life. . . . For the exact sciences, Edinburgh is worth more than Oxford and Cambridge together.'

had fallen since the early years of the reign of Charles the First, there was still a tradition of respect for learning. Not only did the ancient schools survive (and some of them, still active in our own time, were even then as much as five hundred years old) but they were faithful yet to the ancient tradition—free access to learning for any man who chose, irrespective of either wealth or social status. Dr James Kerr, who speaks with authority, says

> For more than three hundred years, in a practically continuous record, there is scarcely a burgh . . . in which provision was not made for the teaching of Latin and Greek to all, rich and poor, who were able to put them to profitable use. We are warranted in saying that no other country has such a record.

Yet in the early years of the century, the schools and the universities which fed them were alike in bad case. Their revival again can be dated from that quickening decade of the seventeen-twenties which saw the founding of the Agricultural Society, the Board of Manufactures, the Royal Bank. Six years after the first and two years after the others—that is to say, in 1729—a Dublin schoolmaster of Ayrshire stock, Francis Hutcheson (1694-1746), was appointed to the Moral Philosophy Chair of Glasgow, which had been his Alma Mater. He was not among the great philosophic thinkers, though he furthered that study of ethics in terms of psychology—that is to say, in terms of human nature—which had useful results, and might have had much more if psychology had not been for so long a Cinderella of the sciences, and then fallen into hands clean washed of logic. Hutcheson's greatness was rather as a teacher, and as such he seems to have had uncommon gifts. He is praised above all for having had the courage to lecture in English, not the traditional Latin: it may have been less of a benefit than it seemed, for as in Scotland and England the habit grew common, the old international language of all scholars sank steadily to be a specialist study, and though for a century yet some tincture of classics was a part of any liberal education, the common cultural foundation of Europe began to follow the common religious one. None the less, the immediate effect of Hutcheson's teaching was greatly to quicken the University's life: and the quickening of such life is seminal, for the students of one decade are the teachers and scholars and scientists of many more, and they scatter widely after graduation.

From the point of view of its own time, at least, philosophy dominated the revival. It is possible that this was a misfortune. That century was an age of abstract thinking. It was clear abstraction—one can say so much: the strong French and Scottish influence saw to that. But its very clarity had its own dangers: the lucid reasoning in abstract terms proved so satisfying to the thinking mind as to make it forget that the counters of its game—economic man, or liberty, or the like—had no more of objective existence in concrete living than the square root of minus seventy-three. When such thinkers, or oftener, their enthralled disciples, proceeded to act as if ideas were things, the results were apt at times to be disconcerting. They were enhanced by another tendency which, spreading in the sixteenth century, was a dominant in the thought of the eighteenth, and has a wide and powerful effect today—a sort of negative credulity, which assumes that certain things *cannot* be true because the state of the thinker's personal knowledge does not include the conditions of their being so: thus, iron sinks in water, therefore iron ships cannot float; man is heavier than air, so he cannot fly; he does not walk and talk when he is dead, so the Resurrection of Christ must be a fable. In the scientific and metaphysical fields, such reasoning, in the eighteenth century, was even more common than it is today. And the revulsion from the religious wars left the time happily self-satisfied, secure, in its pleasant formal urbanity, that there would be no more explosions over ideas.

Few ages in history have produced a louder: its reverberations are shaking Europe still. Two of the men who most shaped the age's mind shaped theirs in Scots class-rooms and round Scots dinner-tables. These two were David Hume (1711–76) and Hutcheson's brilliant pupil, Adam Smith (1723–90). Professor Sorley endorses Burton's remark that 'There was no third person writing in the English language during the same period who has had so much influence on the opinions of mankind,' while Leslie Stephen considered Hume to be 'the acutest thinker in Great Britain of the eighteenth century, and the most qualified interpreter of its intellectual tendencies.'

Hume, bred to the law, travelled in France in the mid seventeen-thirties, and there wrote his famous *Treatise of Human Nature*, which gives the core of his philosophy. Professor Sorley considers that 'if he had written nothing else, his claim to rank as the greatest of English (sic) philosophers would not be seriously affected.' It

4

was published in 1739, without success. He worked on through the 'forties, with various diplomatic interludes. His *Philosophical Essays concerning the Human Understanding* (1748) and *Enquiry concerning the Principles of Morals* (1751) brought him repute, confirmed and spread far beyond Scotland by the *Political Discourses* next year. He turned then to a fresh study of history, with a vigorous challenge to the Whig tradition which had been dominant since the last Revolution. The first volume of his *History of England* sold forty-five copies in its first twelve months: after the last one appeared, seven years later, it was reckoned that the work had brought its author more money than any ever written in English. It added also to his wide reputation. When in 1763 he went to Paris in the minor post of Legation Secretary, the Dauphin's children were coached, at his presentation, to greet him with pretty speeches in praise of his work. He remained unspoilt alike by his success, by the bitter jealousy of his English colleagues, and by the rancorous attacks of Rousseau, whom he had patiently helped and befriended: and his charm and wit and generosity made him a leader in an Edinburgh that was rapidly flowering into brilliant life.

Hume was a solvent force, not a constructive: but he so stimulated the thought of his time that his influence was none the less creative. The Scoto-German Kant and the Scot Reid and the English school of Empiricists spring from him, either as pupils or as antagonists. He turned Smith to political economy, in which he himself anticipated Ricardo; his ethics influenced the English Bentham and his theology the Frenchman Comte, all men who powerfully coloured the mind of their own day.

He was followed as leader of Scottish philosophy by his close friend Adam Smith, a Kirkcaldy man, the pupil and successor of Hutcheson, whose chair he received in 1752. (He did much for the reawakening University, giving great help to Watt and the Foulises.) Like Hume he was very much at home in France, where he was a friend of Voltaire, D'Alembert, Turgot, and Necker. His first success was mainly as a teacher: it was not until 1776 that he published what was to be, in the most literal sense, an epoch-making book—one which coloured the whole political thought of Europe, into most of whose languages it was translated. This was the *Inquiry into the Nature and Causes of the Wealth of Nations*, which Buckle called 'in its ultimate results, the most important book that has ever been written.'

It was certainly not that: but it was important. It founded a
new and influential science, that of political economy. The writer
has been dismissed at times by critics as a mere pupil of the French
'physiocrats': but most of his more important theories—of division
of labour, of money, prices, wages, had been worked out before
his contact with these; and though he adopted their formula *laisser
faire*, he worked it out upon no abstract basis, but on a concrete
and detailed examination of law, history, and actual trade conditions. He directly challenged accepted theory, pointing out that
a nation's wealth lay not in its treasure but in its productive power,
and went on thence to seek for the best means to prosperity, both
national and international. His system had the faults of pioneer
work, and his uncritical followers did much harm, for they took
to reasoning not in terms of man, but in terms of a different and
non-existent creature—that is to say, of economic man: and when
theories true of the non-existent abstract are applied to an existent
and complex concrete, the practical results may be unexpected.
But for the purposes of his own study, the abstraction may be considered justified, and he cannot be blamed for his followers'
limitations.

No third name stands with those of Hume and Smith, though
Thomas Reid (1710-96) of Aberdeen may be mentioned. He was
Hume's opponent, re-synthesising some of his disintegrations by
basing philosophy on psychology instead of a metaphysical scepti-
cism: his influence on French and Italian thought, in his own
time, was very considerable.

The practical turn of mind of the period, which affected even
its abstract philosophy, can be seen in the strong and growing
interest in science. Soon after the middle century, one finds that
the old grammar schools are being supplemented by new 'academies,'
in whose teaching the sciences were conspicuous. Perth Academy,
founded in 1760, taught not only mathematics but astronomy,
chemistry, and geography: and the next thirty years brought
similar schools at Dundee, Inverness, Elgin, Fortrose, and Ayr.
The early revival saw two brilliant mathematicians, Robert
Simson of Glasgow (1687-1768), and Colin Maclaurin (1698-1746),
who received the Marischal Chair at the age of twenty: Maclaurin
has been described as 'the one mathematician of the first rank
trained in Britain in the eighteenth century.' James Burnett, Lord

Monboddo (1714-99), anticipated Darwin in his theories of human evolution; James Hutton (1726-97) did great work for geology, of which science indeed he may be called the founder; and Joseph Black (1728-99) is the father of modern chemists and may be called a grandfather of steam-power and at least an ancestor of aviation, since he discovered that a bladder filled with hydrogen would float in air.

The most conspicuous at the time, however, were probably the group of great medical men. In 1720 (again one finds that decade!) Alexander Monroe the elder (1697-1767) was given the Edinburgh Chair of Anatomy. He was to hold it for nearly forty years, and besides important osteological work, he and his son and successor of the same name (1733-1817), with the help of others who soon gathered round them, made their Faculty the chief medical school of the world. Glasgow's was roused in turn by William Cullen (1710-90), among whose pupils were not only Joseph Black but the two Hunter brothers, William and John (1718-83 and 1728-93). The first made important discoveries on the lymphatics and the second was recognised as the chief British surgeon of his day, while his studies of the repair-process of tissues make him the father of modern surgical science, which was to have other major roots in Scotland.

These men were not fugitive and cloistered minds: all, by research and teaching, did great work in developing the general standard of knowledge, not only in their own country, but through the world. The able pupils of the great Medical Schools were soon, indeed, to count as a major export.

The arts were somewhat slower to revive. It was nowhere a great age of creative art, save for German music: and in Scotland, as one might expect, the mind of the time was bent to the solving of urgent practical problems. Yet there was in fact important work in the arts, with powerful results that were felt throughout all Europe. If we trace the roots of the great 'Romantic Revival' which affected all European literature, and indeed other arts, through the nineteenth century, and whose influence is by no means yet exhausted, we shall find that most of them lead to our own country.

The long tradition of genre-verse in Scots which goes back to at least the fourteenth century, and is active, often with lively results, today, had somewhat lapsed during the Civil Wars, but began to revive before they were well over. So early as 1706 the King's Printer, James Watson, had issued his *Choice Collection*[1] of old Scots verse. In 1724 Allan Ramsay (?1685-1758) brought out the famous *Tea-table Miscellany*, a mingling of his own work with the old, which had a huge success and established a fashion: an American scholar, Dr Harold Thompson, has remarked that

One of the striking things about the entire eighteenth century is the fact that a Scottish gentleman in those days could produce a fine song with the same nonchalant ease with which an English gentleman of Elizabeth's day produced a sonnet.

Lady Grizel Hume or Baillie, Mrs Cockburn, Jean Elliot, Adam Skirving, and Dean Skinner, and a dozen others, made songs still sung today. Ramsay's own work is lively and often graceful, with an agreeable Horatian turn, but his real importance (and it is very great) was in being a sort of core or focal point round which a literary society could once more develop. It was he who in 1725 opened Edinburgh's first circulating library and in 1736 her first theatre . . . though both had to be closed for dread of the Kirk, and it was not till 1764 that Edinburgh had a licensed playhouse. Robert Fergusson (1750-74) stands out above the rest for the richness and vigour of his satiric verse: and in the last years of the time which this chapter covers the various strands of Scots 'popular' tradition—racy genre-verse, humorous or passionate song—reached their height in a volume published at Kilmarnock by an Ayrshire countryman of twenty-seven, a farmer of the name of Robert Burns.

The lyric strain, so rare in Europe in that period, appears again, with a wider range, a richer and more 'literary' texture, in the great outburst of Gaelic poetry which marks the mid-century. Iain Lòm had died in 1710: but to him now succeeded Alasdair MacMhaighstir Alasdair (MacDonald) (?1700-70). His work, besides passionate love-song, shows no less passion in its loyalty to the old Scots dynasty and in something that then was very rare in Europe, the deep sense of nature. Duncan Bàn Macintyre (1724-1812) has this again, and with their work stand the love-songs and biting satire of Rob Donn Mackay (1714-78) and the religious poems of Dugald Buchanan (1716-68), considered the greatest Gaelic religious poet, who helped also in preparing the Gaelic New Testament of 1767. The poems of Alasdair MacMhaighstir

---

[1] Not all of it in the 'popular' tradition: it included the courtly poets as well, though these, rather oddly, had less effect.

Alasdair were the first original work in Scottish Gaelic to be printed : they appeared in the year 1751. Rob Donn's were not printed till 1829—fifty-one years, that is to say, after his death : but this is less surprising than it seems, for Church and State made war on all things Gaelic.

Three men who wrote English had immense effect on European letters. From the eldest, James Thomson (1700-48), derive two major aspects of the Romantic Revival. His *Seasons* began with *Winter* in 1726, and no less a critic than George Saintsbury has described them as 'among the most important works in the history of English poetry.' They count more for what they caused than for what they were, though at their best they are true and fine creation: across the gulf they link with Gavin Douglas, the forerunner of all modern nature poets: and though Thomson was contemporary with Pope, they brought back to English the great Renaissance music, the deeper note of Spenser and of Milton. In prose Tobias Smollett (1721-71) ranks as one of the four great founders of the novel in English: his *Roderick Random* comes in 1748. Harsh, almost ferocious, he has a violent vigour that relates him to the tradition of genre-verse. James MacPherson (1736-96) is of another rank from these. His famous, or notorious, versions of Ossian began to appear in the year 1760. They probably did adapt, or rather were based on, Gaelic originals, but were freely upholstered to capture the contemporary taste. They have none the less some real poetic feeling, and what we now consider their defects helped then to make them enormously admired. Napoleon took them with him on campaign, and they had a powerful effect on the literature of several of the languages of Europe.[1]

Later, the novelist-critic Henry Mackenzie (1745-1831) is the completest possible contrast to Smollett. His *Man of Feeling* (1771) epitomises the 'sensibility' which Rousseau was making the rage of cultured Europe: it went into nineteen editions in his lifetime, with immense success in America and France. It is now very dead, and we remember, or forget, the author as the man to whom *Waverley* was dedicated—and who, as critic and patron of other artists, and a man who worked for the good of his native Highlands, was not unworthy to receive the honour.

[1] Percy's *Reliques* (1765) may be mentioned in this context as one of the great influences upon the Romantic Revival. Bishop Percy, of course, was himself an Englishman : but most of the greatest ballads in that important and germinal collection were Scots.

It is not without significance, however, that if we put aside the philosophers, the chief prose form of the time was history—mainly Scots history, and often history seen (as earlier by Barbour and John Major) as essentially the study of human conduct. We have already spoken of Hume's success: but most of the major British historians of that time were Scotsmen. An English scholar, Dr Hunt, remarks that

historical writing was raised by Hume to a foremost place in our prose composition; its right to that place was maintained by Robertson.

Hume's view of history as affording data for the interpreting of human conduct was new to England,[1] and proved stimulating— too much so, in fact, for the comfort of the Whigs: but his sceptical intellectualism worked to narrow, or shallow, his perception of life. William Robertson (1721-93), Principal of Edinburgh, has the same thinness: it was part of the age. But he was the first British historian to give a broad general view of history as a steady process of interdependent event: and (like nearly all the men mentioned in this chapter) he was a great personality as well. There were others—Anderson, Goodall, and Lord Hailes—who deserve that a successor should salute them: but this is not a history of Scots letters.

In most other arts there was less activity: but there was none the less a quick sense of life, and in one something like supremacy in Europe. The time was everywhere an age of music, from the great Germans to the enchanting birdsong or rumbustious jollity of the English songs: and though it was long since mediaeval Scotland had drawn to her students of music from other lands, she was still a singing country, and always had been. Much of the poetry of the time is song, especially in vernacular Scots and in Gaelic—not meant for paper but for the living voice. The lovely passion of Burns's *Red red rose*, the daimonic glee of *Johnnie Cope*, are on paper no more than the photograph of a Turner sunset: half their merit as art is in the utter union of words and music to a single thing. Scots tunes were acclaimed in England before the Union, and Allan Ramsay made them a fashion at home. Later on, in the 'sixties, the Reverend Patrick MacDonald made a pioneer collection of Gaelic ones. Everyone sang: it was almost part of a

[1] Not, as Dr Hunt says, to Britain. Barbour's *Brus* is a thoughtful study of leadership, worth reading as such by a soldier of today.

gentleman's table manners. Outside song, there was good dance-music, but not much else, save that in the Highlands, though the pipes were illegal, the great tradition of *ceol mòr* was . . . remembered.

The supreme Scots art of the time was undoubtedly building. The vivid native tradition of architecture was changing its form, as living things always do: but it had suffered least from the long desolation. Sir William Bruce, who had brought to it a new classical inspiration, had lived to 1710. He was followed by Colin Campbell (d. 1729), whose *Vitruvius Britannicus* extended and confirmed the classical mode, and by James Gibbs (1682-1754). Gibbs did most of his more important work for England[1]: but he built the West Church of St Nicholas, Aberdeen (without fee), for regard to his native city. Sir William Chambers (1726-96) also did most of his work furth of the country: his masterpiece is Somerset House in London.

By his day, however, poverty was passing. Scottish building had begun again on a large scale, and found in Edinburgh a noble site. The Nor'loch was drained in 1763, and the fierce old city strung upward to the Rock threw out an arm to the slopes that ran to the sea. The North Bridge was built in 1772, and (laid out by James Craig) the superb New Edinburgh began to grow and spread in the sea wind: the first house was three years older than the Bridge. The time came to flower in the work of the elder Adam and then in that of his greater son, Robert Adam (1728-92), whose lovely designs show the classical inspiration as perfectly tuned to the idiom of its day as that of the great early phase of the French Renaissance. No finer urban domestic architecture can be found (and that was a noble age of it) than Charlotte Square, to name only one example.

The exquisite detail of Adam's decoration is the time's chief sculpture, and links in a curious way with the beautiful miniature portrait work of James Tassie (1735-99) and William Berry's (1730-1783) delicate intagli. Painting had never been very strong in Scotland, though there had been more than we commonly recognise. There was now a deliberate attempt to foster it. In 1729 (once more the 'twenties) the School of St Luke was founded in Edinburgh, and gave his first training to the younger Ramsay. The

---

[1] St Mary le Strand, the beautiful tower of St Clement Dane's, and the stately St Martin's in the Fields, all in London, are his ; also the Radcliffe Camera at Oxford.

Board of Manufactures also founded a School of Design, which had much to do with the success of their work: and the Foulises in 1754 established a second School of Art in Glasgow, under the wing of the University. William Aikman (1682-1731) had returned from exile so early as 1712. His contemporary John Scougall painted portraits of grace: but the greatest name among those of this time is Allan Ramsay (1713-84), son of the Ramsay who did so much for letters. He is all the more Scottish for being very French[1]: he has a controlled grace of sensuous enjoyment and the delicate clear colour of East Scots light, but he can be virile as well as exquisite, and like all these men, he was personality as well as artist, the friend of Rousseau, Voltaire, and Dr Johnson. Other names come later, who deserve but cannot receive here more than mention—Robert Strange (1721-92), who revived the long-lost art of etching and was one of the finest of European engravers; Alexander Nasmyth (1758-1840), a fine portrait painter; Gavin Hamilton, Jacob More, Alexander Runciman, leading on to the appearance of Henry Raeburn, who properly belongs to the age of Scott.

It is worth while giving the catalogue in some detail, in order to show the wide range of the whole revival. The swing-plough and latent heat and Paisley gauzes, *Johnnie Cope* and *The Wealth of Nations*, lymphatics and engines, Ramsay's playhouse and Lindesay's essays on linen-weaving, Hailes's *Annals* and the grace of Charlotte Square, Glasgow's School of Art and her deepening of the Clyde, are all of them parts of one great national movement.

It was very national. It was so in temper, in the rich interest in humanity and the sense of life continuous with the past which show not only in Hume or Robertson but in Ramsay's gathering of the old songs. It was so in that double feeling we share with France, so valuable when both sides are present, so deeply dangerous when one stands alone—in that interest in the abstract principle one sees in Hume again and Adam Smith, and in that sense of concrete circumstance which has a hundred varied manifestations, from the nature-poetry of the Gaelic lyrists, Allan Ramsay's painting of his sitters' lace, or the fiction of Smollett to Hutton's geology or John Hunter watching the healing process of wounds.

[1] When his work was thrust among that of English painters at the Louvre Exhibition of 1938, French critics remarked that he was out of place there.

It was national also in another sense. No less than Ormiston or Patrick Lindesay, these men of the intellectual revival were consciously and deliberately working for the renewal of their country's life. One notes how many of them were actual teachers, and the rest had what is the teacher's greatest gift, the power not only of expressing thought but of stirring and quickening the minds of others. And it was most truly national again in that, as mediaeval Scots life had done, it saw itself as an integral part of Europe . . . and made Europe see it as European *and Scots*.

IV

THE HIGHLAND TRANSITION

FORTY-ONE YEARS: 1748–89

He was hardly guided by them that might have used him better—and
they haena made their plack a bawbee o't, neither.
                                        Sir WALTER SCOTT, *Rob Roy*.

WHILE the sunlight grew and broadened in the South, the North
and West presented a different picture. At the time of the Union,
the clan feuds were over (save so far as their afterglow coloured the
Jacobite risings) and the Highlands seem to have been in better
case, for the first quarter of the century, than were the Lowlands.
Our main authority (and it is a good one) is a book which had been
published in 1703—Martin Martin's *Description of the Western
Isles.*

Martin was very well qualified to write it: he was a Gaelic-
speaking Skyeman, a scholar, and a well-trained man of science,
M.A. of Edinburgh and M.D. of Leyden, who had written papers
for the Royal Society. His book is not a collection of curiosities
for the patronising urban, and the Sentimental Traveller was not
yet: it is an early and excellent example of scientific ethnological
field-work, with a close, sober, and first-hand account of all the
Isles, from Arran to the Shetlands. He knew them both from
within and from without: and one of the few occasions when his
scientist's calm permits him to show heat is in a comment on the
Southern charge that the Islesmen were 'savages':

> I am not ignorant that foreigners, sailing through the Western Isles,
> have been tempted by the sight of so many wild hills, that seem to be
> covered all over with heath and faced with high rocks, to imagine that
> the inhabitants, as well as the places of their residence, are barbarous;
> and to this opinion their habit [=clothing] as well as their language has
> contributed. The like is supposed by many that live in the South of
> Scotland, that know no more of the Western Isles than the natives of
> Italy.

The Highlands in the early century were of course bitterly poor, like all Scotland else: but—to quote Mr W. C. Mackenzie, the foremost living authority on their history—

Notwithstanding their privations, the people were singularly healthy . . . they were athletic; they were musical; they were hospitable; and they were no doubt happy.

The impression one gains is of a life hard indeed, yet not lacking even among the very poor in the grace of fine manners and the love of beauty, not only in nature but also in music and a 'literature' that was none the less fine for not being committed to paper, and whose living books were listened to at the *ceilidh* with a discriminating appreciation . . . though already the schools and the Church made war on Gaelic, and were opening the way to that civilising process which was, within a couple of hundred years, to bring to Stornoway the speech of the crooner.[1]

Is this picture too idyllic? Possibly. But it is time someone stressed the positive side. Most strangers who wrote of the Highlands in that time were in the first place stunned by the scenery and dazed by the sheer discomfort of travelling through it. Then the people wore an odd dress and—poor savages!—found it as hard to express themselves in English as the average English gentleman did in French. And—one hears less of this, but it can be seen today—the Highlander's natural dignity of bearing makes him a difficult person to patronise: a sometimes exasperating quality. Yet not all strangers suffered from these troubles, and along with the picture of the native Martin, but three-quarters of a century later in time, stands that of a very English Englishman, which supplements Martin's and, though much had happened in the interval between the two, confirms it. Dr Samuel Johnson, as a distinguished scholar and the friend of a well-known Scot, had the *entrée*, and his shrewd warm insight permitted him its full use. He naturally gives a good deal more attention to what Martin takes for granted, the life of the gentry, whose scholarship and fine manners delighted him . . . except that they would give him Cheshire cheese with tea!

The Highlands, like the Lowlands, had their problems. Yet the two differed. Poverty was the same. Communications were worse, and the Highland soil; though on the other hand the popular

[1] Some people (so Dr Johnson testifies) objected to Gaelic versions of the Scriptures, on the ground that they would prevent the decay of the language: and even already, after 1690, the rents of the suppressed Bishopric of the Isles were assigned to schools ' for the extirpation of Erse [=Gaelic] and other pious purposes.'

'culture' was on a higher level than in the Lowlands, and that of the gentry was at least no less.[1] The Highland gentleman, being commonly Catholic or Episcopalian, was debarred from the universities of his country, but he frequently went to France for his education. There was, however, nothing to call trade. In the Lowlands, during the decades just after the Union, it was so to speak economically absent. In the Highlands the absence was psychological: men did not think in terms of a trading world. There was a little trade with the South in black cattle, and a certain importation of 'luxury' goods—tea, claret, the laird's table-silver and queen's-ware plates, his books, his wife's one silk dress, perhaps furniture. But for the ordinary needs of life, each community, almost each household, supplied its own, from meal and shoes and blankets to amusements.

The major difference between Highlands and Lowlands was less economic than in the social structure. It was feudal, in the strict historical sense—in the Scottish historical sense, not always grasped, which combines the feudal nexus of land tenures, organised on a military basis, with another, not found conjoined with this out of Scotland, and which historians, in consequence, are apt to overlook or under-rate. Land, in law, was held by the chief, and in general social assumption, held for the clan. The chief held it as the leader of his people, and especially as their commander in war. He leased it out to the clan's officers, the gentry who were his own more or less close kinsfolk, and these in turn to their personal followers, who mostly bore their name and wore their badge, and were accounted also as humble kinsfolk, but kinsfolk none the less, with a share in the name.[2]

Now this patriarchal government could work. It did not always: no sort of government does, since all in the long run, as we often forget, are composed of men who are fallible human beings. There were tyrannical and oppressive chiefs: but there were also ways of dealing with them, from cold iron to even more effective songs;

[1] Dr Johnson observes, ' I never was in any house in the Islands where I did not find books in more languages than one.'

[2] It is characteristic of Scotland, and of great psychological and social importance, that while family pride is proverbial in our country, there are no exclusively aristocratic surnames. If a servants' agency offered an English housewife a cook called Tudor, a housemaid called Plantagenet and a parlourmaid called Guelph, she would call the police. If a Scotswoman found that her domestic staff were respectively Bruce, Stewart, and MacAlpin, she might be mildly amused at the coincidence, but the names would not strike her as being anything odd: and the three would certainly take due pride in them.

and a man whose life and property depended on the willing service of his followers, and whose only police were those same followers, had to behave himself reasonably well, so far as they at any rate were concerned. He might murder his wife or carry off his neighbour's, burn another chief's castle or rise against the King: but to do these things, or prevent someone else from doing them to himself, he had to depend on the clansmen who were his tenants, who were Highlanders with a sense of their dignity, and as much right to the tartan as himself.

In the old days of personal chieftainship, the chief's obligations had been recognised. The magnificent Colin MacKenzie, first Earl of Seaforth, used to go on a progress through his vast lands with very much the state of a sovereign prince: but his last words to his brother and successor were 'above all to be kind to his men and followers, for that he valued himself while he lived on their account more than on all his great estate and fortune': and after the 'Fifteen those same followers stood loyally by his nephew, then the Chief. The latter's factor, Donald Murchison, collected his rents for ten years in the Government's teeth, and carried them to the Earl all the road to Spain. Sometimes it needed more than a little fighting: but the people were willing to risk life and goods, not by force, but in face of force, for their exiled Chief. And in 1725 the Commissioners for the Forfeited Estates had to report that they could not sell those of Seaforth, since they could not get possession in order to do so. In some places to which the red soldiers had easier access and the clansfolk were forced to pay rental to King George, they, desperately poor, raised a second rent, of their own will, for their forfeited chief overseas.

Now, men do not do these things for callous tyrants who have been removed from the power to do them harm. But by the mid-century, the system was changing. The meaning was going from military tenure. Many chiefs and gentlemen had gone into exile after 1690 and again after the 'Fifteen. Those who remained, and still more those who returned, came to feel themselves not leaders of a people, but as they were in law, owners of land. And the tacksmen, once the link between chief and people, now acted rather as a block between them: they held land, but their interests lay elsewhere, in the professions or the services. Both 'had to' have money, and the need for it grew as the rest of Scotland steadily grew richer and the standard of living consequently grew higher.

The portrait of Fergus MacIvor in *Waverley* shows with Scott's accustomed sense of the social relations a type of such men, between one world and another as their fathers had often been, but unlike their fathers, belonging to neither rather than to both.[1] The still unshaken loyalty of Evan is not 'romance' but straightforward manners-painting: only the manners are those of a world that was fading.

Some men—Lochiel of the 'Forty-five and his brother, John Duke of Argyle and Duncan Forbes of Culloden—were stirred by the new movements in the South, and tried to translate them into Highland terms. Culloden's objection to the Rising, in fact, was less on political or religious grounds (neither he nor Argyle had much cause to love the House of Hanover) than from fear of the consequence of more civil war to a country beginning to recover from it: and Lochiel, though he joined the Rising, felt the same. But some were conscious only of more need for money and tried the simple expedient of raising rents. Even so early as 1737, Culloden, then Lord President, told Argyle of 'oppressive and unmerciful exactions' which threatened to 'unpeople' the Isle of Tiree. His remedy—that of all the more enlightened—was more security for the sub-tenants, definition of vague and oppressive 'services,' and of course, better methods of agriculture.

In 1739 an odd thing happened, that the Outer Isles recall as the Raiders' Ship, the *Long nan Daoine*. MacLeod of Harris and MacDonald of Sleat (it was these two who kidnapped Lady Grange) decided to deport to the Plantations a number of objectionable clansmen. They described them later as thieves, but brought no proof. A hundred and eleven, counting their families, were forced on board a ship, and so despatched. But the ship called at Donaghadee and they escaped, and there was most properly a first-class scandal. Sleat and Harris denied their part. Culloden, who appears to have known the facts, contrived in some way to stop a prosecution: and Mr W. C. Mackenzie suggests, with reason, that six years later this inconvenient knowledge was used to keep the two out of the 'Forty-five. Now, this story has a double point to it. It is clear that even before the 'Forty-five there were chiefs with small heed to their responsibilities: but it also shows that

---

[1] Scott saw the Highlands from a Lowland standpoint, and the 'Forty-five from that of 1812: but he was too much of a Borderer not to understand a good deal of what he saw, and no one has had a keener eye for men as they move through their native environment.

before the 'Forty-five there was a public opinion sufficiently strong to make a pair of very tough specimens nervous lest conduct that fifty years later would appear as a natural, even praiseworthy, proceeding should be attributed to them.[1] No one thought of blackmailing the Marquis of Stafford for doing much the same thing only a lifetime later.

The Rising brought down the whole structure of the Highlands. The abolition of military tenures and of heritable jurisdictions appear as reforms. No doubt they were necessary: but those two things had been the social cement, and nothing was supplied to fill their place. The Jacobite chiefs were exiled, and the Whigs were already finding a centre of gravity furth of the Highlands. And the familiar externals of life were suddenly and forcibly abolished. The Jacobite clans were almost to a man Episcopalians or Roman Catholics: their clergy were more effectively hunted down. War was declared on their music and their language, on their very dress. Suppose Hitler had conquered London, and forced every man in it to shave his head, keep it shaved, and go about without shoes and collar, under penalty of a concentration camp? Yet the shoes and collar of the Londoner, and even his hair, carry no proud historic association: the tartan was part of a man's pride in his race, the kilt of his manhood: now, to wear either of them involved being sold as a slave in the Plantations. The changed dress was a continual reminder that the government people knew was rooted out and that its successor was hostile to all they cared for: its most immediate contact with themselves was through the atrocities of the Butcher Duke, of Cumberland— the methods of the Nazi.

The psychological effect was profound. The whole life of the people had been broken up: their leaders were gone, and 'no man cared for their soul.' At the same time, there were new lands overseas, and some men turned their back on their own, grown tarnished and hopeless, and made their way there to build up a new life. The poverty and the sense of wreck at home were at first the main cause of a popular movement, though sometimes there were further stimuli. Many Catholics of South Uist emigrated because their convert chief would have forced their conversion: and

---

[1] The Lord President's blackmail is conjectural: but there is good contemporary evidence that Sleat and Harris were very badly scared when word of their activities got about.

a body left Lewis in 1773 to escape a bad factor unchecked by a young chief who was then in India on military service.

These movements began in the years about 1760, after the failure of a well-meant but inadequately thought-out project to establish a linen industry in the Highlands. In 1770 six shiploads of people went—about 1,200: and in the next five years there were more emigrations, some of whole communities, headed by their tacksmen. Some men realised that the country was being bled of a vigorous and valuable stock, and there was alarm—Dr Johnson speaks of it—at the 'epidemicall fury' of emigration, and a proposal for an address to the King to beg for action against its 'fatal effects.'

The Government took none. There were plenty of Highlanders for Army needs, and nothing else about the Highlands mattered. Things came to a climax in 1782, with the almost total failure of the crops. Then for some years the tide seemed to turn again. In 1783, thanks to Henry Dundas, the tartan and the kilt were again made legal. At the beginning of 1784 certain Highland gentlemen, led by Grant of Grant and the famous novelist-critic Henry Mackenzie, set to work and founded the Highland Society, Mackenzie setting forth its purposes as

1. An inquiry into the present state of the Highlands of Scotland and the condition of their inhabitants.

2. An inquiry into the means of their improvement by establishing towns and villages—by facilitating communications through different parts of the Highlands of Scotland by roads and bridges—advancing agriculture and extending fisheries—introducing useful trades and manufactures—and by an exertion to unite the efforts of the proprietors and call the attention of Government towards the encouragement and prosecution of these beneficial purposes.

3. The Society shall also pay a proper attention to the preservation of the language, poetry, and music of the Highlands.

It seemed to be the beginning of better days. And at first things went well. Just after the Society was founded the Forfeited Estates were restored to their heirs, and the Treasury was even induced to commission Professor James Anderson to report on fishing. In a letter to George Dempster [1] a little later the Professor shows with

---

[1] A Lowland M.P. turned Highland laird, and a very attractive and enlightened one. His letters to Sir Adam Ferguson of Kilkerran, recently edited by Mr James Ferguson, younger of Kilkerran, are full of the best aspect of the time, and much of them is topical today.

unofficial frankness how the Highland fishing was ruined by 'absurd laws' which favoured Dutch and Irish in Scots waters but 'tied up the hands of the natives' and wrecked Scots trade. Dempster took matters in hand in the House of Commons. He extracted a promise of Highland lighthouses, and in 1786 a Fishery Act, which led to the foundation of the British Society for Extending the Fisheries and Improving the Sea Coasts of the Kingdom—a body including many Highland lairds. It set about a large and ambitious programme for the creation of fishing communities, for which various lairds were willing to grant free sites.

By the late 'eighties, the promise that in the South was already achievement seemed in a fair way to spread to the Highlands also. Even the Government had been stimulated, by Henry Dundas, into showing something of interest: in 1789 the Highland Society, which had then been in existence for five years, even received a grant of £3,000 to pay for their initial inquiry. But the Rights of Man that year came to the fore, and in that passionate preoccupation, the mere rights of Highlanders tended to be shelved.

V

THE CHURCH STANDS BACK

FORTY-ONE YEARS: 1748–89

Concerning the Bounds of Unity; the true placing of them importeth exceedingly. There appear to be two extremes. For to certain zelants all speech of pacification is odious. . . . Peace is not the matter, but following and party. Contrariwise, certain Laodiceans and lukewarm persons think they may accomodate points of religion by middle ways, and taking parts of both, and witty reconcilements; as if they would make an arbitrement between God and man.

FRANCIS BACON, *Of Unity in Religion.*

As was said in the opening chapter of this book, the first half of the eighteenth century shows the overlapping of two very different ages. The religion and politics of the period which ended with the collapse of the 'Forty-five have thus been considered in the previous volume. There followed a revulsion from religion. For two hundred years it had spelt civil war, from whose consequences all the best men of the time were working devotedly to free the country. *Abusus sustulerat usum* for many of these, and a large number, led by David Hume, were professing sceptics of any form of religion. So popular indeed was this attitude that Dr Gregory says in 1760 the creed most fashionable at the time was 'absolute dogmatic atheism'; and a few years later no Edinburgh printer dared publish Professor Beattie's reply to Hume, though Beattie was a scholar of repute.

There were still men whose faith was sincere and deep, from the gentle and devoted Thomas Gillespie, who led the secession called the Relief Synod, to the saintly Episcopalian Lord Pitsligo: but many of the more scholarly ministers and most of those gentry who were neither atheists nor Episcopalians were, often quite frankly, what the time called Deists—believers, that is, in a righteous First Cause of Things, and taking for granted the Christian code of ethics, but without belief in what is called 'revelation.' The ministry of the Church, from their point of view, was a scholarly, leisured, and beneficent profession . . . and they did not forget the

47

first, nor the third, of these attributes; men like Principal Robertson and Dr Carlyle were not only scholars of wide and mellow culture but men of fine character, with a very real sense of social duty, tempered by charitable tolerance.

These Moderates had increased since 1700, and by 1760 were the ruling party. In 1736 their 'opposition,' the Evangelicals, were still sufficiently strong in Edinburgh to be able to close Allan Ramsay's theatre. In 1756 a minister of the Establishment became the author of a successful play, although he had, to be sure, to resign his charge: and the Reverend Dr Carlyle went boldly to see it, though the General Assembly rebuked him for it. In 1784, when the Assembly met, the great Mrs Siddons was in Edinburgh: and its hours of session had to be adjusted so that it should convene when she was not playing.

The Evangelicals or High-flyers were backed by the growing middle class of the towns and a largish number of Lowland country-folk, who held, in its religious part at least, very much the creed of the former Covenanters, and abhorred the very sound of the word ethics. The grim negative ritual of the Covenant Sabbath was still enforced with a fantastic minuteness, and the use by a minister of the Lord's Prayer was still, as late as 1773, matter for grave suspicion of 'heretical pravity.' In High-flyer parishes kirk-session rule was, for the humbler folk at any rate, very little less fierce than it had been in 1650: and the popular reaction to a grimness which had now no longer temporal power to support it was often a defiant laxity, a good deal enhanced by the hard-drinking habits of the most alcoholic era in British history.

Though they remained within the Establishment, the High-flyers in fact were really further from their Moderate brethren than they were from the Presbyterian forms of Dissent. These had increased. There was still the remnant of the old Cameronians, who had remained outside in 1690, and now were known as the Reformed Presbyterians, and had no dealings with any other kind. There were also at this time three secession bodies, who had broken away from the Establishment. The Associate Synod, called generally Seceders, had begun in 1740 with eight members, and in 1765 had a hundred thousand: the question whether or not the Burgess Oath, 'to maintain the true religion professed within this realm,' involved recognition of the Establishment had already split them in Burghers and Anti-Burghers, who were mutually excommunicate. The small Relief Synod broke off in 1761, as a protest against the system of patronage, but contrived to retain for the church which they had left an attitude of Christian charity which speaks to the character of their leader Gillespie.

As for the illegal Dissenters, for many years after 1748 the Episcopal Church was driven underground. Her people held faithfully to non-resistance, and worshipped in small groups in private houses or outdoor conventicles in secluded places. (One country house in South Scotland still has the Prayer-books which were buried in the garden on Sunday night and dug up again on the following Sunday morning.) Their number is rather difficult to assess. In the last quarter of the century, the Presbyterian Ramsay of Ochtertyre says that at Linshart in Buchan, Dean Skinner's parish, eight hundred commonly made their Easter Communion: the North-east, however, has always been the Episcopalian stronghold, and the numbers south of Forth were certainly lower, for the slow and quiet strain of the Penal Laws was more telling than a dramatic persecution. The heaviest weight of the Laws pressed on the clergy, who, with no resources abroad, no access to the universities at home or in England, were in time worn down. In the early century there had been six hundred: by 1784 there were less than fifty. And the layfolk, deprived of their ministers and pastors, tended either to conform to a legal religion, or to leave off religion altogether, while others again tried an expedient which, though it safeguarded them somewhat at the time, was to lead to considerable trouble later. The Penal Laws applied only to men in Scots orders, and as the Church was—informally at least—in communion with the Episcopal Church of England, some congregations sought to parry them by bringing in ministers ordained in England, owing no allegiance to the Scottish bishops, and sharing not their Arminian [1] tradition but the Latitudinarianism of England.

The accession of George III in 1760 eased the pressure somewhat, though several years later the congregation of Bishop Forbes at Leith was forcibly dispersed by the dragoons. But the death of Charles Edward in 1788, and his brother's renunciation of claims to kingship, removed political reasons for persecution: the clergy

[1] 'Reformed Catholic.'

respected George's character and were grateful for his efforts to protect them, and all but one bishop and one presbyter decided to acknowledge him as king.

One outstanding event took place before that time: in an upper room in a slum in Aberdeen was founded, in the year 1783, the great Episcopal Church of America, which now has a hundred and sixty-eight dioceses. When the American War came to an end, there was no bishop in the new Republic. Dr Samuel Seabury was therefore elected, and applied to the English bishops for consecration. They would not give it, fearing the temporal law. The Bishop-elect, though an Englishman by blood, was however a graduate of Edinburgh, and had shared as a student in the hidden worship of the congregation now of Old St Paul's.[1] He begged the Scots bishops to give the Western World 'a free, valid, and purely ecclesiastical episcopate,' and on 14th November 1783 he received it, next day signing a concordat 'between the Catholic remnant of the ancient Church of Scotland and the now rising Church in ~Connecticut.' The Concordat still holds, and the American Church still uses a Liturgy based upon the Scottish.[2]

Roman Catholics also were heavily penalised—more severely, indeed, than were Episcopalians, although as some set-off to the greater pressure they had access to resources from abroad. After 1760, however, in their case also the laws were commonly applied with less rigour. In England some of the harshest of such laws were repealed altogether in 1778, on the condition that they abjured Charles Edward and the temporal jurisdiction of the Pope: and they were now allowed to inherit land and even bring up their children in their own faith. Proposals were made for a similar act for Scotland. The General Assembly, whose predominant Moderates were no persecutors, voted for it, by 118 to 24. There was none the less a riot in Edinburgh. The military had to be called out; and the General Assembly changed its mind, and found that repeal would be 'inexpedient, dangerous, and prejudicial to the

[1] We hear of the young Seabury in Edinburgh asking his host for an Episcopal church, and being told ' Take your hat and follow me. . . . Do not come near me, keep me barely in sight.' ' So following his guide at a distance . . . the stranger at length saw his host disappear suddenly into a dilapidated building . . . and following still the sound of footsteps into the fifth or sixth storey, there worshipped God according to his conscience.'

[2] The Scottish Liturgy of 1637 received a revision in 1764 which made it substantially that in use today.

best interests of religion and civil society in this part of the United Kingdom.' The measure for relief was accordingly dropped.

The English movement known as Methodism had made a spectacular appearance in Scotland as the great Cambuslang 'revival' of 1741, which made much noise. It took little hold, however. John Wesley himself made a preaching tour in 1751, and found a great many listeners but few converts. His Presbyterian hearers were repelled by his outspoken dislike of the Scots Reformers—'May God deliver us from Reforming mobs!' was his comment on the ruins of Arbroath—and he found them in turn, especially the Seceders, 'more uncharitable than Papists.' Episcopalians were less unfriendly, but though he admired the 'decorum' of their worship, they considered him to be a good man misled. It was not until a later generation that his tenets began to make any headway in Scotland.

VI

SLEEPING PARTNERSHIP

THIRTY-FIVE YEARS: 1748–83

When we had a king and a chancellor and parliament-men o' our ain,
we could aye peeble them wi' stanes when they werena guid bairns. But
naebody's nails can reach the length o' Lunnon.
Sir WALTER SCOTT, *The Heart of Midlothian.*

To the general stir of active and vigorous life in the third quarter
of the century there is a very notable exception. All through that
quarter and well into the fourth there was much interest in theories
of conduct; there was much interest in past human conduct, seen
in concrete and often also in national terms; there was a very wide
and active interest in the country's welfare, in national terms again;
but though much of the future political life of the world was being
shaped by Hume and Adam Smith and Watt, there was hardly
even a glimmering of interest in the government that should guide
the nation's conduct or represent its collective activity.

This is strange at first sight. Past Scotland, though ill to
govern, had not by any means always been ill-governed. The old
Scots theory of government had been very unlike that hallowed by
Whig tradition—democracy veiling a practical oligarchy. From
Malcolm III onward, and from at least David I quite consciously,
it indeed fought a running war against oligarchies. So long as the
union between them truly held (as again and again it did for long
periods of time) the joint rule of the Sovereign and the Estates
had, in practice, succeeded, in spite of the stormy factions who
strove to overthrow the essential balance between the varied elements of the nation. Mediaeval Scotland was indeed for long
perhaps the best-governed country in all Europe: and the ideal
which had made her so survived the anarchy after 1286 and even
David II's disastrous reign and the constantly recurring minorities
that staggered the subtle poise which it demanded.

Two centuries of constant Whig propaganda—that is, of anti-
national propaganda—have caused these facts to be generally for-

gotten. One would not claim, of course, that the old Estates were perfect as a political machine: but a hundred years ago a very distinguished Scots historian, who was also a lawyer of much eminence,[1] spoke of their achievement in the light of current political agitations:

The wisdom and public spirit of the Scots Parliament anterior to the Union had not only procured for the people of Scotland all the elements of real freedom, but had effected a settlement . . . of all the great questions which it is the professed object of the Liberal party to resolve in a satisfactory manner at this time. It appears that above two hundred years ago the Scots Parliament had not only effected a settlement . . . of the difficult and complicated tithe question . . . but established an admirable system of poor laws, the efficiency and security of which have been proved by the experience of two centuries, till they were obliterated by . . . the Court of Session; provided an efficient remedy against arbitrary or illegal imprisonment; established a complete and universal system of public instruction; introduced a humane but effective system of criminal law; given the meanest person, charged with an ordinary offence, the same privilege which the English law concedes only to State offenders accused of high treason; awarded to all prisoners the right of being defended by counsel and heard by them upon the evidence; provided for the protection of the poor in litigation against the rich; . . . afforded a humane relief to insolvent debtors, so as to check the evils of prolonged imprisonment; extended their care . . . to the aliment of poor prisoners in jail; established that retrospective period in bankruptcy which English wisdom did not for a century after; given absolute security to cultivators of the soil in the enjoyment of their leasehold rights; . . . prevented the oppression of the husbandman by the exactions of middlemen, or the distraining for more than their own rents by the owners of the soil; never admitted the hideous injustice of the corruption of the blood in the case of high treason . . .; established an admirable and universal system of registration for all titles and mortgages relative to real property; introduced a lucid and intelligible system for the conveyance of landed estates; brought cheap justice to every man's door by a . . . system of local courts; provided for the just and efficient prosecution of crimes by the establishment of [a public prosecutor]; [made matters easier for creditors].

It is an impressive list: and he adds as comment

Whether these were important objects to have been gained, great and glorious attempts to have been made by the parliament of a remote . . . and distracted kingdom during the fifteenth, sixteenth, and seventeenth centuries, we leave it to our readers to judge; but . . . if they were not, then is the whole Liberal party of Great Britain at fault . . . for almost

---

[1] Sir Archibald Alison, Sheriff of Lanark, an historical writer of European repute in his day, who refused the office of Solicitor General.

the whole objects for the acquisition of which they profess such anxiety for England in the middle of the nineteenth century were secured for Scotland by her native legislators before the end of the seventeenth. If the English legislators should continue a course of wise and practical legal improvement, they will perhaps obtain by the year 1900 most of those advantages which the old Scots Parliament had secured for their country two centuries before.[1]

And one marked feature of the old Estates, until well on in the seventeenth century, had been a noble type of nationalism, not aggressive, ever ready for friendliness, but facing aggression with steadfast dignity. We all know the great Declaration of Arbroath: it is but one of many such pronouncements.[2]

The passing of an effective Crown from Scotland, the concentration of politics on religion, or rather on a conflict of religions, overthrew the balance on which all depended. Politics came to mean the mere struggle of party: and for a lifetime before it came to an end, the old Government had been far from admirable, whichever of the parties headed it.

Yet if Saltoun and Belhaven—and the Scots people—had succeeded in getting their way in 1707, the rousing of political consciousness which was bred of the Union struggle might have borne fruit. One can hardly feel that the intelligent, brave, and devoted men who brought a hopeless country to life again would have shown themselves fools and knaves when they came to rule her. But they had no political machine.

The whole post-Union government of Scotland is in fact a remarkable phenomenon. We are too well accustomed to even its oddest aspects to realise how very odd they are, or how curious a thing is our modern status. Before 1707, the Estates comprised, besides the representatives of the Church, 153 hereditary legislators and 154 elected ones, meeting together in the capital. Now this was changed. Officially, the governing machine consisted, after the Union, of two chambers, one composed of some 600 foreigners (and frequently very hostile foreigners) among whom forty-five Scots floated submerged, the other of an assembly of foreign peers, to whom the Scots peers were allowed to add sixteen elected from

---

[1] Sir Archibald was perhaps a little sanguine. England still lacks, for instance, that useful official the Procurator Fiscal.

[2] Cf. for instance the replies of the Estates, in the minority and after the death of James V, to the threats of Henry VIII : and compare again the tone of the Scots and the English Parliaments, after 1603, with regard to the projected Treaty of Union. See *The Scotland of Queen Mary*, pp. 14, 17, 69, 270-72.

their own 153. This body met well over three hundred miles on the outer side of the Scottish frontier, and any letter from its place of meeting took nearly a week to reach the capital. There was no telegraph, no telephone, no radio, and there were very few newspapers, whose news was stale when it reached the readers' hands. Officially, Scotland now was part of a United Kingdom of two nations: but in politics that were common to them both—as for instance, 'peace, war, and general taxation,' in which the nation had long ago claimed a voice—she could not make her collective opinion felt; while in those concerning purely Scots affairs, the vast majority of her governing body was completely lacking in any contact with these. The interests of foreigners overrode her own when there was any difference between the two, while their interest was seldom roused by Scotland, except when she chanced to prove an inconvenience.

One is not surprised that by the mid-century, when the sons of those men who had seen the Union had grown to political age, there was taking shape a still very common attitude of mind, which caused a modern Historiographer Royal, writing a general History of Scotland, to exclude 'the history of the United Kingdom' as something with which Scotland was not concerned, even (he makes the exclusion in that connection) when it deals with a war in which many Scotsmen died, and which has affected all our history since.

By the mid-eighteenth century (as the historian mentioned in the last sentence remarks with an apparent disapproval . . . though, to be sure, on another page of his work) the average Scot 'had neither political ideals nor any living concern in the government of his country.' The Scots members of Parliament shared his frame of mind. At first Lockhart of Carnwath and a few men like him had stirred them to act together on Scots affairs. But two things were needed for that policy—a measure of control by constituents and considerable skill in obstructive tactics; and unfortunately neither of them was present. Before long the Scots members gave up the struggle, merely voting *en bloc* for whichever Government had control of the House. Only Walpole's insults over the Porteous Riot roused them to take any sort of national standpoint.

Yet with her organs of government thus excised, Scotland was governed; and even, by lucky chance, surprisingly well, though in still more surprising manner when one remembers that the cardinal article of the Whig credo was consistent exaltation of Parliament as against rule exerted by a single man. It was the age of the Benevolent Despot: and in practice, Benevolent Despots governed Scotland—more absolutely, in domestic matters, than any Lennox Stewart had tried to do, or even Cromwell in full Dictatorship.

There was in fact something to be said for the method. It ensured that Scotland should be ruled by Scotsmen, and for much of the time by two very able Scotsmen. If it favoured nepotism and corruption, Parliamentary government, as then practised in England, reeked of them both. Its immediate results were not ill: but the ultimate results were to be grave, for the sense of responsibility towards their country died out from among the general mass of men, as it always does when dictators rule in peace.

The office of the Secretary for Scotland had been abolished in 1746. From that time until 1827 the nominal head of Scots administration was the Home Secretary, who was always English. In practice, however, 'a deputy was king'—one of a series of 'managers.' The first of them was Archibald Duke of Argyle, called Congé d'Élire, who held the post until his death in 1761. He held it firmly, though his status depended almost entirely on personality and a disillusioned gift of handling men, backed by a complex system of patronage. A man could consider himself sure of promotion 'whether he was [King George's] friend or foe, if he would go to hell for the Duke of Argyle.'

Congé d'Élire, though he used his power for his personal satisfaction (as the luckless James of the Glens found out in course), yet took heed to the general well-being of the country, especially of the neglected Highlands. When in 1752 a number of the forfeited estates were annexed to the Crown, he made a real attempt to bring it into that relation with them, of the Chief, which had been the strength of James the Fourth. Unluckily, however, George the Second, though not a bad specimen of the junker type, was hardly the man for the experiment, taking no interest whatever in the kingdom except in so far as she might have 'nuisance value.'

Later, Argyle had to deal with a small storm. In 1757, for defence against a possible French invasion, a citizen militia was formed in England. Its extension to Scotland was however refused: and in 1760 the French attacked Carrickfergus, apparently seeking a base against the Clyde. There was general anger at Scotland's lack of protection, and a fresh demand for a national militia, which greatly annoyed the Whigs, since these considered that the Jacobites were backing the proposal in order to show their acceptance of the new King, and feared lest they might be rewarded with loaves and fishes. Accordingly, the militia was still refused.

Much the most notable of Argyle's successors was Henry Dundas, who was later Viscount Melville. Becoming Lord Advocate in 1775, he for thirty years was the uncrowned King of Scots—and, one may add, no constitutional monarch. He was a man of strong personality, outstanding even in that vivid age, with uncommon charm, a remarkable head for claret, and magnificent talk in the rich and racy Scots which still survived as the 'curial' speech of the nation. 'Tory and Whig agreed in loving him,' and his ripe humanity was no mere mask. He had his country's interests at heart, and strove to serve them according to his lights, which if cynical were very far from dull. He took the corruption of politics as he found it; but if, in the India, War, or Home Offices, or at the Admiralty, he profited by it, he used it also to do much for Scotland.[1]

On his arrival in power he at once abolished an ugly blot on the Scottish social system—the seventeenth-century institution of 'bound' colliers and salters, who, with their children, were thirled for life to the salt-pan and the pit. In 1782 he procured the repeal of the act forbidding the Highland dress and tartan, and two years later managed to secure that twelve annexed estates were restored to their heirs, on repayment of the sums which had been expended. (The money came to £90,000, part of which built the beautiful Register House.) His powerful influence in the affairs of Whitehall extracted useful grants from the Treasury for canals and harbours and for Highland schools, and even in aid of the Highland Society.

Nevertheless, in the early days of his reign the Sleeping Partner in the United Kingdom began to stir a little, uneasily. A wind from across the Atlantic was blowing in France, and an eddy began to drift through the northern stagnation. But the events which fanned it belong to a sequence which opened beyond the frontiers of Scotland, and the new political interest of the 'eighties can be better explained at the end of a later chapter.

[1] There survives a private list, made in 1788, of 2,662 country voters, with the names neatly annotated : ' Has a family ' ; ' Wants a commission for a younger son ' ; ' Married to a niece of Mr Dundas,' and so forth.

VII

THE DISTANT SCENE

THIRTY-FIVE YEARS: 1748–83

Pitt recognised the genius of Frederick the Great, and resolved to give him firm and energetic support. . . . The Londoners hung after Pitt's dismissal from office on his carriage wheels, hugged his footmen, and even kissed his horses.

J. R. GREEN, *A Short History of the English People.*

THE foundation-stone of our present-day Europe was laid on the 16th December of the year 1740, when Frederick 'the Great' invaded Silesia. It was tamped down in 1757, when the British Government repudiated the agreement made with France at Klosterseven, and just in time, saved Frederick from crushing disaster. As a result of these things, in the present year, small children have been shot down in Scottish streets.

The war called 'of the Austrian Succession,' opened by that invasion of 1740 and Frederick's breach of his recent guarantee, was over by the year 1748, and falls before the period of this chapter: but it must be recalled in this place, none the less, for with it opens a sequence of event which must now be sketched, if only in bare outline.

The Europe which emerged from the confusion of the sixteenth-century religious conflict was based on a principle which begins to show (it was very clearly grasped by our own James IV) in the long and tangled European war which preceded and partly included the Reformation—the war in which Flodden was an episode. This principle was that of the balance of power—of a balance, as seen then, between France and the Empire.

It was called into play in the sixteenth century, as counter to the preponderance of Charles V. In the seventeenth it stood against Louis XIV, and at his death in 1715 the whole of the political structure of Europe was grouped round the two poles of Vienna and Versailles. The recognised policy of the United Kingdom was to preserve that balance in constant being by swinging her weight to one side or the other. But the plan was based on the fundamental ideas that France would be always the France of Louis XIV, and that powers which were secondary would remain so: and before the eighteenth century was half through, both of these factors were beginning to change.

France had broken the immense strength of the Hapsburgs, though they still held that nominal hegemony of the Empire which was implied in the Imperial title: their actual domains were a curious patchwork—Austria, Hungary, half the Low Countries, the Duchy of Milan. But the French effort to build a Bourbon Empire of France and Spain and the latter's vast possessions had also been decisively defeated. In the centre of Europe, within, for the time, the Empire, a new power challenged France and the Hapsburgs both—a Slav-Teuton state with its centre at Berlin and the Hohenzollerns for its dynasty. And British, or rather English, interests already spread beyond the marches of Europe.

Since the Reformation, and largely because of it, the power of the Hohenzollerns had steadily grown; and in 1701 their already wide dominions had become the considerable kingdom of Prussia. In 1740 its throne fell to Frederick II, a cold thin machine of a man, devoured by greed, and of a quite unscrupulous ambition, great military and organising gifts, and a cynical understanding of human nature and of human passivity under the *fait accompli*. He loathed everything German—would not even speak the language: but Prussian aggrandisement spelt Frederick aggrandised, and he bent to it that acute efficiency. Almost at once he decided that his advantage lay 'in robbing an ally whom he was bound to defend,' the young Archduchess of Austria, Maria Theresa; and so, on the 16th December 1740, he marched his armies into Silesia.

For eight years that war swept across the centre of Europe,[1] France, opposed to Austria, supporting Frederick, and England, opposed to France, supporting Austria. And there grew from it a Franco-British conflict whose terrain spread far, to east and west overseas. Then in 1748 this war had been halted by what was called the Peace of Aix la Chapelle.

It was virtual, but temporary, stalemate. The only power which gained by it was Prussia, who still retained her loot Silesia, and whose programme in the Empire was only begun. France and Britain had laid the foundations for new war, over claims in India and America. In the former, it was to open very soon, for India,

---

[1] The 'Forty-five, from a European point of view, is one of its sideshows.

as so often in history, was being torn in pieces by quarrelling native powers, with a foreign threat behind them to the north. Its nominal suzerain yet was the Muslim Great Moghul[1]: but the Moghul Empire was now gravely threatened between the Hindu Mahrattas to the south and the Afghans and the Persians to the north, and was breaking up into separate quarrelling states.

Time out of mind, the vast wealth of the Indies had been a proverb. Since Vasco da Gama reached Calicut in 1498, Europeans had sought to possess a share in it, but they came and went not as colonists but as traders. Now that the Moghul Empire was dissolving, French and English intervened in its politics in order to protect their trading stations: and each hoped to be heir to the crumbling central power, which for ages had gone to invader after invader. 1748 saw Dupleix, representing France, in virtual control of South India, as ally of Hyderabad and the Carnatic.[2] England was helping the latter's enemies, and in 1751 Clive took and held Arcot its capital, and the English and French in India attacked each other, though their governments at first were not greatly concerned.

Then the same war stirred on the other side of the world. The British—still rather the English—colonies formed a deep strip from Nova Scotia south to Georgia, and inland, vaguely, to the St Lawrence and the Alleghanies. The French controlled the basins of the St Lawrence and of the Mississippi, beyond the Alleghanies, and the region of the Great Lakes that joined the two, thus encircling the coastwise strip of colonies. The weak link in the continuity of French land lay south of the Lakes, along the Ohio River: and British settlers established themselves there. The governor of Virginia, Robert Dinwiddie, sent the young George Washington to build a fort in order to make the occupation effective. French settlers repulsed him, and built the fort themselves, on the site of what is now the city of Pittsburg. The British Government next year expelled the French *habitants* from Acadie, the French colony north of the New England States, which had been French for a century and a half. There ensued a state of semi-official war, with Montcalm, the Governor of French America, pressing hard against the British colonies and threatening to enfilade the coastal

---

[1] The Moghul Empire of India was founded in the sixteenth century by the invader Mahmoud Babar, and reached its height about the mid-seventeenth, with Shah Jehan.
[2] Pondicherry, the main French post, and Madras, the chief English one, were both upon the coast of the Carnatic, the eastern shore of Peninsular India.

strip by the fort which he had built at Ticonderoga, in the pass between the St Lawrence and New York.

European war began to loom again, and George II grew anxious for his loved Hanover, which was inconveniently close to Prussia.[1] In 1755 he therefore agreed to back Russia against Prussia, and wished Austria, as a further counterpoise, to strengthen her Netherlands.[2] Frederick decided that Britain and Russia together were too much to tackle: accordingly, in 1756, he offered a guarantee for Hanover, in return for a British guarantee of Prussia. Austria, alarmed, made haste to reconcile herself with France: and the moment France's alliance with Prussia expired, France and her ancient enemies the Hapsburgs made another for their common defence against the new threat from the North European plain. It was meant to prevent war: it brought it on instead. Frederick, anticipating 'encirclement' and Austria's recovery of Silesia, marched into Saxony, west of Silesia, between Austrian and Prussian territory, and began what was to be the Seven Years War—1756 to 1763.

We need only outline that complicated business. Scotland, as such, had nothing to do with its conduct, and though Scots troops, of course, took a share in it, the Government had been scared by the 'Forty-five and their part was less than in two earlier wars, of the Spanish Succession (1702-14), when the Scots Greys took seventeen standards at Ramillies, and the Austrian Succession, when for the first time in its history the *Maison du roi* lost its colours, taken by the same regiment at Dettingen. But the war's consequences, none the less, and the politics concerned in its conclusion, both involved Scotland, and importantly: indeed, they involve her still at the present day.

Britain supported Frederick's aggression, whereon France attacked Hanover and beat Cumberland—the Cumberland of the 'Forty-five, that is—who saved his army by giving his parole that he would disband it. Once it was safe, he promptly broke the parole, with the concurrence of his Government, and the French were driven back across the Rhine. Pitt, who for some time had

---

[1] It lay directly south of the ' stem ' of Denmark, though not marching with it, and unlike Prussia, had a useful stretch of coast on the North Sea, including one shore apiece of the estuaries on whose rivers stand the great towns of Hamburg and Bremen : and Prussia already held patches of territory to the west of it, while she actually marched with it on the east.

[2] The Austrian Netherlands were more or less equivalent to modern Belgium.

6

been out of favour, not only as an ally of the King's heir but because he wished to concentrate against France, unencumbered by concern for Hanover, became Secretary of State in 1757, and virtual leader of the Government. He found Prussia exhausted by the economic and military strain of her conquests. Her defeat at that point— and she was very near it—might well have altered all subsequent history. Two things saved her: one was Pitt's financial help, the other the death of the Empress Elizabeth, whose half-mad successor, Frederick's fervent admirer, lived just long enough to draw Russia out of the war.

In 1758 and 1759, Pitt proved himself a brilliant war minister. He blockaded France and carried the war overseas, endeavouring to strip France of her colonies, in what was now a deliberate bid for world-power. His terrain was the globe: he kept going half a dozen campaigns at once, far apart, but all elements in one design. In 1759 Wolfe took Quebec: he was killed there, but his Scots successor Murray carried on the war, and next year Canada, France's chief colony, was in British control. In India, French diplomacy was mishandled. France lost Indian support; and in 1761 Eyre Coote took her chief base in India, Pondicherry. In Bengal the English settlement at Calcutta and the French one at Chandernagore lay close together. There were complications with the native princes; and Clive, by some creditable soldiering and some less creditable diplomacy, had broken French influence by 1760, and made Great Britain mistress of Bengal. In barely five years, Pitt had strangled the trade of France, had seriously harmed that of most neutrals, and enormously increased the trade of England: the great commercial doctrine of the Whigs, that war meant wealth, seemed amply justified. He had also achieved the security of Prussia, of a new type of state whose dominant principle was desire for power—not power as a means, but power as an end in itself. The conception is Eastern rather than European, but it had Western efficiency now behind it . . . and under it also that rankling sense of her inferior culture which had long already marked North Germany, and in fact was undoubtedly one of the strongest emotions that ever troubled Frederick's icy brain.

By 1762 there were, however, fresh factors emerging in home politics—the new young King and his chief adviser Bute. Both disliked the 'bloody and expensive war,' and the steady piling up of the National Debt. Bute seems too to have seen what was growing up in Prussia, and desired not only to check her aggrandisement but to make peace with France upon such terms as should make possible future alliance with her. The rival policies clashed when in 1761 the Bourbons of France, Spain, and Naples made an alliance, and Pitt wished therefore to make war on Spain. The King refused: Pitt resigned, and Bute succeeded him—to be faced at once with Spain's declaration of war. Spain, however, had no success, and in 1763 Bute found it easy to induce both France and Spain to give up the fight: and he forced Prussia out of it as well, for though, as he was bound to do as an ally, he made it a condition of the Peace that France should evacuate Prussian territory, he also withdrew Pitt's subsidy to Frederick, who could not afford to carry on without it. The Peace of Paris left Britain enormous gains. Canada, Cape Breton Island, and Prince Edward Island were taken from France—that is, almost all her American possessions—and she also yielded Minorca, as Spain did Florida, while in India Britain was left as the major power alike in the Carnatic and in Bengal. Bute, however, declined to use the advantage of victory wholly to strip the conquered. Spain, in exchange for Florida, had the return of Havana and Manilla; France kept her various Indian 'factories,' her West Indian Islands, and her rights in the fisheries of Newfoundland.

The Peace exploded a political conflict which had been going on, though more or less under the surface, since the young King's accession in 1760, and was now to threaten the Whig Dispensation and greatly embitter Anglo-Scottish relations.

These last played a very important part in the business. The 'fifties had brought the countries almost to friendship: the old antagonisms were dying down. In 1758, indeed, Horace Walpole, very much an Englishman and the son of a notable Prime Minister, had gone so far as to say publicly that the Scots were 'the most accomplished nation in Europe.' The administration of the United Kingdom had begun to be that of a Union of two kingdoms. Scots were given a place at last in the services as something more than mere regimental commanders. In 1756 one became British Ambassador to Prussia, another Commander-in-Chief in America. In 1759 General Murray had succeeded General Wolfe, and became Governor of Canada. Sir James Douglas distinguished himself at Dominica, Sir Hector Munro was launched on a brilliant career, and Pitt had been using Highland regiments, and talking of their 'fidelity and honour,' both of which qualities they had amply proved.

These successes chilled the new affection of England, and she also had a more legitimate grievance, for one or two Scots had lately been preferred to places which in fact were purely English. It was not perhaps of very much importance that Robert Adam should be Court Architect or Robert Strange President of the Academy: but William Murray, later Earl of Mansfield, had become, in the year 1756, Lord Chief Justice of England, which was serious. And the young King, making his first speech from the throne, had added to it of his own accord, 'born and educated in this country, I glory in the name of'—not *England*, but *Britain*. And now a Scot became Prime Minister, and what was worse, he threatened the power of the Whigs, which ever since the Glorious Revolution had been considered as a law of nature.

The culprit was John Stuart, Earl of Bute. Bute is an interesting and tragic figure, rising strangely in the politics of the age, his position completely incomprehensible save against a background of Scottish history. He was grandson of an anti-Union peer and nephew of the Argyle called Congé d'Élire, had been bred on the outer fringe of politics, and was—the point is not irrelevant—a man of quite uncommon charm and good looks, a shy scholarly half-recluse and book-collector, living very quietly on somewhat narrow means when by a sheer accident of the English climate he was brought in contact with Frederick, Prince of Wales. Frederick liked Bute: so did Frederick's unhappy wife, whom the King hated worse than he hated Frederick himself, and whose widowhood a little while thereafter left her very seriously in need of friends. Their son George, whom his father's death made Heir-apparent, was a gentle, bullied, rather stupid youth, and gave Bute the pathetic, half-hysterical adoration such a lad often feels for a brilliant elder who is kind and patient . . . the more as the Princess of Wales was by no means patient, and constantly harried the boy to assert himself and to break out from the obscurity in which his grandfather and the Government would alike have kept him.

Bute found the pair—the angry, ill-treated Princess and her gentle, earnest, conscientious son—dependent on him for both counsel and comfort. He took seriously his position as their friend, trying to restrain the Princess's indiscretions and to train the young

Prince for his future position. For instance, we know that he borrowed the unpublished MS. of Blackstone's *Commentaries*—the Bible of English lawyers—for George to read, attempted to cultivate his taste for the arts, and with more success, to make him feel himself not German but British, as neither George I nor George II had ever been, by birth or by their personal inclination.

Now Bute, standing on the rim of politics and profoundly revolted by what he saw from it, had his theory of a possible reform. The Sovereign was now the mere puppet of a party—of a party that stood for a portion of the nation. But the Tories no longer supported a rival King, and Jacobitism was, in practice, dead. Suppose that George III, when he should come, a native-born king, to the throne, should draw about him a government of both parties, standing not only for England but for Britain, and take his place at the head of Parliament as the leader of national administration? It was in fact not far from the old Scots conception, of the Crown as apex of a balanced structure embodying all the elements of the nation [1]: and there is no inherent reason, at least, why it should not have been able to work in England, where indeed the national talent for compromise, for finding a working balance of differents, would seem to give it a likelihood of success.

But Bute, as Samuel Johnson (whom he befriended) said later, was 'a theoretical statesman,' and George the Third was far from being David the First. George came to the throne, a young man of twenty-two, in 1760, and attempted to put Bute's ideas in practice. The Whigs went into a panic, redoubled when Bute became Prime Minister and desired that the Government should have place in it for men of both parties and of both the kingdoms, and, which was nearly as terrible, for the King.

Bute had to be pulled down, and he was attacked by a swarm of pamphlets, speeches, newspapers, directed to whipping up the mass-hysteria to which, in that century and the seventeenth, the London mob was exceedingly addicted. They were wholly unscrupulous. Burke, who was Bute's strong opponent, admitted later that most of the charges brought against the Scot were unjust

---

[1] In practice, under the old Scots constitution, the Sovereign was ' member ' for those not otherwise represented in the Estates—a development from the old Gaelic idea of the Chief. Nearly all sovereigns recognised the fact, though as always the quality of the representation depended on the quality of the man. It was precisely this intimate relation of Crown and *populus* which made the development of absentee monarchy so peculiarly disastrous to our country.

or frivolous. John Wilkes, in private, expressed his disbelief of the very stories he was so busily putting about in print. 'I thought him a good Minister,' said he, 'but it was my game to attack him': and he did, with all the resource of an able Yellow Press.

There were a good many lines of the attack. The Peace of Paris was an easy one: England had trounced the Froggies, and that 'bloody Scotchman' had traitorously omitted to strip them bare. Then Bute wanted to let the King share the Government, and the English, by now, had a blind and ingrained terror of any power being wielded by the Crown.[1] Then Bute was also quite indecently handsome, a distressing quality in a public man: and of course he must be the Princess Dowager's lover: a Jack-boot and a Petticoat, hung from a gallows, were the signs of popular righteous indignation. Then he was poor, which was extremely shocking: and when his wife inherited a large fortune, the new riches were the result of taking bribes. But the gravest charge, the one easiest to exploit and impossible to rebut, was that Bute was a Scotsman. Not only was Wilkes crying out on the one hand that a Hottentot had as much right to preferment in England, but the lately pro-Scots Horace Walpole was laying down the law that no Scot could lead the British Parliament; and the Duke of Bedford was vociferating that there was an end of England for evermore if a Scot should be appointed as the Speaker. These are among the mildest of the attacks. Much of the flood is beyond any decent quotation. Cartoons showed Britannia choking on a thistle, and Cumberland grew popular with the mob *because* of his brutalities in Scotland.

Bute, proud, shy, sensitive, and by now aware that his pupil the King had not the qualities to achieve their plan and that the Tories lacked the political training which would have enabled them to give support, bowed to the storm, and resigned within a year. It did not end the enmity of the Whigs. Whenever they happened, in the next twenty years, to require a red herring, Bute was brought out again. In 1770 he was still caricatured as trampling, decked with thistles, on Britannia. Even in 1780 he was accused of being a Jacobite, and forged letters, alleged to be from the exiled James, were shown to back the charge. 'This envenomed Sirocco' pursued him to his death: and his project for a united government and for

---

[1] Not really unnatural, considering their history, though it goes oddly with their traditional veneration for Elizabeth and Cromwell and their affection for Henry VIII.

better international relations between the two partners of the United Kingdom achieved the precise reverse of his design.

In addition to this unhappy sequel at home, the Seven Years War was soon followed by another, which seemed to shatter Pitt's vision of an Empire, and which did help to wreck the monarchy of France and both directly and through French repercussions long and powerfully affected British affairs. This war began against British colonies, but France and Spain and indeed great part of Europe were to be involved in it before it ended.

Its beginning comes with the Whig assault on Bute. Bute had brought into the ministry George Grenville, who was a Whig and the brother-in-law of Pitt. On Bute's resignation Grenville succeeded him, and was faced, of course, with the task of paying for the war—not one that ever endears a government—while, as fresh complication for the Treasury, an unexpected demand came from overseas.

The American-British colonists by now were something like a couple of million strong—a third as many again as the people of Scotland. Many, now, had been born and bred on American soil, and felt America to be their country. They desired the advantage of being British subjects—protection, especially, from their enemies: but they had a forcible and growing objection to being governed from across the Atlantic, and in local affairs by men sent from across the Atlantic, responsible not to the Colonies but to Whitehall and a government who had never seen their country.

Now, Bute's Treaty of Paris had left in British hands a huge new stretch of American territory, from the Alleghanies to the Mississippi. In 1763-64 the Indians there (who included the formidable Iroquois) rose against their new masters. The Colonists refused to defend themselves, and a handful of regular troops had to deal with the rising. It was clear that a frontier garrison was needed. The Colonists objected to paying for it, and also objected, no less forcibly, to any restriction from home upon their trade and to any legal protection of Indian interests.

The unhappy Grenville, forced to retrenchment at home and confronted with the piled-up debts of Pitt's war, had to find the money to guard the colonies. Now the war had been fought very largely for colonies, and it seemed to him to be less than reasonable to pay a heavy price for their enlargement and then to make them a burden on the State. He proposed therefore to make them self-supporting, and if possible, contributory as well, in return for protection by the mother-country: so he asked for a British monopoly for their trade, and desired from them some kind of direct tax also, on whatever commodity they might choose themselves. They refused to choose; and in 1765 Grenville proceeded to pass the famous Stamp Act—a small direct tax on legal documents, such as already was in force in England. The Colonists objected violently, and shifted the basis of the whole dispute by protesting that a British Government in which they were not represented had no right to tax them, even for their own advantage . . . and at this point the young King suddenly went mad, and a quarrel over the question of regency brought down Grenville, who was replaced by Rockingham.

Pitt who, better than either Grenville or Rockingham, grasped the new issues now raised by the dispute, induced the latter to repeal the Stamp Act: but serious damage was already done. The vague and not all justified discontents of the Colonists had found a formula which went behind them and subsumed them all in the fundamental question of national status. The Colonies were aware of themselves as a nation—as one, to be sure, of a British Union of Nations, but none the less, or all the more, a nation: yet Westminster treated them as a mere possession, and could not, apparently, see why they should resent it. For the rest of the 'sixties there was constant friction, and a growing interest was roused at home in the fundamental rights and wrongs of the matter. Pitt (now Earl of Chatham), Hume, and Adam Smith all strongly supported the Irishman Burke in preaching that the Colonists had justice on their side, and that freedom was likely to be the strongest chain in holding the unity of an overseas Empire. But the Government had the law upon their side; and the shocking insolence of the Colonists' claim to an equal citizenship with themselves fired many good people to scandalised indignation, especially in the English ruling class.

The problem was frittered with for a number of years. The Government were not at all unwilling to grant concessions on points they understood. They could understand well enough an objection to taxes, and by 1770 all but one were repealed, though with the new Prime Minister North protesting that he must leave that on tea by way of token that Westminster could legally impose them.

Chatham, Burke, David Hume, and Adam Smith, and a number of other men, made forcible protests; but North had the King behind him,[1] and held firm. The Resentments piled up then for three years longer: but on the 16th December 1773 there took place the famous 'Boston Tea-Party'; the East India Company's newly imported tea was thrown into the water off Griffin's Wharf.

It should have been a warning. It was not. North promptly suppressed the government of the State. Then, to make sure of Canada's loyalty, her Catholic French were given religious freedom: and the Calvinists of New England were horrified. Then the Colonies' agent in London, Benjamin Franklin, was grossly insulted by the Privy Council. For months ill-feeling piled up steadily; and at last, in April 1775, armed Colonists and British regulars clashed—ironically, at the village of Concord. Next winter the Colonists hoisted their own flag: and on the 4th July 1776 their representatives at Philadelphia signed a formal Declaration of Independence:

These United Colonies are and ought to be free and independent states: and all political connection between them and the state of Great Britain is and ought to be dissolved.

The war swayed on for six years, drawing in, as wars commonly do, more belligerents. The American part was for the most of it a thoroughly muddled affair, on both sides alike. At the end of a year, America was not winning; but Britain was clearly losing, and deserved it. Her troops were ill-led, ill-supported, and ill-supplied, and in October 1777 General Burgoyne had to surrender with his army.

The insulted Franklin had meanwhile gone to Versailles, where he appealed to many sentiments, from the fashion for 'Nature' and the Noble Savage through the new doctrine of the Rights of Man to the lingering resentments after the Peace of Paris. In March 1778 France entered the war as ally of the new nation. North offered terms to America, but too late, and the dying Pitt believed that he was watching the complete collapse of that Imperial power for which he had carried on the Seven Years War.

Spain, France's ally, declared war also next year, and attacked Gibraltar, the key to the Mediterranean and the Near East. The Franco-Spanish fleet commanded the Channel. The Scots-

[1] George's first attack of insanity was brief.

American privateer Paul Jones (later the founder of the U.S. Navy) was actually raiding the Scots coast, and the French were threatening an invasion of England. In spite of the fervent efforts of the press-gangs, whose activity was now extended to Scotland, the British fleet could not cope with the situation. Holland was added to the enemy, and in the same year—that is, 1780—Russia, Prussia, Sweden, Austria, and Denmark and Norway made a League of Armed Neutrality against Britain.

The grim situation was to be saved, however, by a Scottish soldier and an English sailor. General Eliott, of the family of Stobs, was shut up in Gibraltar in 1779; and he held it for three long years against France and Spain, against blockade, bombardment, and starvation, thus occupying many enemy ships. And in the January of 1780 Rodney defeated the Spaniards off Cape St Vincent, did a good deal of damage to their fleet, and greatly lessened the naval odds against Britain.

Yet he could not regain control of the Channel, or prevent French ships from reaching America with men and munitions. Mahan, the classic writer upon sea-power, declares that America owes her independence to the fleet of France, and he is clearly right. In the October of 1781 the American issues of the war were decided, by the surrender of Cornwallis at Yorktown.

A couple of other wars had sprung from the main one. A luckless campaign was in progress in the West Indies. In the East, Warren Hastings was fighting the Mahrattas, and Hyder Ali, Sultan of Mysore, had in 1780 fallen upon the British, and endangered their hold in Southern India. Sir Eyre Coote, however, fighting against heavy odds, held him, and next year began to win this war, though peace was not made till 1784.[1]

Before that, things had improved in the West Indies, for in the April of 1782 Rodney encountered the French fleet at Les Saintes, and in a hard-fought battle achieved the defeat of the brave and able French admiral, De Grasse: and a few months later Eliott, still holding Gibraltar, was relieved by a British squadron under Lord Howe.

All the parties to the war were by that time weary. Britain was beaten by the Colonists, but had contrived to draw with France

---

[1] In that year Pitt's Bill took the real power in British India out of the hands of the East India Company and gave it to a Board whose President sat *ex officio* in Parliament.

and Spain. The very serious damage to her fleet inclined France to peace. St Vincent and Gibraltar had cost Spain dearly. On 27th September 1782 Britain admitted that the Colonies, from the Atlantic shore to the Mississippi, were now 'free, sovereign, and independent states.'[1] Sixty thousand Loyalists, left on American soil, were allowed to make their way to Canada, which in spite of its very largely French population, had not joined the insurgent colonies. Next year peace was also made with France, Spain, and Holland. By the peace terms, several of the West India islands were restored to the French and Dutch, and Minorca and Florida went back to Spain. But thanks to Eliott, Britain still held Gibraltar.

The Peace caused a furious outburst of wrath at home. There had been incredible mismanagement, amounting to mass-murder of our troops. Cowper sang of the tragedy of the *Royal George*. But no squall heeled her: her bottom fell out at anchor in calm weather,

> And Kempenfelt went down,
> With twice four hundred men,

. . . nor was any dockyard official hanged for their murder. And she is only one example of many. Scarcely more creditable is the way in which the politicians concerned in the mess stirred up a smoke-screen to protect themselves by blaming the men whom they had sent to their deaths. Blame of the living was devoted also to the party called the King's Friends, who had led the war, and who were the ghost of Bute's planned coalition. They deserved blame: but it did not reflect back credit on those who bestowed it, for the Opposition Whigs cheered in the House when they heard the glad news that Britain had been defeated and the Government were delivered into their hands.

[1] They were federated in 1789.

VIII

THE RETURN OF POLITICS

SIX YEARS: 1783–89

As there are certain hollow blasts of wind and secret swellings of sea
before a tempest, so are there in states.

FRANCIS BACON, *Of Seditions and Troubles.*

THE Whigs returned, and a young man of twenty-three, the son of
Pitt, was given the Chancellorship of the Exchequer. He was an
ardent pupil of Adam Smith, and his vigour and foresight at the
Treasury saved defeated Britain from the post-war collapse of the
finances which in France was to have such momentous consequences.
Smith's influence, and perhaps that of other Scots, shows in his
attitude to French relations, for only three years after the peace
with France he brought forward a Treaty of Commerce with that
nation, designed to be the first step of a friendship which might
link the two powers of France and Britain in future as France and
Scotland had been linked in the past. But events which no one at the
time foresaw were to intervene and bring something very different.

Although Pitt would have called himself a Whig, he led the new
movement, then beginning to stir, which was to destroy the old
Whig oligarchy. The word 'beginning' there applies to Britain.
In France it had been in progress for a lifetime. Voltaire in the
'thirties, Montesquieu in the 'forties, had idealised what they saw
as the freedom of Britain under a limited constitutional monarchy,
and the former had brought his lucid negative mind and his formidable wit keenly to bear on all the weaknesses of the French state. His
temper ruled the *philosophes* of the 'fifties—Diderot and the other
men of the *Encyclopédie.* That influential compendium of knowledge had a solvent effect on all accepted values, and challenged all
accepted institutions. Those men who made it, like Voltaire himself,
had minds like a steel blade, keen, clear, and thin. Nothing existed
that transcended 'reason,' by which highly emotional word they
understood a logical exposition of such facts as were within their
own power of experience. They respected man, not as bearing

72

within him a spark of the divine, but as a substitute for the divine—
a simplification which commonly makes for trouble. Ignoring the
divine, they ignored sin also: all that was needed for perfect human
life was good law, or later, as Rousseau came into fashion, no law.
All men were born both free and equal.

They attacked a good many most genuine abuses, and also many
familiar assumptions: and when the space of these last had been
swept and garnished Rousseau obligingly filled it with many others,
delightful to believe. Natural man is naturally good. Civilisation
has corrupted man, who in his primitive state is a dignified, robust,
and noble creature, 'with pity in his heart.' Back therefore once
again to the Noble Savage, and give free rein to the sacredness of
Emotion! (We ourselves saw it again in the nineteen-twenties,
though with other labels on its deities.) And the Encyclopaedists,
who believed in Progress, were intensely shocked at this blue-print
for it, Voltaire remarking, with his acid sweetness, 'On n'a jamais
employé tant d'esprit à vouloir nous faire bêtes.' [1]

None the less, Rousseau ran away with the movement. In
1762 his *Contrat social* caused an immense furore: like Calvin's
Institutes, *Das Kapital*, and *Mein Kampf*, it became the Koran of
an impassioned creed. He was turning, however, from his former
idea of *l'homme dépravé par la société*. Society now is not evil in
itself, but the result of a contract for mutual protection. The
individual is no longer free: society now has supreme power over
him. Force as a sanction, however, is illegitimate. All government
must be by the general will, which legislators merely formulate.
The best government is by an elective aristocracy: election will
naturally secure to it uprightness, understanding, experience, and
all other claims to eminence and esteem. Christianity is still only
fit for slaves; but the Government should enforce upon all men, if
necessary by the death penalty, a civil religion based, according to
Reason, on all the proper social sentiments.

It took like wildfire, conquering all the 'advanced,' including,
in that time of deflated religion, many eager souls who were hungry
for a faith, and who, forbidden by the pressure of fashion to believe
in God, sought a substitute in man or in reified, often deified,
abstractions of states of being, like Progress or Liberty. As in all
such welters of new negatives, men took out of it what their tem-

---

[1] 'No one has used so much wit to make us stupid'—the last word has a
ferocious double meaning, as *bête* means not only *stupid* but *animal*.

peraments demanded—an inspiring hope for the betterment of the world; licence for licence or for self-assertion; a generous ardour to defend the oppressed; a satisfaction for envy and resentment, made dignified by being raised to the status of virtues. Common to all was a sense that much was wrong, and a feeling that with a little intelligence it could quickly (if those at present in power were removed) be all put right and bring the millennium. And since much, in plain objective truth, was wrong, and some of it flagrantly very wrong indeed, the more speculative elements in the creed were all taken as being thereby confirmed in full.

The successful issue of the American War brought these ideas from the sphere of ardent talk in study and salon and round the dinner-table to that of immediate concrete politics: and not, by any means, only in France. Their effect in London was considerable: in Edinburgh it was, in some ways, greater still, for in the third quarter of the century the old intercourse with France had been renewed, and Scots men of letters—Hume, Robertson, Adam Smith—had been lionised in Paris and Versailles.

The major principle of the American struggle had been that men were not responsible to a government not responsible to them. Britain saw the issue, as it bore on her political theory, in terms not of a community, however, but of the rights of the individual man. That difference had a profound effect on Scotland. But the statement of the individual's rights in face of any form of government was a congenial conception to Scots, who since the dim beginnings of their nation were accustomed to the idea of the clan, in which, though status might vary, each man had status, a recognised place within the corporate whole, and the caird was entitled to speak his mind to the chief.

The moment men came to think of that conception again as one needful in the political pattern, it grew even fantastically evident that it was left out of the present constitution of both the countries of the United Kingdom. In England in 1775 twenty-five great landlords returned a hundred and sixteen members of Parliament. The non-existent burgh of Old Sarum, with a single voter, sent up a couple of members, while Birmingham, with a hundred thousand people, had none at all. There was nothing quite so glaring as this in Scotland: yet much was clearly crying for reform. The million and a half of the Scottish people were represented by forty-five members of Parliament, of whom thirty sat for the country areas. In 1790, the country voters who elected these numbered barely over three thousand—and nearly half had been created voters for the occasion, by a legal fiction, voting 'to oblige' and for the receipt of due consideration. Of the sixty-six burghs, only Edinburgh possessed an individual member. The town's population was some 80,000, and its representative in Parliament was elected by twenty-five out of that number, 'the pleasure of Dundas being the sole rule of every one of them.' Glasgow, now near the same size, shared a single member with three other burghs, whose joint population was 11,000: each of the four had equal voting power, and their total of voters was well under a hundred. And all these scarce votes were saleable property, quite frankly saleable and quite frankly sold.

By 1780 societies were being formed to urge the consideration of these matters. Their delegates met in London and sent up a petition to the House of Commons, who, finding the extant arrangements good enough, rejected it. In 1782 Pitt moved for an inquiry, but was defeated. The subject, however, by now was 'in the air': and the men who had led intellectual revival were philosophers as often as *gens de lettres*, and had left a deep imprint on their successors' minds. French political writings were current in Edinburgh, and native pamphlets also began to abound, quoting not only Hume and Adam Smith, but Locke, Montesquieu, the Encyclopaedists, and Rousseau. In 1782 and the following year an Edinburgh man, Thomas MacGregor, and an Aberdonian, by name John Ewen, were busily conducting a press campaign, and a pamphlet declared that

the great body of people are in relation to civil affairs excluded from the exercise and enjoyment of the rights of freedom

... although, at the same time, it observed with regret their 'total indifference' to the deprivation. The old question also of patronage in the Church was raised once more—avowedly, now, because the popular election of ministers would provide political training for future voters.

These new demands did not pass unopposed by those men who were interested to maintain the extant, and convenient, state of affairs, or by others who deplored the new appetite for such an irrelevancy as politics. A gentleman who signed himself Atticus wrote in the *Caledonian Mercury* that

It is to *trade, industry,* and *improvement of the soil* that poor Scotland must look for salvation, not to the nonsense and distraction of the turmoil of politics.

But the scandal of the system of election smelt worse and worse the more it was turned over. The effluvium, indeed, appeared to daze men slightly, for (it was now a lifetime since the Union) the disputants never seem to have considered whether, how wide might be the electorate, representation by a small minority in a large foreign assembly would secure the benefits ascribed to a broader franchise. The vague sense of grievance had focussed upon The Vote, and the word had captured and fired the imagination. The vote was seen, rightly enough, as the recognition that the individual had his place in the state: but as often happens in times of general excitement, the symbol was rapidly becoming a fetish, whose possession would bring the millennium at once.

The Merchant Company of Edinburgh was converted, and began to agitate. Thomas MacGregor formed a burgh committee. In March 1784 the thirty-three royal burghs sent delegates to hold a joint convention, and next year they discussed the draft of two bills, for municipal and parliamentary reform. They decided to drop the latter for the time, and tried to get Fox, as a very prominent Whig, to bring forward the other in the House of Commons. He refused, but Sheridan undertook to do so, and was thwarted by the influence of Dundas, though fifty-three burghs were now supporting the bill. The interest, though keen, was still confined to comparatively few, and as it strengthened, so did the opposition. In 1788, the General Assembly went out of its way to observe with satisfaction that the British Constitution, as it stood, was 'the wonder and the envy of the world.'

Soon, however, the disturbance was flattened out by the impact of one far greater. France was stirring. The last two wars had completely wrecked her finances, which in addition had been badly managed and now were in a ravel beyond all sorting. Her imminent bankruptcy precipitated the ideas which were floating in solution—all the new theories and old grievances (and many of these were very real and oppressive), all the hopes and the hatreds, the generous endeavour and the envy, the sincere belief in the new Religion of Man, and the rancour of the Court faction who hated the Queen and spread ugly scandal about her through the nation.

Very few of those who made the French Revolution had even the slightest intention of doing so. Some of those who had done most—adored Voltaire, petted Rousseau, and made a lion of

Beaumarchais—were the very people whom it first destroyed. Men talked happily in pleasant candle-lit salons, tossing the new words, feeling themselves 'advanced.' But the words were creating assumptions, as words do—true assumptions and false, taken equally for granted as the only beliefs that intelligent men could hold. And on these beliefs they would act when action was stirred, as before very long it was to be by the desperate condition of French finances, which grew worse and worse, the appalling deficit mounting and mounting still as Turgot, Necker, Calonne, Brienne tried to check it.

In 1788, as a last expedient, the honest, stupid, and badly worried King was induced to call the old Estates General, the elected representatives of the nation, who had not assembled since 1614. In an atmosphere of hope and hostility, shot with the new political ideas, they walked in stately procession through Versailles on the 4th May of 1789.

That atmosphere was a highly explosive one, and in less than six summer weeks the spark had touched it. In four more, a white-faced man drew the King's curtains with the news that the Paris crowd had taken the Bastille. 'C'est donc une révolte?'—'Non, sire, une révolution.' The thunder rolled through Europe for twenty-six years before its first lull, and the debris still are flying.

II
SUMMER
FORTY-THREE YEARS: 1789–1832

Edinburgh was a true capital, a clearing-house for the world's culture, and a jealous repository of Scots tradition. . . . Below the comely surface there were new forces working, of which even the illuminate Whigs knew little; but the surface was all cheerfulness, good fellowship, and a modest pride . . . an agreeable cosmopolitanism . . . (but) the scene was still idiomatically Scottish.

JOHN BUCHAN, *Sir Walter Scott.*

IX

SUNSHINE IN PRINCES STREET

FORTY-THREE YEARS: 1789–1832

> There sometimes comes a period in the life of a nation when material
> and intellectual forces are finely balanced, when wealth is esteemed not
> as an end in itself but as a key to the full rich life of a civilised com-
> munity. Such a period, despite the destruction of foreign war, despite
> the political stagnation of the Dundas despotism, revealed itself in
> Scotland during the closing decades of the eighteenth century.
>
> G. PRATT INSH, *Scotland*.

FOR some time, in Edinburgh, the thunder of the captains and the
shouting were no more than a stimulating roll of drums. A lifetime
before, the windy city strung on its ridge of rock had seemed to
have little life in it but the wind's: in 1789 it looked, and was,
one of the leading capitals of Europe . . . save that it did not contain
a government. In the splendid new streets that matched its
splendid site, the *perfervidum ingenium Scotorum* had flowered in a
garden of rich personalities who speak to us in the memoirs of the
age, in its portraits that seem to leap from the wall with life.

It was still intensely itself, intensely of Scotland. Certain men,
in the 'sixties, had sought to anglicise 'the Scottish idiom of the
British tongue': but others, who agreed with MacKenzie of Rose-
haugh that it was 'more fiery, abrupt, sprightly, and bold,' 'more
massy and significant' than English, still kept to the old courtly and
curial Scots, even when on paper they wrote—and even were at pains
to write—a language indistinguishable from English. Adam Smith
and Joseph Black used an anglicised speech: but Hume, Robertson,
Hutton, the elegant waspish Jeffrey,[1] and Walter Scott showed
their nation in their tongue, and so did most of the delightful
women whom foreign visitors praised as whole-heartedly as Ayala
had done their far-off ancestresses . . . women whose charm did not
pass with their youth and beauty, as Scott's enchanting Mrs Bethune
Baliol and a score of Raeburn's and Ramsay's portraits remind us.
And the city's vigorous nationality was bred of no narrow provincial nationalism—the nationalism of inferiority-complex, such as

---

[1] Jeffrey and Hume, however, deliberately *wrote* a carefully anglicised language.

poisons Berlin today, and even Rome. No less than the Edinburgh of James the Fourth, that town of great talk, vivid humanity, and broad full interests turned her windows on Europe, and shone light from them fully as much as she received it.

The reawakening intellectual life which had stirred from its long winter in the 'twenties had increased in volume and variety through the middle decades of the century. Now for a generation there was summer—summer not without storms, but ripe summer none the less, with full life in it, though a less creative life. In the 'nineties, the literary impulse of the revival shows a kind of pause. There was keen and general enjoyment of literature; there was vigorous and scholarly criticism; there were men of letters, and those of no small having. But there was no Smollett, no James Thomson, no David Hume. Much was being written, in both Scots and English: the Scots included the later work of Burns, but in English, though there was a mass of writing, it only once touches a high creative level, and that was not in poetry or fiction but in biography, though, to be sure, in one which ranks with the greatest books of its age.

The philosophic tradition, by this time, was becoming tradition rather than new growth: but Dugald Stewart (1753-1828) was still continuing it as a great teacher, who drew many foreign students to his class-room: those who came from England included men as famous as Lord Brougham, Lord Palmerston, and Lord John Russell—a future Lord Chancellor and two very notable Prime Ministers. During much of the generation, Henry Mackenzie was still the acknowledged Dean of Scottish letters: his European fame lasted out his lifetime, and he was in fact a really notable critic, whose criticism took the practical turn of discovering and encouraging work of merit. Another conspicuous figure was the man whom Johnson found 'the best company in the world,' the advocate James Boswell of Auchinleck, whose *Life of Johnson* (1791) is still the greatest biography in the language. There were others of celebrity in their day, successful or fashionable in two or three capitals, whose work has long since died with the change of fashion. One may mention, perhaps, Thomas Campbell (1777-1844), though less because some fragments of his work survive in the more conscientious anthologies than because of his service to English education, on which he left a deep beneficial print.

In the last decade of the century, the 'pure' literature with most claim to permanence is the song and genre-verse in Scots, of which Burns (who died in 1796) was acknowledged king. His creative greatness is not the originator's: he owes it rather to the very fact of being so intensely derivative as to distil the quintessence of the 'kind'—of two of the several and various traditions of Scots.[1] He was too truly Scots to be narrowly Scots. There is much of Rousseau in him, something of Shenstone (a man important as originator), but he is greatest when most national, as in the superbly controlled crescendo of abandonment in *The Jolly Beggars*, or the ballad union of colour with a stabbing bareness of line that characterises the greatest of his songs. Round him is still a garland of lesser names, from the Duke of Gordon to Tibbie Pagan the alewife, who turned off Scots songs as the fancy took them—songs that are still as fresh as meadow grass.

Through the first third of the nineteenth century the general picture is still very much the same—keen interest and magnificent conversation, a great deal of lively and good, but ephemeral, work, and much very sound and useful scholarship. The creative impulse was returning, however, and one great figure was to tower over Europe.

With his exception and that of another man, the work of most permanent value was the least lively—the sober results of historical research, especially that carried out by the Bannatyne Club, founded in Edinburgh in 1823, and its Glasgow sister, the Maitland Club, five years younger. No subsequent writer of Scottish history but is deep in their debt for their work in preserving, editing, and printing a great body of valuable source-material, which without their good offices might well have perished. Jameson's *Dictionary of the Scottish Language*, published in 1808 (and inspired by the Iceland scholar Thorkelin), is no doubt in part a product of the same interest, as are the Gaelic Societies of Edinburgh (1811), Glasgow (1812), and Inverness (1818). The leader of the historians in general was Patrick Fraser Tytler (1791-1849), whose *History of Scotland* (1828-43) did some long-needed justice to 'the Jameses.'

It was an age of great journalism. Francis Jeffrey (1773-1850), editor of *The Edinburgh Review* and later Lord Advocate, ranked as

[1] His success had the unfortunate effect of concentrating attention after his time on these traditions alone, and consigning others, not less worthy intrinsically, to oblivion.

the foremost critic of his day. 'Christopher North' (John Wilson, 1785-1854) and Scott's son-in-law J. G. Lockhart (1794-1854) stood close beside him during their own lifetime. (Modern opinion would change the order of merit, leaving Lockhart an easy first.) Their vehicles were the Whig *Edinburgh Review* (1802) and the Tory *Quarterly* (1807) and *Blackwood's Magazine* (1817)—all of them read far beyond the marches of Scotland, yet all vigorously, intimately, of Edinburgh. *Chambers's Journal* was added to these in 1832, to reach a more 'popular' but still intelligent public. The journalism of those full-blooded days was to ours what all-in wrestling is to croquet. The Tories were in revolt, and as Professor J. H. Millar observes,

the liberty of thought and speech for which every Whig was prepared to go to the scaffold, or at the very least to send his king thither, has generally been denied to a Tory, except on pain of provoking the most withering scorn and indignation.

The remark was intended for a later time, and indeed has not yet lost validity: but a modern editor would tear his hair at the energy with which, in the eighteen-twenties, the *Edinburgh* and *Blackwood* tore each other's.

The great publishing houses belong to this time also. That of Oliver and Boyd was in business already, but Archibald Constable (1774-1827) and William Blackwood (1776-1834) both come now, to be followed at the very end of the period by the two brothers William (1800-83) and Robert Chambers (1802-71), whose first books were published in the middle 'twenties.

On the later side of 1800, the outstanding names in literature were four. Two ladies who lived well into Victorian times need not detain us. Joanna Baillie (1762-1851) was a most fashionable and successful writer of 'closet drama,' immensely admired, especially in London, and now quite dead. There is still life in the novels of Susan Ferrier (1782-1854), who leads on (for she fore-ran them in actual writing) to the great names of John Galt and Walter Scott.

Galt (1779-1839) comes late, for he did not publish work of any importance till 1821. *The Annals of the Parish* were actually written in 1813, the year in which Scott set to work at *Waverley*, but were refused publication on the grounds that there was no possible public for Scottish novels. By 1820 Scott had proved this judgment spectacularly false, and the book appeared. *The Provost* comes in

1822, *The Entail* next year, with a whole mass of lively minor stuff. They show the old genre-tradition expressing itself in the new form of prose fiction . . . and incidentally they also show how much could be accomplished in that medium in a language which was definitely Scottish: and all, careless as they are and slackly constructed, have remarkable vigour, life, and humanity, and an unmistakable 'quality' in the writing.

The towering figure is of course Walter Scott (1771-1832), who entered letters in the year 1802, as editor of a collection of Border ballads,[1] and between 1805 and 1813 wrote narrative poems which had immense success. They are not great: as a poet Scott was only great by snatches, though the Waverleys. would be less great than they are if the man who wrote them had not been a poet: but they are of much historical importance, since they trained a reading public who could accept the greater work of the Romantic Revival. His really great work comes between 1814 and 1819, in a wonderful pageant of novels of past Scotland. He touched their level again in 1823 and the following year; and in fact wrote novels almost to his death, though none of the rest, save only *Kenilworth*, can be put on a level with those whose scene is Scotland. I have written elsewhere:

All the old strands of our letters join in him . . . the folk-strain whose climax is in Burns . . . the darker and loftier side that is in the ballads . . . *Wandering Willie's Tale* goes back . . . to *The Tarne Watheling* as surely as Claverhouse or Fergus MacIvor is in line of descent from Barbour. . . . The delight in pageantry recalls the makaris, as the frame and setting sum up the lettered and scholarly Scots eighteenth century, which had not lost, even in douce little Jamie Thomson, Gavin Douglas's eye for the zest of a wild landscape, the tang of the old cramped and bickering Edinburgh that is underneath Scott's superb eye for a crowd, or remembrance of old and stately loyalties.

. . . Add that Scott was a most lively (if before 1670 a most inaccurate) historian, a great editor, a critic of quality . . . and always a superb personality. He sums up the rich life of that generation, fusing in himself what seem to a foreigner its antinomies, speaking for his time to his country and for his country to Time:

and his influence was immense all over Europe, from Russia to Spain, though greatest in France and England . . . if in the latter

[1] It is worth remembering that, twenty years after Watt had mastered steam and while the first steam-boat actually floated, the ballads were still current among the people, forming their scale of values and their outlook as the radio and the cinema do today . . . though, to be sure, the minds of the truly pious, who were beginning to multiply again, were not allowed to be contaminate by them.

at least his weakest work was very considerably the more esteemed, to the detriment of his subsequent reputation.[1]

Gaelic literature lived mainly on its past, though in 1800 nearly every district still had its local poet. The most notable names are those of Ewen MacLachlan (1775-1822), who was the Rector of Annan Grammar School and who, though in the main a nature poet, also translated Homer into Gaelic; John Morrison (1790-1852); and Peter Grant, whose sacred poems—*Dain Spioradail*, 1816—went into twenty editions. Gaelic had spread to the New World by now, with the Nova Scotians James MacGregor and John Maclean.

Of the other arts, it is not uncharacteristic of the time that the outstanding one was portraiture. Sir Henry Raeburn (1756-1823) is the greatest name, corresponding to Scott in letters, and very like him in the robust enjoyment and interest in character that mark his work. Andrew Geddes (1783-1844) was at his best not far behind him, and helped to revive the neglected art of etching. David Scott (1806-49) recovers the vein of the fantastic, and John Thomson (1778-1840) laid the foundations of Scots landscape painting. There is a long catalogue of other names, including the popular Sir David Wilkie (1785-1841), who seems to be reviving in reputation, the animal-painter James Howe (1780-1836), and many more, who were successful but now are dead enough; though one may give a passing mention to William Dyce (1806-64) as the first Scots religious painter for centuries—perhaps since the one who painted St Joan's loved banner. There were also a fair number of practising sculptors, in the neo-classic manner of Thorwaldsen: but none was of much account.

Robert Adam lived until 1792. With him the great tradition of architecture began to pass. The decline was slow at first, for W. H. Playfair (1789-1857) still achieved much beauty and dignity of proportion: he completed Adam's work for the University of Edinburgh, including the Dome, and designed the fine classic National Gallery—not the best 'kind' but excellent in the kind. Thomas Hamilton (1785-1858) showed the same qualities, with a freer handling, in the gracious and stately Edinburgh High School. David Hamilton (1768-1843) did notable domestic work in Glasgow;

---

[1] His reputation has also suffered badly by the fact that most of us are forced to read Waverleys—and generally the wrong Waverleys—in our early youth, and so never read Scott after. Yet Scott, like Horace, and Shakespeare's Roman plays, is one of the compensations of middle age. He is definitely not for boys and girls.

and one should not forget Archibald Elliot, who brought the Calton Hill into the scheme of Edinburgh's New Town (the beautiful terraces were designed by Playfair), Robert Reid (1776-1856), who built the stately church in Charlotte Square, or Gillespie Graham (1777?-1855) who was the architect of the splendid Moray Place and the streets around it.

For most of the time the classic inspiration was dominant: and already it was beginning (though, as we may see by the High School, only beginning) to change from a tradition inspiring artists to an archaeology that fettered scholars. Another, even less fortunate in its results, was soon to be set beside it by Scott's success. In his own country, as in France and England, he had caused a fashion for 'the Gothick taste.' [1] In Scotland it took the form of Scots Baronial—i.e. Abbotsford Gothic. The real stuff can of course be magnificent, and almost always has an arrogant vigour: the nineteenth-century imitation, however, ranged as a rule from the timid to the ghastly, though its worst comes later than this time—and lasted long. Graham worked in this style as well as in the classic, but is something a good deal better than typical of it. His use of the seventeenth-century tradition in the beautiful façade of Murthly Castle rather suggests that the movement might have taken a happier turn, and developed, as its analogue did in Sweden, into living tradition with its roots in the old. But the Victorian Age was to be too powerful; and Graham's best work is less typical than that of William Burn, whose St John's Episcopal Church in Princes Street is conscientious and quite dead scholarship.

Music was still a part of normal life: but Scots music is a very difficult subject. The seven-volume *Oxford History of Music* has no mention of Scotland anywhere in its index, nor even in the long article on folk-song, though in beauty Scottish folk-song yields to none. Everyone sang: but one cannot say if there was much new music. The Highland Society set going a fashion for Gaelic airs that saved many lovely things from what otherwise might well have been extinction.

In science the former eminence continued, though less in pure science at this time than in applied. Its results, which were to affect the entire world, can more properly be discussed in a later

---

[1] Not new in England, where it goes back to Horace Walpole : but Scott's influence immensely and tragically popularised it.

chapter. Scots medicine was still in very high repute: the medical schools drew pupils from all over Europe. It was during this period that a Scottish surgeon laid the foundations of the R.A.M.C. This was Sir James MacGrigor (1771-1858), who was in charge of the Medical Service in the Peninsula. Napier says of him:

During the ten months from the siege of Burgos to the battle of Vittoria, the sick and wounded numbered 95,348. After James MacGrigor arrived, the army marched ten days to the enemy, and then a month after it had defeated him, mustered within thirty men as strong as before, without reinforcements from home. The ranks had been filled up by convalescents.

In education, one point worth remark is the mutual interaction of Scotland and England. The Scots schools were still honourably open to all: in 1803, William Wordsworth and his sister were astonished to find a barefooted herd-laddie quoting Greek. Meg Dods, no doubt, would have had a word for it: but in England already the mediaeval tradition had collapsed, with results that were impinging upon Scotland, where they were to have an unfortunate effect. That of Scotland on England was to be happier: England, indeed, owes to Scotland the third and largest of her universities. At this time Oxford and Cambridge seemed moribund: decayed in scholarship and discipline, and wholly unworthy of their great traditions, they had sunk to the level of mere 'snob' institutions to which young men were sent to be out of the way and make friends who would be useful to them later. In 1824 Thomas Campbell the poet set on foot a scheme for a new university in London: University College was founded two years later, King's in 1829, both on Scottish models. They have since grown into a vast organisation.

At home, the new life of the universities had by this time considerably quickened the schools. The school system, however, was still far from systematic. In 1803 the masters of parish schools were granted a minimum stipend—£5, 11s. 1½d. sterling, with a rise after twenty-five years, and a house and garden: there were also scholars' fees, but these were small. An investigation of 1818 found that in spite of this inexpensive equipment many thousands of children, especially in the Highlands, were not so much as being taught to read and write. Six years later the General Assembly tackled the problem, and built a number of 'Assembly Schools' in the Highlands and Isles. The Church still controlled most part of the schools system, and the parish teachers all had to subscribe the Westminster Confession. So had the staffs of the universities.

The foundation of modern Scottish school education was laid in Glasgow in 1828, by a Paisley man, David Stow, who in that year founded the Infant School Society, from which developed very soon thereafter a seminary for the training of teachers in the actual methodology of teaching—the first 'Normal College' in the United Kingdom.

Scanty as was its equipment, none the less the old haphazard plan had its qualities. Many escaped education altogether—or education by books, at all events: and no doubt some of them might have gained by it. But most lads of parts could get it if they desired: and to think of it as something deserving effort, something that called for a certain amount of adventure, instead of something laid on like the town's water, was perhaps not altogether a disadvantage, the more as in that age of lively minds there were many who desired to make the effort, and relished the fruit none the less for having to climb.

X

TOWARDS RELIGIOUS FREEDOM

FORTY YEARS: 1789–1829

Nothing contained in this Act or in any other Act applying to the Church of Scotland shall prejudice the recognition of any other Church in Scotland as a Christian Church protected by law in the exercise of its spiritual functions.

The Church of Scotland Act, 1921.

AT a first glance across this period, the major elements in church history appear as the waning power of the Moderates and the increasing tendency, marked already, of the Presbyterian bodies to split and secede. These were, in fact, both conspicuous and important: but behind them is something wider—a frame of mind utterly foreign to that of Knox or Melville, of Cant and Donald Cargill and Richard Cameron. It shows in the heat of the very secessions themselves, for however acrimonious their disputes, there was never a single threat of taking arms for the forcible conversion of opponents or the imposition of a creed on the state. Instead, we can see a steady and broadening growth in the temper of Robert Baillie and Robert Leighton, that temper expressed in clear and generous phrases in the passage from the Church of Scotland Act which is quoted as the motto for this chapter. And the change brought back once more the religious freedom, for all men to worship as their conscience bade them so long as they did not force other men's consciences, which Scotland, after so brief a possession of it, had lost with the deposition of James VII.

The influence of the French Revolution upon religion was twofold. A few men were confirmed in an acrimonious hatred of all religion. Many more were startled to a new sense of its need, and becoming more conscious, less apt to take accepted points for granted, grew aware of the dilemma of Moderatism, of the intellectual ambiguity, to put it no more strongly, on which it was based. The general turn of mind of the Moderates revolted at much in essential Calvinism. Their generous and humane system of ethics could accept only a benevolent God, and their logic forbade the use of the adjective for one who created men on purpose to damn them to eternal torture for his own glorification. This position was very difficult to combine with subscription of the Westminster Confession: yet to revise the Church's formularies would inevitably bring about a split, and perhaps ejection from the Establishment. Accordingly, the Confession was not revised, and the Moderates were compelled to signify their assent to doctrines in which they did not believe, and which their teaching frankly contradicted. Further, in times of stress, men need a God, and some definite notion of their relation to Him; and the Moderates' extremely uncertain relation to what was their own official theology made them uneasily vague in point of dogma. Thus their authority, moral and theological, weakened as men began to note these things. Those who only a very little earlier would have accepted their teaching contentedly either lost hold of even a nominal Christianity; joined the now legalised Episcopal Church, where they could be Christians without being Calvinists; or turned to the 'Highflyer' ministers, who accepted the Westminster Formulae sincerely, and were not afraid to preach a clear-cut dogma. Part of the growth of 'Evangelicalism' has also been assigned to the influence of a popular *Life of John Knox*, which was published in the year 1811 by an Auld Licht Anti-Burgher minister, Dr McCrie.[1] It cast a romantic glamour, not yet lost, on the Left Wing of the Reformation Church, 'whose very excesses were held up as an example instead of a warning'; and it probably owed a good deal of its popularity to the fact that it gave revolutionary fervour, which was in the air, a 'respectable' peg to hang on. Indeed, it well may have contributed to the growing dominance of the Highflyers. But a change in social balance also helped. As Scotland became a manufacturing country, the middle-class, and its influence, increased: and then, as earlier and later, it was they for whom Calvinism had the strongest attraction.

The Moderates, too, had another disadvantage. They had all through the eighteenth century been willing to accept the patronage system as the price of their position as the State Church. By the older Highflyers, who inherited the Covenant tradition of a State in complete subordination to the Church, this lay control had always

[1] He is the gentleman who attacked Sir Walter in what is perhaps the longest review on record—85,000 words, the length of a sizeable novel. But it was an age of heroic editors.

been strongly resented. Now the younger saw in it class privilege also: and already the new claim that the Rights of Man included a vote in secular legislation was leading, as a logical consequence, to a similar claim in ecclesiastical. Thus even within the Establishment itself, at least the later part of the period was marked by a steadily increasing tension.

The Presbyterian Dissenting Churches present at this time a picture of constant flux. The Seceders, as we have seen, were split already into the Burghers, or Associate Synod, and the Anti-Burghers, or General Associate Synod. The former of these, in 1799, divided once more. The issue was that of literal adherence to the Covenants and the Westminster Confession on the authority of the magistrate to impose a form of religion upon the lieges. A New Light majority of the denomination announced that they did not desire their ordinands to agree on this point with the Covenants and the Confession, or approve of 'compulsory measures in religion.' An Old Light minority stood by the Covenants and by Westminster, approving in principle of such compulsion, and seceded as the Original Associate Synod. The point was purely academical, as the State was not in any likelihood of compelling assent to the Seceder tenets, and had even ceased, for the last seven years, to enforce that to Presbyterianism in general: but in 1806 the other Seceder body, the Anti-Burghers, also divided on it, their Auld Lichts withdrawing under Dr McCrie as the Constitutional Associate Presbytery. Their New Lichts for a while retained their title of General Associate Synod: but in 1820 they were disrupted once more. Their majority joined the New Licht Burghers (the Associate Synod) taking the name of United Secession Church, while their minority joined the Constitutional Associate Presbytery, calling themselves now the Original Secession. The Original Associated Synod (the Auld Licht Burghers) in 1839 went through a similar process of fissure and junction, their majority then becoming reconciled to the Establishment, while their minority, after a short while, joined with the Original Secession Church, which now became the United Original Seceders, and continues to exist under that name.

The first secession of 1733 had thus in a little over a century produced no fewer than five sub-secessions and four partial re-unions: between 1806 and 1820, in fact, there were—counting of course the Reformed Presbyterians, who had no dealings with any other sect and who threw out no branches of their own—no less than seven Presbyterian Churches, each holding precisely the same theological standards and the same polity and mode of worship: indeed, there were henceforth never less than five. But it is worth remarking, none the less, that in the first place two of these secessions were caused by assertion of the principle that compulsion in religion was unrighteous: and in the second that even the movements of those sects who wished for compulsion were accomplished without so much as the threat of arms. There might be—there was—some bandying of hell-fire: but of temporal weapons hardly so much as a divot.

The incoming denominations from England slightly increased. A few more converts were made to Methodism, and Independency (Congregationalism), which since its first introduction by Cromwell's troops had died out, was revived a little before 1800 by two ex-navy men, James and Robert Haldane. In 1808 these gentlemen changed their faith, becoming Baptists, and drew with them certain of their followers: the rest, in the year 1813, were organised into the Congregational Union.

For the illegal Dissenters—the Roman Catholics and Episcopalians—the growth of tolerance brought better days. We have seen already that the death of Charles Edward in 1788 had achieved the release of the Episcopal Church from its long and dear-bought loyalty to the Stewarts. His brother Henry Benedict still lived, and was to do so until 1807; but he had stated his own claim to the Crown in a form which amounted to its renunciation, and as a Cardinal of the Roman Church he could pass it on to no posterity. In 1789 the Episcopal Church therefore acknowledged the House of Hanover, and petitioned for relief from the Penal Laws. Times had changed a great deal in the last forty years. The Moderates were still in the ascendant, and gave a ready and generous support: Principal Robertson of Edinburgh and Principal Campbell of Aberdeen both used their great influence on the side of repeal. It was opposed by the Seceder bodies, but not very widely or heartily even by these: indeed, it is worthy of note that the strongest of the opposition to it came first from the 'qualified' English clergymen whom some southern congregations had imported, and then, and forcibly, from the Church of England.

Indeed, repeal was refused, for the time being. The Commons

8

passed it, but the Lords, where the English bishops sat, threw out the bill, the Lord Chancellor making the somewhat remarkable statement that there could be no bishops without the King's authority. The question was raised again in 1792; and Thurlow (the Lord Chancellor just mentioned) tried to make it a condition of repeal that the clergy of the Scottish Church in future must be ordained by English or Irish bishops. A Welsh one—Bishop Horsley of St David's—dealt with him firmly: ecclesiastical arguments being useless, he told Thurlow that this would break the Treaty of Union. As a matter of fact, it did nothing of the sort, for the only Church protected by the Treaty was the Presbyterian Establishment: but war threatened with France and revolution at home: Thurlow feared to antagonise Scotland, and surrendered. Repeal was passed on the 15th of June, on condition the Scottish clergy would subscribe to the general drift of the Thirty-nine Articles.[1] There were still—indeed, there are still—penalties for Episcopalians who attended a service at which the King and his heir were not prayed for by name, and others also for any Scottish cleric who should officiate on English soil, though none for English who should do so in Scotland.

The terms of the repeal were to cause trouble. Such life as there was at that time in the Church of England (which was then passing through a phase of decadence) was in her Left Wing, who had Calvinist sympathies, and who read into the Thirty-nine Articles a markedly Calvinist interpretation. The Scottish Church had for standards, outwith the Scriptures, the Creeds and the Prayer-book: and her ministers threatened now to refuse the Articles, and rather remain beneath the Penal Laws. The much revered Bishop Jolly of Aberdeen pointed out, however, that the Articles might be read also in a non-Calvinist sense; and the condition was thereupon accepted, though with clear emphasis on the sense of acceptance. The Church of England still was not satisfied, and tried to put pressure on the Scottish Church (in whose concerns she had no authority) to abandon her own Liturgy for the English. This was firmly refused. But now a fresh problem threatened, that of the 'separated' congregations, twenty-four which had sought to baulk the Penal Laws by bringing in clergy who were in English orders and refused to recognise the Scottish bishops.

---

[1] The principal subordinate standard of the Church of England, after the Scriptures and the Creeds.

The Scottish Church was now in formal communion not only with her daughter Church of America but with the Churches of England, Ireland, and Wales: on this basis, Jolly drew up a formula for reunion of these 'English' congregations, allowing them the English Liturgy on condition they recognised the Scottish bishops. Thirteen of them, accordingly, came in [1]; and as token of the concordat, in 1806 an Englishman was made Bishop of Edinburgh.

It was a false step, and they had to regret it. The Church of England had swung towards the Left, and tried to thrust Calvinism on her Scottish sister, whose very existence was a protest against it. In 1826 a group of English Evangelicals arrived on a preaching mission to Edinburgh, and attacked the teaching of the Scottish Church and in special the use of the Scottish Liturgy. Nor was this, by any means, the last of such trials.

Church Law was codified in 1811 by a Code of Canons, revised in 1818. Close relations with the American Church continued, and the Scottish Church now consecrated a bishop whose charge was those members of the various Reformed Episcopal Churches who were scattered through Europe. In accordance with the spirit of the time, the demand that laymen should have greater voice was expressed among Episcopalians also.

Complete religious freedom, or very nearly, was attained in the year 1829, with the repeal of the laws against Roman Catholics. The English Test Act was repealed in the previous year, and a public meeting was held in Edinburgh—not now to denounce the relief of Catholics, as in 1778, but to support it. In March 1829 the Assembly Room was crowded by a large gathering of Whigs and Tories, who approved the measure of Peel and Wellington for complete emancipation. 8,000 signed a petition in its favour. It is true that rather more than twice as many signed one against it: but the Government, having decided on repeal, in order to conciliate the Irish, declared that those who had signed the first petition were 'of a higher and more varied class.' The Act was passed, and at length all the people of Scotland were free to worship as their conscience bade them, without, in practice, being penalised by the Law.

[1] Some of the remaining eleven persisted for a long time : the last was only recently reconciled. One or two, notably St Thomas's, Edinburgh, claimed to belong to the Church of England ; and all were in the habit of sending their young people to England for their confirmation by an English bishop.

XI

MEN AND MACHINES

FORTY-THREE YEARS: 1789–1832

> The minds of men were excited to new enterprises, and there was an erect and outlooking spirit abroad, that was not to be satisfied with the taciturn regularity of ancient affairs. Even Miss Sabrina Hookey, the schoolmistress, though now waned from her meridian, was touched with the enlivening rod, and set herself to learn and teach tambouring, in such a manner as to supersede by precept and example that old time-honoured functionary, as she herself called it, the spinning-wheel, proving, as she did one night to Mr Kibbock and me, that if more money could be made by a woman tambouring than by spinning, it was better for her to tambour than to spin. JOHN GALT, *The Annals of the Parish,* for 1788.

ON the intellectual and spiritual side, the period shows rather a ripening than a change. On the material there were to be great changes, which in time affected the other aspects of life. To the work of man and his familiar tools was now to be added the work of the machine.

In appearance, the steady progress was continued. The work of the 'twenties, the 'thirties, and the 'forties had built up a structure of prosperity which had weathered the shock of the American War and was now to withstand the strain of Napoleon's blockade and the trade slump that followed the war with France, and emerge, to all seeming, stronger than ever before, with the promise of new and rich developments.

Its strength was tested early in the time. The outbreak of war in 1793 caused a run on the banks, and some of them went under: and 1797 brought further strain. Pitt had underestimated the cost of the war, and was forced to borrow from the Bank of England, which went off gold, causing something like panic among British 'business'—a panic made worse by the imminent threat of invasion. There was a widespread hoarding of currency, which resulted in so great a shortage of coin that pound notes torn in quarters had to be used, and Spanish dollars were put in circulation, at a value of 4s. 6d. Private banks suffered badly, and many of them had to go out of business. Within a few years after the war, however—that is to say, by about 1820—trade was reviving. 1825, indeed, brought a general boom, followed almost at once, in England, by collapse, and an extremely acute financial crisis. The Government declared that the banking system needed drastic amendment, and proposed henceforth to limit the Bank of England to notes of £5 and over, and forbid private banks to issue notes at all. The plan threatened disaster to the Scottish banks, with regard to which it was wholly unnecessary: her more advanced and elastic system of banking had brought Scotland through in much better case than her neighbour.[1] The Government declined to be at the trouble of differentiating between the Kingdoms, and wished also to force upon them a uniform system, which naturally was that in practice in England. Sir Walter Scott intervened, with a vigorous pamphlet, *The Letters of Malachi Malagrowther*, and led such a storm among Scottish business men that the Government was cowed into surrender. The Scots pound note was saved: though even today, when pound notes are again familiar in England, it is not legal tender in that country, and has to be changed in a bank and at a discount.

The country's general economic sett showed a new and valuable development taking place among the working-class consumers. From time out of mind, handicraftsmen had been used to band together for various socio-economic ends[2]: and many of these mediaeval sodalities had an element of what we call mutual assurance, against death, sickness, injury, or unemployment. After the Reformation these open guilds had revived again as Friendly Societies: and these now were finding a new activity. In 1769 the weavers of the village of Fenwick in Ayrshire joined in a band for the wholesale purchase of goods, to be resold to members at cost price. Other such groups soon followed: the Govan weavers in 1777 founded one which endured until quite recently, and that of Lennoxtown, founded in 1812, is still extant. At a suggestion from Alexander Campbell,[3] an English group at Rochdale in Lancashire

---

[1] Eighty English banks failed, and only three Scots, one of which in the end paid up in full.

[2] These sodalities (for which many names were and are used) must be distinguished from the trade and craft guilds. They were purely voluntary organisations, as a rule with a strong religious element and also one of communal merry-making. The *solempne and greet fraternitee* whose *lyveree* was worn by men of five different trades among Chaucer's gathering of English pilgrims would be one of them.

[3] Robert Owen's manager, and a founder of the Glasgow Trades Council.

moved on from this to trading with sharing of profits. The Scots soon followed, and the movement grew. By 1830 there were between three and four hundred of these Co-operative Societies, as they were now called. Their efficiency varied somewhat from place to place. Some were unstable and rapidly collapsed, but many grew into large businesses, soundly managed, a great help to the thrifty working-class housewife, and a source of both interest and profit to her man, and of valuable administrative training.

Until the end of the eighteenth century, Scotland's major 'working' interest was still the land. In 1801 the total population was 1,608,420: of these, half a million (31 %) were occupied in one branch or another of farming. Farming still throve, and its immense importance was recognised. In 1790 a Chair of Agriculture was founded in Edinburgh University (incidentally, by a lawyer, William Johnstone) for the scientific study of its methods. The Societies continued a lively existence, and were supplemented in 1793 by a new government-supported Board, whose first President was a Caithness man, Sir John Sinclair. It sponsored research in scientific farming, and encouraged skill by premiums and exhibitions. Its first ploughing match was held in 1801, and in December of 1822 it held its first Show, of fat stock. The gate-money came to £51, 10s.: in 1919 it was to be £17,000.

Land reclamation went on steadily. Round Kelso, for example, in 1790 there were 21,000 acres in cultivation, worth £84,600: by 1837 there were 32,000, and the value had risen to £174,600. Cobbett, visiting Scotland in 1832, was astonished at the high standard of Scots farming, which by then was world-famous, and contrasted Scots farmers, much to their advantage, with 'our Suffolk chawbacons.'

The increased population meant more mouths to feed. The war brought greater demands from England for exports. Scotland could feed herself, with a large surplus of grain and potatoes, of cattle and of sheep, for her neighbour's needs. As transport improved, trade steadily expanded.[1] By the 'thirties, Perthshire alone was sending to London 10,000 tons of potatoes a year. Stock farming gained even more by the better transport. In 1750 Aber-

---

[1] The roads, etc., will be dealt with later in this chapter. It may be mentioned, however, that vehicles had very greatly improved. In the first quarter of the nineteenth century the Scots farm cart could do twice the work per horse of the clumsy waggon then in use in England.

deenshire had brought its oxen from the South. Less than a life-time later its own cattle were celebrated to the English Channel, and Aikie Fair set 6,000 on the road. Ayr, the other great centre, sent 100,000 beasts yearly over the Border. The coming of steam transport helped this trade further, and enormously increased the value per head. Sheep which had formerly taken fourteen days, losing value daily, from Wick to Edinburgh, now came easily and quickly by the steamboat. In 1820 Fife cattle went lean to England: fifteen years later they were being shipped ready fatted. The post-war slump did some damage to the market, as England could not afford such high-class goods: but in 1825 it was estimated that Carlisle at the time of its great annual fair would see eighty to ninety thousand pounds change hands.

One change was coming, which greatly affected the Highlands. The steady enlargement of the English wool-trade, the development of the Scots, and the better transport, increased the value of sheep. Galashiels market in 1775 had sold 772 stone of wool: before the century had reached its end this had already risen to 5,000, and the value of wool per stone had doubled also. The result was a general rage for sheep-farming, whose results will be discussed in the next chapter.

The French war dealt a blow to fisheries, which were only just beginning to revive. The stocks of the Fishery Society fell, and its working was also seriously hampered by the fact that, since it was an Anglo-Scottish body, its shareholders insisted on its being managed from London, by men ignorant of immediate local con-ditions. As result, it was crippled before it began to go. In 1807 a Fishery Commission was appointed to replace it, and did so with a spectacular success, producing large quantities of useful food and a valuable commodity for export, creating employment, and training first-rate seamen. In 1807, 90,185 barrels of herring were cured, about a third of them for the export trade. By 1820 it was 442,195, of which 294,805 were sent abroad.

Fishing was carried on mainly in the West: in 1816, 510 boats out of 726 were Clyde registered. In 1808, however, Sir John Sinclair, on Telford's plans, founded a fishing settlement at Wick. In twenty years time it was the largest of its kind in Europe, and the East Coast ports were busy from Eyemouth to Lerwick. Most of the fish, in the early days of the trade, went either to the West

Indies or to Ireland. The abolition of slavery in the former lowered exports thither from 67,000 barrels a year to 5,000: but the Scots curers turned instead to the Baltic, and captured its extensive trade from the Dutch, who had so long exploited the Scottish grounds.

In 'industry,' till after 1800, the major interest was still in textiles. At the beginning of the period, linen still stood foremost, linked, as it had been, with the revival in Scots agriculture. It had outgrown the supply of Scots flax, however, and had to import a good deal of its raw material: in 1830, 15,000 tons of flax from other countries arrived in Dundee.[1] The sett of the industry, being well established, was only slowly affected by new conditions. Machine spinning began just before the French Revolution: a Bervie firm spun by machine in 1787. It was used only for coarse fabrics, however: the finer continued to be spun by hand, and generally by women working at home. Power-looms for weaving came in even more slowly: it was not till after the slump of the eighteen-twenties that linen became a factory industry.

Its rival, cotton, however, was that from the start. Cotton, and textile machines, reached Scotland together, as we have seen, just before the French Revolution. The new trade had no traditions, good or bad: it was rapidly and deliberately imported to fill the gap left by the loss of Glasgow's tobacco. It found at once a body of highly-skilled workers, used to making lawns and gauze of an exquisite fineness; and it was handled by men of enterprise, who, though it required an imported raw material, steered it through the dangers of Napoleon's blockade and the U.S. Embargo Act of 1809. It was sometimes close sailing: in 1811 half the Glasgow weavers were out of work through the shortage of raw cotton. But the trade revived, and by the end of the 'twenties had become a good deal larger than that in linen.

The spinning-machines came in at the very start. They were worked by hand-power at first, in the cottages; but before the 'eighties were past water-power was being used, and was gathering the mule and the jenny and their workers into great buildings holding the source of power: these were called popularly 'factories.' By 1796 there were thirty-nine, employing no less than 182,000

---

[1] That city was also beginning what was to become an enormous trade in coarse fabrics made from jute.

people—nearly two-fifths of the number of those on the land. Water-power had its disadvantages: and the Glasgow firm of Scott and Stevenson were already experimenting with Watt's engine. The innovation made slow advance, however: it was easy enough to devise an effective machine, but very difficult to get it made, as at first there were no regular mechanics, let alone works for the production of engines. Each firm had to put together its own contrivance: and the standard of adjustment of many of these, as of course the number of resultant breakdowns, would bring tears to the eyes of a modern Greek tramp's oiler. In 1800 there were still but eight steam-engines in the trade—only twenty-three in Scotland, for all uses. Thirty-one years later, the city of Glasgow alone had 107 mills spinning cotton by steam-power.

For some time longer the weaving of the yarn remained as a domestic industry, very highly skilled and proportionately paid. The fine weaver was the aristocrat of craftsmen, with three or four times the common run of wages: he worked, very often, no more than a four-day week, and came out on Sundays braw in blue coat and brass buttons, with fine lawn ruffles and his hair in powder.[1] The great days of hand-weaving were round about 1800, when Glasgow merchants employed 15,000 looms, over a district going as far as Stirling.

The first power-loom was invented in 1787, by an English clergyman of the name of Cartwright: but though Horrocks of Preston and others worked on it, it remained for long in the experimental stage, and it was not till after 1800 that it was capable of commercial use. Its use spread. By 1813 there were 1,500 power-looms in the country: by 1830 Glasgow alone had nearer 15,000. Yet even so late as 1838 there were over 51,000 hand-looms in the Lowlands, of which all but 2,400 were weaving cotton. The effect of the power-loom in the lowering of wages was felt much more slowly in Scotland than in England. The power-loom was used at first for the coarser stuffs, which had made up the bulk of the English trade. The Scottish firms had specialised in the finer, in 'fancy articles for show and taste': Paisley, in the 'thirties, made £600,000 worth of exquisite shawls a year, and in 1834 had not one power-loom. The impact of the machines was also lessened by subsidiary highly-skilled handicrafts, to which, in the manner

---

[1] The Paisley weavers, as one can almost guess from the sight of their fabrics, were enthusiastic gardeners, with an especial passion for carnations.

of Miss Sabrina Hookey, the women could turn when they laid aside the wheel—'white Ayrshire flowering' and tambour embroidery of an almost incredible fineness of execution, on Scots muslin as delicate as a wisp of cloud.[1]

By 1800 a third class of textiles was growing. There had always, of course, been much weaving of wool in Scotland: her climate saw to that. But until after the rise of linen and cotton, her woollen fabrics were mostly made at home, or by the 'customer weaver' for home consumption, from the spinning of the goodwife and her maids. Only a little coarse cloth had been made for sale, though that, to be sure, was an export of old standing. Now the Tweed valley began its famous 'tweels,' soon changed to 'tweeds' by the happy blunder of a London clerk. It was sheep country, with the wool at its doors; and the new trade, beginning at Jedburgh, soon spread to Hawick and to Galashiels—helped greatly, it is said, by a pair of checked trousers with which Sir Walter Scott set off a fashion. Its highest reach was in the Paisley shawls, which were now made also in wool and in silk and wool, with most wonderful colouring and charm of design.

When the French wars came to an end with Napoleon's fall— that is to say, in the year 1815—cotton was the chief industry of Scotland, linen still throve, and wool was rapidly rising: and Scottish products in all were deservedly famous, their greater part being in the 'luxury' class, and notable both for quality and for beauty. The supremacy of textiles was, however, very soon to be challenged, for the 'heavy' industries were drawing ahead.

As we have seen, they were already established. Even at the beginning of the war, the Carron Ironworks had 2,000 employees, and was using 800 tons of coal a week. The war brought a greater demand for both coal and iron, and before the trade slump which followed the peace could be felt, the industry found new scope in a new Scots invention, for which all Europe was soon to be in the market.

Between 1788 and 1806 the eight Scots blast-furnaces rose to

[1] Philosophy, dress-making, and economics can mix oddly. One great benefactor of the Scots cotton trade was Rousseau. The fashion for 'nature' and 'sensibility' led to a rage for white cotton dresses. The ladies of Raeburn's portraits, Jane Austen's novels, and Josephine's court went to balls in fine 'worked muslin,' and it superseded lace for their caps and kerchiefs and for the five-foot christening-robes of their babies.

twenty-nine, and their output from 7,000 tons to over 23,000. In 1801 David Muschet discovered the use of the black-band ironstone: and in 1828 James Neilson's invention of the hot-blast furnace trebled the output of iron for the same coal-consumption.[1] Between 1796 and 1828 the output of Scots iron-works had already doubled: in the ten years after Neilson's invention it quadrupled again.

The trade received an enormous impetus from the new developments in shipbuilding. That also had increased by 1800. In 1776 the largest ship with a Clyde registry was still of no more than seventy-seven tons. By 1800 it was 500 tons.[2] The number, and the tonnage, increased, though but slowly. In 1820 Scotland had 2,851 ships, of which nearly a third were still of foreign building. The port with the largest tonnage was Aberdeen. Greenock came next, and only three per cent. of Scottish shipping was registered in Glasgow.

Already, however, great things were in train, and Glasgow had prepared herself to meet them. In 1796, 58,980 tons of shipping tied up at Glasgow Bridge. Rennie, called in in 1799 to supplement the excellent work of Golbourne, wrought so effectively that in 1806 this figure had risen to 83,683: and his new dock at the Broomielaw served so well that in 1831 12,000 ships with a tonnage of over a quarter of a million entered the port. But by then, Glasgow stood for steam.

In the seventeen-eighties, John Fitch in America had tried to apply Watt's new steam-engine to ships. His experiments failed, and he killed himself at last: but his Scottish rivals were more fortunate. William Symington, a young Scots engineer, and Patrick Miller of Dalswinton, his patron, on the 14th October 1788 sent a steam-propelled vessel across Dalswinton Loch. It took years of work to perfect, but in 1802 their *Charlotte Dundas*, the first practicable steamship of the world, was launched upon the Forth and Clyde Canal, where she proved herself capable of the amazing feat of towing two barges of seventy tons apiece for twenty miles in no longer than six hours.

Fitch's successors ran a very good second. A Scots-American

---

[1] Coal was saved from feeling the effect of lessened consumption by William Murdoch's invention of coal-gas lighting, which began to be used, though very tentatively, in the last decade of the eighteenth century. Edinburgh streets bloomed gas-lamps in 1817.

[2] 139 years later, the Clyde built one of 86,000 tons.

of the name of Fulton had been experimenting on the Seine, and in 1807 his *Clermont* (with engines manufactured by Boulton and Watt) was running between New York and Albany, on the Hudson River. The first regular passenger steamer of the Old World was the work of a Torphichen man, Henry Bell (1766-1830), whose *Comet* in 1812 ran regularly between Glasgow and Greenock. Her three-horse-power engines did only four miles an hour, but as set-off she carried a library of the classics . . . perhaps because her commander on her first run was the parish schoolmaster of Helensburgh, William MacKenzie. She was wrecked off the coast of Argyle in 1820, and her engines are now preserved in an English museum.

The new thing grew. In spite of the French wars, Scotland built nine steamships in the next two years; and the *Marjory*, built by Denny of Dumbarton, had been sent to London—the world's first steamship to sail the open sea. The first steamship to leave an English port was the Scots-built *Caledonia* in 1817, owned and commanded by the son of James Watt. Next year Denny's *Rob Roy* was on the Belfast run, and the Calais-Dover packet crossed under steam; while the next year again—that is, 1819—the *Savannah* made the crossing of the Atlantic, though as yet the very heavy coal consumption compelled her to make part of it under sail.

The centre of steamship building was the Clyde, and its great pioneers are the two Napier cousins, David and Robert, Dumbarton men by birth. David set up in 1821, at Camlachie, experimenting on the hulls: he invented the tank still used in testing 'lines,' and the beautiful 'fine bow,' which gave greater speed. He built the world's first steamship dock at Lancefield, but was lured to England then. Robert took over. He also made history, but later history, that falls to be discussed in another chapter. One must mention a third Napier here, however: he was James, Robert's brother, who in 1830 solved the crucial problem of fuel consumption, and therefore space, at sea, by the invention of the tubular boiler, which by cutting out nearly a third of the coal required made possible long voyages under steam.

Of the great Scots share in the Revolution of Transport, the steamship is the most spectacular item. It was not, however, to be the only one. Before the keel of the *Charlotte Dundas* was laid, Scots had made possible the modern roads which in turn were to make possible motor transport. Even in the third quarter of the eighteenth century, the steady growth of trade and manufactures was causing new roads to push their way through Scotland. In the fourth they branched and spread as a tree grows, but faster; and they went on steadily growing. Between 1796 and 1810 three hundred miles of new road had been constructed in the one county of Aberdeen alone: and in the century after 1750 no less than 350 'local' acts were passed to provide new turnpikes. Travelling, accordingly, grew easier, and public transport better organised. In 1788 a coach already ran between Edinburgh and Glasgow: two years later one joined Edinburgh and Aberdeen: and it speaks to the improvement of road conditions that the fourteen days from Edinburgh to London had shrunk, in fine weather, to something like forty-eight hours.

After 1800 advance was much more rapid. In 1803 the great engineer Thomas Telford (1757-1834) was surveying the Highlands. His genius for the laying out of roads was well seconded by the work of John Loudon McAdam (1756-1836) in devising a surface that would stand up to weather and traffic. The two brought road-making, quite suddenly, to a level that it had not reached in Europe since the barbarian tribes under Alaric came marching down the Flaminian Way on Rome—that is to say, for about fourteen hundred years. It has been well said that Telford was more than a craftsman: he was something too of a statesman and an artist, and he and the men who made the great Roman roads would certainly have understood each other. In eighteen years he made 920 miles of Highland roads, with 120 bridges. The Caledonian Canal is part of his work, the great Dean Bridge [1] a mere trifle in its sum. Abroad, he built the first docks of London River—St Katharine's, close by the Tower, and the Menai Bridge, and the 120 miles of the Gotha Canal, which is still the pride of Sweden's waterways.

The demand for the transport of bulky and heavy goods focussed attention, for the time, on canals. That between Forth and Clyde was proving its value, in spite of the early storms of its career: in 1816 it was paying its shareholders sixteen per cent. Its success tempted Telford to the great enterprise of a ship canal down Glenmore, that should link the ports of the Clyde with those of the Baltic. It was unfortunate from the first, however. After long struggle, it was opened to traffic in 1822: but an unfriendly government

[1] Over the valley of the Water of Leith.

strangled it, and it never fulfilled what had been its major purpose.

Very soon, too, the canals had a powerful rival. An English engineer of Scots extraction,[1] George Stephenson (1781-1848), invented in 1825 a machine which could use steam-power to propel a vehicle. Long already, trucks had been running upon rails: now this engine, the *Locomotive*, was set to draw them, at twelve miles an hour, between Stockton and Darlington: and a Scots engineer made the startling prophecy:

It would be rash to say that a higher velocity than twenty miles an hour may not be found applicable,

though many were terrified at the idea: it was impossible that the human frame could endure the impact of such terrific speeds. But the twenty miles was soon reached and surpassed, for the *Rocket*, five years after the *Locomotive*, achieved the incredible pace of over thirty.

Scotland was quick to add railways to her steamships. The first Scots line to adopt the new mode of traction was Monkland to Kirkintilloch, a ten-mile stretch, in 1826.

Railways, the steamship, the 'heavy' industries, the thud of engines in the factories and the growing pall of smoke across the Midlands . . . while Scott laboured with his last strength to pay his debts, the scene was being set for the Victorian Age. And already, from behind the dramatic surface, came the rumour of other changes, no less profound.

[1] His father was the son of an emigrant Scot.

XII

MACHINES AND MEN

FORTY-THREE YEARS: 1789–1832

Though there was no doubt a great and visible increase of the city, loftier buildings on all sides . . . I thought the looks of the population were impaired, and that there was a greater proportion of long white faces. . . . In that same spirit of improvement which was so busy everywhere, I could discern something like a shadow, that showed it was not altogether of that pure advantage which avarice led all so eagerly to believe.   JOHN GALT, *The Annals of the Parish*, for 1791.

IN the half-century after 1780 men were striving earnestly to increase their power by the invention of more and more machines. And before those fifty years had run their course, the machines were already showing their power over men.

There were growing changes in the national balance. One which no one, looking at the time, can miss is the steady drift from the country to the town. So far, in the whole course of our history, towns had existed for the sake of the country: they held its machinery of administration, its markets, its sources of higher education, and (though less in Scotland than in most other kingdoms) they were nuclei of its system of defence. But now the change was already setting in from a mainly rural economy to an urban, in which the towns are thought of as being central, and the country as merely a source of food for them—or in our day, as a source of their amusement, as somewhere for leisure, in holidays or retirement.

The total population showed already the beginnings of the huge nineteenth-century rise. In 1701 it had been about a million. By 1801 it was well over one and a half; and this growth was by no means generally spread, for more and more it concentrated in towns. These were still, however, small to a modern eye. Edinburgh, whose fine New Town reached as far west as Castle Street, had risen from 30,000 to 86,000—about half the size of modern Aberdeen. Glasgow had grown now to very nearly as many, and an industrial district was rising round it. Dundee had taken almost a century to recover from Monk's sack in 1651: in 1750 it had only 12,000, which in

1800 had risen to 26,000—about the size of modern Inverness. Paisley had risen very markedly, from 4,000 to something like 17,000. But at the beginning of the new century, only three more towns, Dunfermline, Perth, and Greenock, had populations of more than 10,000—that is, were larger than modern Wick or Elgin. And at that time, as we have seen already, thirty-one per cent. of the people were on the land.

Between 1801 and 1840, however, something like 350,000 people —nearly four times the 1801 population of Glasgow—settled in urban conditions in the Clyde valley. From a fifth to a fourth of the total population was suddenly, within the half of a lifetime, crowded together in one small area: and no preparation was made to receive that influx, save the hasty building, without plan or design, of exceedingly inadequate shelters for them, and the pro-vision of new kinds of work, from which certain familiar elements were omitted.

Beneath this material shift there were certain others. It is im-portant, but they were far more so. One is again an alteration of balance, which was to lead to a bitter and shameful conflict. The old Scotland, assuredly, had been full of conflict: but the lines of cleavage were so to speak vertical. Men fought each other for religious creeds, for opposition or loyalty to the Crown, for loyalty or for treachery to the State; and clan fought clan, in Lowlands and in Highlands, for possessions, prestige, or plain pugnacity. But there was no *horizontal* line of division: no social class fought another social class—and certainly not because the Scottish peasant was unable to handle the spear as well as the spade. There had been strong distinctions of class and class: but also there had been strong bonds between them. They fought, and often played, side by side with each other; they tholed their paiks from the same school-master, sat side by side upon the college benches, bore the same name and took equal pride in it, and in the Highlands wore the same badge and tartan. Whatever distinctions there might be between them, Jamie Telfer and Buccleuch spoke as man to man.

That was the basic thing, which again and again had saved Scotland against long odds: and now it was going. Even on the land, the lairds were leaving their people. In the formless aggrega-tions of the towns, men were disappearing in a nameless mass. And under the new prosperity of Scotland, something very old was taking a new pattern. The Seven Deadly Sins were familiar enough, and that called Avarice as common as any. Now it took a new shape, and at the same time was given a new cloak, that enabled it to masquerade as virtue.

In the middle years of the eighteenth century, the leaders of revival had been men who worked for their country as often as for themselves. Now that spirit was rapidly becoming rare, the more as the broad, deep-rooted sense of the nation, as a thing for whose safety all men were responsible, was tending now to weaken and disappear—most of all in those who not so long before would have been the natural officers in its defence. Again, the reviving strength of Calvinism, which was strong in the class engaged in manufactures, not only strengthened that negative code of ethics in which thrift and hard work are exalted as ends, not means (that is to say, as virtues in themselves) but turned from the New Testament to the Old—not the Psalms or the Prophets but the Pentateuch, with its emphasis on material gains for the Chosen. And again, the whole eighteenth-century turn of mind ran to the abstract and the general: to a man to whom it was a point of virtue to concern himself passionately with growing rich, it was therefore easy to pass from 'my men' to 'my hands,' the more as imagination was dominated by the magical power of all the new machines. And the eighteenth century (probably enough by reason of this abstract way of thinking) was a peculiarly brutal age—far more brutal, both in theory and in practice, to the weak than ever the Middle Ages had been.[1] Philosophy also justified avarice. The doctrine of *laisser faire* had been intended to mean that a man was free to sell goods or labour in whatever market was most profitable: in practice, it meant that the strong oppressed the weak, and no one had any right to interfere.

Take all these together (and all were in action together) and they meet at one point, which is the ultimate of human wrong—the denial of manhood, of personality, the regarding of men and women as merely things, or what is even worse (it tempts ourselves worse), as mere abstract terms in an economic equation.

It was not, of course, a new sin: it underlies the ancient in-stitution of slavery, and many things more, from murder to bad manners. In lands of the Christian tradition it had, however, been recognised and condemned for what it was. The truly terrible thing about that age is that decent people began to take it for granted,

---

[1] Cf. the code of popular manners, or lack of them, revealed in the novels of Smollett, Fielding, and Fanny Burney.

as a normal, respectable, attitude of mind—even, indeed, as that proper and praiseworthy. As result, though Scotland in the eighteen-thirties was many times richer than in the seventeen-twenties, a large and growing proportion of her people were far worse off than ever they had been.

In the landward districts of the Lowlands also there was a further complicating factor, and one very difficult to deal with justly, even if attempt had been made to deal with it. The pioneers of the new agriculture had hoped that their efforts would enrich the country, and greatly enlarge the national food supply: and in both these aims they had met with amazing success. As a consequence of that success, however, the able men who had practised the new methods got more and more of the land into their hands. The farms enlarged, and more and more of the people fell from the status of peasant cultivators to hired labourers, or were driven to the towns.

The rural population began to fall. In Clydesdale, for instance, in 1755 there were 599 people in the parish of Wandell and Lamington: in 1840 there were 331. In others the downward slope was even steeper. Roberton and Weston, in 1755, had 1102 people: by no later than 1791, there were but 740. In Crawfurd parish fifteen families had lived where in 1791 there were none at all. On Tweed-side, Drummelzier went down by a third in the time, Traquair by a half. In Roxburgh, in the parish of Oxnam every village vanished.

Yet the Lowlands were far less affected than the Highlands. Revival there had come late, but it seemed to be coming: in the seventeen-eighties the Highland Society appeared to promise new and better times, which in some places had very soon begun. In 1794 George Dempster could write triumphantly from Skibo:

You would wonder at the change the little tenants have made in their houses and farms since they knew they were not to be removed or *raxed*.

The hope was not fulfilled. Soon Ramsay of Ochtertyre, recalling 'the lively and cheerful people' of the Highlands, has to add with a sigh, 'They have no longer that gaiety and airiness of manner which struck the most superficial observer in visiting their country' . . . but which has rather rarely struck him since. To lairds (and their wives) living out of touch with the people and faced with the expense of Southern life, the new demand for wool came like manna from heaven. Sheep were the thing. The hill ground, under sheep,

gave rich return: and to men who had come to think in abstract
terms, whatever made more money was 'improvement'—a name
which implied that to practise it was a duty. Therefore, clearly,
nothing must stand in the way of sheep.

Very little did. 'The improvements in the Marquis of Stafford's
Estates' [1] were praised by Mrs Harriet Beecher Stowe, the famous
exponent of the Rights of Negroes, as

an almost sublime instance of the benevolent employment of superior
wealth and power in shortening the struggles of advancing civilisation.

They consisted in replacing men by sheep. And that process was
going on all over the Highlands. The people were simply turned
out of their crofts and houses: their crops were left to rot, their
rafters burnt, and to make sure they did not settle again, any man
who gave evicted tenants shelter was threatened with eviction for
himself. In some places also marriages were forbidden, lest men
should be born to take up ground required for sheep. Women in
childbed were turned out in the rain, while their furniture was
broken up behind them, their meal-arks emptied into the nearest
burn.

It was done on no small scale, for the thing spread in an evil
epidemic. One laird felt justified by the one before, and he did
not see the thing happen, being absent. The factors who were
directly responsible were as a rule incomers from the Lowlands,
small men in authority, resenting the local people, glad to show
power. Some of the evicting lairds made a real attempt to mitigate
the impact of the blow: Lord Stafford himself allowed those who
would emigrate to sit rent-free for two years before they went, and
spent a good deal of money in the provision of alternative employment.

None the less, the people were driven from the land, and that
in the two senses of the last word. In 1801, 3,000 were evicted in
Inverness-shire. Between 1800 and 1806, 10,000 went from the
West and from the Isles. Sleat was cleared altogether in 1811; and
between that year and 1820 the Sutherland Clearances got rid of
15,000. These were the worst. But in 1828, 600 left Lochmaddy,
and two years later 900 more were driven from Sutherland.

In places, there were efforts at resistance. In 1792 there had
been riots in Ross and Sutherland, and a Crofters' Committee was

[1] Lord Stafford had married the Countess of Sutherland, who owned large
lands in that county.

buying gunpowder. In Coigeach, the women set on the police, disarmed them, and burnt their batons . . . and Coigeach stayed. Again, in 1820, in Glencalvie, the people in a body refused to go. The military were called in, and fired, killing a girl, whereon the crofters charged, breaking the troops and reducing the Sheriff's coach to shattered wood: and they stayed also. But these were exceptional cases, for two reasons. In the first place, the time of the worst Clearances is that when most able-bodied Highland men were—as Pitt said of them to their detractors—'showing fidelity equal to their honour' in service in those Highland regiments who bore themselves nobly through the long years of war, and who on general parades for punishment were formally exempted from attendance, 'no examples being needed for such honourable soldiers.' The other reason was that the Highland people, profoundly religious, obeyed their ministers: and the patron lairds had put in 'the right type of man.' In 1845 the *Times* Special Commissioner, reporting on the discontents of the Highlands, was able to observe with satisfaction that although these tiresome people did object to being driven out to Canada or the Gorbals, the Church had the situation well in hand:

It is owing to the influence of religion alone that they refrain from breaking out into open and turbulent resistance to the law,

and retaining their crofts as the folk of Coigeach had done. Starvation, too, was taming them by that time. In 1822 General Stewart had written:

Ancient reputable tenants, possessing stocks of ten, twenty, and thirty cows, with the usual proportion of other stock, are now pining on one or two acres of bad land, with one or two starved cows.

In 1831 the Sutherland folk, driven from the fertile soil to the edge of the sea, were living on shellfish and broth made of seaweed and nettles sprinkled with meal. It is a cooling diet to the blood.

Between 1797 and 1837, Skye alone—and that is a fraction of the Highlands—gave the British Army, in a crucial war, twenty-one lieutenant-generals and major-generals, forty-eight lieutenant-colonels, six hundred other commissioned officers, and ten thousand other ranks, not to mention one Governor-General of India, four Governors of British colonies, a Lord of Session, and a Chief Baron of England. At the beginning of that period, the country north and west of the Highland Line contained a fifth of the kingdom's population. At the present day it contains a twentieth. That is to say, while the whole population of Scotland has more than trebled, that of the Highlands has shrunk, not relatively, but absolutely. And the psychological effect on the Highlands of the course of affairs from Cumberland's invasion to the end of the Clearances has not yet been assessed. Perhaps when that of these last few years on Europe has been studied, we shall be nearer comprehension.

Of those cleared, the more vigorous and enterprising went overseas, many of them to Canada, but many also to the United States, where they were lost to both Scotland and the Empire. The rest drifted to the towns, where the growing factories offered the hope of subsistence. But the new machines were in the factories, and the work that once had been skilled and well-paid labour could largely be done by children. It was so done. Even in the enlightened mills of New Lanark, in a business run by a professed humanitarian, 500 children were working a six-day week, thirteen hours a day spent tending the machines, and then two hours of compulsory education. In some mills children of five worked a thirteen-hour day and spent their Sundays cleaning the machines. In the Forfar flax-mills it was sixteen hours. It was what they were for: 'no man cared for their soul.' Boys and girls of the age of puberty were herded together at night in the locked bothies. And the Reverend Nathaniel Paterson of Galashiels observed with a comfortable satisfaction that 'there is no training for the volatile mind of youth equal to that maintained in the factories.'

Others, however, admired the system less. Sheriff Watson of Aberdeen, John Maxwell of Pollok, and the Glasgow Tory paper *The Courier* [1] protested fiercely at this state of affairs, and demanded legislation to amend it. They were hotly opposed. To pass such legislation would interfere with the individual's rights, and blaspheme the sacred doctrine of *laisser faire*. None the less, in 1802 Sir Robert Peel (who as a Tory cared less for the Rights of Man) succeeded in getting through the first Factory Act, which enacted that the 'parish apprentices'—pauper children sold in batches to

---

[1] It is worth noting that most of the social legislation of the nineteenth century comes from the Tory or Conservative side. The Liberals, in spite of their professed humanitarianism, represented mainly the town and the town employers. The Tories represented the country interest : and apart from the fact that they did not directly profit by the mills, they were used—the better of them at any rate—to a more personal contact with their people, while their general creed was less based upon abstractions.

employers, as was the common custom all over England—should work only a twelve-hour day. Those who were not paupers were not to be interfered with: but the principle of legal regulation had been introduced, though it was to take another seventeen years before Peel and Owen got the Act extended to forbid any child under nine from factory work. Even so, the extension had to be limited to cotton and wool mills. Children were still permitted, in the sacred name of individual freedom, to work in coal-pits as soon as they could walk, their pregnant mothers dragging trucks beside them, crawling on hands and knees through the galleries, a chain passing between the legs from an iron waist-belt. And the enforcement of the Factory Act was left in the hands of Justices of the Peace, who in towns were very commonly factory owners, and sincerely agreed with the Reverend Nathaniel Paterson.

Vast hordes of people were gathering in the towns, reinforced, on Clydeside, by many more from Ireland. The men brought their families, hoping to find work. But it was not the men who found the work. It was the bairns who were the bread-winners, at any rate in the textile industries. A weaver's wages, at the beginning of the period, had been forty or fifty shillings a week, which then was a good deal more than it is now. By the end, they had sunk to 10s., or even 4s. 6d. In 1834 some were actually receiving 3s. 6d. for a week of fourteen-hour days. And something else happened, which is less often remarked on. The farm labourer and the handicraftsman of old might be ill-paid and work in hard conditions: but far the greater number of labouring men were engaged in work that called for skill and gave interest. No day on a farm repeats another day, while the mason, the wright, the weaver, and the smith had each the satisfaction of *making* something. Their work, however humble, was creation; and the man who creates has that impact on his world which is one of the deepest of all human needs, and thwarted, breaks out in terrible morbid forms of cruelty and tyranny and destruction, or atrophies, rotting till it poisons manhood and leaves slaves crying for state-supplied bread and games. Now, for too many, 'work' was to mean no more than a meaningless sequence of mechanical actions: and nothing else, outside the factories, supplied the mental vitamins it lacked.

There was worse than material squalor in the cities, where vast poverty-stricken masses herded together, barely sheltered from the rain, in appalling filth, which the water-supply and the housing conditions between them made inevitable even to those women who retained the self-respect, and the energy, to make some kind of attempt to cope with it. Many, small blame to them, did not make the attempt, and took 'the short way out of Glasgow' instead. The eighteenth century was a hard-drinking age. Gin spread in England ('Drunk for a penny, dead drunk for tuppence') and whisky in Scotland, where before this time it had been used as a medicine or a liqueur. By about 1800 it was said that every twelfth house in Glasgow was a drink-shop.

Poverty, drink, unemployment, unspeakable housing, enhanced each other in a vicious circle, while the highly respected Malthus was proclaiming that 'no man has a right to subsistence where his labour will not fully purchase it.' But to let men actually die of starvation because they had sought vainly for employment was pushing *laisser faire* a little too far. To prevent them from dying was not, however, easy, especially in the trade slump after the war. In wealthy England by 1831—that is to say, in the richest country in Europe—ten per cent. of the whole population were 'on relief,' in spite of the dreadful conditions on which it was granted, conditions that were designed with a careful science to remove every vestige of human dignity, and human freedom, from the recipients. In Scotland the system was both better and worse. The Kirk Sessions attempted, and as a rule with a decent humanity, to keep body and soul together in the disabled: but able-bodied men who could not earn could only starve till they ceased to be able-bodied.

These things grew and festered under the brilliant surface until they broke stormily through into politics. We rarely realise quite how explosive was the atmosphere in the British eighteen-twenties. The French Revolution might very well, indeed, have been paralleled on our side of the North Sea. Only, the mass of the people, when it happened, were by no means so badly off as they were later: and by the time they had reached the pitch of revolt the process of the Industrial Revolution had opposed the middle class to those oppressed.

XIII

THE RIGHTS OF MAN

TEN YEARS: 1789–99

Liberté, égalité, fraternité.
Motto of the French Revolution.
Sois mon frère cadet ou je te tue.
An onlooker's translation of the above.

THROUGH these forty-three years the French Revolution and its consequences were a dominant factor in British politics. In Scotland they had one important, and evil, result. For a long lifetime after the Treaty of Union, Scotland was still a European country— much more than England had been since the Middle Ages. Especially, the old close connection with France, which had weakened in the seventeenth century, had revived again, with stimulating results. Now the Revolution caused it to be broken, and severed Scotland from the Continent. The only country with which we had close relations, for more than a century, was to be England.

The larger implications of the fact can more conveniently be dealt with later. It is enough to say here only that Scotland became in time more insular than England, while also her sense of national being grew weaker. As result, when the country's lost political sense revived, and intensely, it had no longer, at its very core, the idea of the nation, but was bent upon abstract political principles or the rival interests of opposing classes.

It is ill for men to think, in politics, of the nation alone, as we know to our cost today. For health it must be constantly related to things which are greater than itself, and less—which are ultimately as great as humanity and as little as the individual man. But to leave out the nation and think but of these extremes, that of which it is part and that which is part of it—or still worse, of either alone— is a disaster. And it was this which began to happen in Scotland; although, till the end of the war with Napoleon, it had not indeed gone beyond beginning to happen.

We have already seen in Chapter VIII how agitation for a wider franchise, begun under French and American influence, was stirring here and there in the seventeen-eighties. The summoning in France of an assembly which was far more representative of the nation than the British Parliament was even of England, was very warmly welcomed in this country. Not only Burns, but the leading men of the Scots universities—Thomas Reid, Dugald Stewart, Principal Robertson—expressed strong sympathy with the new French movement. The venerable Tory Henry Mackenzie, the young Sir James Macintosh, young Thomas Christie, were eager to combat Burke's aspersions on it. Sir James's *Vindiciae Gallicae*, in fact, won him an honorary grant of French nationality.[1] When the Third Estate broke away in a few weeks to re-form itself as a National Assembly, the Dundee Whig Club sent its congratulations; and the fall of the Bastille, which ensued soon after, was celebrated in Edinburgh, Glasgow, and Dundee by wildly enthusiastic public dinners. The Earl of Lauderdale, in the Paris streets, made impassioned speeches in praise of liberty. Lord Sempill offered 6,000 pairs of shoes to the army that should defend the young Revolution.

Meanwhile, in France, that Revolution spread. The Bastille fell in July 1789: three months later, in the *journées* of October, the 'people' took the King in their own hands, and brought him, a virtual prisoner, into Paris. Now, the Revolution had been first begun by aristocratic anti-royalists, by middle-class men who desired a 'constitution,' and by wealthy ones with less status than they liked or a desire for good fishing in troubled waters. Once they had shaken the power of the Throne, however, control passed rapidly to the Paris mob, led by men who professed desire for a republic, and who did desire a new class domination, with themselves as dictators. In June 1791 the Civil Constitution of the Clergy—state control of the expropriated Church—forced a violent crisis. The King sought to flee from France, to join the exiled Royalists over the border, but was captured at Varennes and brought back to Paris. By September, however, there seemed to be promise of peace. Louis accepted the new constitution, and for just under a year of general hope, France was a constitutional monarchy. The republican

---

[1] Strictly speaking, unnecessary. The French Consul for Scotland, Comte Alfred de Curzon, lately pointed out in the *Journal des Débats* that the grant of French nationality to all Scots, originally made by Louis XII, was confirmed again and again by successive kings, and has never been rescinded, while Louis XIV specifically decreed that no war between France and the United Kingdoms should affect its validity.

doctrinaires and would-be dictators were intriguing on one side and rising into power, helped by the fact that a revolution which began in an attempt to redd the finances had succeeded in reducing these to chaos and causing a first-class economic crisis. The Queen and the emigrant friends of the old regime were intriguing on the other for foreign invasion, under her brother the Emperor Leopold, in company with his new ally the King of Prussia. For a moment, the threat of a German invasion of France united the Revolutionary factions: they did not wait for the invasion to come, but on the 20th April 1792 declared war on the Empire, attacking the Netherlands. It was not quite three years since the Estates had met, and the war thus begun was to last for twenty-three, and to draw in all Europe before it reached its end, to say nothing of India and the United States.

France was ill-prepared, but the war was popular there. The Royalists wished the defeat of the Revolution. The Moderates hoped it would buttress their shaken power. The Extremists hoped it would play into their hands. Nor were any of them made easily afraid: whatever one may think of the Revolution, one is forced to admire the proud unshakeable courage that was common to men and women of all parties.

The French offensive in the Low Countries failed. At the end of July the Prussian Duke of Brunswick was marching on the frontier of France, announcing that he would give Paris to sack by his troops if the city did not surrender to King Louis. It doomed that King. The people flew to arms, and on the 10th August seized the royal palace. The King was deposed and a prisoner in the Temple . . . and the mob of the Sections was by that same act above the new *Assemblée législative*. And meanwhile the Prussians were marching through Champagne, on a country in disorder and with no army. There were cries for the Government to flee from Paris. But Danton took the people in his strong gripe. The surrender of Paris, he cried, was surrender of France:

the guns you hear are the drum-beat of the charge on France's foes. To beat them, to strike them down, what do we need but daring, daring again, and constant daring—*de l'audace, encore de l'audace, toujours de l'audace.*

France gave him that—though the *audace* extended to a massacre of Royalists in the prisons, that horrified Europe. It had other manifestations besides, however. A strange rabble of an army sprang out of the ground. It seemed that their chief weapon was a song: but that song was the *Marseillaise*, and it took them to Valmy. The enemy troops had already forced the Argonne. But Dumouriez led his tailors and counter-jumpers, with their few guns, against the Prussian flank: and it was the Duke of Brunswick who fell back, and on the morrow gave orders for retreat. *L'audace* had won, and Dumouriez went forward to Jemappes. On the 13th of November he was in Brussels.

The victory went to the head of the Convention, who had by this time replaced the Assembly in Paris, and who stood for the full tide of Revolution. They offered to help any nation against any king, with a promise of *fraternité et secours à ceux qui voudraient recouvrer leur liberté*. Within a month more, they were already announcing that in any country occupied by their troops they would establish the sovereignty of the people and abolish all privileges whatsoever, except those incident to that sovereignty . . . and that they would confiscate to the French Republic all royal and ecclesiastical property. The boast was not vain, for by a few weeks later the Armies of the Republic were on the Rhine, and were sweeping over the march into Savoy.

Already the British Government were alarmed. The French held the Scheldt, that 'pistol pointed at the heart of England'; and Britain also had a treaty with Holland. Pitt told the Convention that if France desired British friendship

she must show herself disposed to renounce her views of aggression and aggrandisement and to confine herself within her own territory, without insulting other governments, without disturbing their tranquillity, without violating their rights.

But by this time there was no holding the Republic. The reply was 'Jetons-leur en défi une tête de roi,' and on the twenty-first day of 1793—a little less than four months after Valmy—the slow kind man who was the King of France went through the streets of his capital to the scaffold. Pitt gave the French ambassador his passports. On the 1st February France declared war on Britain, on the 9th March on Holland and on Spain. On the 22nd, the Emperor declared war on France.[1] It was not quite four years since the Estates had met, and already six powers, as result, had gone to war.

While Europe flamed, there were lesser fires at home; and as

---

[1] Up to this time he had been fighting what from his point of view was not even a *de facto* Government.

usually happens at such times, the penalty exacted for their raising fell on those who desired a merely moderate blaze, that should cook the dinner without removing the roof. We see those four years from this end, and know their events. The men who lived through them saw them from the other: and the attention of many of them was focussed on the gallant hope and generous emotion that underlay much of the fervours of 'Eighty-nine, on the noble abstract principles of its creed, and on the ungenerous and ignoble corruption that was the note of British politics. Societies of eager men were forming to apply the principles to the corruption, as a rule in no extremist frame of mind. The Constitutional Society studied problems of representative government. In 1791, that year of delusive hopes, a Larbert man of the name of Thomas Hardy formed the London Corresponding Society, to work for short Parliaments and middle-class votes; and a society called the Friends of the People was founded by a young advocate, Thomas Muir, supported by Lord Daer and Colonel Dalrymple—all men who sympathised with the new hopes, yet, alarmed by the violence already lifting its head not only in France but on our side of the water, desired, while working with vigour for reform, 'to counteract the more radical tendencies.' The society had no republican aim, and it was strongly against the use of violence.

The point of view was very popular, and the society spread rapidly. In 1792 the leaders decided to call a convention of delegates in Edinburgh. A hundred and forty arrived, representing eighty such societies, in thirty-five places. They meant peaceably: but they chose their time, and name, quite remarkably ill, for in that month King Louis was put upon his trial, and in France *l'Ami du peuple* meant Marat, the bloodiest of the wildest Republicans: and by way of driving home these unlucky facts, they began with the Revolution's favourite gesture, a solemn oath *vivre libre ou mourir.*

It was folly: and the Government answered by panic. Muir, as leader, was arrested for sedition, and released on bail—which he used to go to France, and plead, at the risk of his neck, for the King's life. The Friends defiantly called another meeting, for April, a date no more fortunate than the other, for by that time we were at war with France. In August, with feeling blazing at its height, and the French 'Terror' in active operation for the last year, Muir was tried before the notorious Lord Braxfield, a roaring brute with a brutal sense of humour . . . which hardly appears in his remark at the trial, that beyond all doubt

The British Constitution is the best that ever was since the creation of the world, and it is not possible to make it better.

Even Braxfield, in the middle of the Terror, did not go so far as to sentence Muir to hang: he transported him, however, for fourteen years, and an English minister of the name of Palmer was given a seven years sentence at the same time for writing an address against the French war on behalf of the Dundee Friends of Liberty. And a gentleman who reported Braxfield's speech with a faithful reproduction of his accent was given three months for his accuracy.[1] They were brutal sentences, cruelly unjust. All wars in which what we call ideologies cross national divisions breed such, however, and in justice (even to Braxfield) one has to remember that the sentences on 'Fifth Columnists' in France were a good deal more numerous, and drastic, and paid no greater heed to the equities. Having said which, it is as well to recall that Fouquier-Tinville does not whitewash Braxfield, any more than Braxfield whitewashes Fouquier-Tinville. *Arcades ambo:* and the generous young Muir was the man who suffered.

The war continued, both at home and abroad, and soon gave the Government reason for its terror. France seemed at first to be in hopeless case. Nearly all Europe was united against her. Scandinavia, Venice, Turkey, Switzerland, were the only neutrals: and she had no allies. But the history of France is like our own. Again and again both countries have seemed to be ruined, by *force majeure* or by a disease within: and again and again they have risen in new strength, by some indestructible force in the nation's spirit.[2] So it was now. Austria recovered Belgium. The Prussians recrossed the Rhine. The Spaniards were in the glens of the Pyrenees. The Piedmontese were marching through Savoy. The British and Hanoverians together were drawing the siege lines about Dunkirk. A Royalist insurrection blazed in the West. Toulon, the major

---

[1] If it were not so highly improbable, Muir's subsequent career would make a very exciting romantic novel. The French Directory sent a warship to rescue him, which failed. Washington sent another, which succeeded, but thereafter was wrecked. After many adventures, he died in his early thirties, a naturalised and somewhat embittered Frenchman.
[2] Paris was yielded on the day I wrote this sentence. I do not take it back. It is still true.

naval base of the South, surrendered to the British and Spanish fleets. And meanwhile the Government had gone to the scaffold, and all France was torn to pieces by the Terror.[1]

By the end of August she seemed completely crushed. But again her armies sprang from the very ground, and she had in Carnot a genius for training them. By the end of that year, 1793, the civil war in the West had been put down, crushed in the terrible Christmas at Savenay: and a week before that, young Colonel Napoleone Buonaparte had taken Toulon again for the Republic, and been promoted to Brigadier-General. The tide was turning, in spite of Lord Howe and 'the glorious First of June' the following year, when the French fleet was badly mauled off Brest. Only a few weeks after Howe's victory, the battle of Fleurus, to the south of Brussels, threw open the Low Countries to the Republic: and the 28th July, the 10th Thermidor, brought the Terror to an end, with Robespierre's fall.

Against this crashing background, restlessness, fomented by the Government's harsh measures, continued in Britain. In England also there were 'Friends of the People'; and undeterred by the heavy sentence on Muir, the Scottish and English societies together held a joint conference in Edinburgh, in the October of 1793: and the challenge, coming straight on Muir's condemnation and against the background of the Terror in France, further exasperated the Government. There were more arrests. Two Englishmen, Joseph Gerrald and Maurice Margarot, and a Scots country laird of the name of Skirving received the same sentence as Muir. Skirving died on the convict ship that took them out. The English society called a convention in London, to support the men on trial in Edinburgh, and frankly proposed an armed association. In May 1794, with the war still in favour of the Revolution, Parliament showed its sense of domestic danger by suspending the Act against Wrongous Imprisonment and its English equivalent, that of Habeas Corpus :

---

[1] The Terror appalled its time : and it was appalling. But by modern standards—Russian, Spanish, German—it seems now almost humane and civilised. Torture was not used, and except in occasional outbreaks of mob-fury or isolated cases as at Nantes (and Carrier shocked the violent of his own party) the victims were killed painlessly, in daylight, and with some regard for human dignity. There is a good deal of moral difference between being guillotined publicly, in form, and being shot in the back, in one's underclothes, in a cellar, even without preliminary torture. Fouquier-Tinville would not have dined with Himmler.

and the drastic measure appeared to be excused by discovery of a formidable plot. A government spy of the name of Robert Watt had, it seems, turned genuine revolutionary, and become a leader in a group of men who planned simultaneous risings to take place in Edinburgh, in London, and in Dublin. Edinburgh Castle was to be seized, bodies of armed men were to surround the soldiers and arrest the Lord Provost and the magistrates, who were then to be put on their trial. The Post-office, banks, and public-houses also were to be seized, the two latter to be given *centinels*: and when the three capitals were thus controlled, a petition should be presented to the King, exhorting him to remedy abuses. The plans had been worked out in elaborate detail, and pike-heads were being forged to serve as sanction.

Watt, and Downie, Treasurer of the Friends of the People, were immediately arrested, and tried for treason. Dundas kept the trial out of Braxfield's hands, but Watt went to the gallows none the less. Feeling blazed high on both sides, and the blaze was fanned by the constant news of France's victories. By the early months of 1795 she had overrun Holland and made of it 'the Batavian Republic.' [1] The Prussians were driven back across the Rhine. Savoy was cleared. France counter-invaded Spain and Italy, while wars were breaking out in our colonies. Before the summer of the year was ended, the Alliance against France collapsed like a card-house. At the end of the year four widely severed powers, Britain, Austria, Portugal, and Sardinia, alone held out: and France had established a new constitution, whose five Directors knew extremely well that in France without credit or commerce or industry (and all of them had been wrecked by the Revolution) only war, and successful war, could save their heads.

At home the atmosphere still was full of smoke. There were pamphlets in hundreds, and some of the Left extremists were preaching the doctrine of political murder. Harvests were bad, and prices were rapidly rising. In Edinburgh, one in eight of the people had no resource but to live on charity. The bitterness grew: already,

[1] This campaign saw what was probably the only instance in history of a fleet being captured by hostile cavalry. The Dutch fleet, frozen in in the Texel, was taken by French hussars who crossed the ice. It also saw the Black Watch win their famous red hackle. The 11th Dragoons, stationed to cover a retreat, lost their guns to the French. The Black Watch recovered them after hot fighting, and though all the gun-horses were killed, brought them safely back : whereon King George took their red hackle from the 11th Dragoons, and gave it to the rescuers of the guns.

in the previous year, '94, the Government, raising a militia in England, had been afraid to extend the measure to Scotland. In 1795, as the war worsened, the law of treason was specially enlarged to cover not only any speech or writing directed against the King's authority, but also any sort of political meeting of which notice had not been given in advance. Feeling ran so high that the brilliant Whig lawyer Henry Erskine, a man of wit, scholarship, and the finest honour, son of the Earl of Buchan and Dean of the Faculty of Advocates, lost his Deanship for opposing the extension; and scandal raged against even the venerated Dugald Stewart, who six years before had approved of the young Revolution.

The new danger had a steadying effect, however. Already, when a militia had not been granted, Volunteer corps were forming in case of an invasion: and the Tory Scott and the Burns who had wept with joy when the Bastille fell took part with an equal keenness in their raising. By 1796 forty-one districts had joined to raise and equip 'a promiscuous armed democracy' of all parties.

Still the external danger pressed on Britain. Beneath the Directory the Revolution was passing through the customary change. Six years from the first meeting of the Estates, a wild extravagance and ostentation, as flagrant as those of the *ancien régime*, but lacking its grace, mocked the poverty of the masses. The sacred Sovereignty of the People was the rule of the profiteer, the bureaucrat, and the soldier. In theory, men were still equal before the law. In practice, *la carrière ouverte aux talents* remained as a general working principle . . . but now in the form of every man for himself, and the Devil, or the guillotine, take the hindmost.

The starving mob soon rose against their new masters. On the 4th October 1795—by their calendar the 13th Vendémiaire—these were saved from destruction by a 'whiff of grapeshot' directed by the young General Buonaparte. They showed their gratitude for his services, and incidentally got him out of the way, by giving him the command of the army in Italy. He was then a little over twenty-six: and in four years more he was Dictator of France. In eight again, he was master of most of Europe. In eight more, he was prisoner on an Atlantic island. And for eighteen years all British history passed in the shadow of that small grey figure with the broad cocked hat, pale face, and keen black eyes.

XIV

BRITAIN AND A DICTATOR

TWENTY YEARS: 1795–1815

DICTATOR, n.   Absolute ruler, usually temporary . . . of a State, especially one who suppresses or succeeds a republican government.

Concise Oxford Dictionary, *1914 edition.*

Why, man, he doth bestride the narrow world.

WILLIAM SHAKESPEARE, *Julius Caesar.*

BEFORE the end of 1795, nothing stood against France but Austria and Britain. Next year, the Directory struck at these in turn. Austria came first. The Armies of the Rhine and of Sambre et Meuse failed badly, but Bonaparte in Italy (he had by that time gallicised his name) in a series of startling campaigns drove the Austrians back until he was barely eighty miles from Vienna; and by 18th April 1797 he had forced them to make an unwilling peace with France. The attack on Britain came later, and was a fiasco. Hoche, no mean general, led an invasion of Ireland. The weather broke up its fleet, and it did not land. A small force actually arrived in Wales, but was unsupported and very easily dealt with.

Yet Britain stood alone now, against a France who in little more than two years had fought and defeated the greater part of Europe. Pitt thereupon opened negotiations for peace: but the Directory refused his conditions. Britain has rarely faced more pressing danger than in the dark year of 1797. The Bank of England could not pay its debts. There was extremely serious trouble in Ireland, and widespread hate of the Government in Britain. The very powerful orator Charles James Fox, the leader of the extreme Whig opposition, declared that it was the real enemy, and that the danger from France was a mere myth: and many were contented to believe him. The Army and the Navy were in revolt against their horrible conditions of service.[1] And

[1] H.M.S. *Revenge*, in a nine-year commission, had over three hundred floggings, of anywhere from six to five hundred lashes. Food and accommodation tallied with this conception of discipline. A young officer of the time writes to his mother, ' We live on beef which has been ten or eleven years in the cask, and on biscuit which makes your throat cold in eating it, owing to the maggots, which are very cold when you eat them ! like calves-foot jelly or blomonge—being very fat indeed. . . . We drink water the colour of the bark of a pear-tree, with plenty of little maggots and weevils in it.' The Army discipline, except in Highland regiments, was the same, and the food and accommodation not much better.

10

France, with the powerful fleets of Spain and Holland as well as her own, was preparing an invasion.

Had those fleets joined, it would almost certainly have been successful. On St Valentine's Day, however, off Cape St Vincent, Admiral Jervis met the Spanish fleet, and thanks largely to the valour and seamanship of two young English captains, Nelson and Collingwood, drove it back, badly battered, into Cadiz. Those of France and Holland were still in being, however: and when on the 15th April the British fleet was ordered from Spithead, the men refused to sail and went on strike, and it took the best part of a month to restore them to order. They had been back on duty for only two days when those at the Nore struck also, blockading London, seizing ships, and even sacking private houses. The infection of mutiny then spread to Yarmouth . . . and the Dutch fleet was just about to sail.

The commander at Yarmouth was a Scot, Admiral Duncan. The men of his own flagship and one other stayed loyal and would not join the mutineers. With these two ships Duncan sailed to stop the Dutch fleet; and coming off Texel before they had weighed anchor, stood on and off with his masts just in sight of them, flying signals to a non-existent squadron. The Dutch, who could have blown Duncan out of the water, were bluffed successfully, and stayed in harbour, giving Pitt time to deal with the mutineers by a judicious blend of concession and rope.

The time that Duncan had won was of crucial value. The disaffection in Britain was growing worse. In Scotland a formidable secret society, the United Scotsmen, had recently been founded by George Mealmaker, a weaver of Dundee: and apart from that, the new Scots Militia Act, which demanded the raising of 6,000 men, was intensely unpopular with the working people, whose agitators had contrived to convince them that it was a class measure, planned by their oppressors—a conception to which conditions in the forces, as described above, gave a good deal of support. There were riots. At Tranent on the 28th July a charge of English cavalry down the street killed eleven people. And besides the general working-class disaffection, the Whig opposition in Parliament preached surrender, and Pitt was forced to offer peace again, abandoning his previous conditions.

It was refused, and the outlook grew steadily worse. On the 17th of October the Treaty of Campo Formio left France completely mistress of North Italy. She had annexed Belgium, given Venice to Austria, and made the greater part of Italy into two republics, her protectorates: and now Bonaparte was brought to deal with the North.

He was just too late. Six days before that triumphant treaty was signed, Duncan, the true descendant of Wood and the Bartons, had put a fatal spoke in the wheel of France. He sailed out again with the penitent mutineers, forced the Dutch fleet into action off Camperdown, and pounded it till it was completely useless.[1] There were nearly eighteen years of war to come yet, but that victory, none the less, marks a vital turn, like the Marne in the September of 1914. It saved for Britain that control of the seas which in the end was to be her salvation.

The Directory had now, thanks to Jervis and Duncan, been deprived of the aid of their two allied fleets. They failed, however, to grasp the point's importance, and proclaiming Great Britain the enemy of world freedom, put Bonaparte at the head of a new army, which with the concurrence of Fox and his Fifth Column, should dictate the terms of Republican peace in London. General Bonaparte, however, knew better than they what was implied in naval command of the Channel, and being well aware that Republican principles had badly damaged the fighting efficiency of the lately admirable fleet of France, decided to strike at Britain through her Empire, attacking Egypt as the key to India, and stirring up war in India itself.

Bonaparte's Eastern campaign threatened grave danger: but again sea-power proved too much for him. He seized Malta from the Knights, took Alexandria, and occupied Lower Egypt with a strong force. But on the 1st August 1798 Nelson destroyed his fleet at Aboukir, irretrievably harming his communications. Bonaparte knew his Egyptian plan had failed, and swung it against Syria instead . . . and again was baffled by the British fleet, which came to the assistance of the Turks. His whole Eastern venture in fact was collapsing now, for the war that he had stirred in India had been crushed by a vigorous Scot, Sir David Baird, who in fact added something like 20,000 square miles to the British dominions in the

[1] There is a tale of a worthy Scot, Captain Inglis, who when signals grew confused in the heat of the fight, flung the code-book on the deck and roared cheerfully, ' Damn signals ! Up wi' the helm and gang into the middle o't.' Nelson perhaps remembered Captain Inglis in his famous general order before Trafalgar— not the rhetorical ' England Expects ' (which by the way was hoisted by a Scot) but ' in case signals cannot . . . be clearly understood : no captain can do very wrong if he places his ship alongside that of an enemy.'

course of it, and confirmed the British hold upon the coast and the central part of the great Southern plateau.[1]

The Government were in need of some success, for they were far from popular at home, and trouble, well deserved by long oppression, had sprung up in Ireland. The attempt at invasion in 1796 had led to reprisals against its sympathisers, and some ugly atrocities by British troops. In 1798 there were dangerous risings in the unhappy country, and a few French landed, defeating a British general. The Directory failed to reinforce them, however. They were surrounded and obliged to surrender, and the Irish rising was crushed, by no means gently. The United Scotsmen also were put down, their leader Mealmaker being transported; and the Combinations Acts of 1799-1800 struck at associations of working men. But with more effect than measures of repression, a realisation of the foreign danger was now beginning to unite the country. The union, however, did not come at once. In 1800 and 1801 again there were 'meal riots,' led by an English officer named Cartwright: and the agitation for Reform continued, the *Dundee Advertiser* being founded to express it. But as the war went on, the disturbance sobered, and it was not until about 1808, when economic pressure began to be felt, that it showed signs of breaking out again.

The war situation was ambiguous. By the middle months of 1799 the Eastern danger had been firmly dealt with. In Europe, however, France's success was alarming. Northern Italy was in her hands already, and now she drove out the Pope and the King of Naples, made their domains protectorate republics, and went on to do as much for Switzerland, which had never before, in her history, been conquered. The Powers were startled out of their supineness, and Britain's successes on the Eastern fronts showed that she still was a serviceable ally. While the Syrian campaign was still in the balance, at the beginning of 1799, Russia and Austria joined forces with her in a Second Coalition against France. Russian-British forces under the Duke of York were defeated in Holland and had to surrender *en masse*. But the Russians defeated the French in Italy, and the Austrians did the same in Germany, while a British fleet engaged what was left of the Dutch one off the Texel, and put it out of action.

---

[1] It was Baird who earlier, as a prisoner of Hyder Ali, drew from his mother the classic ejaculation ' Lord help the man that's chained to our Davie ! ' But his men adored him.

The new threat stirred Bonaparte to cut his losses on the Eastern front, and hurry back to France. He found the Directory discredited, and on the 10th November, the 19th Brumaire, he threw it out by a bloodless *coup de main*, and established in its place a new constitution, with himself (he was then thirty and four months) [1] as First Consul, the head not only of France's armies but of her civil constitution also. He was virtual President of the Republic: and he very soon was to rule it as dictator, and soon thereafter as something more than that.

Already, hampered by the Directory, Bonaparte was a legend and a terror. Now he proved himself a superb administrator, and one who could win the genuine love of his people, not merely by force and fear (though he used both), nor even the dazzlement of his success, but by his sheer gift of handling and leading men and reconstituting a shattered, tormented nation. Through all the changes of her constitution, his code of laws governed France until 1940, freely accepted: and his achievements of peace, in a dozen directions, survived the wreck of his military triumphs and became a part of the national foundations. Had he been, as a soldier, a little less brilliant (or even as brilliant and a happier husband), he might have died on the throne of Charlemagne and founded an enduring dynasty. As it was, he was with power for thirteen years yet, and it took three more to complete his overthrow.

He was faced now with Pitt's formidable Coalition, and he offered peace 'as between the two most enlightened nations in Europe,' disclaiming *les idées de vaine grandeur*, and speaking of peace as the first of needs and of glories. It is possible that he was in fact sincere: but Pitt, strong in the Coalition, refused with violence. Bonaparte thus had to fight the three Powers: and he fought them. By the end of 1800 Austria had seen her army crushed at Marengo and Hohenlinden: the French held Belgium and Northern Italy. Russia withdrew, and with Sweden, Denmark and Norway, and Prussia, formed a new League of Armed Neutrality. Britain tried to invade both France and Spain, and failed, and had for sole consolation, at

---

[1] It was a war of young men. Of Napoleon's twenty-four marshals (leaving out Poniatowski) nineteen were Generals of Division before they were forty, fifteen before they were thirty-five, and MacDonald, Marmont, Suchet, and Grouchy when they were still in their twenties. General Hoche was twenty-nine when he was killed, General Duphot twenty-seven. Napoleon was only forty-five at Waterloo.

the moment, the belief that she had settled the Irish Problem by the establishment of a United Kingdom of Great Britain and Ireland . . . which at once deprived her of her leader Pitt.

The Union dates from the first day of 1801, on which occasion George III at last discarded the quaint custom by which the sovereign of England bore the arms and used the title of King of France, even when he happened to be that monarch's ally. The methods by which the Treaty were brought about were similar to those of 1707, but the terms secured by Ireland were much better. She was given a hundred members in the Commons, and thirty-two in the Lords, while her taxes were lighter than those of England or Scotland. The mass of the Irish were bribed to acquiesce by a promise of Catholic emancipation, which, as in 1691, at once was broken. Pitt, who had made the promise, refused to concur in its breach, and resigned his office: and his fall appeared to bring defeat much nearer.

Britain, however, turned and took the offensive, striking north and south. The Powers of the new League were told that their 'armed neutrality' was in fact a mere disguise for belligerency. The Danish fleet blocked the entry to the Baltic, the road to attack upon Russia and Prussia both; and when it refused to give British ships free passage, Admiral Parker was sent, with a British fleet, to deal with it in Copenhagen Roads, arriving there upon the 1st of April. Parker was cautious: but one of his captains was Horatio Nelson, who turned a useful blind eye to the flagship's signals, and being comfortably unable to make them out, proceeded to act according to his judgment. The Danish fleet went effectively out of action, and the League too, for the Czar Paul, who was its main support, had been murdered by his subjects the week before. On the south of the map, that tough old Scots veteran of the Seven Years War, Sir Ralph Abercrombie (who had come close to wrecking his career by a protest against the Government's handling of Ireland), had been sent to Aboukir a month before. On the 21st March, a little more than a week before Copenhagen, he defeated the French Army of Occupation, and though he was killed, another Scot, General John Moore, succeeded him and carried on the campaign; and in June the remaining French troops in Egypt surrendered.

It was not victory: but it was not defeat. Britain had saved her power in India, and she still retained the mastery of the sea. Negotiations for peace were already proceeding, and the diplomatic and military position inclined the First Consul now to what both sides knew was likely to prove no more than an armistice. 'Peace' was signed at Amiens on the 25th of March 1802, on terms which included the surrender by Britain of all captured overseas in the various sideshows, except for the islands of Trinidad and Ceylon.[1] France in turn gave up her claim to the Papal States and to Naples: but she still retained Switzerland and North Italy, very conveniently on Austria's flank, and the Low Countries, close alongside England.

This armistice marks a definite psychological turn in the war. Till then, though nominally a war of nations, it was in origin a war of ideas, and had turned, as such are very apt to do, into a war of international parties, with civil conflicts running beside and within it and providing what we call 'Fifth Columns' in every country. Such makes for uglier and more complex problems. The higher the motive, the worse the war, as a rule, the religious ones being the most vindictive of any, and political wars between professional armies or those undertaken for mere love of fighting being comparatively decent and humane.[2]

Pitt had emphasised all along that he was fighting not France but the Revolution. Many, even in England, held much the same point of view, which was naturally congenial in Scotland. Conversely, many, in Scotland and England both, accepted the tenets of the Revolution, and would have been very willing to see them triumph. Now, however, the temper of France herself was changing. She had grown very sick of violent freedom, with its numberless tyrants, and welcomed a Dictator who could give her good government and victory. The ink was barely dry on the Peace Treaty when Bonaparte, by three and a half million votes against eight thousand, had been elected Consul for his lifetime: and the votes had a genuine popular feeling behind them.

The change reverberated across the water. Those who had honestly opposed the war for the sake of *les principes de* '89 saw them cast into the shadow by a new sun, which much more strongly resembled *le Roi soleil*. It is never very difficult, in England, to

[1] Ceylon had been annexed from the Dutch in 1795, by Hugh Cleghorn, the former Professor of Civil History at St Andrews, and another Scot, Major Agnew, who with a remarkable audacity brought off an almost bloodless *coup de main*.
[2] Germany, of course, is an exception. Whatever her motive has happened to be for war, she has always shown herself a dirty fighter. Froissart expresses his opinion with vigour.

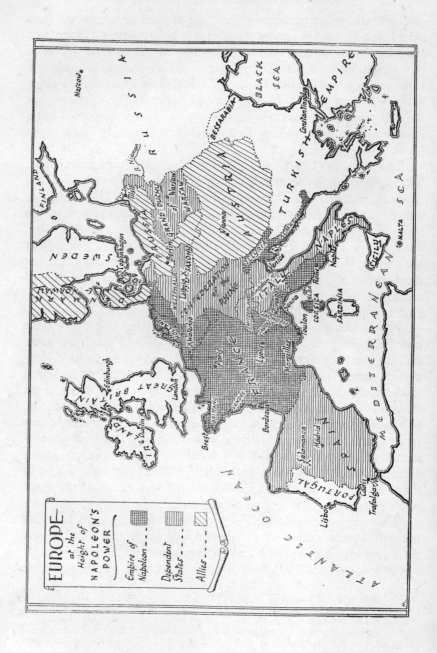

EUROPE
at the
Height of
NAPOLÉON'S
POWER

Empire of
Napoleon-----

Dependent
States------

Allies-----

rouse anti-French feeling among the mass of the people: the memory of long unsuccessful wars can print a nation's subconscious very deeply (witness England's attitude to our own country) and the *Johnny Crapaud* tradition soon revives. It rose now, besides sentiments more creditable—a refusal to be forced, against one's will, into the Empire of another power, and a knowledge that the alternative was to fight, most probably against odds, till the point was settled. And since this latter attitude at least was one familiar in Scotland for centuries, she, being in the same danger, shared it now, so that in the two British countries alike the antagonisms of class and of opinion which had hampered their former efforts were blotted out, and the two countries themselves drew closer together than they had ever been since 1291.

The prospective danger soon was actual, for Bonaparte's power was going to his head. He was a great war-leader, a virtual king: and the man who can take these offices soberly, without being born to them, is hard to find. He showed quite openly that he held the Treaty as an armistice dependent on his will, kept his troops in Holland against its explicit terms, and made preparations that could only be meant as preliminaries to an invasion of Britain. Pitt therefore declined to hand over the island of Malta, whose transference to France was a term of the Treaty. The Consul insulted the British Ambassador, and Pitt thereon seized 1,200 French and Dutch ships, declaring war on Bonaparte five days later, on the 18th of May 1803.

The declaration came as a surprise—to no one more than the 10,000 unfortunate British subjects who were travelling or resident in France, and were left to be interned for eleven years. Bonaparte also had been caught unready. He went on for the rest of the year with his preparations, and they were formidable. An army of 150,000, trained men and well accustomed to victory, was gathered on the cliffs beside Boulogne, with a huge flotilla of flat-bottomed barges. No detail was neglected. Even a medal, finely designed, was struck, with the confident inscription, *Frappé à Londres:* 1804. All was ready for the magician to wave his wand.

But magic does not cross water easily. The spell worked in India, where Bonaparte had stirred up the Mahrattas: but the *Armée d'Angleterre* had to wait for the weather, and meanwhile the British fleet cruised in the Channel, with an eye on the menacing white rows of tents.

The pause gave Britain essential time to prepare. Four hundred thousand volunteers were training, without distinction now of class or party. Scotland rattled from end to end with the clink of side-arms. Professors drilled their classes in the quadrangle: the advocate's wig and sober bombazine barely veiled the splendour of his gold-laced chest, and the draper's musket stood beside the yard-stick, as *lang wepponis* had done long ago in Edinburgh. It has been the fashion to laugh at them, looking back. But such, after all, were the men who fought under Bruce: and an age that has seen the heart-warming heroism of elderly Air Raid Wardens, men and women, will be less inclined to despise their enthusiasm.[1]

There were these, and the fleet which had made time to drill them, and was now blockading the French naval ports. And the Indian war, after all, went in Britain's favour. Baird's brilliant pupil Sir Arthur Wellesley won in September, largely with Highland troops, the hard-fought costly victory of Assaye, at odds of five thousand against thirty thousand.[2] Lake, further north, was equally successful, taking Delhi, the capital of Hind, which with Agra now came under British control: but that war ran fiercely on for some years yet.

The summer of 1804 moved towards autumn, and still the tents stood on the cliffs above Boulogne. In May Pitt again had become Prime Minister: and so much had the ultra-Whigs now changed their temper that Fox would have joined him had the King permitted. In May too France, less than eleven years after abolishing all monarchy, made her First Consul hereditary monarch, by a vote of some three million against three thousand . . . though he dared not risk the title of King of France, but (probably recalling Augustus Caesar) took that instead of Emperor of the French, thus saving prejudice, snubbing Austria, and paying tribute to the classics, all in a phrase.

His major aim was still the invasion of Britain. And still British sea-power stood in the way of that. In December 1804 he forced

[1] When in 1804 the Home Castle beacon was lighted one night in error, the Border volunteers turned out almost to a man, some riding forty or fifty miles before dawn : Scott rode a hundred in the twenty-four hours. And the women whose men were by chance away from home sent off uniforms, horse, and arms so that their husbands and sons might make better speed.

[2] The 74th Highlanders (later 2nd H.L.I.) received the title of the Assaye Regiment in consequence of their conduct in this battle, where all their officers were killed or wounded. To them, to the 78th Highlanders (now the Seaforths) and to the English 19th Dragoons, the East India Company presented a third Colour, in recognition of their services, ' to be carried at Reviews, Inspections, and on Gala Days.'

Spain to join him. Her fleet, joined to his, gave him parity with the British, and cancelled at once its easy supremacy.

The next year, 1805, was deeply anxious. Pitt, looking ahead, worked hastily to make a Third Coalition, with Austria and Russia once again. He accomplished it by the summer, with the result of forcing Napoleon now to act against Britain before Austria should come against his flank. The French and Spanish fleets were therefore ordered to slip through the British blockade, which was not very close, make for a rendezvous in the West Indies, return conjoined, and hold the Channel open for the barges. And a fortnight thereafter Napoleon in London should dictate his terms of peace to a prostrate foe.

It was the strategy of a great . . . soldier. Had the fleets been under steam (and the *Charlotte Dundas* was already at work on the Forth and Clyde Canal) it might well have succeeded: but manœuvres under sail in the broad Atlantic are ill to time punctually, and it needed timing.

It very nearly succeeded as it was. Admiral Villeneuve duly broke out of Toulon, dodged Nelson, and got clear across the Atlantic, dodged Nelson again, and doubled back to Europe, there joining with the Spanish fleet from Cadiz to cut out the rest of the French ships blockaded in Brest. On the 22nd July he was off Finisterre (the Spanish, not the Cape of Brittany) with only Biscay between him and the Channel. Sir Robert Calder, another Scots admiral, met him there, and challenged. Villeneuve had ten frigates and twenty sail of the line, Calder fifteen of the latter and no frigates [1]: but the four-hours delaying action was effective. Villeneuve had to turn into Cadiz to refit, where Collingwood pinned him in with a fresh blockade. Pitt and Calder had wrecked Napoleon's chance of invasion: and the Emperor knew it, for Austria was already on the move. He relieved his emotions on poor Villeneuve, then broke up at last the huge camp at Boulogne, and marched his troops to meet the Austrian armies.[2]

The menace of invasion was postponed. Not cancelled yet, so

[1] The ship of the line is roughly equivalent to the modern battleship, the frigate to the light cruiser. Both, of course, were much easier to build than their modern analogue, and navies therefore had many more of them.

[2] Calder received very little gratitude. He was charged with having broken off action too soon (Villeneuve had orders not to fight, and tried to obey them) and had to demand a court-martial to clear himself. Nelson showed what he himself thought of the charge by sending him home to it in command of his own ship, ill though it could then be spared.

long as the British fleet was inferior in strength. But the fresh French war against Austria and Russia gave a new importance to the Mediterranean. In October, Napoleon accordingly called Villeneuve from Cadiz: it is only a short distance from Gibraltar, and the French fleet might well have slipped through the Straits: but Nelson caught him, at odds of two to three, on the 21st October, off Cape Trafalgar. The fight cost the life of England's greatest sailor, one of the great sea-commanders of the world: but nineteen of Napoleon's capital ships were taken, and another blown up. A fortnight after that, Sir Richard Strachan, another of the Scots admirals of the time, captured five more of them which had escaped. The French fleet, as a fighting force, was ruined, and Britain had won back her control of the sea.

It did not end the war, for the Third Coalition failed to do what had been expected of it. Napoleon had been defeated in the West, but in the East he advanced triumphantly. In a little more than three weeks after Trafalgar, the Emperor marched as a conqueror into Vienna: and within three more, on the 2nd of December, the Austrian and Russian armies were destroyed in the chilly winter sunlight of Austerlitz.

It killed Pitt. He was only forty-six, but ill and worn. 'Roll up the map of Europe,' he said at the news. 'It will not be wanted again for these ten years.'

The 'ten years' was an accurate prophecy. For three, Britain's part in the main war was nil. She carried on, however, some useful sideshows, saving Sicily for the unpleasant King of Naples, while General Stuart's victory at Maida cleared the French from Calabria. In 1806 Sir David Baird took the Dutch colony of the Cape of Good Hope: and the Spanish possessions in South America were also attacked, although with smaller success. Auchmuty, a wandering Scots-American, took Monte Video, to see it lost by his successor Whitelock. Buenos Aires was also taken and lost. But all these, save perhaps Baird's annexation of the Cape, were minor affairs, obscured by the thunder of major events in Europe.

The immediate consequence of Austerlitz was that Bavaria and Wurtemberg and thirteen of the minor German states formed a Confederation of the Rhine, and surrendered to Napoleon as Protector. Napoleon was thereby master of most of the Empire . . . and after just over a thousand years existence, on the 6th day of

August 1806, the Holy Roman Empire ceased to be: Francis II was forced to resign the Imperial Crown.[1]

Napoleon's Empire steadily increased. Prussia still held out: but in just under a year after Trafalgar, she also was beaten, on the field of Jena, and Napoleon rode as a conqueror into Berlin. In the next year, 1807, Eylau and Friedland accounted for Russia also; and in July she and Prussia were forced to sign the Treaty of Tilsit, becoming Napoleon's allies, or rather vassals.

He was now, in effect, the master of three Empires. He celebrated his new accession of power by abandoning the lip-service his title had paid to *les principes de* '89, and assuming that of King of Italy; made his eldest brother Joseph King of Naples; and tossed another kingdom, that of Holland, to his brother Louis, who was now the husband of the Empress Josephine's daughter, Hortense de Beauharnais.

From the North Sea and the Baltic to the Danube, from the Portuguese march to the inner recesses of Russia, he was, and for five years remained, the master of Europe. Only Britain, Sweden, Portugal, Sardinia and Sicily (then kingdoms), Montenegro and Turkey were holding out against him: and Britain, of these, was the only first-class power.

He had not forgotten her during the past two years. Even when he was too much occupied elsewhere for actual war on her he attacked her trade. By the Berlin Decrees of November 1806, no French ship, or a ship of a French ally—Prussian, Italian, Russian, Dutch, or Spanish—was to trade in any way with the United Kingdom: and all British property reachable was to be seized. It was not meant as a 'starvation' blockade (for Britain, in those days, was able to feed herself) but to strangle exports to the Continent and so produce an adverse balance of trade, which by forcing gold abroad should dislocate commerce. In January of 1807 our own Government considerably helped him, by insisting that neutral ships trading with France, or her allies, must first put in at a British port—a proceeding which later on, in 1812, caused a three years sea-war with the United States, at a time when it was extremely inconvenient.

The Berlin Decrees were already harming our trade, and Glasgow in fact was suffering severely, when Canning, then the

[1] Francis, two years before, had proclaimed himself also Emperor of Austria— i.e. of the Hapsburg domains within and outside the Empire. He kept this title.

Foreign Secretary, learned that the Treaty of Tilsit was to be used to force the neutrals Portugal, Sweden, and Denmark to join the blockade. The Danish fleet had recovered from Nelson's attentions; and Canning, guessing that France and Russia would seize it to make up for the heavy losses of Trafalgar, offered Denmark alliance with Britain. Denmark refused, and he promptly fell upon her. It was not magnificent, but it was war. By the 9th August (a month and two days from the signing of the Treaty) a strong British force was off Elsinore, demanding the Danish fleet. It was refused. Copenhagen was then bombarded for four days: the fleet and its stores were seized and carried to England . . . and Denmark declared war (a formality with which Canning had not troubled) and joined Napoleon. Britain replied by seizing Heligoland, as a useful smuggling base for British goods, and then declared a blockade of the Continent.

By this time Portugal, England's oldest ally, had defied Napoleon. In October he agreed with Spain to divide her, invaded the little country, and annexed it, the royal family and many refugees fleeing overseas in British ships to Brazil. The affair seemed a mere incident in his conquests: but looking back, one can see Napoleon's star, though it still blazed, cross the zenith at that moment. It was then that he achieved the one thing too much that tilts the balance for all who suffer from ὕβρις, from the arrogance that makes men take their stand with gods.

Four months after Portugal was in his hands, he turned on his ally Spain, kicked out her King, brought Joseph Bonaparte from Naples to rule her, and tossed Naples in turn to his brother-in-law Murat. Spain rose. In one fortnight after he entered Madrid, King Joseph found it advisable to leave. Portugal was up too: and before Joseph's fortnight had quite reached its end—on the 1st August, that is, of 1808—Sir Arthur Wellesley landed at Mondego with a British Expeditionary Force, and the five years of the Peninsular War had begun.

It began badly. There was a brief but vigorous campaign. The victories of Roliça and Vimiera defeated that excellent soldier Marshal Junot, and had the French armies pinned into a corner, when their fruit was lost—one regrets to say, by a Scot. Political intrigues against Wellesley had sent Sir Hew Dalrymple [1] to super-

---

[1] A great-nephew of that Master of Stair who assisted William III in planning Glencoe.

sede him: and Sir Hew made with Junot the Convention of Cintra, by which, though the French agreed to evacuate Portugal, they were given passage home in the British fleet, and still left free for any further action.

Another Scot saved the situation, however. Moore by this time had landed in Portugal, and was making to join the northern Spanish armies. Soult and Lannes defeated these before he could do so, and Napoleon himself had arrived, and was in Madrid. Moore found himself in an unattractive position: no less than four French armies, each larger than his own and expertly led, were converging on him. He had either to surrender or to retreat: and retreat itself seemed wholly impossible. Moore none the less determined to save his army for further use: he achieved it, he and his men, by forced marches in bitter cold, through two hundred and fifty miles of terrible country, to Coruña on the sea, where he could embark. The white spats of the Highland Regiments are in memory of the tatters of their shirts, bound over their bleeding feet on that cruel road.

At Coruña, Soult came down on the embarkation. The battle that followed, on the 16th January 1809, cost Sir John Moore his life: but he had succeeded, and the troops got clear. The Retreat to Coruña stands with Mons and Dunkirk among the great rearguard actions in British history: and the defeated Soult recognised its valour, for finding Moore's hasty military grave, he set up a monument, that honours both.

Austria, seeing Napoleon occupied in Spain, took what seemed a chance of throwing off his dominion. But his star still blazed. He turned on her in person, and in May had ridden once more into Vienna. In July he defeated the Emperor Francis at Wagram [1] and in October dictated his terms of peace, which included his marriage, in the following spring, to the Emperor's daughter, the Archduchess Marie Louise.

In 1810 the Little Corporal cast a taller shadow than ever over Europe. That year he made the Pope his prisoner, and next year the Emperor's daughter bore him a son, the King of Rome. The title of King of the Romans was by the tradition of nearly a thousand years that commonly borne by the Emperor Elect.

1810-12 seemed the topmost of his power. Britain was left: but

---

[1] The French guns were commanded there, and brilliantly, by Law de Lauriston, son (like Napoleon's Marshal MacDonald) of an exiled Scot. He later commanded the rear-guard in the Retreat from Moscow.

Britain, if not yet annexed, had been defeated. Not only had her armies been driven from Spain in the beginning of the year 1809, but later in that year her counter-attack had been made, on a large scale, only to prove a very costly.and spectacular failure. Napoleon had been preparing Antwerp and Flushing as bases for the long delayed invasion. General the Earl of Chatham (Pitt's elder brother) and Admiral Strachan were sent to deal with them, landing at Walcheren. Pitt's ghost did not haunt the Cabinet, however, or if it did it failed to establish contact. The Cabinet made a hideous muddle at home. Chatham's sole strength was *vis inertiae.* Strachan, a capable and distinguished sailor, was not strong enough to make up for Chatham's defects: and in November what fever and the French had left of their force had to limp back across the Narrow Seas. The unlucky Strachan was made the scapegoat for it. Only Cochrane's naval action in Basque Roads contrived to give the year's war news some comfort.[1]

Yet none the less, on the edge of his huge dominions, that was in progress which sapped Napoleon's strength. Moore had given Spain a chance for her second wind, and in the April after his retreat, Sir Arthur Wellesley landed with fresh forces. For nearly five years he held resistance together in the Peninsula, with varying fortune, but with intermittent and cumulative success. The Peninsular War was, strategically, a sideshow. In fact, it 'struck the dragon's soft underside.' It sapped Napoleon's strength where that was weakest, and its very slowness made it more effective, for it led Napoleon, now full charged with ὕβρις, to under-rate it, and make an enormous blunder.

In March of 1812 Russia and Sweden had begun to show a certain recalcitrance, and refused to carry on the blockade of Britain. The Czar Alexander disliked exceedingly, also, new French advances in North Germany, which were creeping very close against his march. He followed the refusal, therefore, in April by a demand for the evacuation of certain of the frontier provinces. And Napoleon took the demand as an excuse for the actual conquest of the Russian Empire.

---

[1] 'Cochrane the Dauntless,' later 10th Earl of Dundonald, was the most brilliant Scots sailor of the time. In May 1801, with fifty-four men, he took a Spanish frigate of three hundred and nineteen men and thirty-two guns. In thirteen months, his little *Speedy,* of a hundred and fifty-eight tons, ninety men, and fourteen four-pounders, took fifty enemy ships with five hundred and thirty-four prisoners, besides killed and wounded, and a hundred and twenty-two guns.

Napoleon defeated himself, as such men do. Had he satisfied the Czar, and turned his whole force on Spain and then on Britain, we should have been lost, for the terrible strain of the war and the long blockade was bleeding us sorely. But he saw beyond Russia the road to India, and mastery of another continent—Alexander's Empire (it was a classical age) joined to those of Charlemagne and Barbarossa and the half-mythical splendour of Muscovy. Spain could wait: his capable marshals would deal with that. Britain could wait : her new American war (which began in that June) would keep her occupied, and weaken her so that she dropped into his fingers.

He led an enormous army to the eastward, on a summer triumph, by roads he knew well already. Already Persia and the Arab chiefs were responding to effective diplomacy. In Dresden, three Kings and an Emperor were his clients . . . and he himself was not yet forty-three. But Spain's resistance was proving, as such does, infectious. Turkey and Sweden, on either flank of Russia, announced that they intended to stay neutral: and Russia, safe to north and south, laid her plans.[1] On Midsummer Day Napoleon crossed the Niemen. The Russians steadily withdrew before him, and he followed them through the vast plains towards Moscow—and winter. Almost he won. The impatient Czar superseded Barclay de Tolly by Kutusov, whom Napoleon caught and beat at Borodino, at the end of September, with huge loss on both sides. Forty-seven French generals were killed or wounded: Napoleon's High Command did not lead from the rear. A week after it, the *Grande armée* was in Moscow.

The city was all but empty. Soon it was burning. It burnt for five days. Napoleon waited in the Czar's capital for the Czar's peace terms: but the capital was ash, and so were his hopes, for the French were far from their base, in a stripped country, and the Russian winter now was hard at hand. It was beginning when he turned in October. The Retreat is one of the nightmares of history—heroic nightmare, for there was magnificent courage. But of the *Grande armée* of 500,000, not 200,000 crossed the Niemen again

---

[1] It is worth noting that the Russian strategy is precisely the application on a large scale of a method more than once employed by Bruce, and that the main Russian Army was led by a Russo-Scots Minister of State, Barclay de Tolly. Scots, in fact, played a very prominent part in making Russia a military power. Her navy (like that of her later rival Japan) was created by a Scot—in her case Admiral Greig, who also built the great sea-fortress of Cronstadt.

when they reached it on the 20th December. These had not been defeated. In all the bitter fighting of the Retreat, they had held firm. But Napoleon had been defeated.

The world knew it. In the spring it was easy to form a Fourth Coalition, of Prussia, Russia, Austria, Sweden, Britain. And already the French armies in Spain were crumbling. In June Wellesley, now Earl of Wellington, with Sir Rowland Hill and Sir Thomas Graham of Balgowan as his seconds, broke Jourdan at Vitoria in the North, and drove the French against the Pyrenees. Soult tried to counter, but could do no more than keep Wellington out of France until the autumn. In August Graham stormed San Sebastian, the bulwark of the last French power in Spain. October was decisive in East and West. On the 10th of it, Wellington was on French soil. On the 16th, Napoleon's last levies from drained France met outside Leipzig the enheartened troops of Austria, Prussia, and Russia, joined together. In a huge three-day battle he was defeated. He fell back fighting, but on the last day of that crucial 1813, Russian, Prussian, and Austrian troops invaded France: and Wellington was almost at Bayonne. On the last day of March 1814, Paris surrendered. The last action was fought at Toulouse on the 10th of April, when Wellington defeated Marshal Soult. The day after that, Napoleon abdicated; and on the 30th May the Treaty of Paris set on the throne of France Louis XVIII, the brother of the guillotined Louis XVI. Napoleon's conquests had shrunk to one small island, scarce twenty miles long, off the Italian coast: 'and kings crept out again to feel the sun.'

A Congress met at Vienna next January, to tidy up the Europe he had left . . . and on the 1st March he landed once more in France, and an army which had no love for Louis XVIII or for his foreign backers sprang around him. Europe rocked, but acted: and this time finally. British, Dutch, Belgian, and German allied troops, with Britain and Prussia carrying the major weight, gathered under Wellington in the Flanders plain. Four days fighting there brought the Hundred Days to an end, on the 18th June, near Brussels, at Waterloo. In four more, the Emperor again had abdicated. On the 6th July the Allies were in Paris, and soon Napoleon was on the long sea-road to the desolate lonely island of St Helena, where he was to die in 1821. Even at his death he was not yet fifty-two.

XV

THE VOTE ONCE MORE

SEVENTEEN YEARS: 1815-32

No name, no power, no function, no artificial institution whatsoever, can make the men of whom any system of authority is composed any other than God and nature and education and their habits of life have made them. Capacities beyond them the people have not to give. Virtue and wisdom may be the objects of their choice; but their choice confers neither the one nor the other on those on whom they lay their ordaining hands.

EDMUND BURKE, *Reflections on the Revolution in France*, 1790.

WHEN a great flood, driven by a great storm, falls, it leaves behind it an untidy landscape. Now, though the flood of the widespread war had sunk, the wind of the Revolution that had stirred it blew still across the litter of the wrecked fields. The industrialising of so much of Scotland had brought a new class division to the country. The French Revolution made men aware of it. Repression and the danger from overseas—the latter more than the former—had driven the conflict out of sight for a while. But repression heals nothing; and now that the war was over, the struggle revived in an aggravated form, not only in Scotland but all over Europe.

The blockade enriched the farmers and the lairds: but otherwise, town and country suffered by it. War taxes and ruined markets wounded trade. Unemployment was rife. The disbanding—a polite word for turning adrift—of the great armies added to beggary. In Dundee, one in six of the people were destitute. The price of bread was fantastically high. And unwarned by Revolutionary France, the landed interest in the House of Commons forced through, the very moment war seemed ended, an Act to prohibit the import of foreign corn until wheat should have risen to famine prices.

The law, a most rigid guardian of property, seemed to care nothing for men's souls and bodies. Scotland did not hang children for stealing a loaf of bread: but at one session a twenty-three shilling theft was punished by a sentence of ten years, and a case of culpable homicide by seven—the same sentence as that for stealing a cotton

143

gown.[1] All was ripe for Cockburn's 'sedition of the stomach': and in the generation after the war, Britain came very close to revolution —much closer than we are apt to recognise.

Before the war, and through its early years, attention had focussed on one panacea, the possession of a parliamentary vote. The war had quietened the agitation for that, but it was not forgotten. The *Edinburgh Review*, founded in 1802 by a group of young men, revived Pitt's policy, although without effect on Parliament. In 1809 an English member, Sir Francis Burdett, brought forward the question in the House again: but only fifteen members would support him, and when he later defined the House of Commons as 'a part of our fellow-subjects collected together by means which it is not necessary to describe,' he found himself committed to the Tower, after a riot in which one man was killed.

The classes who were most directly oppressed had already tried, as a substitute for unprocurable legislation, to apply immediate pressure to their employers by that organised withdrawal of their labour which is called a strike: but the Combinations Acts of 1799-1800, passed during the war, forbade unions for this purpose. Even to join one involved a three-month sentence. Parliament having taken from them their only sanction in a 'free' bargain whose scales were loaded against them, they applied for its help to compensate for the loss. In 1808, with prices already risen, the Scottish miners begged for a minimum wage. The House went so far as to appoint a Committee: and these declared that it would be 'injudicious.' In 1811 a suggestion was made of boards to arbitrate between masters and men: the masters, however, would not even consider such infringement of the individual's rights. The workmen waited hopefully for a while, but nothing was done; and the end of the war left matters worse than before it, with no prospect that anything ever would be done. At length, after showing a very real patience, they began in despair to turn to violent action.

There were, it seemed, two possible means of help. One was direct pressure on those employers who exploited them, applied by concerted action through trades unions. These were illegal, but they now revived, and being illegal ran easily to violence. The years

---

[1] This ratio between the values of person and property lasted long. In Glasgow in 1864 a man who had killed another with a poker was given six months, a girl who stole fourpence-halfpenny got fifteen. Even in this present century, in England, suffragettes served eight months for breaking a pane of glass worth half a crown, while men who had raped small children got off with three.

between 1816 and 1824 saw a number of trade union outrages:
employers were shot at, several mills were fired, and black-legs were
killed or attacked with vitriol. The other means was the checking
of abuses by legislation: but legislation was withheld from men who
could bring no pressure to bear on Parliament. It was a natural
enough belief that the vote alone would enable men to do that: and
they certainly could not do it *without* the vote, save by violence,
which the saner and more responsible men misliked.

The agitation for a wider franchise, which before had been almost
confined to the middle-class taxpayer, who wanted a voice in affairs
in return for his money, spread rapidly among the 'working class.'
Within a year or so of the end of the war, there was hardly a village
in the whole of Scotland where some men were not preaching
'Radical Reform'; and a daily newspaper, the famous *Scotsman*, was
founded in 1817 to press for it.

The Government continued its policy of ignoring inconvenient
demands, and in Scotland and England alike, ill-feeling grew. In
1819 there was a violent crisis.[1] Great popular meetings—6,000 men
gathered at Airdrie—scared the Government at length into taking
action: but unluckily it was the type of action which had led to the
transportation of Thomas Muir. A young Forfar laird, Kinloch of
Kinloch (M.P. for Dundee after 1832), was charged with sedition,
and had to flee to France. At Neilston a band were arrested and
imprisoned merely for playing *Scots Wha Hae* in public. Explosives
piled up: and then one morning every kirk door in Glasgow and
for forty miles round bore a formidable placard, issued by nothing
less than a Committee for forming a Provisional Government:

Compelled to assert our rights at the hazard of our lives . . . let us
show the world that we are not a lawless sanguinary rabble, but a brave
and generous people determined to be free. Liberty or Death is our
motto, and we have sworn to return home *in triumph*—or to return
no more.

And it called a general strike for the 1st April.

Some blamed the placard on *agents provocateurs* of the Government, as the Moderate Presbyterians of the seventeenth century had
blamed the dying speeches of Covenant martyrs on the Roman
Catholics. But it sounds authentic, and its immediate results were

---

[1] In England also. It was the year of the Peterloo Massacre at Manchester,
when the soldiers rode down the mob and there were some deaths ; and the
next year brought the Cato Street Conspiracy, to murder the whole ministry.

widespread alarm, even in those who like the Government were ignorant of past Scottish history. (Scott, who by no means shared that ignorance, considered that civil war was inevitable: and in fact disturbances much less than this had opened such wars, and serious ones, in the past.) Next day, in the crowded industrial district round Glasgow, hardly a man was at work, and many were being openly drilled and armed. Suburban families were fleeing into the city, where huge crowds waited the signal for uprising: and in places hopeful Utopians were proclaiming that no one was any longer to pay rent.

Troops were sent in haste—three English battalions and the Rifle Brigade. But 'the Radical War' came to little after all. A skirmish of troops and strikers at Bonnymuir saw fifty strikers wounded and some killed. The revolt, however, broke up from within. A cry was raised that Government *agents provocateurs* were at work: and the suspicion of treachery in the leaders dissolved it as no repression could have done. Two of the leaders, none the less, were sentenced to the ghastly English penalty for treason, which the Act for Improving the Union had forced on Scotland. Another was hanged, and eighteen more transported. The violence, for the next few years, died down, though a general ill-feeling against the Government persisted still, and was not at all improved when in 1820 the old King, long hopelessly mad, died at last and left his throne to the Prince Regent, whose relations with his wife, and his creditors, were only a fraction of the many scandals, mostly well-based, which surrounded the Royal House.

The agitation for Reform continued, but with the attack now narrowed and concentrated on what seemed the easier question of the burghs. Petitions for municipal reform were accumulating from all hands; and in 1819 Lord Archibald Hamilton contrived to obtain a Parliamentary Committee to consider them. The Radical War scared it out of action, however: it decided that municipal reform would involve a breach of the terms of the Treaty of Union.

1822 brought a curious incident. King George the Fourth arrived in his northern kingdom, and was received with a general enthusiasm which at first sight is surprising. It seems even stranger that the man responsible for the visit was Scott, whose general code of ethics scarcely resembled that held by the First Gentleman in Europe. Yet neither Scott nor the people of Edinburgh were either as merely silly or as snobbish as some indignant commentators would make them. The kingdom which for centuries had been used to regard her king as a clan regarded its chief had suffered now for more than two hundred years from a very vicious tradition of absentee kingship: in fact, since the year 1651 no reigning sovereign of Scots had set foot in Scotland, and none since Anne (and she only as a girl) had ever been at any time in the kingdom which all through the long wars of that period had provided many of the best of his soldiers. Scott desired to bring this cold-shouldering to an end: and the growing improvement of Anglo-Scottish relations, beginning before the war and strengthened by it, and now, it seemed, confirmed by the frenzy of England over his own long series of novels, seemed to provide an opportunity. It was an idea based on sound statesmanship: but like many such, it failed to take into account the nature of the man on whom it depended. The king available was not adequate. His charm, and his kingship, roused a passing fervour: but the episode was to prove—an episode: and in recollection, an episode slightly absurd.

The movement for municipal reform continued in vigorous action; and the resistance, led by the Lord Advocate, was growing proportionately more obstinate, based frankly on the fact that Burgh Reform would certainly lead to Parliamentary also. As a sop to the growing restlessness, however, an act was put through by which the burgesses were allowed the right to indict corrupt magistrates before the Court of Exchequer. Cockburn sums up the general reaction:

It first excited the hopes and then the indignation of the people. It began by disclosing the trustlessness of Town Councils, and ended by hardening them in their protected abuse of power.

In 1823 Lord Archibald Hamilton raised again the question of the county franchise, sorely embarrassing the Government. They found that to intermeddle with the franchise would be a serious breach of the Treaty of Union; and observed that Britain must be seen as a whole, and that if Scotland had not enough members of Parliament, the lack was made up by Ireland's having too many.

Next year a concession was made to the Trades Unions. Francis Place, an English Radical, supported by Joseph Hume, a former surgeon of the East India Company, and John Ramsay M'Culloch, Editor of *The Scotsman*, procured the repeal of the Combinations Acts: but the repeal at once was qualified by the prohibition of any combination which could be used to 'intimidate' employers. It was not till the next year again—1825—that strikes were legalised for raising wages and protesting against the reduction or changing of terms: 'molesting' or 'obstructing' the process of business were still, however, specified as crimes. The legal position of any body of strikers was thus, to say the least, ambiguous still: yet the principle of the strike had been recognised.

The Tories fell in 1827. The Whigs who succeeded them were pledged to Reform: but their tenure of office this time was very brief, and the Tories returned, with Wellington as the Prime Minister. For a time the stormy state of affairs in Ireland ousted Reform from the centre of the stage, its place being taken by Catholic Emancipation. That was granted, as we have seen, in 1829. The next year brought the King's unregretted death, and the accession of his brother William, who was proclaimed in Scotland by a title which ignored the whole course of her history—so much for Sir Walter's attempt to give us a sovereign! It brought also a violent storm through most of Europe, for that which had lulled for a while in 1815 had lulled, not ended: the winds of '89 rose again to gale force in the year 1830.

When Napoleon fell, the Congress of Vienna had settled Europe to their satisfaction. The settlement was based avowedly on a reaction from the idealisms which had plunged Europe in so long a war. Indeed, idealism was not its failing. It was based frankly on the theory that strong monarchies would keep the general peace. Their territories must therefore be restored. As for the rest of a very new-fangled map, which for twenty-odd years had been shifting like a transformation-scene, republics need not be taken seriously, and minor sovereignties, however ancient, were for the greater powers to dispose and arrange as might conveniently serve their purposes.

This principle saved the worst blunder, at all events. Prussia was furious with France for defeating her, and demanded now a huge indemnity, as well as large areas of French territory, and the blowing up of the beautiful Pont d'Iéna.[1] Great Britain, however, had at last grasped the fact (which had been well enough known to James the Fourth) that France's integrity was the core of any European

---

[1] Louis XVIII saved the bridge by declaring that if it was to be blown up, he would take his stand on it and go up as well: so Prussia had to be content with a (temporary) change of name to the Pont de l'École militaire—a choice perhaps not wholly without malice.

balance; she stood now against a vindictive settlement, insisting that France 'belonged' to Louis XVIII, and must therefore keep all that was French in 1790. She backed the affirmation by returning all the French colonies that she had captured, save such unconsidered trifles as Mauritius and a couple of the Caribbean islands [1]; and also insisted that the indemnity should not be vindictive.

The map was considerably re-drawn, however. Some three hundred minute but sovereign states of the Empire were massed as the Rhineland and Westphalia, and handed over to Prussia as her reward. To Austria was given Lombardy, and also the old independent republic of Venice. She also was appointed as the head of a new confederation of thirty-eight German states, though the Emperor remained merely Emperor of Austria. Another old independent republic, Genoa, was given to the King of Sardinia and Piedmont. The States of the Church went back to the Pope again, the Kingdoms of Naples, of Portugal, and of Spain to their old dynasties. Belgium was given to Holland, and Norway taken from Denmark and given to Sweden. Poland, however, which in the course of the last two generations had been absorbed by Austria, Prussia, and Russia, was not given back her old historic status as an independent kingdom. Britain expressed some pious hopes on the point, but 'the robbers were not in the dock but on the bench,' and final judgment was given accordingly. Lastly, Great Britain, Austria, Prussia, and Russia formed a Quadruple Alliance for twenty years to maintain the Treaties of Paris and Vienna—those giving effect to Napoleon's abdication and to the new map of Europe drawn by the Congress.

It might, no doubt, have been a great deal worse; and would, if Prussia had had the guiding of it. But now on the old struggle, yet unappeased, between theoretical republicanism and practical class-conflict on the one side, and despotic monarchy, not always benevolent, upon the other, there was superposed a new and intricate pattern of traditional racial antagonisms. Italy, split as she had always been, agreed in common hatred of Austria, and Naples also detested her dynasty. The Catholics of Belgium and the Calvinist Dutch yoked ill together. Poland resented her abandonment. And

---

[1] She retained, however, the Cape, Ceylon, and British Guiana, taken from the Dutch; Heligoland, which had belonged to Denmark; the Ionian Islands, which since 1789 had experienced a variety of owners; and Malta, which at the time was nobody's bairn, since the Knights of Malta (the successors of those of St John of Jerusalem) were dissolved after their expulsion by Napoleon.

France, dubious enough of the moderate Louis XVIII, strongly disliked his autocratic brother, soon his successor, and began to recall
those *principes de* '89 which their immediate result, the Directory,
had made her, for a generation, forget.

For fifteen years tension steadily increased. 1830 brought explosion. Poland rose. France turned out her King in the 'Three
Glorious Days of July,' and Belgium broke suddenly away from
Holland. But the disturbance, on this occasion, was brief. Poland
was ruthlessly crushed. France, having expelled the absolute
Charles X, replaced him with a constitutional cousin. Belgium's
claim to be an independent kingdom was allowed by the Powers,
who saw in it an opportunity to neutralise for good the cockpit of
Europe. Lord Palmerston found her a king in Leopold of Coburg,
son-in-law of George IV and brother-in-law of Edward Duke of
Kent, the brother and sometime heir of the King of Great Britain;
and in 1839 all the Great Powers joined to guarantee her neutrality
for ever.

These changes were to affect our future history. At the time,
their immediate repercussion on Scotland seemed merely to return
the King of France to his previous exiled quarters in Holyrood.
But the brief storm was noisy while it lasted: the British cry for
Reform grew more insistent, and the Government looked abroad
and were alarmed.

In November of 1830 Wellington's Government fell, and the
Duke was succeeded by a Whig, Lord Grey. In the following month
Lord John Russell, Dugald Stewart's distinguished pupil, brought
in a bill for English reform at last; and it passed its first reading, by
a single vote. Next day Francis Jeffrey, now Lord Advocate,
brought in a corresponding one for Scotland. The bills were thrown
out in the later readings, however: and Grey induced King William,
who favoured Reform, to dissolve the Parliament, and call a new one.

The General Election was a rowdy one, with a good deal of
'brickbat and bludgeon work at the hustings.' Two hundred petitions went up to Westminster. A hundred thousand supporters of
Reform marched in procession through Glasgow; and in Rothesay
the owner of the cotton mills (who employed many children under
five years old) was so carried away by zeal for the Rights of Man
that he stirred up the crowd to stone the carriage of the Marchioness
of Bute, who was a Tory. The actual management of the election

was largely in the hands of one Robert Ellice, an exceedingly efficient Scots-Canadian, to whom the credit was given for its result: the privileged voters of both Scotland and England returned a large majority for Reform.

The House met again on the 14th June of 1831, and passed Russell's bill by 136. In October the bill reached the Lords, and was thrown out by an adverse majority of forty-one. There were riots. In England, Nottingham Castle was burnt, and many public buildings also in Bristol, where the soldiery killed or wounded some scores of people. Scotland was quieter, but only relatively. The crowds smashed dummy crowns on Glasgow Green, and a hundred and twenty thousand marched through the city, bearing banners inscribed with *Liberty or Death*.

The bill was brought up again in the next March, again passed the Commons, again was thrown out in the Lords. Grey resigned, but was at once restored to office by Wellington's failure to form a Government: and now King William was induced to promise that if the Lords threw out the bill again, he would create sufficient Reforming peers to ensure a majority in the Upper House. It brought the Lords to heel. On the 7th June of 1832 the English Act received the Royal Assent: on the 17th July, so did the Scottish.

The seats were redistributed, and the fifteen burgh members increased to twenty-three, which brought the total now to fifty-three. The 'Parchment Barons,' or *ad hoc* landholders, who created artificial county votes, were abolished. The county vote now went to all £10 freeholders and £50 tenants, and the burgh vote to all £10 householders—a standard so high, by the values of the time, that in seventeen towns the electorate was actually diminished. And the first Reformed Parliament, meeting in February 1833, at once made short work of the question of Burgh Reform, for in August it enacted that in future the Town Councils should be elected by residents of the burgh who possessed the parliamentary vote. The ballot and shorter Parliaments, however, were refused as needless and inadvisable. And Lord John Russell, happily satisfied, declared that the thorny question was settled for good, and that further Reform would be a breach of faith.

So the (fairly) peaceful, and partial, revolution was accomplished, without much bloodshed after all. 1832 marks the opening of an age: and the bell that tolled for Scott in late September sounded also the passing of much that had marked another.

III
AUTUMN
EIGHTY-TWO YEARS: 1832–1914

In all time of our wealth,
Good Lord, deliver us.

The Litany.

XVI

PROGRESS: THE SURFACE

EIGHTY-TWO YEARS: 1832–1914

The successful elaboration of means towards an end unknown and unconsidered.

W. H. MARWICK, *Economic Developments in Victorian Scotland.*

FOR a century before 1832, the material wealth of Scotland had been increasing, and for a long lifetime more the increase continued, reflected in the growing volume of trade. In 1851 the tonnage of goods that passed through Scottish ports was five and a half million: in 1884 it was nearly twenty, and by 1913 a good deal over thirty. In 1864 the Scottish railways carried nearly eighteen million tons of goods: in 1912 it was sixty-seven million. Scottish exports, in 1801, had been worth three million. In 1851 this had risen to five, in 1883 to twenty-one, and in 1913 the figure for four ports alone was more than double this—forty-seven and three-quarters—while several others drove a vigorous trade. One has, of course, to take into account the fact that the population more than doubled, rising from two and a third million in 1831 to over four and three-quarters in 1911. But that increase, remarkable as it is, bears a small proportion to the expansion of trade.

The commercial prosperity of the country at large is reflected in the strength of its banking system and its power to withstand occasional heavy strains. These were to come, for the age of cyclic 'crises' was beginning. Industrial crises were of course nothing new: as far back as economic history reaches, war, revolution, famine, disease, or weather have shown themselves capable of creating them; and Scotland had never been able for very long to ignore the fact, as we have seen already. With the Industrial Revolution, however, there entered a new, unharnessed complex of factors, to produce what is called 'the boom-depression cycle,' through which countries appear to swing in a regular rhythm of oscillations covering about a decade.

None the less, throughout the nineteenth century, the Scottish financial system faced these strains, though there was a growing tendency for the banks to seek shelter from them by amalgamations. In 1843 there were twenty-five independent Scots banks: in 1861 there were but fourteen, and by 1883 no more than ten.

Their activity was considerably hampered by the general attitude of Parliament, which never quite succeeded in grasping the fact that the Scottish system differed from the English, and was indeed a good deal more soundly based: bank failures in England were a commonplace, while in Scotland, though they occurred, they had been rare. The Bank Charter Act of 1844 attempted to concentrate note issues into the Bank of England. The Scots banks succeeded in obtaining their exemption; but new Scots banks of issue were forbidden, and the note system was further regulated by the Bank Act of 1845.

That year and the next saw a wild epidemic of speculation in railways, which were by that time spreading hither and yond. Hundreds of schemes for new ones were rushed out, and thousands of speculators rushed into them, without much critical heed to the schemes, or the schemers: and on top of this, there was a sudden fall in the price of wheat, when a good season followed on a bad one, with heavy foreign purchases between. Wheat played a greater part then than it does now in Scottish farming; and the result of the two disturbances was a serious crisis in 1847, with business houses failing right and left. Many English banks were exceedingly hard hit: the Scots ones kept going, though not without difficulty. A number of 'Exchange Companies,' however (a new institution which, unlike the banks, would advance on the security of stocks), had been wild-cat affairs, and many of these went under.

1857 brought a more serious crisis. It began in the United States, where many firms failed and were unable to pay their British debts, while a number of British firms held American stocks. As result, the Western Bank failed on a large scale, and the City of Glasgow Bank had to close for weeks. The former, however, paid up in full in the end, and the latter recovered, only to fail, through sheer ill-management, in the greater crisis of 1878, when thousands were ruined. Its fall, however, had the beneficial effect of drawing attention to the principle of limitation of liability, embodied in an act of the next year, which made all the Scots banks limited liability companies.

From 1864 the Scots banks showed a growing tendency to establish branches in London. These were successful, in spite of the efforts of their English rivals to procure legislation that should check their advance. The English banks thereon made an attempt at counter-invasion, but did not succeed. Their revenge was to come otherwise, and later.

The swing from agriculture to industry continued steadily through the century. In 1801 thirty-one per cent. of the people were on the land: in 1901 it was four and a half per cent., and falling still. Yet though agriculture lost its pride of place, it did not deteriorate in quality, though its economic fortunes fluctuated. It was hit by the trade slump after the French war, and recovering, lost in 1846 the artificial safeguard of 'protection.' Prosperity was recovered in spite of this, but brought its own perils: the good years of the later 'fifties and the 'sixties caused rents to rise by something like fifty per cent.; and a run of bad harvests that followed in the 'seventies caused this rise to become a considerable hardship.

None the less, progress in quality continued, and the extent of farmed land greatly increased. In 1857 there were 3,556,572 acres under cultivation, in 1877 4,668,221. The expansion was due partly to improvements in the system of land drainage, devised by the cotton-miller James Smith of Deanston, and partly to the work done in the 'forties by the German chemist, Baron Justus von Liebig, on artificial fertilisers, which stimulated much further research in Scotland. Towards the end of the century arable farming was heavily hit by overseas competition. Wheat showed a spectacular fall from 223,153 acres in 1857 to but 81,185 twenty years later: and the decline continued. Barley fell also. Stock-farming, however, advanced, thanks largely to the Highland Society. The Clydesdale horse became the best heavy draught breed in the world, and was largely exported. Scots cattle—Ayrshire, Polled Angus, Galloway—won equal fame: a Scots farmer at Paris in 1878 gained the world's championship, and a few years later Scottish cattle, for breeding, were selling for as much as 500 guineas.[1]

The relative decline in the place of farming came from no carelessness in its technique. There already Scotland had become supreme: and she kept the skill that had won her supremacy, and

---

[1] This price has been greatly increased. In 1920 one Scots ten-month calf fetched 6,600 guineas.

12

greatly extended her scientific resources. The machine entered farming in 1827, when the Rev. Patrick Bell, minister of Carmylie, evolved a practicable reaper. Soon after, Lord Tweeddale attempted a steam plough: his experiments were unsuccessful, however, and the use of steam was for long confined to thrashing. Machines worked by hand, or by teams of horses, increased: but 'power' of any sort was little used until well on in the twentieth century, after the coming of the petrol engine. In the chemical and biological aspects of farming fine work was done. We have seen that so early as the seventeen-eighties the scientific side of agriculture was recognised in the universities: and the Highland Society helped the Edinburgh Chair of Agriculture to grow into the headship of an important Department; did much for the Agricultural Colleges of Glasgow and Aberdeen; and urged on the development, from a grant made by Thomas Dick in 1833, of the great Dick Veterinary College, founded in 1839 and now among the most important in the world. The Society's work did not end there, by any means. It saw to the provision of County Council lecturers and demonstrators to keep the farmers in touch with the newest science, and in 1856 it received a charter permitting it to examine and give diplomas. In 1872 it appointed examiners also in forestry.

One should add that a number of subsidiary but potentially important industries were now springing up on the land, besides farming proper—market-gardening, fruit-growing, the making of preserves, and the canning and salting of meat. All these gave employment, broadened purchasing power, and increased the nation's supply of wholesome food, for home consumption and for the export trade. In a country where farming stood at so high a level much could and should have been made of all of these. There were great opportunities: and nothing like full use was made of them.

What damaged Scots farming was no lack of skill or science, but an inadequate sense of the place of 'the land' in a healthy national economy. Nearly all the advances which had taken place had been the work of individual men or of combinations of private citizens. These could do much to improve methods of farming, but they could not tackle the framework of agriculture. And the laws of tenure were long overdue for reform: as Sir Isaac Connell puts it:

If the tenant, by the use of expensive manure, had brought up the land to a high state of fertility, if with or without the approval of his landlord he had spent money on additions to buildings, or in drainage operations, it was quite open to the landlord at the end of the lease to claim all the improvements as belonging to him, and in some cases the tenant had the option of quitting the farm and leaving behind him the capital so expended, or of paying a rent increased in consequence of [these] very improvements.

Legislation, however, for long could not be obtained, for the Scots members, as a rule, were Liberals: and the Liberal party, taken as a party, was urban in outlook and little concerned for the farmer. The slump of 1878 at last forced the Government to consider abuses in farming. In 1883 the Agricultural Holdings Act (extended in 1900 and 1908) removed this one, gave more security of tenure, and brought in the principle of minimum prices. Yet though a legal injustice was remedied, there was no attempt to envisage, in terms of the nation, the place of the land-worker, large and small—to determine it, and as far as might be, safeguard it. And yet all that men eat comes somehow out of the land: and men cannot achieve very much unless they eat.

By 1832, as we have seen, the change from a rural to an urban nation was well under way. Industry grew for the whole of the next long lifetime, going, like farming, through prosperous years and lean, but over the whole time, taken as a whole, increasing in total volume and total wealth.

Within that whole there were none the less great changes. The most marked of all was a steady and increasing change in balance, as textiles gave way to the new 'heavy' industries. In 1830 textiles still held the lead, though linen already had lost its pre-eminence. A linen industry existed still. Hand weaving, of high quality, continued: in 1836 there were still some five thousand hand-looms making linen. It declined as they did. Power came, but in 1890; although the population of the country had risen from about two and a third million to well over four million, there were only ten factories, with six thousand hands, and a third of the trade was gathered into Dunfermline, which still kept up its high repute for damask.

Out of linen, however, grew a considerable subsidiary, the trade in jute, which began in the early 'thirties in Dundee, and was stimulated by the Crimean War and later by the American Civil War. In 1838 it used 1,136 tons of raw material; in 1858 some 30,000; in 1868, 58,000; and by 1890 no less than 206,759. Then

Indian competition caused it to shrink, but till the end of the time it was still important: in 1910 it employed 68,000 people. From jute in turn grew a flourishing minor trade, Kirkcaldy's floorcloth and linoleum, which was begun in 1847.

Cotton, at the beginning of the 'thirties, could still be called Scotland's major industry. It suffered from, but weathered, Napoleon's blockade, to be stricken ruinously in the 'sixties by the results of the American Civil War. In 1861, just before that war, the imports of raw cotton from the States had been 172,055 cwt., and the export of fabric 150 million yards. In 1864 the imports from America were only 7,216 cwt., and the exports fell to 94 million yards. Also, the market was beginning to shrink: other countries were learning to make their own cotton fabrics. Scotland now suffered more seriously than England, for the latter had made chiefly the coarser fabrics, for which there was still a large market in the East, while Scotland worked for the finer 'fashion' trade. In one point, thread, she retained supremacy, the great factory of Clark and Coats at Paisley remaining still the largest in the world.

The wool trade, for much of the time, was still very active, making tweed, flannels, shawls, hosiery, blankets, and carpets, all of high quality. By 1890 there were 282 factories, and the South of Scotland Technical College at Galashiels was doing excellent work. Then, however, there was a very serious slump. Between 1895 and 1910 Hawick, the heart of the trade, had to close half its mills, and in those of Galashiels employment fell from 19,000 to about 15,000. Again, as with linen and cotton, a trade which had specialised in the finer fabrics was caught by the rise of foreign competition and by inelasticity in face of fashion. Women's fashions were made in Paris and Vienna, men's in London: and the Scottish mill-owners had let themselves get out of touch with their high-priests.

Many lesser industries flourished on a small scale—not so small, either, in the case of printing and its adjunct paper-making, for Edinburgh was still the head-quarters of the British trade. The rest ranged from glass and pottery to whisky. The chief were those broadly described as 'chemical,' which grew as the coal-trade's important by-products developed in both quantity and use. They ran from explosives through paint, rubber, fertilisers, to soap, fine drugs, and dyes, in which last important research was done at Perth.

More and more, however, the 'heavy' industries—coal, iron, and

stccl, and the new and growing uses of these metals—were rising
to primacy above the rest. Scotland's lead with the steam-engine
brought them new importance, though at first their movement had
been rather slow, partly because of the strong interest in textiles,
but mainly because Scots coal was inferior in carbon to that of
England. The hot-blast furnace made up for this defect. It had
come in 1828, with the railway, and the two caused a rapid increase
in the output of iron. In that year Scotland produced only five per
cent. of the total British quantity of pig-iron: but within twenty
years it was twenty-six per cent., which in proportion to her population meant more than double the production of England. The actual
figures of output went up in leaps. In 1836, it was 75,000 tons; in
1845, 475,000; in 1855, 820,000; in 1865, 1,164,000; in 1870,
1,206,000. Then, however, a decline in bulk set in, and much
less Scots ore was used: between 1880 and 1913 the amount mined
fell from over two and a half million tons to something like a fifth
of that amount, while imports of ore, already 42,000 tons at the end
of the 'seventies, had risen by the end of the century to about a
million and a half a year.

Steel in Scotland was hardly worked before the 'fifties, and for
twenty years longer was of minor importance. The first steel ship
to be built upon the Clyde came in 1879, and thereafter the growth
was steady and very rapid. In 1885 the output was already 241,000
tons a year, and in fifteen years more this had risen to 960,580.
The steel ship was mainly responsible for the increase: in 1879
ten per cent. of those built on the Clyde were made of steel, but
ten years later, ninety-seven per cent.

Coal rose with iron, and the growing use of gas for illumination
gave a further stimulus. So did the railways. Indeed, their effect
was three-fold: coal was used not only to build them but to drive
them, while they greatly simplified its handling in bulk. By 1855
the number of collieries had risen to 367.

By 1880 the change from textiles to 'heavy' trades was completed, and the main industrial activity was concentrated upon coal
and iron. The actual production of these two was now no more
than a part of it, however. By 1832 the age of machines needing
coal and iron to make them and coal to drive them was well begun.
Scotland, in spite of her place as their pioneer, was a little slow at
first in their manufacture. Save for Nasmyth's steam hammer and
Fairbairn's steam riveting, the machine-tools needed were mostly

of English devising: the finer quality of Scots handicrafts also slowed the introduction of machines, which at first were incapable of equal precision. Scotland, however, soon began to make them, not only for herself but for all the world—machinery for brass-founding, sugar-refining, textile work of all kinds, with sewing-machines (made on a very large scale), and sanitary, agricultural, lighting, and heating equipment, for all of which new inventions made growing demands. The greatest market, however, for Scots iron goods derives from the immense revolution in transport. Locomotives were made in Glasgow from 1831. Eighty years later the North British Works alone had made 7,346—for India, Japan, America, South Africa, Germany: in that one year of 1911 the company made 2,351, the Glasgow and South Western Railway Company's works the same number, and those of the Caledonian Railway Company 2,758.

The crown of Scots metal work, of Scots work for transport, was none of these, however. It was ships. We may not, possibly, pass for a maritime nation (though those who know the Minesweeper Patrol may conceivably have a different opinion), but since the *Charlotte Dundas's* first engineer, a little nervous, laid hand on her throttle lever, the world's best ships have been built in Scottish yards. In that sooty age of the nineteenth century, it is ships that give Scotland her chief cause for pride.

Even in 1820, one ship in three on the Scottish register had been built abroad: and this number included the greater part of the large ones. A lifetime later one ship in five built in Scotland was sold abroad. The Austrian Lloyd Company, by 1876, had bought no less than fifty-seven Scots ships: the great North German Lloyd Company of Bremen had twenty-six built at Greenock in ten years. In 1913, some 80,000 men were at work on ships, and that year's total tonnage of shipbuilding was well over three-quarters of a million. In the next year Russell (now Lithgow) of Port Glasgow held the world's record for a single firm—an output of 78,000 tons in one twelvemonth.

The growth in size and power of the ships themselves was no less steady. In 1819 the largest steamship of the year had been the Clyde-built *Waterloo* of sixty horse-power and two hundred tons. In 1839 was launched the *India*—the first ship to reach India under steam: and her engines were of three hundred and twenty horse-power, her tonnage twelve hundred. By 1848 the *Europe*, of 1918 tons, had a good deal more than double the *India's* power.

Before the *India* had slipped down the ways (with a twenty-one gun salute to see her off) a vital new invention had been made. In 1836 the Swede John Ericsson and the Englishman Francis Smith invented, simultaneously, the screw propeller. Its advantages, for ocean-going ships, over paddle-wheels were manifest at once: but the wooden hulls could not stand up to its drive, and for several years it made its way but slowly. The prejudice against ships built of iron gave way, however: the Clyde had already, indeed, begun to make them, and in 1845 the first iron screw steamer, the Bristol-built *Great Britain*, crossed the Atlantic.

Already the great steamship lines were forming. In 1840 Samuel Cunard of Halifax, Nova Scotia, was drawn to the Clyde by the fame of Robert Napier, and founded, mostly with Glasgow share-holders, the great Transatlantic company he named.[1] The English owners were acutely jealous, and did their best to strangle the new venture: but he succeeded in gaining the mail contract, and in July 1840 the first Cunarder, the *Britannia*, triumphantly crossed the Atlantic in a fortnight. The time under sail was thirty days—with luck.

Thereafter the only rivals to the Clyde were two Scoto-English firms, Laird's of Birkenhead and Fairbairn's of London River. Even the Admiralty had to look north: from 1838 Robert Napier was building for the Navy, for which he made, at Govan, its first iron ships. The mid-century saw an enormous shipping boom. The Clyde had everything—a noble sea-way, iron, coal, railways, skill, and above all men with a passion for their work and the enter-prise to seize all new ideas and develop them to their utmost. Between 1846 and 1850 nearly as many steamships were built on the Clyde as in the whole previous quarter-century: and between 1850 and 1853 the tonnage exceeded by something like 40,000 the total of all built since the *Charlotte Dundas*.

Steam, however, had not yet won supremacy. The greatest age of the sailing ship, in fact, overlaps its first growth. Nothing more beautiful has moved on the waters than the great China clippers of the 'sixties, built for fast voyages over the longest trade-routes. They were miracles of an age-old intricate craft: and again the greatest of them were built by Scotsmen. The splendid Boston clippers are no exception, for the finest of these were the work of Donald McKay.

---

[1] It operated from Liverpool, not Glasgow, though his partners, George Burns and David M'Ivor, were Scots.

That glorious brief meridian of sail begins with the dainty little clipper packets built by Alexander Hall of Aberdeen for the coastwise run to London in the late 'thirties. The first of the great bluewater clippers that followed was the *Torrington* of 1845. The famous tea-clippers, the flower of all, began with the *Stornoway* in 1850. The names of those that ollowed are sea-legend—*Thermopylae*, *Lancing*, both Clyde-built, and *Cutty Sark*, built at Dumbarton in 1869, and *Ariel*, *Taeping*, *Sir Lancelot*, all of Greenock. In the famous tea race of 1866—the major event of all the seaman's year— the *Taeping* won the hundred days race over the *Ariel* by twenty minutes: but in another race the *Ariel* broke the record between London and Hong Kong by accomplishing the voyage in eighty days. But speed was not their only quality. Underlying it was a superb endurance. Take the *Lancing*, built in 1865. She had won fame in sail when the Compagnie Générale Transatlantique bought her, and had her engined by David Napier. As the *Pereire* she gave twenty years service in steam in the North Atlantic: then she went back to sail, and covered the Christiania-Melbourne run in sixty-five days. In 1916, being over fifty years old, she could still make the crossing from Newfoundland to Scotland in something a little under seven days.[1]

The career of these lovely creatures was short, however. In the very year that the *Cutty Sark* was launched—that is to say, in 1869—the new Suez Canal cut the long sea-road to the East by the Cape of Good Hope. Its great cargo space and lower running costs kept the sailing ship on the seas for some time yet: in the early 'nineties there was indeed a sort of revival of sail, for 185 sailing ships were built then in the Clyde. Some live even yet, in the hands of Finnish and Scandinavian owners, who love them for their old and noble tradition, and make them pay by using them for timber: in the last decade, crossing by the night boat out of Boulogne, I have met one standing southward through the Straits, a barque with every cloth set, like pearl in the moonlight, leaning to the breeze. But as power and speed and economy of fuel grew in their rivals, they were clearly doomed . . . though the fashionable cant that seamanship would die with them has been handsomely proved a lie.

Already, in 1854, before the great clippers, John Elder, Robert Napier's chief draughtsman, and Charles Randolph of Govan had

---

[1] It is pleasant to add that Joseph Conrad's *Narcissus*—the real one, in which he sailed as Second Mate—was Clyde-built.

built the first compound engine, and lowered coal consumption thirty to forty per cent. The screw-propeller came steadily into use, though it was not till after 1860 that the Cunard Company discarded paddles. The steel ship came in the later 'seventies, when Elder's built two cross-Channel packets with steel hulls. The triple-expansion engine, in 1882, increased power greatly. And only six years later the turbine engine, which now rivals, though it has not yet superseded, that based on the piston in the cylinder, was invented, this time by an Englishman, the Hon. C. A. Parsons. It was very slow in developing, however: not till 1901 did Denny's of Dumbarton build the first turbine steamer in commercial use, the *King Edward*, for the Turbine Steamer Company, while the first turbine liner, the Cunard Company's Clyde-built *Carmania*, was not launched till 1905. Two landmarks fully as great as the turbine engine come at the very end of the period. In 1911 the internal-combustion engine was used afloat; and next year the first oil-burning steamship, the *Selandia*, was built in Denmark, to revolutionise the whole economic basis of sea-transport.

One can sum the whole process by comparing speeds. In 1840 the *Britannia* startled the world with an Atlantic crossing of a fortnight. By 1889 the *City of Paris* had already reduced this to something under six days—a record broken five years later again by the Cunard sisters, *Campania* and *Lucania*, while again in 1910 the *Mauretania* brought it down to less than four days eleven hours. All save the last-mentioned of these famous ships, like the *Lusitania* and the *Aquitania*, and the *Indomitable*, which in 1908 broke the Atlantic record for a warship, were born of the skill and science of Clyde yards.

Shipping, of course, was not the only aspect of the nineteenth-century revolution in transport. In 1832, roads and canals were still responsible for most inland carriage. The latter, by then, were near their maximum use. The Forth and Clyde, in 1837, was paying a dividend of thirty per cent., and two years later three thousand ships went through it in twelve months. The Paisley Canal ran an hourly passenger service, which in 1836 carried well over 400,000 people. The Caledonian ran a regular goods and passenger service between Glasgow and Inverness. But the fall came quickly. In 1842 the Edinburgh-Glasgow Railway was completed, and the great days of canals were at an end—unless the petrol barge may yet bring revival.

Road traffic, at the beginning of the 'thirties, was well organised. In 1834, sixty-one stage coaches reached and left Glasgow daily, carrying half a million passengers in the year. (One may add that thirty-seven local steamboats plied in and out of Glasgow by this time, and carried more.) But already Scots trains had been running for six years past, and on the Fast Day of 1834 a Glasgow railway official proudly recorded that no fewer than six of them had left St Rollox, and

Everything went with the greatest regularity: not the least delay, nor did any accident take place, and not so much as one waggon went off the rails. We had 1,250 passengers out, and the whole of the number returned. Collected £60-8-6½.

He does not record what was said by the Kirk Session.

Before Stephenson's death in 1848, the railway was the 'natural' method of transport. Its development, none the less, was a muddled business, financially and in every other way. Neither in Scotland nor in England was there any attempt at bold planning for national needs. Instead, a mess of little local lines ran hither and yond, and only slowly joined into a system. The first Scots line that could be called a trunk one was the Edinburgh-Glasgow, which was mentioned above as having been opened in 1842.[1] The Edinburgh-Berwick, which was in time to grow into the North British, came five years later, the beginning of the Caledonian in 1845, though it was not till 1848 that Glasgow was joined by rail with Perth and Carlisle. North of Tay the first line came in 1838, on the seventeen miles between Dundee and Arbroath. The Great North of Scotland, opening the North-east, dates from 1852, the Highland Railway from 1855, though it did not reach Dingwall till 1863, and twenty years later passengers from the West Coast and the Isles had still to drive to Garve, for it did not reach the West Coast till the later 'eighties. The West Highland line reached Fortwilliam no earlier than 1897, and only some years later was carried to Mallaig. Communications between North and South were to be much shortened by the great Tay Bridge of 1878: but it fell, with a passenger train going over it, in a December storm of the next year, and was not replaced till 1887. The Forth Bridge, a world's

---

[1] Third class fare 4s. sitting and 2s. 6d. standing. The second class 6s. permitted not only seats but a roof : but there were neither cushions nor glazed windows. For some time after this, those who travelled in luxury had their own carriages loaded unhorsed on a truck, and sat in those. Now and then the lashings gave.

wonder in its day, was opened in 1890. The great Waverley Station, once the largest in Britain, was built between 1895 and 1900, a Queen of Scots being turned out of her grave to make way for it.

By 1864 there were some 1,720 miles of Scottish railways. By 1912 it was well over double this. The capital invested had risen also from forty-seven and three-quarter million pounds to a hundred and eighty-five, the receipts from three and three-quarter to thirteen and a half, the number of passengers from twenty to eighty million, the tonnage of goods from eighteen to sixty-seven. The startling speed of thirty miles an hour had long been doubled. In 1895 the East and West Coast trains—our familiar *Flying Scotsman* and *Royal Scot*—raced from London to Aberdeen, arousing much interest. In spite of Shap and the high pass into Clydesdale, the *Royal Scot* was victorious by twenty minutes, and her engine-driver was carried shoulder-high. The whole run took eight hours and twenty minutes, but not for some years yet was this the regular time. The comfort of trains increased enormously. The first British sleepers came in 1873, and dining-cars, gaslight, and heating in the 'eighties,[1] and the general amenities steadily improved: somebody even made the discovery that a railway station did not need to be ugly, and in fact the fine Joint Station at Aberdeen, in building at the end of the period, has a notable comeliness and dignity.

Power transport on the roads is of course much younger, although a practicable form of steam carriage ran from London to Brighton in 1831, and between Glasgow and Paisley three years later. The coach-owners combined to strangle it, and there was a pause till in 1866 the electric engine was invented, independently, by two Englishmen, Varley and Wheatstone, and a German, Siemens. The latter constructed an electric tramway at Portrush in County Antrim in 1883. Scotland began to build them in the 'nineties, to give cheap transport within the growing towns . . . and Glasgow and Edinburgh were among the very few cities of the world which refused to turn their trams into moving hoardings, in spite of the revenue which might thus be gained.[2]

---

[1] Not in all trains. The writer's father, travelling on the old Highland Railway in the 'nineties, used to carry a silver-plated ' traveller's lamp,' which was stuck to the window by a suction disc, and gave light to read by. Well within this century the old copper heaters used to be flung in, dunt after dunt, down the train—very comfortable, too, for those whose legs were long enough to reach them, though apt to cool before the train reached Drumochdair.

[2] Electricity naturally suggests a note on lighting. Gas had already come in, though the friction match was only invented in 1833. In 1869 Glasgow estab-

Other machines were already under way. The bicycle was invented in 1839, by a Dumfriesshire smith, Kirkpatrick Macmillan: it was at first no more than a sportsman's toy, and not till the 'safety' in 1888 did it become a real means of transport, with important social results. Its popularity and usefulness were vastly increased by the pneumatic tyre, invented in the later 'eighties by a Scots veterinary surgeon, John Boyd Dunlop (1840-1921). The tyre did even more for the new 'motor'—the road vehicle driven by the petrol engine, which in our day has become the railways' rival. The engine which was to make it possible is German, Austrian, and French in origin: the first British car was made in England in 1895, at a time when its presence on the road was illegal without a man walking in front with a red flag. Not till 1903 were cars really recognised by the law, and officially licensed and numbered. Even until the end of the period they (with their women passengers shrouded in veils) formed but a smallish fraction of the traffic on the untarred roads where the dust rose up in clouds.

Flying came very slowly. The power of hydrogen to lift a balloon had been discovered in 1766 by the famous Scottish chemist Joseph Black. It was not put to use till 1783, when J. A. C. Charles experimented in France, and for long thereafter very little was done till the internal combustion engine gave motive power. Otto Lilienthal, a German engineer, and Percy Sinclair Pilcher, a Scots scientist, were working in the 'nineties to produce a 'heavier than air' machine, and before Lilienthal's death in 1896, had discovered and used the principle of the glider: Pilcher's odd bat-winged glider, made that year, is still preserved in the Royal Scottish Museum. Farman in France and the Wrights in America carried on their work, and applied the petrol engine, the latter making the first flight by a power-driven 'plane on the 17th December 1903, at a speed of something like thirty miles an hour. Not till 1909 came the first air crossing of the English Channel, made by the Frenchman Louis Blériot; and the aeroplane, till after the Four Years War, was either a fighting weapon or a toy.

Along with the transportation of goods and people, the age brought a revolution in that of thought. Postal systems were old: the Roman Empire had an excellent one. They had always, how-

lished a municipal lighting system : Edinburgh did not follow till 1880. Electric light was used in St Enoch's Station as early as 1879, but until the end of the century gas was the usual illuminant.

ever, been expensive. In the eighteen-thirties a letter cost its recipient from fourpence to one and eightpence, those of peers and members of Parliament going free. In 1837 an English schoolmaster named Rowland Hill wrote a pamphlet advocating a universal penny postage. The scheme was decried as impossible: but a Scots M.P., Robert Wallace of Kelly, took it up with vigour, and succeeded in getting a Royal Commission appointed. They were converted, and in 1840 the system of penny postage was established, and proved at once an overwhelming success. (Our familiar adhesive stamp is, by the way, the device of a bookseller of Dundee, James Chalmers.) The post was soon followed by new means of cutting distance. Between 1837 and 1845 Wheatstone and Cooke in England, Morse in America, invented the electric telegraph: and in 1876 the living voice transcended space, when the Scot Alexander Graham Bell (1847-1922) made the first telephone, in America. Twenty years later, the Irish-Italian Guglielmo Marconi began to send sound, not over a metal wire, but through naked space: it was in the year 1899 that a 'wireless' message crossed the English Channel, and a new force came into politics. For a time, however, it was nothing more than a useful sea-going supplement to 'the wire': its enormous effect on the minds of large bodies of people was scarcely glimpsed for another couple of decades.

The world grew steadily smaller, and Scotland grew richer. Her ships went like shuttles about the Seven Seas, carrying her cottons to England, Turkey, the States, the East and West Indies, South America. Later they took iron, coal, and chemicals, and many things more—public fountains for Calcutta, castings for bridges in India, Italy, Spain, eighty thousand tons of drain-pipes for Brazil: indeed, the great Usher Hall in Edinburgh is built on whisky exported to Japan. Scotland's eyes, indeed, were on the ends of the earth . . . and there were other ways in which that was true.

XVII

PROGRESS: THE UNDERSIDE

EIGHTY-TWO YEARS: 1832-1914

The glittering and resolute streams of Tweed.
RICHARD FRANCK, *Northern Memoires*, 1694.

The town is sewered. All the sewage is collected into an outfall sewer, which discharges into the mill-lade . . . about three hundred yards from the Tweed; there is no attempt at purification of the sewage. The liquid refuse from the mills is discharged into the lade. . . . Below the point at which the lade discharges into the Tweed the water of the river is greatly fouled, the bottom of the river is coated with sewage deposit . . . The river here contains a large amount of refuse of all kinds, such as pots and pans, old linoleum, old iron-work. . . .
Report of the Tweed Pollution Commission, 1906.

NINETEENTH-CENTURY Scotland was, for her size, very rich. But if David I or Alexander III, James II or James IV had come back from the shades to visit the country for whose wealth he had laboured, he would have been far from pleased with all he saw.

The great Kings of Scots had worked for the country's wealth, which means a good deal more than the country's riches. So, as private citizens, working each in his place, had most of the men who had led the great eighteenth-century revival. Material riches, to them, were means, not end. Now already, however, they had become an end: and already, first the Highlands and then the Lowlands had learnt what happens to countries where that is true. Nor was the lesson by any means concluded.

We have seen how the machinery of life enlarged in no more than the space of one long lifetime. But in that same lifetime there were two other changes, one mental, one physical, both significant. In 1845 recruits for the Army were rejected if they were less than five feet six: in 1897 such a standard could be passed by so few that perforce it must be lowered, by four inches, to admit a sufficient number. In 1830 Scotland was known through Europe as a country in the van of the world's thought: in 1910 she was almost bare of the arts, her creative writers, her painters, driven abroad, her philosophers and her scientists known abroad by the name of another country than their own. So much for the effect of the Age of

Machines on the mind and body of the very nation which had first made steam-power a practicable thing. And yet machines are not evil things in themselves. They are merely tools man can use to what end he wills.

The generation round about 1800 had made Edinburgh a magnificent city: but it had not done anything to heal her slums, that festered where once her nobles and men of letters, her scientists and philosophers had dwelt. The generation which succeeded it made the once charming little city of Glasgow into a vast stretch of something, for much of its area, close to Hell. Men could dredge the Clyde, in face of most disconcerting difficulties: but they made no attempt to dredge the Cowcaddens. In forty years, 350,000 Highland and Irish folk, all bitterly poor, all unused to town life, had flocked into lower Clydesdale [1] . . . where for years on end there was serious unemployment. Three-fifths of Greenock in 1842 was out of work, 10,000 for the whole of next year in Paisley. And for long the most that had been done for these people was to give them a bug-ridden roof over their heads, and factories to which they could send their young children.

Slums were nothing new. It would be difficult, for sheer cold horror, to beat Hogarth's *Gin Lane*, which shows an aspect of eighteenth-century London, then the richest of all the cities of the world. But slums on this gigantic scale were new. In 1847 twenty-five people, of whom eight were already down with the deadly typhus, were sleeping in one Glasgow cellar, sixteen feet by ten. That, no doubt, is a case extreme in vileness. But in 1861, nevertheless, that city had 100,000 people in one-room houses—up to fifteen at times in one such house, where they ate, cooked, slept, washed when they did wash, bore and begot their children. Nor was this social custom confined to Glasgow. Next year in Hawick, a town not very large, a hundred houses had two or more families sharing one room between them. In the whole country 226,723 *families* (altogether over a third of the population) were living in houses of a single room: and in very nearly eight thousand of such cases, that single room was a room without a window.

---

[1] In 1840 a quarter of Glasgow's population was Irish, though the flood began to lessen after that, and in 1861 only 16 per cent. were Irish by actual birth. The one fine novel of the young Irish-Scot Edward Shiels, who died in his twenties a few years ago, shows that these incomers, given a chance, are as capable of becoming loyal Scots as any other of the half-dozen races who preceded them, and of bringing their own contribution to national life. Too often, however, they have not had a chance.

Glasgow's water-supply, till 1855, came for its greater part out of a river well flavoured by the general refuse and drainage of thirty communities of between them 116,000 people. A bill, indeed, had gone up to Parliament three years before to secure Loch Katrine water: but it met so much inertia, and opposition, that in spite of furious work by Lord Provost Stewart it took that time to pass. The Edinburgh water was less foul: but it involved, for most of the city's people, long waits in queues at the insufficient wells, and then the carrying of heavy pails up the steep stairs of perhaps a nine-storey land—not the best exercise for a pregnant woman. And without water, decent sanitation, even mere surface cleanness, cannot be hoped for.

As one would expect, the poorer parts of the towns were scourged again and again with epidemics. It was reckoned that in 1843 one in eight of the total population of Glasgow was attacked by the louse-borne typhus: and cholera came turn about with typhus, while tuberculosis and rickets never went. Heroic doctors laboured, and cursed Town Councils: but Glasgow's first Medical Officer of Health was not appointed till 1863, her first Fever Hospital was built in 1865, and her first Sanitary Inspector appointed in 1870. Not till 1890 was the notification of infectious diseases made compulsory. Such blame as was going for cholera epidemics fell not on the Bailies, or those who voted for them, but on Providence: and if Providence had insanitary habits, it was a pious duty to submit.

Yet the Scottish race is singularly tough. Although conditions were even worse than in England (where the Devil may witness, and Dickens did witness, that they were bad enough), the infant death-rate, until 1912, was actually lower than in England. It was, how-ever, more than high enough. At its maximum, in the later years of the 'nineties, it reached a hundred and thirty per thousand born [1]: that is, of a hundred babies born in Scotland, thirteen would die before they were able to walk: and in the 'sixties one child in twelve was still-born. As for Glasgow, *half* of its children, in the 'sixties, died before they were five. Nor are these things, if unhappy, old and far-off. In 1903—that is, in the lifetime of people not yet forty—seven children in ten in the Edinburgh schools showed some kind of mental or physical defect: and of the babies born in 1907, one in eight was dead by the end of 1908.

[1] That of Holland, in 1937, was 38. It is likely to be a good deal higher this year.

These Ramah-figures should be adequate. Any reader with an ounce of imagination can gauge from them the general conditions: and a reader with none will learn nothing from statistics. The moral results were as one might expect. Vice and crime flourished in a Christian country. Drunkenness grew. In 1840 one house in ten in Glasgow was selling 'drink,' which was not honest beer but bad raw whisky, doctored with fusel oil, sheer poison alike to body and to soul. The ratio of illegitimate births was half as high again as that of England, reaching its peak in the decorous eighteen-sixties. In the 'eighties, when it had fallen considerably, one child in ten born in Scotland was a bastard. Nor was this only the fruit of town conditions, for it derives not merely from the housing (which was bad enough in the rural districts also, especially for unmarried farm-workers) but from the lack of decent recreation, for which the Church must bear great part of the blame, since all the amusements left for large numbers of a vigorous people have been summed up, and with sufficient truth, as 'drink, conversation, and fornication.' The highest bastardy figures are not from the towns, but from the old Covenant shires of the South-west, where the rate was one and three-quarter times that for all Scotland.[1]

The rural areas had fresh air outdoors: and water, if it had to be carried in pails, was generally cleaner than in cities. If the houses were crowded, and bad, much of life, even for women, was lived outside them, while food, if coarse, was in the Lowlands at least fairly plentiful for the greater part of the time, and a good deal more wholesome than is common today. There was a tradition, that gave roots to life: and in rural work there was far less in proportion of the deadly monotony of unskilled labour, of mere machine-minding: the landworker had more often than the townsman the satisfaction of a skilled, varied craft. He lacked comfort and leisure, but given security, he was much better off than the submerged masses who congregated in the city slums.

Security, however, he lacked too often. The dwindling of the proportionate importance of the land in the national economy drove him into the towns, or else away from Scotland. Often, even yet, the compulsion was less indirect, for the Highland Clearances continued still: in the forty years after 1841 some 18,000 people left

---

[1] The Highland counties kept down the total figure, and the large Irish element in Glasgow that for the towns: the general rate for Ireland has always been much lower than that of Scotland or England.

Inverness-shire. There was a famine in 1837 in the Highlands, another in 1846: the grave poverty caused a number of fresh evictions of those no longer able to pay their rents. The 'seventies brought in a further motive. The growing wool-exports of Australia threatened the sheep for which men had been cleared away: and wealthy foreigners had begun to discover the thrill of the Highland sport of stalking deer. To the Englishmen, who made up the bulk of these, any sport with shooting involved implied 'preserving.' Scots lawyers were a little dubious of its legal application to red deer, but money talks louder than lawyers—and mere Scots lawyers. Huge areas, preserved, let at high rates, and others were very soon cleared of sheep and men, to be let beside them. In 1883 already two million acres were under deer.

A good deal of nonsense is talked about deer-forests, on both sides. Much of that ground was quite useless for cultivation: and preserving had at least the useful effect of keeping it free from the paper and empty tins and broken bottles with which an educated democracy is apt to embellish all places it has been told are beautiful. Yet none the less, in that year 1883, a Royal Commission was obliged to admit that about a third of these two million acres was capable of being used for cultivation—was fit, that is, to support those men and women whom Scotland was driving off, or out of, the land.

Emigration, indeed, was still regarded by the Government as the panacea for all Scottish ills. If people were poor or ill-housed, the remedy was to take the most energetic and enterprising, the young and active, and shift them out of the country, in a drain of six successive generations—thousands of them, the pick of a small country's rural stock, of the men who in any sort of sane national whole would have been charged with the nation's defence and feeding and the carriage of her products to other nations, and given a fitting status in the kingdom their forefathers had won for Robert Bruce.

Not all, however, took this remarkable view of the method by which to tackle Scotland's ills. If the larger portion of those better off were ignorant of these horrors, or ignored them, or considered them the will of Providence (which is no great blasphemy in a Calvinist), there were yet men and women in all classes, from great lords to courageous dwellers in Glasgow slums, who saw horrors round them and would not turn away, but threw off their coats and went to work to fight them, and not without some measure of success.

Not enough was done. Yet much, none the less, was done. One would not desire to rejoice that conditions in England were for much of the century very similar: if Glasgow was rather worse than Liverpool, the English slum areas were of more extent. But the fact that the same ills were suffered by both countries made it easier to force Parliament to act. Those ills which were peculiar to Scotland, the most flagrant being the stripping of the Highlands, were but inadequately remedied: yet Glasgow profited with Liverpool by a large body of useful legislation; and the spontaneous movements among 'labour' for its own help were common to both countries, though these for long showed more national differences.

These movements for redress can best be described in the chapters concerning the politics of the time, when their consecutive process will show more clearly. We may leave the material aspect for a while now, and concern ourselves with those things of the mind and the spirit which are also part of the texture of national life, before we consider it in its total workings, in what we are used to speak of as politics.

XVIII

THE CHURCHES

EIGHTY-TWO YEARS: 1832–1914

A spirit of greater liberality than the world knew before, bringing men of adverse principles and doctrines into a more human communion with one another, showing that it's by the mollifying influence of knowledge that the time will come to pass when the tiger of papistry shall lie down with the lamb of reformation, and the vultures of prelacy be as harmless as the presbyterian doves ; when the independent, the anabaptist, and every other order and denomination of Christians, not forgetting even those poor wee wrens of the Lord, the burghers and anti-burghers, will pick from the hand of patronage, and dread no snare.

JOHN GALT, *The Annals of the Parish.*

FOR a generation the history of the Churches had been marked by an increasing tolerance, yet by a tendency, no less evident, for new denominations to be formed by secessions from those already in existence. The contradiction is more apparent than real. Those differences which, in the sixteenth and seventeenth centuries, produced a violent strife within first of all the general Reformation Church of Scotland [1] and then within the Presbyterian body, for the supremacy of one party or other, were now solved by their frank acknowledgment and a peaceable separation of the dissentients— not always, certainly, without ill-feeling, but at least without even the threat of civil war. Indeed, in two cases, these very subdivisions were caused by the growth itself of tolerance, for in each case the majority concerned desired the abandonment of that principle of state compulsion in religious matters which was part of the essence of the Covenants.[2]

In the latter half of the nineteenth century, this tendency to subdivide was reversed, and among the various Presbyterian churches there was a general seeking for re-union. Before that time had been

---

[1] A good deal of popular confusion is caused by a failure to realise that until 1638 Episcopalians and Presbyterians formed one State Church, much as Anglo-Catholics and Evangelicals do today in England.

[2] See the text of the National Covenant in the Appendix to *The Scotland of Queen Mary* and that of the Solemn League and Covenant in that of *The Passing of the Stewarts,* and contrast with the points at issue in the Seceder divisions of 1799 and 1806, for which see p. 92 of this volume.

attained, however, the Establishment suffered the greatest religious division since 1638—that of 1843, known to its generation as *the* Disruption.

The cause was no new problem: it was, in essence, the old strife of the *regnum* and the *sacerdotium*, recurrent since the eleventh century, and nowhere more violently than in the Scots sixteenth. This time, however, the issues were clearer than common, though the situation was made more difficult by the consequences of the Treaty of Union.

In the Establishment, by 1830, the predominance, as we have seen already, was passing from Moderates to Evangelicals. These had always opposed that system of patronage established by the Act of 1712, whereby the ministers of the parishes, although inducted by the presbytery, were appointed by the local heritors. The agitation for wider political franchise had already done much to strengthen a growing desire to supersede this method of appointment by one in which the minister's congregation might at least refuse an unwelcome nominee. A couple of months before the Reform Act passed, the greatly respected Professor of Divinity in the University of Edinburgh, Dr Thomas Chalmers (1780-1847), had directly moved, in the General Assembly, that an adverse majority of (male) heads of families in a congregation should invalidate the heritors' presentation. The motion was lost, but only by twelve votes: and in 1834 the Assembly passed it.

This opened what was called the Nine Years Conflict. Next autumn Auchterarder, in terms of this formal ruling of the Assembly, refused acceptance of a presentee, and the Presbytery accepted their refusal. The presentee and his patron thereupon carried their case before the Court of Session; and after a long delay, the Court decided against the Presbytery. The sole Court of Appeal was the House of Lords, and to these the Assembly, supporting the Presbytery, took their cause: and the House of Lords upheld the Session.

Side by side with this dispute, there had been others. Before the Session case had reached a judgment, the Presbytery of Marnoch in Strathbogie had also rejected a vetoed presentee: and the Assembly had sustained their rejection. The Court of Session commanded them to rescind it: they obeyed, and thereupon the Assembly suspended seven of their members, and on these appealing to the Court of Session, deposed them outright for contumacy.

By 1840 there was a glaring deadlock, and the Church was in a manifest false position. She, the State Church, was defying the law of the State. Conversely, that law was supporting her ministers in defiance of her supreme authority on a question of her internal discipline. The situation was impossible, and there were other factors to make it worse. It was true that the Church whose supreme governing body was the Assembly represented the State Establishment in religion. But on the other hand, it was also true that since the general rights of citizenship were now enjoyed by non-members of the Church, the decision that a civil authority might override decisions of the Assembly on points of her internal discipline was obviously unjust in principle. Moreover, if the civil authorities should intervene in the Church's internal affairs, the ultimate one was the British Parliament: and the 'nation' of which the Church was the State religion was one-ninth of that which elected Parliament. In effect, a body eight-ninths of whose constituents were foreign and the great majority non-Presbyterian controlled the internal affairs and discipline of a Presbyterian and Scottish church.

Charles I, in his least constitutional intervention, had ventured nothing like so far as this. It is not surprising that very strong feelings were roused: and Parliament showed an exemplary lack of tact. Attempts to modify the Settlement and achieve a concordat between the conflicting parties were made, and in good faith by both of them. Peel, however, was bored by the subject, and Melbourne more so: and Parliament refused consideration.

In the Assembly of 1842 Chalmers put forth a *Claim, Declaration, and Protest*, which affirmed, in terms moderate but precise and clear, that all Acts of Parliament concerning the Church were 'void and null and of no legal force' if they changed her government and discipline or were passed without her consent or that of the State of which she was the 'established' religious form. It summed the situation with masterly clearness; and the General Assembly accepted it, by a majority of a hundred and thirty. The Government, however, took no heed.

In November, the ministers who supported Chalmers—four hundred and fifty of them—drew up a memorial, which was formally despatched to Westminster. But Peel and Lord John Russell still ignored it, and a proposal made in Parliament for a Committee to consider the question was negatived by the English majority.

On the 18th May of 1843 the Assembly met in St Andrew's,

Edinburgh, with Dr David Welsh as Moderator. He declared that the Assembly was not free, as the civil legislature had negatived the Claim of Right which was passed by its predecessor. He summed the issues with clarity and force, and ended by a solemn affirmation that he could not accept the benefits of Establishment when he could not agree to the conditions 'now deemed to be thereto attached'; and having ended, he bowed to the Commissioner and walked out, more than four hundred ministers going with him.

Four hundred and seventy came out altogether, leaving manse and stipend: some abandoned charges worth £1,000 a year. Many of their congregations came out also, and the secession was soon constituted into a body which proudly claimed the title of the Free Church. The claim was justified. The Disruption was by no means a mere endeavour to achieve the dominance of a party or faction, and the freedom it claimed was not freedom to persecute. It was a real stand for real freedom, carried out with as great generosity as courage: and whatever the later influence of the Free Church, it remains an outstanding event of its century, for which all Scots can feel profound respect.

The pity is that it should have been forced. Had Parliament acted with honesty and reason, it need never have happened: the blame was not the Assembly's. Parliament did act at last, but just too late. Only three months after the Disruption took place, Established congregations were given the right to object against presentees. The patronage question then lapsed for many years, but in 1869 the General Assembly once more condemned the principle. Five years later, a government then headed by Disraeli cancelled at last the Act of 1712, and abolished the system of patronage altogether.

Unluckily, this did not heal the schism, for by this time there had grown up in the Free Church a tradition hostile to the Establishment. Before patronage was revoked, in 1872, the Free Church Assembly had already voted, by 322 to 84, that even the abolition of patronage must leave the Disruption exactly where it stood: and the year after abolition had taken place, they voted, by a larger majority—397 against 84—in favour of disestablishing their rivals. The latter, none the less, attempted re-union, and in 1878, 1886, and 1893 made overtures to the Free Church Assembly, which however were successively repulsed.

The Free Church, immediately on its constitution, took the lead among Presbyterian Dissenters. Though times were hard, its members and adherents raised something like half a million in one year, and rapidly organised, on a national scale, a system of churches, schools, and colleges beside and rivalling the Establishment's.

For the rest of the period, as we have noted, the time was one of re-unions . . . though, to be sure, nearly every re-union also meant a division. Before the Disruption, in 1839, the majority of the Original Associate Synod (the Old Light Burghers) re-joined the Establishment: their remaining minority amalgamated with the Original Seceders (the Old Light Anti-burghers), the conjoined body now becoming the United Original Seceders. In 1847 the United Secession Church joined the Relief Synod as the United Presbyterians: this time there was no dissentients on either side, and for half a century 'the U.P. Kirk' remained a considerable and important body.

In 1852 a majority of the United Original Seceders joined the Free Church, and in 1876 a majority of the Reformed Presbyterians (the former Cameronians) did the same, though in each of these cases the older and smaller communion left a 'continuing' body bearing its name, which still exists. The outstanding union, however, was that of the United Presbyterians with the Free Church in the year 1900, which had stormy results. Negotiations between the two communions had been in progress since 1863, and the whole of the United Presbyterians had been brought to approve of the amalgamation. A small minority of the Free Church still dissented, however; and six weeks after the union their representatives appeared in court to claim that, as they alone stood for the principles of 'Forty-three, the great endowments of the Church were theirs. The Outer House, perhaps of the opinion that this claim for a secular authority to intervene in the Church's internal affairs was hardly in the spirit of the Disruption, gave for the majority, now the United Free Church. The 'Wee Frees' thereon appealed: and the Inner House sustained the former judgment. They thereupon took their claim to the House of Lords, and though the Scots judges before whom the case had been twice tried already had been unanimous, the House of Lords saw fit to reverse their verdict, and gave the great trusts and the many substantial buildings and institutions in the old Free Church to the tiny minority, who could not man them or administer them. There was fiery feeling—in fact, such an explosion that (the Prime Minister now being a Scot, Lord Balfour) the Government was forced to appoint a Commission, which in 1905 decided for division. A Parliamentary Committee was set up to allocate the property, and though neither party was well satisfied, an arrangement was arrived at, and carried out.[1] The Free Church remained determined separatists: but the United Free, by 1914, were steadily moving towards a reconciliation with the Establishment, though it did not come to pass until some years later.

In the Establishment and the United Free Church, the period brought some change in externals of worship. Congregations ceased to stand during the prayers, and sat instead, in a forward-crouching position. Organs, in spite of fervent opposition to an instrument which (unlike the tuning-fork) was unscriptural, came slowly into use in both communions. Their entry was encouraged by an increasing interest in church music, which inspired a number of very fine new psalm-tunes, such as the lovely *Kilmarnock*, *Rest*, and *St Kilda*. The Metrical Psalms of the good Provost of Eton ceased to be the sole permitted form of praise: in 1898 the three major Presbyterian communions authorised a *Hymnary*, which grew through successive revisions into a fine and scholarly collection. From 1857 onward there was a movement for the use of a liturgy; but it was strongly opposed, and though it persisted it never spread very far. The great traditional feasts of Christendom (though not the fasts) began, however, to be noticed again, and there was a significant change in the form of churches. To all the Reforming divines of the Left Wing, preaching had been the core of public worship, to which prayer and the reading of Scripture alike must give place: now in many new churches, or churches newly restored, the pulpit ceased to dominate the interior, the communion table taking its place of honour.

In the Episcopal Church during the 'thirties the centre of gravity still was Aberdeen: all its six bishops belonged to the North-east, and three of them indeed resided there, the most notable being George Gleig, Bishop of Brechin, the first editor of the *Encyclopaedia*

---

[1] The sort of situation produced can be seen at the village of Garrabost in Lewis. The minister and most of his flock accepted the Union, retaining possession of the church and manse. The Wee Frees built themselves a wooden church alongside the old one. On the Lords' decision, they took possession of the old church and manse, and refused to allow the United Free congregation to rent the wooden building. These therefore built an iron church beside it, and subsequently a stone one beside that : and the four, representing the same theological standards, the same mode of worship, and the same polity, stood side by side for years along the road.

Britannica. His successor in the middle century was another North-eastern man, again Bishop of Brechin, Alexander Penrose Forbes, again a fine scholar, and a bishop whose social conscience stirred Dundee to work for which he is still remembered with honour by men of all communions in that city.

The Oxford Movement in the Church of England, which began in the year 1833,[1] drew closer the Church's relations with that body, or at all events with its 'Right' or 'Tractarian' wing, which stood in general for the same principles as the Scottish Church. The Oxford men also sought for a revival of external forms which by long Christian tradition had expressed these principles: and a similar movement now stirred in the Scottish Church, especially in the North-eastern dioceses. Since the Civil War, the sole *external* difference between Episcopalian worship and Presbyterian had been the use of a liturgy and the prose psalms, and the fact that the lay-folk shared prayer as well as praise, and in doing so 'knelt before the Lord their Maker.'[2] Now they began to break from the long domination of the verbal, and restoring ancient symbols and ceremonies, gave sight and movement also their share in a worship which had for long been confined to voice and hearing.

Relations with England were not all friendly, however. The English Church was split in opposing factions; and the Left, which was strongly affected by Calvinism, resented Scottish friendship with the Tractarians, and redoubled their attempts, already made, to intervene in the Scottish Church's concerns. They sent up clergy of English ordination, who claimed the right to officiate in Scotland without obeying either the Scottish bishops or the Code of Canons of the Scottish Church, and they tried to stir up Protestant prejudice to prevent the use of the Scottish Liturgy. The interference, indeed, became so flagrant that the Scots Church was forced, in 1844, to send the English one a vigorous protest against

sending her agents to Scotland . . . to countenance men who have set up schismatic altars against the lawful authority of Scottish bishops.

---

[1] Nothing to do with the modern ' Oxford Group Movement,' which indeed has very little to do with Oxford.

[2] This for some reason, in spite of the Scripture command, was peculiarly offensive to Presbyterians. Episcopalian children at school were long apt to be pursued by the rhyme,

Pisky, Pisky, boo and ben',
On your knees and up again.

. . . to which the traditional retort was

Presby, Presby, dinna ben',
Sit ye doun on man's chief en'.

The protest, however, had very little avail. The English 'Left,' from whom the offence proceeded, held all places of authority in their church, and were strongly supported also by the Queen, who greatly disliked the Episcopal Church of Scotland, and considered that it ought to be abolished. Working upon the growing anglo-philism of the laymen of the landed and professional class, who were a very strong element in the Church, they slowly anglicised the episcopate, even the priesthood, especially south of Forth: and in places the old but quite unhistoric taunt that the strongly nationalist Church was 'English' began to find a certain justification. It would none the less be quite unfair to imply that all those Englishmen who sought charges in Scotland were of this type: several entered the service of the Scottish Church because she was free of the bonds of establishment, and these as a rule accepted her traditions loyally, doing devoted and honourable work.

The re-opening of the universities to Episcopalian students was among the greatest of the benefits procured by the repeal of the Penal Laws. In 1853 the lay professorships also were thrown open to men of all religious denominations—an action which was to permit the great service to Scotland of, among others, the Irish Dr C. S. Terry, the English Dr George Saintsbury, and the Scot Sir Herbert Grierson. In 1841 the Liberal leader William Ewart Gladstone and James Hope-Scott of Abbotsford began to work for the founding of a Theological College at Glenalmond in Perthshire, to which a boys' school was attached. (The college was later removed to Edinburgh.) Many more schools were built, up and down the country, and in spite of the Church's poverty, many new churches. Religious communities also were established, as foci of prayer and a great help in the Church's social work: the first was that of St Mary and St Modwenna, which was founded in Dundee in the early 'fifties by Bishop Alexander Penrose Forbes. Almost all the remaining traces of Penal Laws were rescinded in 1864, 1871, and 1887: and though nearly all Episcopalians still are liable, technically, to two years prison, the law has long lapsed from any effect in practice, and Sheriffs and Law Lords break it with perfect calm.

In the early stages of the period it was natural that there should be a growing claim by the laity to possess a greater voice in the administration of the Church. It had been expressed so early as the 'twenties by John Skinner of Forfar, but made little headway till Gladstone took it up in 1852. Eleven years later, laymen were given

a vote in the election of the Scottish bishops; and in 1876 the founding of the Representative Church Council gave them also a share in
administering the property of the Church. It was not, however,
until 1905 that the establishment of the Consultative Church Council
gave them a voice in legislation also.

The end of the period brought an important change in the
Prayer-book. For most part of two centuries the English book had
been used for all services save the Eucharist. (The Scottish one,
being illegal in both countries, had been hard to come by.) There
were, however, many distinctive uses which involved departure from
the English forms, and in 1912 these were defined and regularised,
and incorporated in a new Scottish Prayer-book, as prelude to a
much more thorough revision which was to take many years of work
to complete.

The number of Roman Catholics greatly increased. Those of
Glasgow, between 1805 and 1846, had risen from 1,000 to nearly
70,000. The great majority of these were Irish; and the Irish and
native Scots authorities agreed none too well. There was a good deal
of external friction also, first in the 'forties over a Government grant
to the Irish Catholic College of Maynooth, and again in 1850 when
it was proposed that the bishops of the Roman Church in Scotland
should bear Scottish territorial titles. Indeed, there was such a flare
of hostility that an act was passed forbidding them to do so. It was
repealed, however, in 1871, and seven years later a hierarchy for
Scotland was established—two Archbishops, of St Andrews and
Edinburgh and of Glasgow, and four Bishops—and the change was
now accepted without protest. For the rest of the time the Roman
Communion in Scotland underwent a period of quiet and steady
growth: many schools were built, and many religious houses, which
often did admirable 'social work,' especially among the very poor.
In 1911 the number of Scottish adherents to the Church was
reckoned at 520,000—that is, roughly one in nine of the population:
only some 25,000, however, were Scots by descent, and the greater
number of these belonged to the traditional 'Catholic Belt,' stretch-
ing from Uist and Barra across to Mar, in which last district the
adventurous and shifting seminary for the training of priests found at
last a peaceful home, at Blairs, soon after the Penal Laws were repealed.

All the different communions were more or less affected by the

new movements in scholarship and science which were stirring
Europe. To the general mind, the very base of Protestant religion
was belief in the literal inerrancy of every statement made in Holy
Scripture. The Church was supposed to depend upon the Scriptures, not vice versa: accordingly, when the new sciences of geology
and biology seemed to conflict with the Book of Genesis, many
worthy people believed, with joy or horror, according to their attitude of mind, that the basis of Christianity was threatened. The
storm began in 1844, when Robert Chambers, the Edinburgh
publisher, produced his *Vestiges of Creation*, and first made widely
known to the general public the principle of the evolution of man.
It increased to fury with Darwin's *Origin of Species* fifteen years
later, and from then till after the end of the century, 'the opposition
of science and religion' was firmly believed in by superficial thinkers,
and often caused real spiritual distress, and as often a brash and
shallow arrogance which was no great help to any efficient thought.

The development of textual scholarship and its (sometimes
rather unchastened) application to the study of Scripture caused
another conflict: to show that the Pentateuch could not be written
by Moses or that one book of the Bible contradicted another overthrew, it seemed, all the authority of religion. Dr Robertson Smith,
Professor of Hebrew in the Free Church Divinity College, Aberdeen,
and one of the foremost scholars of his day, was a leader of 'the new
criticism'; and his views as expressed in an article on the Bible,
published in 1875 in the *Encyclopaedia Britannica*, brought him a
resounding trial for heresy. He was acquitted, but in the next year
another article on Hebrew Literature was followed by his deposition
from his chair.[1]

During the latter part of the century there was once more a
reaction against Calvinism, which led, in the various Presbyterian
churches, to more heresy trials. This widespread but largely un-
formulated movement had much to do with the vigour of another
which derives its first impulse from the ethical interest of the best
of the eighteenth-century Moderates—the growth of missions and
of 'social work.'

This was not peculiar to any denomination. In the Roman
communion such activities were part of the tradition of the Orders:
in the others, the broad-minded and large-hearted Dr Norman

---

[1] He became Associate Editor of the *Encyclopaedia*, then Editor in Chief, and
Professor of Arabic at Cambridge.

MacLeod and Principal Caird of the Establishment, the saintly Dr Guthrie of the Free Church, and Bishop Penrose Forbes led their own people and inspired each others' in a vigorous attack on social evils. Those missions abroad which the Establishment in 1790 had refused as being no part of its function were now undertaken, and with no small success. The missions of both the Establishment and the Free Church did extensive work in China, Africa, and India, and the Episcopal worked in Africa and took charge of the Indian diocese of Chanda. The increasing interest in social reform did much to weaken old intolerances, by enforcing contacts in work for a common end. Intolerance did not die, and is not dead: but by the beginning of this century, there was a real and growing friendliness between the authorities of the four chief communions, and a spirit tending to that which General Monk described as 'unity in things necessary, liberty in things unnecessary, and charity in all.'

XIX

THE MIND OF SCOTLAND: I

EIGHTY-TWO YEARS: 1832–1914

I believe we should think of things in terms of the intelligence and
conscience of man, not of blind forces of nature.
Professor R. W. CHAMBERS, *Man's Unconquerable Mind.*

IN the long lifetime between the first Reform Act and the beginning
of the Four Years War, the intellectual life of this country of ours
presents a picture of odd anomalies, whose results are still conspicuous today.   For a great part of the period there was still a
broad and lively interest in things of the mind, and a general and
healthy respect for them, which excited the admiration of other
countries.   It was not the prerogative of any class, nor was it confined to those who were scholars themselves, or even those who
would desire to be thought so.   More, probably, than any country
in Europe, Scotland kept true to the mediaeval faith that learning
was an honourable thing, and must be accessible to all who sought
it.   The survival of this attitude in Scotland, as a thing taken simply
for granted everywhere, is the more remarkable and the more to her
credit in a time when English influence was stronger than at any
other in our history: for England was that, of all the countries in
Europe, in which this tradition had died out most completely.
Hardy's *Jude the Obscure* presents us with a picture (corroborated
by much other evidence) of conditions almost incredible to a Scot,
and impossible alike in modern England and at any time in the
history of Scotland.   There Shon Campbell, who would be Jude's
analogue, may sometimes have died of scant fare and overwork,
but he much more generally warsled through by the proud and
willing help of his family and one of the very many bursaries, which
had been loyally kept to their proper function of helping the lad
who joined parts with poverty.

Any young man of brains and resolution could reach the means
to a decent education, and that he should choose to do so was
approved.   Education, however, was limited, in the main, to those

187

who sought it, or who had parents who desired it for them. How far this was evil may be arguable: but two sets of forces joined throughout that age to cause it to be counted as an evil. On the one side were two of Scotland's best traditions, respect for learning, respect for the status of man simply as man: and the broadening of the political franchise, closely linked with the second of these, implied some need for the formal education of the voter in a certain minimum of the tools of learning. On the other hand, it was naturally held (though this belief was implied rather than stated) that the future voter, whether he chose or not, must be bred from the start to the right shade of belief, at all events in matters of politics and of history on which politics are based, so that when the time came he should vote in the right direction. Between these two, there was much activity in the broadening and in the systematising of the whole scheme of national education: and some of this work was undoubtedly beneficial.

In the Established Church the Moderates had roused a lively interest in education, which did not pass with their supremacy, and which the Free Church honourably retained. Already, in 1824, the Assembly had begun to found schools in the Highlands and the Islands. As the State Church, engaged in a State function, she had a fair claim to financial help from the State, which in 1836 was duly forthcoming. With this support, it did not take her long to return to the excellent plan for a national system whose theory Knox had framed in 1561 and whose practice had been attempted, with some success, by Archbishop Spottiswoode in 1616—to be wrecked by the long years of civil war. In 1839, with the Government's concurrence, the Church set to work at an extensive scheme, which aimed at providing a school for every parish.

After 1843 the Free Church at once began to establish a parallel system. The support of Government could not be invoked, but the Church's adherents gave generous support, and in seven years they had built no fewer than 626 schools, with two Normal Colleges to train their teachers. The Episcopal Church and also the Roman one built schools for their own children where practicable, also training their teachers: and besides these schools there were several founded, mainly in the Highlands, by the Society for the Propagation of Christian Knowledge, and in the towns a number of private ventures, especially for girls and the younger children.

By the middle years of the century, in fact, Scotland was over-schooled: the reduplication was seen to involve great wastefulness of resources. Opinion began to favour a State system, undenominational in religious outlook, at least so far (this was commonly taken for granted) as the various Presbyterian communions. The important Act of 1861 placed the main school system in Government control, under what was called the Scotch Education Department, with Government inspection and Government grants, and opened it to all Presbyterian teachers, who were guaranteed a minimum salary of £35, which might rise to £70.[1]

The Act was by no means wholly beneficial, since it took over from the English Code the vicious system of payment by examination results, which stereotyped and shallowed education, by reducing it to a process of *ad hoc* cramming. To Scotland's credit, it was much disliked. A Commission which sat in 1867 found that of half a million children in Scotland, very little more than a couple of hundred thousand were attending Government-inspected schools . . . and, what was much less to the national credit, more than 90,000 went to no schools at all.

Reform was taken vigorously in hand. In 1872 another act gave popular control of education, by elective School Boards in every parish and burgh, with power to impose a cess for education, to enforce school attendance for children of five to thirteen, and to receive grants from the Education Department. The genuine popular interest in education caused this democratic system to work, on the whole, to good effect. The deadly institution of child labour was coming to be recognised for what it was, and a forward step was made in 1878, by banning employment of children under ten. In 1890 the very bad arrangement of payment by the results of one examination was at last got rid of.[2] Three years later education was made free for all children from three years old up to fifteen, though it was not till so late as 1901 that the limit for compulsory attendance was raised to fourteen. Finally, 1908 brought in at last

---

[1] One has to remember prices. Even at the very end of the period, when they had risen, schoolmistresses in the country districts lived in decent comfort on £80 to £90, and some, though one would think hardly in comfort, on £45 a year and a free house. In Aberdeen in the last years of the time, it was possible to have a comfortable bedroom and sitting-room in a residential quarter, with fire, light, food, and baths, for £1, 1s. a week, and a parlour-bedroom in a respectable working-class quarter, with fire, light, and food, though probably a tin bath, for as low as 11s.

[2] In that year also the Boards assumed responsibility for the education of deaf-mutes and the blind. Those partially deaf had longer to wait, however, though their difficulties in large classes of normal children were very great.

14

some (badly needed) attention to the physical well-being of the children, their examination by medical officers, and provision of meals for the necessitous.

The important Act of 1872 was not limited to primary education. Its aim was provision 'for the whole people of Scotland'—a national outlook, in more senses than one. The old burgh schools were put under the School Boards, though the 'Academies' and other institutions which had their own governing bodies and endowments were excepted, and carried on in their old tradition, continuing often to do excellent work. The Episcopalian and Roman Catholic schools also remained outside the Government scheme. It was not, in fact, until 1892 that the State took much interest in secondary schools; and its dealings in their concerns were not always happy, though there was certainly excellent intention in the purpose, formulated about this time, of making a direct educational ladder from the infant school to the university. The uniform Leaving Certificate for the country, established first in 1888, was intended as the half-landing of the stair for those who went higher, and for those who did not, as a state hall-mark, a sort of minor degree, corresponding to the French *baccalauréat*. An Intermediate Certificate, taken half-way through the secondary course, was added in 1906, and though it had the defect of all such uniform tests for a whole country, it also acted as a useful filter to limit the higher classes of the schools to those who might receive their benefit. Both avoided the worst form of stereotyping by considerable range in the choice of subjects.

The Presbyterian churches, by the 'sixties, had lost direct and formal control of the schools: but the loss was a good deal less real than apparent, as up to 1905 the training of teachers was largely in their hands. There were nine Normal Colleges—three Established, three Free Church, one Episcopalian, and one Roman Catholic, with St George's, Edinburgh, for secondary teachers. Most men also took university degrees, and of women many worked for the St Andrews L.L.A.[1] and after the turn of the century, for degrees. Even before that time, they had come to outnumber men in the profession.

In 1905 the Education Department took the Normal Colleges into its grasp as well, and handed them, re-christened Training Centres, to the control of large Provincial Committees. Unluckily,

[1] Diploma of Lady Literate in Arts, founded in 1890 and conferred on results of local examinations. It died out as the universities opened more widely to women.

at the same time it established an odd, and pernicious, plan of training teachers. These began their career at school at the age of fifteen,
and were passed on, as by a conveyor belt, to leave the Training
Centres five years later as Certificated Teachers, more or less trained
in the technique of teaching, but often very little trained in its
substance, and with very little vocation for their task. Those who
were naturally adapted to it picked up something on the way and,
all honour to them, made good and able teachers. Others did not:
but a Department which had spent Treasury money on a student's
training refused to 'waste' the result by discrimination against those
unfit to teach, who indeed might be more or less illiterate, unable,
when they received their certificate, to grasp the sense of a page
of simple prose, much more to write one without gross mistakes.
The effect of the system on the schools it staffed, and on the nation
which was trained in them, was therefore rather considerably varied.
Quite first-rate work was done—at times in exceedingly unlikely
places: over the rest we may draw a decent veil. It accounts for
the large sales of some periodicals.

The Universities, through the period, underwent a good deal of
active reconstruction. The important Commission of 1858 reduced
them to four by accomplishing, not without stour, the long-discussed
fusion of those of Aberdeen. It did much else, for it changed the
constitution of them all, erecting University Courts, senior to the
Senatus and with financial control, and a General Council in each,
of all graduates, whose functions were to be sure a little vague, but
which had power to initiate legislation. The Commission dealt too
with the Arts Curriculum, drawing up one of six subjects (seven in
Aberdeen), which if inelastic was both broad and well-balanced.
For the greater part of the nineteenth century, the Arts Degree gave
the student a general grounding in the foundations of academic
knowledge. The cry for specialisation was being raised, under
German influence, and they yielded to it so far as to establish
Honours courses; but these for long were very wisely guarded by
a rule that the Pass course must be taken as well.[1]

---

[1] This excellent tradition survived the regulation which compelled it. If a
personal comment may be permitted here, the writer, if asked to choose between
an Honours course which she greatly enjoyed and in which she took a First Class,
and the six Pass subjects in which her attainments varied from 4th prize to the
bottom of the Merit List, and in which she was occasionally bored, would choose
the second as the better value. Some experience of an English university at which
specialisation reached fantastic extremes confirms this judgment.

The later Commission of 1889 gave a wider choice of Arts subjects. In part it was needed, for the teaching of modern languages had begun, and of such 'new' subjects as political economy. But the greater choice was not too well safeguarded, and the innovation opened too easy a road to 'soft options,' vocationalism, and ill-judged combinations of subjects. Science was made a separate faculty, conferring its own degrees. With this step to the modern went also a useful return to the mediaeval—that is, to a recognition of the students as members of the *Universitas*[1]: four Students' Representative Councils were set up, which could deal in the name of the whole student body with the Senatus and University Court.

An important innovation was that women, who had lately made their appearance in the class-rooms, were now to be admitted to degrees. It was not, however, till twenty years thereafter that Edinburgh consented to admit them to medical classes. In the other three, they received full membership, on equal terms with men: and in 1903 Aberdeen appointed a woman as a member of its junior teaching staff. Queen Margaret College for Women, founded in 1883 by Mrs Elder, became part of the University of Glasgow. Another new academic institution, University College, Dundee (founded in 1880), was joined with the University of St Andrews, becoming its Medical School and Department of Science.

The Carnegie Trust, founded in 1901 to administer a gigantic benefaction by the Scoto-American steel magnate of that name, did a good deal for staff and for scientific equipment, and gave valuable endowment of research. It also, by a scheme for the payment of class fees, made university education almost free, as far at least as tuition was concerned. Its benefits in this have been considered by those acquainted with its consequences to be offset by the fact that it encouraged the swamping of the university classes by large numbers of students unfitted to profit by them: its benefits and disadvantages are both still, possibly, matters for debate, though its value in aiding research work is undoubted.

Besides these formal changes, there was another, which at the

---

[1] It is perhaps characteristic of our country that Aberdeen is the one university in Europe which retains, though in a rather shadowy form, those once important officials the Procurators, elected by the students of each Nation; and that these elect the head of the supreme governing body, the University Court.

time took place almost unregarded, but which we now recognise as of great importance. This was the effect of the English public school. That much and hotly debated institution, in the modern sense of the term, at any rate, is a product of the mid-century reaction from the social standards of the Regency: we can date it from the year 1828, when Thomas Arnold, a man of scholarship and high character, began the task of regenerating Rugby.

The essential merits and defects of the system need not be discussed here: but three of its qualities had much to do with its effect on Scotland. Its great merit (and it is a very great one) is that it did succeed in inculcating a very strong sense of responsibility, or to use a shorter word, a sense of duty, as the essential obverse of privilege. Its great defect was a snobbery so naïve as to be merely innocent and amusing, were it not that some awkward consequences followed. And its predominant, in which faults and virtues were alike included, was that it was intensely national—that is to say, essentially of a nation whose mind, whose racial blend, and whose history are quite remarkably unlike our own.

The second, and least pleasing, of these three, needs a word of comment, for it was to matter. These schools were meant to train a governing class, and therefore made a very strong appeal to those upon the verge of such a class, who are always, from the uncertainty of their status, most likely to breed the snob. (He can only exist in groups where social status is uncertain.) There are few old families in England, and none of them large. 'Gentility' therefore consisted not in blood but in rank and behaviour: and behaviour, the more as England was very rich, included ownership. It was not so crude a thing as mere worship of wealth: but to be accepted as 'a gentleman,' a man had to do and possess a number of things that were all, as it happened, more or less expensive.

Now the transfer of the Government to England meant that those Scottish families whose tradition involved a share in it were forced to seek that in England. There they found a world of quite different social values, in which this one, of possession, was taken for granted: and as most of them were, by English standards, poor, and as English people were ready to seize excuse for contempt of a Scot, they suffered accordingly. (This had a good deal to do with the Clearances.) England had too, like all countries, her own conventions, the more rigid from her insular position, which oddly enough had affected her far more than our own greater distance from the Mainland of Europe had affected Scotland. Men of another tradition, other conventions, thus found themselves regarded, in the extremely significant English word, as 'outsiders.' Being Scots, they were sensitive, and adaptable: and the pressure to adapt themselves was severe. To win any part in the political game, or peace-time promotion in the Services, the adaptation was a *sine qua non*. Moreover, politics and the Services were alike, by fixed tradition, the preserve of a closely organised society. Careers depended on knowing the right people, and on being a person whom they would willingly know.

The upshot of these cumulative factors (there were others, but they are less relevant to this chapter) was in fine that Scottish boys of the 'gentle' class tended more and more to be caused by well-meaning parents to abandon the old national education, with its wide social contacts, its roots in the home,[1] and to be sent, at their most impressionable age, out of Scotland, to schools which would forward their future career. The results were far from happy, for them or for Scotland. In them the conflict between nature and nurture, going on below the surface of consciousness, had only too often a queer frustrating effect, decreasing their possibility of stature, and twisting their perception of the world. The fierce social pressure put on the foreigners (for children are merciless to the unfamiliar) forced in them too an anxious abandonment of those things which made them 'different'—that is, their Scotsness, which appeared to their minds as not Scots but merely wrong. In defence, they learned a snobbery more aggressive than that which the schools bred in their English pupils: and the strong sense of duty which is the schools' great merit, being (naturally and rightly in its place) a sense first and foremost of duty towards England, increased in them timidity over Scotland. They were bred to take for granted that England was right in all things from international relations to the absence of tea-bread or of the letter r; and that it was a violent solecism to mention what she was unwilling to consider—that is to say, to press any Scottish interest that did not strike her as pleasantly picturesque. They would wear the kilt, on the recognised occasions, whether the tartan was their birthright or not: but they would not force Parliament to take the trouble to discuss, for instance,

---

[1] The sending of children to be educated away from home is an English tradition much older than the modern public school: foreign observers remark on it in the early sixteenth century, as common to all classes.

trawling in Scottish waters. It was not done—in both senses of the phrase.[1]

Apparently there did arise, after a time, some sense of the danger, for public schools upon the English model—Loretto, Fettes, Merchiston, and Glenalmond—were founded in Scotland. Unluckily, to win equal recognition, they were forced (as girls' schools of the early Women's Movement had to be slavish copies of the boys') to be rather more English than the English ones. Looking over an old prospectus of her brother's, of a year at the end of this chapter's period, the writer observes that all masters on its staff were graduates of either Oxford or Cambridge.

The analysis of this factor in Scots education has been made here with a certain amount of detail, since the matter was of great practical importance, and its results are only now recognised. Not only did Scotland lose her 'officers' corps,' but England was presented with an excuse for the neglect of the Scottish point of view. It may be said that she did not require one: but though that was true of much of the century, the enemy of Scotland nowadays is less the Englishman, who is often her friend, than the Anglo-Scots Quisling, who is always her foe. Nor were politics, alas, the only sphere in which this alienation was to matter. The growing anglicisation of the gentry was copied by the wealthy middle class. It was not 'the thing' to go to a Scottish school, or even a Scottish university. Thus to the native system of education (which with all its faults was as good as any extant) there began to be attached a social stigma . . . with the result, of course, in the tougher-minded of making them dourly cling, in the name of Scotsness, to many things that really did need changing, thus producing an inverted snobbery which was no less harmful than snobbery direct.

And for final result of the whole pernicious system, those who should have been patrons of a native culture, those who by breeding, environment, and means possessed the needful leisure and breadth of outlook to make them effectual patrons of the arts, of the 'liberal'

[1] A Scot trained at an English public school fell foul of the author for having given the details of Edward III's dealings with Scotland, although without them the story of the reign of David II is not only incomplete but meaningless. He did not deny her facts, as indeed he could not (the less as the chief authorities for them were English), but he considered they ought to be suppressed, because Edward in England is a popular hero, and English historians commonly do suppress them. He saw nothing remarkable in this attitude . . . and he was no fool, but a man of unusual intelligence, with high (English) academic qualifications, and, what made the whole thing even more curious, with a perfectly sincere affection for Scotland.

elements in education—all these were turned away from such a function. The arts, as is often forgotten (save by artists), have an economic element involved, particularly pressing in small countries: but now there was no Lord Kames or Henry Erskine. So the national culture, the national education, passed into the hands of the lower middle-class, which in Scotland as elsewhere had real and substantial virtues, but in Scotland as elsewhere, and more than in most countries elsewhere, was an unsuitable guardian for many things without which a nation's spirit is in fetters.

XX

THE MIND OF SCOTLAND: II

EIGHTY-TWO YEARS: 1832–1914

Compulsory inclusion in a larger society of alien interests and laws
tends to mutilate—or at least to cramp—the spontaneous development
of social life.   L. T. HOBHOUSE, *Liberalism.*

FOR very long, there have been two sides to Scotland. On the one
is the Scotland of Knox and the Covenanters, on the other that of
the Jameses and Montrose: or if we are to take it in terms of culture,
on the one is the Scotland of the Metrical Psalms (Scots only by
adoption, to be sure, but at least by a congenial adoption), on the
other that of the Gaelic songs, the ballads, Gilbert Hay and Robert
Henryson and Dunbar. And at this time, when in all the countries
of Europe the machine which Scotland had loosed upon the world
was making its first attack upon the arts, those elements which were
most nearly related to the Scotland which made the ballads and the
songs were being siphoned, by emigrant ships or English schools,
from the general reservoir of the national life.

Those which were left had their virtues, and real virtues. For
certain important elements of a culture few but the wildest and
crudest of Covenanters ever lost a profound admiration and respect.[1]
That tradition remained: and in those elements no country, probably, has ever stood at a higher general and popular level than did
late eighteenth- and much of nineteenth-century Scotland. The
general public really could, and did, read widely and solidly, thought
about its reading, and talked about it—talked, very often, superbly.
It was interested in politics and science, philosophy, theology, not
as a pose, but as something often a good deal more like a passion:
and those who were not interested themselves considered it but
natural and right that their neighbours should be, and thought no
worse of them for it.

---

[1] It is true that in their triumph during the sixteen-forties there were
Covenanters who did decry ' human learning ': but Henderson and still more
Baillie were fine scholars. Melville, the real founder of their party, was counted
the greatest Hebraist in Europe, and Knox, who was Melville's spiritual father,
though not himself a man of notable learning, drew up the scheme for national
education which Archbishop Spottiswoode was to put in action.

But the interest was only in certain elements. Learning was honoured and sought, with high results. The creative arts, which in a healthy nation go hand in hand with that, were ignored or distrusted, to a degree that is unparalleled in a civilised country of native intelligence. And partly for this reason, partly for others (of which one was given a few pages back), more and more of those artists and even of those scholars who should have led Scotland's intellectual life were forced to join the unhappy diaspora which throughout that age bled the nation's vitality, while others were born of parents who had already been driven out by the 'epidemicall fury of emigration.' Many even ceased to consider themselves Scots, even to be so considered in their own country: and among them are men who were leaders in their age in their own province. To count these 'lost Scots,' from Ruskin to William MacDougall or Sir James Frazer, is enough to show clearly that the slums of Glasgow or the depopulated Highland glens were symptoms of a disease that went deep and wide, for countries do not drive out their ablest children save by some strange compulsion, and at their peril. They stone their prophets, as is but natural: but they rarely drive them into lifelong exile, and commonly they edify their tombs, and give them a proud if posthumous recognition.

To take the best, the already brilliant tradition of science and philosophy was retained, and even, in the former at least, enhanced. The notable Scottish triumphs in the 'applied' sciences of metallurgy, agriculture, and engineering have been discussed already, but should be recalled here: and there was added another to their number, with as great an effect upon the entire world as that of steam, and more purely beneficial. In Scotland was born modern surgery. As with all the very great discoveries, more than one nation shared in its foundations: but two of the four great pioneers were Scots, and a third an Englishman who worked in Scotland, while the final step which brought it to full being was taken by a Scot, in Scotland also. Sir James Young Simpson (1811-70) in the later 'forties made anaesthetics practicable in use. The French Louis Pasteur (1822-95) discovered the principles of bacterial growth, with immense effect not only on surgery but on medicine proper. The great English surgeon Joseph Lister, Lord Lister, working in Glasgow, began in 1860 the use of antisepsis in surgery: and it was his Scots successor Sir William MacEwen who passed on from antisepsis to asepsis, and demonstrated the scope of what was achieved by being the first man in human history to operate with success on the living brain. Even if we leave out this gigantic achievement, the record of Scottish medicine is superb, and no less varied than high in quality. Foremost perhaps are Sir Patrick Manson (1844-1922) and Sir Ronald Ross (1857-1932) who in the last years of the nineteenth century discovered the cause of those malarial fevers which have played so disastrous a part in history. Sir Patrick, in fact, may be called the real founder of the important science of tropical medicine, which has far-reaching political and economic repercussions: and Sir David Bruce also did valuable work there. There are, quite literally, dozens more—Sir Robert Muir, head in his day of British bacteriology, Professor C. H. Browning, hardly less brilliant, Sir James Mackenzie for work upon the heart, Sir Alexander Ogston in medical jurisprudence, Sir Robert Christison in toxicology, Sir Charles Bell in neurology, Sir James Mackenzie Davidson in radiology, Sir Arthur Keith in anatomy and anthropology, and a string of brilliant operative surgeons—Liston, Fergusson, Marnoch, and many more besides.

In science as a whole the achievement is little less great and quite as varied, from James Aitken's (1829-1919) work on meteorology to that of James Braid (1795-1850) and the 'lost Scot' William Mac-Dougall (1871-1938) in the mental sciences. The greatest achievements, probably, were in physics, for even if we leave out the towering figures of the Ulster Scot Lord Kelvin (1824-1907) and the New Zealand Scot Lord Rutherford (1871-1937), there are Balfour Stewart (1828-87), a founder of spectro-analysis, W. J. M. Rankine (1820-72) in thermodynamics, Sir William Ramsay (1852-1916), who won the Nobel prize for work which included the discovery of helium and neon, Sir David Brewster (1781-1868), one of the founders of the British Association, Sir James Dewar (1842-1923),[1] and perhaps greatest of all, Sir James Clerk Maxwell (1831-79), whose work (so Einstein was to say of it later) 'changed the whole axiomatic basis' of science. But there were others in other sciences—Sir Arthur Thomson (1861-1933), a most brilliant teacher of biology, Sir Patrick Geddes (1854-1932), again a biologist, who founded the modern science of town-planning, Sir Archibald Geikie (1835-1924), the geologist, who directed the survey of the United Kingdom, and another lost Scot, who bears like William MacDougall a Highland

---

[1] He earned much popular gratitude as the inventor of the ' thermos ' flask.

name—Sir James G. Frazer (1854-1941), the doyen of European ethnologists: and these are only the names at the very summit, for a great body of sound and excellent work, and of equally good teaching, was being done.

There are notable names still in philosophy, though none who stand out like Hume and Adam Smith. James Hutchison Stirling (1820-1909) by his work on Hegel 'begins a new era in British philosophy,' and another prominent Hegelian was the lost Scot J. M. E. McTaggart (1866-1925). Andrew Seth, later Pringle-Pattison, (1856-1931), was a stalwart critic of Hegelianism. Alexander Bain (1818-1903) was in his day the father of British logicians, and William Ritchie Sorley (1855-1935) did much to refashion the whole science of ethics, while John Scott Haldane (1860-1936) worked on the biological base of philosophy. Two who did work of merit are more widely known for their place in politics—one a Prime Minister, Arthur James, Earl of Balfour (1848-1930), and the other an outstanding War Secretary, Richard Burdon, Lord Haldane (1856-1928): and a third, though a philosopher by profession, ranks high in our political history—John Stuart Mill (1806-73), a lost Scot again, whom Continental critics still consider as the chief British philosopher of this age.

The group of historians acts as a kind of bridge between philosophy and creative letters. One indeed, the brilliant Thomas Babington, Lord Macaulay (1800-59), had a mind more creative than an historian's should be. Others did sounder if less spectacular work—George Finlay's (1799-1875) on the later history of Greece, Sir William Mitchell Ramsay's, of great importance, on that of the early Church, Sir George MacDonald's upon Roman Britain, Sir Archibald Alison's, early in the time, on European history at large, Sir James Ramsay of Bamff's on the English constitution. Those who worked on Scots history, with results of varied but sometimes of great merit, are in this age too numerous to list, but one must include three general histories of Scotland—the racy if prejudiced work of that delightful person John Hill Burton (1809-81), that of Andrew Lang (1844-1912), which though ill-arranged and lacking in proportion has some fine miscellaneous feeding in its by-ways,[1] and that of Peter Hume Brown (1850-1918), which perfectly reflects the middle-class Whig outlook of the time, and therefore was enormously

---

[1] Lang was much happier upon smaller subjects. His *Maid of France*, for example, is an excellent piece of good scholarship, well handled.

popular. The biographical tradition was well carried on by Archibald Philip Primrose, Earl of Rosebery and Prime Minister (1847-1929). One must mention George Grub's and John Cunningham's work on Church History, E. W. Robertson's and Alan Orr Anderson's on the early history of Scotland, E. M. Barron's splendidly thorough work on Bruce's War and W. C. Mackenzie's on the Highlands: but the list is so long that many men who did sound scholarly work, and others whose work was accepted as scholarly, must be passed by.

The most conspicuous, but by no means the most scholarly, of all, who wielded enormous influence in Europe, was less historian than philosopher—Thomas Carlyle (1795-1881), a strange, powerful, and smoky figure, from Knox's Scotland, with something of Knox's cold and sounding fire. He shows the first swing of what was to be strong reaction from *laisser faire* and from the values, good and bad alike, which had given motive-power to the French Revolution—the turn from liberty and equality to a cry for a strong man, for a Dictator, that later was to be answered, as we know. He believed, and preached, the exceedingly sound doctrine that no sort of human progress was possible not founded on veracity, nature, and God . . . and his great hero, whose many-volumed Life was his magnum opus, was a highly artificial atheist who was one of the finest liars of his age—Frederick of Prussia, commonly called 'the Great.' Indeed, he was a main force in popularising that strong infatuation with all things German which affected the intellectual life of Britain through the larger part of the Victorian Age: and his work was to be read, with great acceptance, in Italy of the early Fascist years and in Germany during the building time of Nazism.[1]

The Elisha to his Elijah, as British prophet, was John Ruskin (1819-1900), although his vehicle was not history but voluminous work, in a magnificent prose, on art criticism—a subject to which, however, he related most of the branches of human activity. He also was a Scot of the Dispersion, and at a further remove than was Carlyle, for he was actually born in England, and held himself, and was held, an Englishman. Like Carlyle, whose pupil in many ways

---

[1] His Germanism is rather amusingly shown in his *French Revolution*: it is a brilliant work which gives scope to his genius for huge smoky pictures, but one never feels one is reading about France. From Louis (who was in fact rather Teutonic) to Marat, every figure in it might be German. It is an odd perversion for a Scot: but the side of Scotland from which Carlyle derives always was rather hostile to the Auld Alliance. It is worth noting, by the way, that though he refused Disraeli's offer of a G.C.B. he was willing to accept the Prussian Order of Merit.

he was (though by no means a blind or uncritical follower) he fought against the doctrine of *laisser faire*, though he approached it from another angle, and with a clearer sight and better balance. Being Highland,[1] he had a vision of the world which had room in it for Mary as well as Martha, and which gave him access to much that his master lacked. Most of his vast bulk of work is direct art criticism, often perishable and at times pernicious,[2] but with a grip of the fundamental truth, then in great danger, that art was a branch of conduct and (in an age which regarded it in the main as the visible receipt for a lavish expense) a vital one to any nation's health. This point of view was to drive him in the end to a political economy based not on economic man but on man—a conception so shocking to the orthodox that when *Unto this Last*, which clearly expresses it, was serialised in the *Cornhill* in 1860, it frightened Thackeray, then the editor, into suppressing it after the first few chapters.

There were other notable critics who, if less prophetic, were often splendid scholars and great teachers: Andrew Lang again, Alexander Dyce (1798-1869), who worked on the early English dramatists, W. P. Ker (1855-1923), the finest scholar in Europe of his day in the literature of the Dark and Middle Ages, and William Archer (1856-1924), a notable London dramatic critic, who gave Ibsen to the English-speaking world, with a profound effect upon its drama. One must mention also as a great teacher of letters Sir Herbert Grierson, happily still with us, and such scholars as John Muir (1810-82) in Sanskrit, Sir Richard Jebb (1841-1905) in the classics, and the monumental work of Sir James Murray (1837-1915) and his successor Sir William Alexander Craigie, for English in the many-volumed *New English Dictionary*, begun at Oxford in 1879, and completed, so far as completion of such work is possible, in 1928.

There was, then, a great deal of brilliant science: there was a fair amount of fine scholarship, though the scientists and even more the scholars had a habit of passing into other countries which would have been wholesome enough had they returned, but which, in fact,

[1] The Ruskins are a small sept of Clan Buchanan, from Lochetiveside.
[2] His influence unluckily helped the disastrous passion for an artificial and antiquarian Gothic, which produced such dreadful results in architecture. If it sometimes achieved things of a real beauty, like the Scott Monument (and even that is incongruous with its setting), it caused, among other things, the destruction of the noble old buildings of Glasgow University, one of the finest Scottish Renaissance works, and their replacement by the mock-Gothic horror which now disfigures such a splendid site.

lost too many of them for good. In creative forms of literature, however, even counting several 'lost Scots' who did work of merit, the barrenness was marked, and was emphasised by the fact that England at the same time was passing through one of her greatest creative ages in letters.

This lack, in a country so intelligent, so prosperous, and with such a respect for learning, is hard at the first sight to understand. One cause would seem to be the draining away and (to adopt a hideous modern usage) the progressive 'de-Scotisation' of those classes to whom the tradition of the Jameses' Scotland would have been natural: and as its converse, the passing of the weight of social control, including the control of education, to one to whom the arts were worse than suspect. The *petit bourgeois*, by his habit of mind, is unsympathetic to them in most countries: and in ours just then he was also undergoing, thanks to the growing power of the Free Church, a strong revival of Calvinist religion. Now Calvin, as recent apologists point out, was not in theory hostile to the arts, any more than, in theory, Herr Hitler is. But Calvinism has been intensely hostile to all forms of art, as to all forms of religion, whose content cannot be expressed in words.[1] Now the content of creative literature—that is, of poetry, fiction, and the drama—is not so expressed. It is *conveyed*, in the long run, by words: but the words, immediately, convey no more than an image of some human activity, and it is by this image, not merely by the words, that the content reaches the percipient.[2] Now there are many types of experience, among them those of most deep and valuable emotional and spiritual quality, which cannot be caught in the coarse mesh of direct words. So a dread of the mythopoeic powers of the mind cuts man away from the food and discipline of the more subtle and profound experience that is necessary to his fullest stature.

Nor did this superstitious terror stand alone. The small bourgeois is often terrifically jealous (the adverb is used in its strictest literal sense) of any equal who dares to set himself up, to assert himself: and all art is, from one point of view, a self-assertion. He is also terrified of approving new things, unless they come to him backed by authority: and all art that is art has something new in it,

---

[1] Music is an exception : but music also, one observes, appeals to the ear.
[2] The distinction seems oddly difficult to grasp, but none the less it is vitally important. Our Lord's habit of teaching by ' parables '—that is, by stories about imaginary people in imaginary situations—as well as by direct statement, may illustrate the difference, though rather roughly.

and when newly born lacks authority from without. Now the artist is an acutely sensitive creature, since without that he has no power to be an artist: and all the pressure of social righteousness, of hostility and suspicion and resentment, and the economic pressure of lack of a public, drove against the sensitive skin of the Scottish Muse, and forced her to silence or a self-consciousness which is sheer poison to artistic creation. And the catalogue of creative letters, therefore, in that period is singularly bare, and contains no name that can rank as of major importance.

It is briefest in drama. Towards the end of the time Sir James Matthew Barrie (1860-1937) wrote many plays, for London, whose brilliant stagecraft is oddly marred and tainted by precisely this quality of self-consciousness and the sentimentality which plays nemesis in societies such as that which has just been described. As Mr E. E. Kellett has pointed out,

The master of all sentimentalists is Rousseau, born and brought up among harsh and matter-of-fact Calvinists, and wielding his influence mainly among a people distinguished, as a rule, by a remarkable combination of logic and practicality.

So Barrie, when he had acquired the authority of prestige won elsewhere, was adored at home, for his worse qualities rather than for his merits: and we may see the same phenomenon again in the attitude to Kailyard Fiction.

In poetry, in what now was well established as the general vehicle for literature, there was more: but little of it is of much importance. In the early part of the period, Macaulay, William Bell Scott (1811-90) and William Edmonstoune Aytoun (1813-65) wrote verse of the minor kinds but with high quality in them: the most truly Scottish thing Macaulay achieved was the *Lay of Horatius*, close cousin to Border ballad. They were succeeded by the unhappy James Thomson (1834-82) who wrote, among much that matters very little, one really great poem, *The City of Dreadful Night*. It is significant that in this prosperous time the high-water mark of Scottish creative letters should be reached by what is an image of despair.

John Davidson (1857-1909) was no happier in temper or in fortune, and a much lesser man in poetry. There are later names— the graceful minor verse (it is not his fault that it is hackneyed now) of Stevenson, the more important work of Lord Alfred Douglas (1870-   ) and Harold Monro (1879-1932)—lost Scots again, hardly to be counted here; or that of Dr Ronald Campbell Mac-

Fie, and the coloured sonnets of Rachel Annand Taylor—a belated Pre-Raphaelite, from one point of view, from another a pioneer in the return that a younger generation was to make to the Scotland of Dunbar and Hawthornden.

The major and most characteristic form of the age, in most countries, was the novel. This was true of Scotland—so far as our literature went. There are few writers, however, even at that, and their work is marred by hack-writing, by clumsiness, or by self-consciousness. With all the more notable figures one feels throughout that they rarely or never did justice to their own gifts. One must mention Margaret Oliphant Wilson or Oliphant (1828-97), who was compelled by economic pressure to bury the exquisite things that she could write beneath a huge cairn of hurried pot-boilers: and the curious marred genius of George Macdonald (1824-1905), whose chief work belongs to the 'sixties and 'seventies. Had he but taken the novel as a form which demanded discipline and integrity, he might well have done work which could stand by Walter Scott's. (Scott's fiction was also a gallop of improvisation, but not for nothing was he trained as a lawyer.) He suffers from shocking construction, conventional plots, and at times from an oppressive didacticism: but he was, truly, a poet and a mystic, with a deep and fervent personal religion that was based on the Gospels, not upon John Calvin,[1] and a rich humanity and dramatic power which are backed by a gift of superb Scots dialogue and create a world which, even when pasteboard thrusts in among flesh and blood, has a solid three-dimensional quality. He is forgotten now: but some of his work would well bear a revival.

R. L. Stevenson (1850-94) shows a difference so great as to make their juxtaposition almost comic. Macdonald's great fault was lack of craftsmanship: one could almost say Stevenson's was too much of it. He combines in a curious way the Cavalier Scotland with the Scotland of the Shorter Catechism: but since he lived and was bred in the latter Scotland he was forced to a self-defensive self-consciousness that gives all but his best work a brittle quality. He shares with Macdonald a fantastic realism and a strong sense of ethics—a very Scots combination: but in his case it was braced by a sense of form. Unluckily for his present-day repute, the facts that he made a reputation elsewhere, that his work was very genuinely Scottish, and that he was a 'romantic' personage made him a fashion among the

[1] He was a Congregationalist minister.

15

sentimental: he became the hero of a sugared cult from which, since the cult was no fault of his own, the modern reaction has been uncritical, the more as critics still tend to overlook the real and enormous service he was to render to the technique of fiction here and in England. He was probably just coming to his feet and reaching his full power when he died, far from home.

His pupil Neil Munro suffered even more from the poisonous influence of self-consciousness, and was less its master. Thus his journalism (he was a most delightful journalist) is better as writing than all save the last of his novels. These had more to them than had Stevenson's, and showed a deep understanding of the Highlands that makes one profoundly regret his technical failure. A finer artist was R. B. Cunninghame Graham (1852-1936), who was, among very many other things, a master of the short story. That again was the form used by Hector Hugh Munro ('Saki') (1870-1916), but his brilliant and sardonic quality shows in work that, apart from the firm clear line of the drawing, is almost wholly anglicised: and there is even less trace of a Scottish descent in the early work of Mr Compton Mackenzie (1883-   ) which in the last years of the period achieved a good deal of success, in London.

There was also a good deal of highly popular work which came to be described as Kailyard Fiction. It is very much the equivalent, in the novel, of the long-familiar genre-verse in Scots, and there is no inherent reason, at least, why it should not have been as good as the best of that, or as Mucklebackit or Meg Merrilees. From the start, however, it was prostituted to the sugared and lachrymose sentimentalism which is the very natural reaction, in a community of strong emotions, to the lack of any healthy outlet for them or of their discipline by an art which can hold them.[1] Sir James Barrie, in his early days, was a leader, but the chief criminal was Ian Maclaren (1850-1907), in the 'nineties. The school produced, very soon, a violent reaction in the single novel of George Douglas Brown (1869-1902), *The House with the Green Shutters* (1901), which very precisely inverts the Kailyard convention in dealing with the same class of subject-matter. In its essence it was quite as sentimental, but those scunnered by Ian Maclaren welcomed it, and it tuned too with the fashion for 'realism' that was sweeping London. It was to have many successors later on: in fact most young novelists of the next

[1] Cf. the way in which the cult of 'sensibility' grew out of what boasted itself as the Age of Reason, or Mr Kellett's remark on Rousseau, just quoted.

generation, when literature was coming to wake again, seemed to feel
it incumbent on them to begin by re-writing it with a local application; and a number of them, having done so, stopped.

In Scots itself, there was very little that counted. The tradition
of the courtly poets was lost. That of genre-verse remained, at times
as a pleasant, accomplished 'little art,' more often as a mixture of
Burns and *eau sucrée* that would have made Burns, sentimental as
he could be, break into language far from suitable to a decorous
Victorian Nicht wi' Burns. One may cite J. Logie Robertson,
Charles Murray, and the joyous extravaganzas of Dr Rorie: and
learned professors still played at the game of turning Horace and
Theocritus into Scots, at times with a marked felicity. The Burns-
cult which linked itself with the tradition is a very odd affair, some
of whose aspects have come in, deservedly, for much damnation:
but it was often a good deal less of a pose than the superior tone of
some of its critics. Burns's worst work—the Saturday Cottar for
instance—had at least the effect of opening him a road through the
inhibitions of the respectable. He was permitted, even to the pious,
being safely dead: indeed, he became a sort of national flag for
those who misliked the growing anglicisation. It was bad for literary
appreciation: but one feels that on the whole it would please his
ghost, even at cost of certain Burns-Nicht speeches.

Gaelic was perishing, apparently. There is a fierce unhappy
nationalism in the poems of William Livingstone (1808-70), and a
sense of revolt in the nature and love-poetry of Evan MacColl (1808-
1878). There were still singers such as John MacLachlan, James
Munro, Dugald Macphail, Angus Macdonald, and Mary Cameron
or Mackellar: but for most of the time they sang against the wind.
There was indeed an interest in things Highland—scholarly, as in
Donald Gregory's *History of the West Highlands* (1836), W. F.
Skene's *Celtic Scotland* (1876-80), and a good deal more in a continuous series to the early work of Mr W. C. Mackenzie: or arti-
ficial and self-consciously 'arty,' as in the perpetrations of 'Fiona
Macleod,' who was actually a Paisley man, William Sharp.

Pro-Gaelic forces were less immediate in Gaeldom than the
impact of the Free Kirk. It came rather late: until the 'seventies,
the Highlands were still rich in song and tale, and many men and
women at the *ceilidh* could go on for nights on end without repetition.
The ministers, however, disapproved: and in 1899 Alexander Carmichael, the saviour of many treasures of old Gaelic verse, could

describe in his *Carmina Gadelica* how he asked a kind hospitable Lewis wife,

And have you no music, no singing, no dancing, now at your marriages?

to which she ('no sour sort') replied,

May the Possessor keep you! You are a stranger in Lewis, or you would not ask. It is long since we abandoned these foolish ways. In my young days, there was hardly a house in Ness where there was not one or two or three who could play the pipes or the fiddle. . . . A blessed change came over the place. . . . The good men and the ministers who arose did away with the songs and the stories, the music and the dancing. . . . They made the people break and burn their pipes and fiddles.

And though Carmichael observed, not without point, 'Perhaps were the ministers to allow them less drink and more music, they would enjoy it better,' the good soul was horrified at the idea: and even today there are many of her mind, and more who secretly share it but dare not show it.

The Education Department was in time induced to allow the teaching of Gaelic in schools, and even a Gaelic Leaving Certificate paper: but the mischief had been done in the generation when girls in Islay, girls fourteen years old, had been tawsed till their hands bled for singing Gaelic songs *after* their school-hours—the years that trained the shepherd Carmichael tells of, who came fifty miles to give him a story he wanted, and when the Sheriff called in the middle of it, fled at once, leaving behind him his staff and bonnet.

Music was frowned on less than the other arts, even secular music—if it was not Gaelic. The keen interest in psalmody has already been mentioned, and the beauty of many fine tunes composed in this time. There was a general enjoyment of music, and it still was common for people to make their own, though in bourgeois circles Scots songs and still more Gaelic were apt to be considered ungenteel: *Fhir a bhata* and *The Bonny Earl of Moray* gave way to *The Maiden's Prayer* and *Asleep on the Deep*. Glasgow, to whom cultural pre-eminence was passing from Edinburgh, formed in 1893 the Scottish Orchestra, which won deserved repute. Two Scottish composers, Sir Alexander Mackenzie (1847-1935) and Hamish MacCunn (1868-1916), did not share the genteel aversion from native music, and created work definitely based on a Scots tradition: and Marjorie Kennedy Fraser, her sister and daughter, did extensive work in collecting no more than the remnants of Gaelic song. The English translations she attached to them were unluckily of a dreadful soulfulness, and the settings of some were unduly elaborate: but her work was none the less invaluable.

It is perhaps odd that the art which flourished most was that of painting—or is it so odd? A painter depends for his sale on one purchaser, while an author needs thousands if he is to make a living. Painting suffers from no language barriers . . . and a painter also can live, without detriment, in the society of his own kind only, a proceeding which is fatal to the writer. Also, while novels were shocking to the godly, a picture was part of the furniture of a house. Not to have pictures confessed to poverty, which was the next thing to immorality: and though no doubt the real popular liking was for pictures which told a sentimental story, snobbery here played a very useful part, for men who made reputations furth of Scotland could sell their work at home for adequate prices.

The early years of the age have few names of note. The genre-painting of Sir David Wilkie (1785-1841) was popular, and not without its merit, and now that the terror of 'subject' in pictures is passing his reputation begins to revive again. There was also some vigour in John Phillip 'of Spain' (1817-67), if less in a shoal of very popular painters of 'historical' pieces. The work of Sir William Quiller Orchardson (1832-1910) carries on the spirit of old New Edinburgh in its sense of pattern, whose slightly sardonic grace belongs to that side of Scotland which touches France.

The landscape painters were headed in the earlier years by John Thomson (1778-1840), John Wilson (1774-1855), William Simson (1800-47), and David Roberts (1796-1864), who all won considerable fame abroad. They went on through the stereotyped Highlands of Horatio McCulloch (1805-67) and the vigorous work of Sam Bough (1822-78): and the influence of the French Impressionists shows in J. C. Wintour (1825-82) and the gentle sentiment of John Mac-Whirter (1839-1911).

Glasgow, between the founding of the Glasgow Institute in 1861 and that of the Society of Scottish Artists thirty years later, developed a very notable school of painters, who though their work shows the influence of France and Holland and later of Japan, have also a strong native quality. The leading men were famous far beyond Scotland, and their fame attracted foreigners to Glasgow, such as Crawhall and Sir John Lavery. Their pioneers were G. P. Chalmers (1833-78) and William McTaggart (1835-1910), whose work parallels that of the French Impressionists, though it does not seem to have derived from them. Later came W. Y. Macgregor (1855-1923), Sir David Young Cameron (1865-   ), Sir James Guthrie (1859-1930), whose best work, like that of Sir Muirhead Bone, was in etching, and the fine decorative painting of E. A. Hornel (1864-1933) and of George Henry. By the late 'eighties the movement was vigorous, and could even maintain, for some years, the brilliant *Scottish Art Review*: and the characteristic union of realism with clear pattern and a brilliancy of colour suggest very strongly the poetic technique of the late-mediaeval makaris, such as Dunbar.

The school faded out as its members drifted away from their own country. There were left, however, the Celtic inspiration of John Duncan, and the early work of the post-impressionists S. J. Peploe (1871-1935), Leslie Hunter (1879-1936) and F.C. B. Cadell (1883-1937).

In sculpture, though Thomas Campbell in his day (1790-1858) was famous and fashionable, there is little to count save the vigorous work of Pittendrigh MacGillivray (1856-1938). In architecture there is a sad declension, though no worse in Scotland than in most of Europe—save that Scotland had more than most, just then, to decline from. She even sank to shame of her own glories, though it was an English *Encyclopaedia of Architecture* which remarked with horror, in 1888, 'it is a fact that the depraved compositions of Robert Adam were not only tolerated but had their admirers.' (In that year the North British Station Hotel was building at the end of Princes Street.) The Romantic Revival had caused everywhere a strong reaction from classical to Gothic. There is no valid reason why such reaction should have made for bad building, any more than the earlier one from Gothic to classical, which had produced great masses of beautiful work. Unluckily, its chief prophet was John Ruskin, who 'wanting all the cathedral but the altar,' played into the hands of the careful antiquaries, who killed Gothic safely and comfortably dead.

A keen interest in older Scottish work, which might have been extremely stimulating, was roused by *The Baronial and Ecclesiastical Antiquities of Scotland*, by the Englishman R. W. Billings, which began to appear in 1845, and by the later work of David MacGibbon and Thomas Ross in the ten years after 1887: but instead of stimulating a living tradition, they bred some horrible 'Scots Baronial,' exemplified, though not at its worst, in Balmoral. Architecture, in fact, ceased to be building, and came instead to be something applied to building—at times, indeed, as anyone who has worked in Marshall Mackenzie's Marischal College knows, to be something that greatly interfered with building. As an American writer has lately put it, 'architects constructed their ornament instead of ornamenting their structure.' The most prominent names are those of David Bryce (1803-76), Sir Rowand Anderson (1834-1921)—who did, however, achieve the beautiful dome which crowns Adam's university buildings in Edinburgh—and Marshall Mackenzie (1848-1933). Later on Sir Robert Lorimer (1864-1929) began not merely to copy the older work, as in his Thistle Chapel (which he made, however, a beautiful thing in its way) but to seek to develop from it a living tradition, recognisably kin to the old, but frankly new and definitely Scottish. Sir Robert's work varies, for there was much to get rid of: but he pointed the way to a return to health. Standing apart from all, and almost unregarded in his own country, though he was to win a European fame, was Charles Rennie Mackintosh (1868-1928), the 'member for architecture' of the Glasgow School, and the founder of modern functionalist building . . . which he based on the principles of old Scottish work. And one should add a note on Douglas Strachan, not as an architect, but as the man who recovered for the world the lost secrets of the mediaeval glass, and used them with a strong sense of design.

Taking it in the broadest sense of the word, Scots culture in the despised Victorian Age has not so bad a record—for a small country, and from one point of view. But that strange lack of a living literature was profoundly and painfully significant, as significant as the steady draining abroad of nearly all the men whose work counted in art, and of too many scholars and scientists. It comes back to this, that for all the elaborate educational structure, there was only a tiny public for native arts: and that is an ill thing to say of any country. It is not a thing that should be true of Scotland. If one thing more than another is marked in our past it is, in all classes and in all sides of living, the union of strong life and strong restraint, and of these with a sharp-edged clarity of perception: and these things are the very basis of art. Now, in at least that large part of the nation which determined the predominant texture of living and had most of the training of Scottish youth in its hands, they were stifled by a timid dowdiness—poison to any nation, and most to ours, in whom timidity and dowdiness are neither of them among our natural vices.

XXI

HOME POLITICS: I—THE FRAMEWORK

EIGHTY-TWO YEARS: 1832–1914

All government is difficult, and government by democracy is most difficult of all. Democracy throws a far greater strain than any other form of government on the intelligence, the loyalty, and the self-sacrifice of the people. Sir ALEXANDER MACEWEN, *Towards Freedom.*

IT has long been a commonplace that the dominant feature of British home politics during the nineteenth century is the gradual extension of the franchise. This is true enough, although the consequences which followed, or failed to follow, on the extension are not always grasped in their relation to Scotland. Nor was this the only change in the machine, for the time saw a weakening in the power of the Lords, the emergence in politics of a third party, and a considerable discontent with the apparatus of Scottish government. Alongside these went a number of varied movements whose general and common purpose was to cope with the social results of industrialisation. There are also two other points worth noticing, though neither was recognised by any new law. One, which affected England more than Scotland, was the change in status of the monarchy: and the other, which affected Scotland profoundly, was her virtual disappearance as a nation.

All these varied factors in the political whole consisted of long and elaborate chains of process which had better be unravelled separately. Let us therefore take first the changes in the machine, in what we may call the frame of politics, and leave their 'content' to deal with in later chapters, including those elements which are not less important because they took the form of vacancies.

The change in the position of the sovereign scarcely touched Scotland till after 1918, and even yet has not deeply affected her: but it was in its essence a return to something which Scotland possessed for centuries, and which England, save for the later reign of Elizabeth, had lost since the death of Edward the Confessor—a sense of the Sovereign as standing for the nation.

Even in Scotland, it had been lost for long. For practical purposes, it may be said to have died with James VI, in 1625. Montrose attempted to recover it, but the material which he had to work on was intractable, and he failed: and though neither of the two sons of Charles I ever quite forgot that he was King of Scots, their small first-hand experience of the country did not greatly endear it, especially to the abler. Later, desire to recover a true Scots kingship was the most living force in the Jacobite effort: but that failed, as Montrose's had done. And it failed too for a very similar reason, that the link between Scotland and the Crown was broken.

Through the Whig domination which succeeded it, it had been a cardinal point in politics that the sovereign and the nation were somehow opposed: and a string of very foreign sovereigns, whose first concern was Holland or Hanover, with England next and no interest in a kingdom in which none of them had ever set his foot, was unlikely to change this. Bute, after 1760, did try to create a 'universall king' of Britain—and failed once more. By 1800, the monarchy was not only negligible, but almost equally contemptible, with

> An old, mad, blind, despised, decaying King,
> Princes, the dregs of their dull race,

and at open, violent, and scandalous odds with each other. 1820 brought the Crown's prestige to its nadir, with the Queen in a trial for adultery which dishonoured her rather less than it did the King, against whom feeling was roused to such a pitch that a gunboat had to be stationed on the Thames to overawe the populace of London. The debts of the Princes were no less a by-word: when the heir to the Throne died in 1827, his creditors got a shilling in the pound. The funeral of George IV in 1830 had been 'a jubilee.' William III was certainly less unpopular: but the mild liking which his subjects gave him was mixed with a genial contempt for 'Silly Billy.'

William died, childless, in 1837, and the throne went to his niece, a girl of eighteen. She was young, pretty, and virtuous, for a change. Her subjects met her with cynical compassion, coupled with prophecies that within a decade Queen Victoria would be Miss Guelph, in a republic. There was even scandal, wholly undeserved, about her relations with her Prime Minister, Lord Melbourne: as she drove to Ascot in 1839 she was greeted with loud shouts of 'Mrs Melbourne.'

She was twenty then. When she died at eighty-two, after the longest reign in our history, she had made the monarchy the best-based in Europe, and given it more real power than since 1603. There had been no formal constitutional change. She never sought to be Prime Minister: but she did become, not in form but in solid fact, the doyenne of a force very powerful in politics, the permanent Civil Service, which holding its office while Governments come and go, continues quietly its experienced work. And she made that headship into a leadership which, in England at all events, recovered something of the old place of the Sovereign as the Chief, embodying the idea of the nation because one with it, its servant and its head.[1]

She was, like her predecessors, German in blood: but she followed less the Guelph strain of her colourless father than the High-German Wettin of her mother: and she married in turn into her mother's house, giving the dynasty which succeeded her the blood of the very able House of Saxe-Coburg. The effect of the match was not only in the heredity of its children, for much of what Victoria achieved was due to her cousin, Albert of Saxe-Coburg-Gotha, whom she married, for reasons of state, in 1840, and loved deeply and devotedly to her death. His surface faults, of excessive solemnity, of shyness in a most difficult position, caused his fine qualities—his honesty, clear vision, and sense of duty, and his wise if in some ways limited statesmanship—to be undervalued, even long after his death: but he did a work for the country and the Crown which is only now being assessed at its just merits.

The Queen's popularity sank very low in the 'sixties, in her retirement after her widowhood: indeed, there was even fresh talk of a republic. As the new sense of the Empire grew, however, the small black figure of 'the Widow at Windsor' came to incarnate the national idea, not only at home but in faraway dominions: and almost unconsciously the foundations were laid of the conception of a group of free nations, bound in free union by a common Crown, that was to be made explicit after her death, and in less than forty years after her death to save at least the principle of freedom . . . although, at the time when these sentences were written, the kingdom whose Parliament had in 1607 drawn up a wise and generous scheme for such union is still the one nation in the British Empire to which that conception has not been applied.

---

[1] In the present year, it may be as well to remind the foreign reader that though the *word* 'Chief' may recall 'Führer' or 'Duce,' the complex of ideas which underlies it differs considerably, and in essentials.

Though she sent her second son to Edinburgh University, gave him the title of Duke of Edinburgh, and revived for her fourth the old royal duchy of Albany, Victoria had small contact with the Scots nation. In spite of her pride in her Stewart ancestry and her passion for tartan (which she even extended to the Balmoral oilcloth) the side that we have called 'the Stewart Scotland' would have shocked her anywhere except on paper. She and the Whigs of the middle class, however, could understand each other. She was, indeed, the Queen of the Middle Class, and they loved her for both her virtues and her defects. In her turn, she had a real affection for Scotland: but it is highly significant, and of much, that to her it was essentially a place where the Sovereign was free of her people and off duty. It was not a nation but a relaxation.[1]

It was hardly even that to her son Edward, who succeeded to her throne in 1901, and following the precedent set by his great-uncle William, was proclaimed in Edinburgh as Edward VII. He was an admirable King of England, and under the mask of a cheerful *bon viveur* was a statesman whose influence on the Continent had a broad and very valuable effect: but though he was liked for his charm and his kindly temper, and the graciousness of his lovely Danish Queen, the quality of his contact with this kingdom was only too well expressed by that numeral VII.

With his son George V came a dawning recognition that the United Kingdom united kingdoms: and since both circumstance and his character brought him, even more than Victoria had done, to represent the Sovereign as the Chief, the position of the Crown began to acquire once more a certain national importance. The change shows more in his later reign, however, and as he came to the throne in 1910, it may better be described in a later chapter.

To the age itself, the main change in the political machine was the continuous broadening of the franchise. It had undoubtedly been made quite clear that if any class or interest lacked the vote, its political and its economic position was, to say the least of it, precarious. And to many people it seemed self-evident also that

---

[1] None the less, her reign saw a return to ancient custom which in time should give us a Sovereign partly Scottish. Queen Victoria allowed both her own daughter and one of the future King Edward's to break the cast-iron rule of the House of Hanover and marry subjects : and in both cases the Princesses' bridegrooms were Scots . . . and the junior one, unlike most of his rank by then, an avowed Nationalist.

the vote was identical with political power, and that, if the people should elect their rulers, they would always appoint those best fitted to guide their affairs.

We know now that it was not quite so simple. Even in England, a town of size and substance may be forced to choose between 'representatives' who have neither of them seen it in their lives until they came to make their election speeches, and who stand respectively for rival programmes which have nothing to do with its most vital needs. In Scotland, when every Scottish adult votes, the representatives those votes appoint may give to the country's urgent and vital problems no more than sixteen hours in the course of a year. None the less, it seems that such things have to be discovered, and that those who think of politics à priori may take some time to make the discovery.

Yet the franchise had its very real importance. A man does not travel far on a sparking-plug, but neither can he go far and fast without one: and the fact that the vote was treated as a fetish must not lure us to what looks indeed in our time to be the mistake that supersedes our fathers', that of treating it as something quite unimportant.

1832 still identified votes with control. And it was very clear that the new Reform Act had merely shifted that control, in the main, from the land-owner's hands to those of the mill-owner, which to the hard-pressed Glasgow working man appeared to be merely a change from King Log to King Stork. The Whig Party, however, were well enough satisfied. They sneered at votes for 'the dregs of the populace,' declared against shortened parliaments and the ballot, denounced the working men's Political Unions as inconsistent with good government, and purred gently over their own accession of strength from the new votes of the class most inclined to support them.

The Political Unions, at the first election, decided to make the best of the situation, preparing 'pledges' for the candidates. Would the candidate, if elected, resign his seat if he were hostile to a measure desired by a majority in his constituency? Did he favour free trade, burgh reform, the ballot, limitation of the working hours for children, abolition of Corn Laws, of patronage in the Church? Would he vote against slavery in the Colonies and the further alienation of Crown Lands?

The programme reveals a good deal of practical grasp, for al

these questions were of immediate importance. None the less, most
Whig candidates refused to answer, and unrest increased, especially
in Glasgow, where a gallant attempt by John Maxwell of Pollok to
get something done for the masses of unemployed had just been
defeated by the Government.

There followed some extremely stormy years, in the midst of
which the new young Queen acceded. By the November of 1834,
popular feeling was blazing once again, and the *Liberty or Death*
banner was raised over twenty thousand people on Glasgow Green.
At the new year, with a general election pending, Lord Cockburn,
a man of sense and experience, was writing 'Everything, not ex-
cepting the monarchy, is in danger.'

The election brought back the Whigs once more to power, re-
christened now by the new, more attractive, name of Liberals: and
there was another huge meeting on Glasgow Green, to listen to the
Irishman Dan O'Connell, to the Reverend Patrick Brewster of
Paisley Abbey, and to George Mills, son of the Lord Provost, who
were hotly demanding 'radical reform.' The phrase made a slogan.
By the end of the next year (1836) the old two-party system had
been challenged: a new party, called the Radicals, was emerging,
in direct opposition to both Whigs and Tories. An Ayr naval
surgeon with a lively career—Dr John Taylor, known as Radical
Jack—John Fraser of Johnstone, Alexander Campbell, and the
eloquent Irish lawyer Feargus O'Connor, formed a National Radical
Association, which declared a boycott of Whig and Tory shops.
The movement spread: in May 1838, when another huge meeting
was held on Glasgow Green, nearly all work in the city was stopped
for it, and representatives of seventy Unions took their places
formally in a great procession.

A similar movement was going on in England. The claims of
both were being clarified by now, and in that year the London
Working Men's Association reduced them to six points—universal
suffrage, annual parliaments, vote by ballot, payment of members,
equal voting districts, and abolition of the property qualification for
members of Parliament. This last point did not concern the Scots
Radicals, but they agreed to support it for England and Wales, and
accepted the Six Points, now called collectively the People's Charter.

The movement by now was widespread and popular, with all the
fervour of a new religion: indeed, there were 'Chartist Churches,'
where lay-preachers discussed with vigour its religious aspects, shock-

ing the more conservative of the godly. 'Hustings candidates' were put forward at elections, who addressed the people but did not go to poll. Shops were boycotted, and Chartist shops were opened. Runs on banks were organised, newspapers were printed, and choirs walked in procession singing the Ninety-fourth Psalm—

> Thy folk they break in pieces, Lord,
> Thine heritage oppress :
> The widow they and stranger slay,
> And kill the fatherless—

producing a problem for the authorities, who could hardly arrest men for singing the Psalms of David in the version officially used by the State church.

The Chartists, in fact, were now in an extremely strong position but the standing weakness of all Scots popular movements very soon set in. In courage, devotion, and intelligence the individuals of their rank and file reach a level no country in Europe can surpass: but we lack the gift of effective common action. There was no one with a clear authority to keep the movement to its central purpose. Instead of concentrating on the Charter, and subordinating all lesser points of difference until that was gained, the Chartists began to split on all sorts of issues, whose variety had no quality in common save irrelevance to Chartism as such. There was 'temperance,' urged with the intemperance characteristic of that well-meaning movement. There was Irish Home Rule. There were Morrison's Patent Pills. Soon the Chartist papers were wasting time, space, and hardly gathered money in virulent abuse one of another, while across all the fissures ran a major split, on the question of the use of physical force. John Duncan and Radical Jack preached red revolution, and the expression of the Charter's demands 'in characters of blood with a pen of steel'; while the New Light Radicals, headed by Dr Brewster and John Fraser, editor of *The True Scotsman*, were strong in deprecation of armed revolt. And besides these there was also a third party, who agreed with Abram Duncan, that the threat of arms was a very useful weapon but that it must not go beyond the threat: 'we must shake our opponents over Hell's mouth, but we must not let them drop in.'

The Government had no desire to drop in, and attempted repression, imprisoning some of the English Chartist leaders. Had they done it sooner, it might well have precipitated revolution. As it was, the movement was losing its unity, and correspondingly its momentum also, while the new agitation for the repeal of the Corn Laws seemed to many Chartists a more immediate issue than the distant prospect opened by a vote. The Chartist leaders denounced it as a red herring, but they were already too disunited themselves to re-impose unity on their followers: and the growing 'Nine Years Conflict' in the Church was opening another split across all the rest. By 1840 Chartism had died down.

The potato famine of 1845 brought acute distress, and closed the ranks again. An interest in the Charter revived once more. The Government were in an awkward position, for now the Whig Prime Minister, Lord John Russell, could not depend on a working majority, and a wave of fierce unrest was sweeping Europe, to culminate, in 1848, in a series of violent revolutions, in Bohemia, Hungary, Prussia, Bavaria, France. There were threats of a similar outbreak nearer home, where the Edinburgh mob were smashing windows and stoning the dragoons sent out to check them; and in Glasgow processions armed with torn-down railings and sporting guns looted from shops were on the march, shouting the slogan of *Bread or Revolution*, and cavalry were charging them down the High Street . . . and these things might well be the foam on a scalding pot, for a petition with five million names was declared to be on its way to the House of Commons, supported by overwhelming masses of people who were marching to London from all parts of Britain, to meet at a rendezvous on Kennington Common.

Respectable London shivered behind its shutters and wondered if the soldiers in Hyde Park could be trusted. The British climate obliged instead. It rained in torrents. The Avenging People sought beer and a decent fire in the nearest pub. The Petition arrived unimpressively in a cab, and on being examined turned out to have but two-fifths of the boasted names, among them being those of such well-known and fervent Chartists as the Queen, the Prime Minister, and the Iron Duke, and many more a good deal less polite.

The tense situation dissolved in ribald mirth, behind which came quieter voices pointing out the shocking behaviour of those dreadful French and the fact that many of the Glasgow Chartists were Irish and still more dreadful Roman Catholics. At the same time the urgent distress of the famine years was passing: and the Liberal Party, very tactfully, put forward a fresh and respectable alternative to Chartism—a group of newly formed Liberal 'People's Leagues,' whose purpose was the Charter softened down by 'such alterations and amendments in detail as shall appear necessary.' Those who loved to hear their own voices licked their lips at such noble scope for further and complex fission. There was a landslide from the original movement. The menacing red cloud of revolution which had hung on the Canongate and Glasgow Green dissolved, and the middle-class voters were glad to forget it. Indeed, they forgot it with such heartiness that Hume Brown, in a *History of Scotland* which perfectly expressed their point of view, dismisses the movement in six and a quarter lines (just after he has devoted thirty-one to one of five acts making easier the breach of entails), and adds that it was in 1856 that 'agitation for Parliamentary Reform *first* assumed a definite form in Scotland.' The italics in the quotation are not his.

In fact, most points of the Charter were won in time, though no Chartist lived to see more than two of them. The property qualification for English members was abolished so early as 1858. The ballot came in 1872, and the payment of members and shortening of Parliaments together, but not till twenty-nine years later; and universal suffrage came last of all, well after the nineteenth century was closed. And none of them brought the lift down to smoor the laverocks. Nor do they seem to have caused the Millennium either.

Though the storms calmed, agitation for a wider franchise continued—vaguely and vainly for a while, since each of the major parties took up 'Reform,' wherefore each in turn denounced it as betrayal of the true and real interests of the country. In sixteen years, five different Governments and seven Queen's Speeches promised a new Reform Bill. Liberal and Tory Governments produced them, and as regularly failed to get them passed.

In Scotland the middle 'fifties brought a new movement—an interesting attempt by Duncan M'Laren, an Edinburgh merchant, and the Rev. Dr Begg of the Free Church to form a new class of small landowners with votes, like the English forty-shilling freeholders, who by this time had a good deal of voting power in the English rural constituencies. They also pointed out some discrepancies of electoral power in Scotland and in England. In England, sixty burghs with a joint population of 392,278 had 22,548 voters and 94 members. In Scotland, sixty-nine, with 329,343 people had a little under 15,000 voters, and 84 members. They had some support: but the still powerful Convention of Royal Burghs considered that its privilege was threatened, and its opposition brought the movement to nothing.

In the later 'sixties, however, Reform looked up. In 1866 Gladstone proposed a bill which (as he was very careful to point out) would leave political power with the middle class. Its provisions were a £7 burgh franchise, a £14 county, and a £10 lodger's. It failed, and his government came down with it. Disraeli, succeeding him at the head of the Tories, brought in next year a wider one for England, and this time succeeded in passing it into law. One for Scotland followed in 1868, giving the vote to all householders who paid the burgh rates, to lodgers in burghs, and in the rural districts to £5 owners and £14 tenants, while seven seats were added, making sixty, which included two for the four universities.

The Scots Liberal Press were shocked by such careless extension. The Radicals, however, were pleased by it, seeing a chance to send up to Parliament men who could speak at first hand for the labouring class. The opportunity was missed, however. Only one Radical candidate was put forward—Alexander MacDonald, leader of the Scots miners: and he failed to win a seat. The heckling, however, showed intelligent interest in the conditions of labour and such matters as government inspection of sea-going ships.

The Radical movement was mainly of the towns, and the 1868 Act satisfied it. Its members now turned in the main to the Liberal Party, in spite of the fact that these had opposed the bill. Thereafter, till almost the end of the century, the dominant of Scottish politics was the influence of William Ewart Gladstone (1809-98), an Anglo-Scot who in spite of Right-wing Episcopal religion was the idol (the word is hardly a metaphor) of the majority of Scottish voters. The 'Tory Radical,' Benjamin Disraeli, who was the leader of the opposite party, was a Jew, and though his personality was in fact no more flamboyant than was Gladstone's, it seemed to the douce Presbyterian middle class not only alien but scandalous: and he had a disconcerting sense of humour. Gladstone's superb head, like an Old Testament prophet, went with a gift of flaming rhetoric supported by a moral earnestness (especially in the concerns of other nations) that deeply appealed to the spirit of the time: and the general temper of the Liberal Party was fashioned by the English Nonconformists, with whom all Scots who held the Whig tradition (now a large majority) were in sympathy. Till the very last year of the century, Scotland steadily sent up to Parliament a solid majority of Liberal members: and this first exception was an ex-

16

ception mainly because Scotland supported the South African War, which the Liberals, in that election, were opposing.

The result at Westminster was rather odd. Scotland could not win attention in Parliament for her own concerns, as urgent as these might be: but she could, and did on more than one occasion, prevent England from being governed by the party in whose interest an English majority had voted. The effect of this on foreign policy was at times considerable and important—an odd by-product of a situation which had made Scotland vanish from Europe's sight.[1]

After the Act of 1868 there was no change in the franchise for sixteen years. Then in 1884 Gladstone's Third Reform Act levelled the county voting qualification with that of the towns, by giving the landward voter household suffrage and admitting him to the 'lodger vote' as well. This enfranchised the agricultural labourer: but by then the voting weight had gone too far on the side of the towns for the balance to be redressed: and the Liberal Party was mainly urban in outlook. Some effort was made in the following year, however, to secure a juster distribution of seats. A new act re-arranged the constituencies, and Scotland was given another dozen members to keep pace with her rapidly growing population.

After this, though 'representation' was still an issue, the question changed face and divided into four. Four movements, overlapping and interconnected as regards their underlying principles, were already being carried on by four groups of people. One of these was claiming the Parliamentary vote for that half of both the countries' populations which because of sex had been excluded from it. One desired that the labouring class, considered as such, should have more voice in national affairs: and within it was developing a party which claimed for this class the *only* voice in affairs. Yet another desired to weaken the power of the Lords in checking action determined in the Commons. And the fourth wished a change in the governing machine, so as to give Scotland control of her own concerns.

After the Act of 1884 had given the vote to most male heads of

---

[1] The inconvenience of the Union to England was much less, at any time, than it was to Scotland : but on occasion it has been real enough, as for instance, in 1928, the action of the Scottish members of Parliament (whom the matter did not in any way concern) in preventing the Church of England from making use of a Revised Prayer-book approved by majorities in her own councils and of the English members of both Houses.

families, men's interest in franchise questions, though not ended, grew more or less academic. Women's, however, was roused, and grew both practical and keen. It had already been shown for a generation. The beginning of the movement came in England, for the position of women in that country, though high in the sixteenth century, had sunk badly, and now, though a woman reigned there, was at its nadir. Blackstone, in fact, the supreme authority on English law, had declared categorically that 'by marriage, a woman's very being or legal existence is suspended.' [1] Her property, her earnings—even those made needful by his desertion of her—her liberty, her conscience, and her children belonged, without conditions, to her husband. Most men, of course, were better than the law, though one notices that when Mrs Gaskell, for instance, received a cheque from her publishers for her work, her upright and generous husband, who adored her, put it in his pocket as a matter of course, kindly telling her that she should have some of the money. Not all wives were so fortunate, however. In one instance, a woman who refused to allow her child to live with her husband's mistress was imprisoned. And in the early nineteenth century, when the Hon. Mrs Norton attempted to get her children away from the exceedingly unpleasant husband who had tried to divorce her on a trumped-up charge, a learned review called her 'she-beast' and 'she-devil.' And those who supported themselves were none too well off. Many worked a sixteen-hour day for four-and-six a week: a twelve-hour day and nine shillings weekly wage was described as Utopian. A governess, accomplished and gently bred, had to save for old age out of £25 a year. Yet there were many women who earned their living. Even in Scotland, in 1833 there were 65,000 in the Lanarkshire mills: and into the 'forties, in Scotland and in England, they worked in coal-mines where men refused to go, and sometimes their children were born deep underground.

The hopes of the French Revolution and of 'Reform' were felt by women. So early as 1791, when the Rights of Man were in everybody's mouth, the beautiful Englishwoman Mary Wollstonecraft produced a *Vindication of the Rights of Woman* which made a resounding scandal in her own country, where men remarked loftily that one would hear next of the Rights of Cats and Dogs. Women played an active part in the Chartist movement, founding Unions

[1] This principle is the root of the odd English custom of denying a married woman any surname : even today she is ' Mary, wife of John Smith.'

of their own to support the men. And while growing interest in philanthropy began to teach those more fortunately placed what were the sufferings of those who earned their living, these latter were beginning to grow aware that legislation would help them, if they could get it . . . and that they were very little likely to get it so long as they had no voice in choosing its makers. From the 'forties, accordingly, a 'Women's Movement' demanded for women better education, a place in the professions, legal protection, and as means to all these, the parliamentary vote.

The tale of their seventy years struggle for the vote is an interesting (and revealing) study in the history of British legislation, and one with many diversions for the cynic. The question of women's suffrage was raised in the Commons so early as the year 1848, when Disraeli spoke very strongly in its favour. Seven years later, Florence Nightingale's cousin, Barbara Leigh Smith, formed an English committee to work for it: and some notice began to be taken of women's claims. An act allowed married women to hold property and to make wills, and in 1857 Englishwomen were permitted the right of divorce, though even then not on the equal terms with men on which Scotswomen had held it from the beginning.

The 'fifties saw a strengthening of the claim to share in professions and social services, and therefore a strengthening of the opposition of those men who feared the entry of possible rivals. Nothing, indeed, is more marked in the whole movement than the terror (the word is not at all too strong) of men, even in Scotland, of 'the weaker sex,' unless it is the innocent lack of logic which declared that while for a woman to work in a coal-mine, much more carry coal-hods up six long flights of stairs, was no derogation of female dignity, she would do an outrage to the whole of her sex if she took a university degree—that while tending the sick was essentially women's work, in which emptying bedpans was gracious and beautiful, to study medicine (and thereby to win not a nurse's pay but that of a physician) would degrade her below the level of prostitution. When in 1857 Isa Craig became no more than Assistant Secretary to the National Association for the Promotion of Social Science, the Press pursued her with ribald commentary.

Yet the movement grew. Its leaders in the 'sixties were the London Scot John Stuart Mill and the eminent English biologist T. H. Huxley. Mill entered Parliament in 1865, when a new Reform Bill was coming into question, and agreed to present a petition for a clause which should include women's votes in the bill's provisions. Committees were formed to support him: that in Edinburgh, which was led by Mrs M'Laren and Miss Mair, grew into a permanent Scottish Association. Inclusion in the Reform Bill was refused: but in 1870 a Suffrage Bill was proposed and debated. It passed its second reading by 124 to 91: but Gladstone (though without giving his reasons) declared that its passing 'would be a grave mistake,' and it failed in Committee by 106.

Advance was being made, however, for the women were fighting their way, very slowly and painfully, in the professions. Just about this time the University of Edinburgh was involved, not very greatly to its credit, in their struggle to win the right to medical training. English women's colleges warsled into existence (Newnham, at Cambridge, had a brilliant Scotswoman, Mrs Henry Sidgwick, born a Balfour of Whittinghame, for its first head) and their students were winning high academic distinction, though the degrees for which they qualified were not conferred on them. In 1869 the municipal franchise was granted to rate-paying women, though they could not themselves sit on town or county councils until 1907. In 1870 they were admitted also to the School Boards, Flora Stevenson being elected to that of Edinburgh.

Agitation for the parliamentary vote went on, but still the official parties opposed it, the Conservatives quite frankly on the grounds that enfranchised women would vote Liberal, and the Liberals because it was well known that all women were Conservatives by nature. A bill came up none the less in 1875, and the personal earnings of Scottish married women were safeguarded two years later.[1] 1881 gave Scottish married women control of their property, and next year the act was extended to cover Englishwomen also. And two years later women's active participation in politics was much increased: the Corrupt Practices Act forbade any payment for electioneering, so it became at once a women's job: the candidate's sister, who could not vote for him, might properly (if she did not get paid for it) cajole the superior sex into doing so. A Women's Branch of the Conservative Primrose League was formed at once; and Mrs Gladstone set going a Women's Liberal Federation, which her eminent husband did not think 'a grave mistake.' This frank admission of women to politics appeared to strengthen greatly their

---

[1] Even in Scotland, in 1881 Lord Fraser remarked, ' why a woman should have money in her pocket to deal with as she thinks fit I cannot understand.'

claim to vote.   Mass meetings in support of 'suffrage' were held—
a large one in Edinburgh.   In 1885 another bill got as far as its
second reading, and another came up in 1892.

The movement was making progress overseas.   In the largely
Scottish dominion of New Zealand women received the vote in 1893.
But at home the Press and the public were bored by it, and though
the election of 1895 returned more than half the House pledged to
Women's Suffrage, bills were blocked or abandoned without much
heed to the pledges: that of 1897, which was backed by a petition
bearing a quarter of a million names, got through its second reading
by 71, and then was talked out.

The South African War interrupted matters then for a few years,
though a National (British) Union of Women Suffrage Societies was
formed.   A 1904 bill was again talked out: and the movement in
consequence entered a new phase.   Mrs Pankhurst, widow of an
English doctor, dissatisfied by the result of half a century's argument,
formed a new society, the Women's Social and Political Union.
Next year another suffrage bill was talked out: and this Union
became, as the word went, 'militant.'   Sir Edward Grey, the new
Foreign Secretary, was speaking at Manchester, and at question time
Mrs Pankhurst's daughter Christabel and a young Labour woman,
Annie Kenney, asked his opinion on the Suffrage Bill.   He did not
answer.   Miss Kenney repeated her question, and was thrown out.
Miss Pankhurst asked again, and again got no answer.   Miss Kenney
returned, and put her question again, and this time both were thrown
out and roughly handled, and attempting to hold a street meeting
afterwards, were arrested for obstruction, and imprisoned.

It broke the long-standing boycott by the Press of a subject
which 'did not interest the public.'   There were horrified de-
nunciations, not of the Minister who had refused to answer, not of
the stewards who had thrown out the girls, but of the unladylike
conduct of the latter.   But, for the first time in years, 'suffrage'
was news.   Four hundred members, two-thirds of the House, went
up at the next election pledged to suffrage: but there was no mention
of it in the King's Speech.   A resolution was put forward, and was
on the point of being talked out once more, when a voice from the
Ladies' Gallery cried 'Divide.'   The police threw out the speaker,
and the Press denounced her roundly for the appalling outrage.
And at this point an amused Prime Minister (Campbell-Bannerman)
received a deputation representing the now great number of women's

organisations, admitted they had 'a conclusive and irrefutable case,' and told them that if they really wanted a vote, the only thing was to go on 'pestering.'

They took him at his word. It was clear now that peaceful meetings, however large, addressed by speakers however eminent, would only take real effect on the converted, and that Parliament would not act unless it was forced, while the average voter heard nothing of the movement, and concluded that only a handful of eccentrics were involved in it. But now two young girls had made it 'news' at last. And the 'suffragettes,' as its members now were christened, decided to keep it news. For ten years they did.

Great processions of women with banners appeared in the streets —one marched through Edinburgh in 1907. Girls horrified their relations by chalking pavements, selling papers on the kerb, wearing sandwich-boards, or making street speeches, mounted on borrowed chairs. What the Press called 'raids' on Parliament were frequent, and reduced that body to an astonishing terror. They were in fact a series of perfectly legal attempts by groups of women to carry a petition to the House. But the terrified Government again and again called out as many as a thousand police to defend them from groups of fifty unarmed women, who were then arrested. One very ugly feature was that roughs were encouraged to knock the petitioning women about. Discovering the value of this defence, the Government forbade the police to arrest, since arrest had the inconvenient result of allowing the women a chance to speak in court. Women, some of them old, were brutally mishandled, and to save themselves made technical assaults on the police—a tap on the chest or a light slap on the cheek—in order to win the safety of Black Maria. The number of arrests steadily mounted, and the Government tried to terrorise the women by refusing to give them the treatment required by law for political prisoners: they were treated as criminals, and when they went on hunger-strike to secure recognition as 'politicals' (which was given to Irish Home Rulers guilty of murder), were forcibly, and very brutally, fed, or had the fire-hose turned on them in their cells. Many were brought to the verge of death by such treatment, and were then released.

In 1908 a suffrage bill again passed its second reading by 179. Asquith blocked it: the women thereupon retorted by a procession of 15,000 through London, and a series of enormous and lively meetings. At the 1910 election the suffrage question was an active issue, and there followed at once the formation of an all-party Conciliation Committee to frame a bill for which all pledged supporters (a large majority of the House) could vote. There was an immediate suspension of 'militancy,' unless a gaily adorned four-mile procession through the streets of London could be counted such. The Conciliation Bill was widely approved. The municipalities of Edinburgh, Glasgow, and a hundred and twenty-nine other British towns sent their official commendation of it, and it passed its second reading by 110. Then Mr Lloyd George and Mr Winston Churchill declared that the measure was not democratic enough: and it was side-tracked. The Liberals fell soon after, but were returned at the second general election of that year: and again the Bill was carried, this time by 167, while three million signed a petition in its favour. It seemed certain to pass: but next year the Prime Minister, Asquith, 'torpedoed' it. The Liberals produced a Male Franchise Bill, and Asquith promised that it should be drafted so as to allow of a women's suffrage amendment, and then allowed it to be understood that he would resign if such amendment were passed. The Liberal members panicked, and withdrew.

The suffragettes considered the truce at an end. Up to this point, in their six years 'militancy,' nobody's person or property had suffered, except their own. They now broke Asquith's windows, and those of many government supporters. Their opponents were in the rather awkward position of being able to call them no worse names than before, but 150 women were arrested, on a charge of conspiracy and inciting to violence, and received sentences going up to nine months. The 'torpedoed' bill came up for its final vote. In spite of both Asquith and the ill-timed action of the suffragettes, it nearly passed. It would have done so, in fact, but the Irish members, who were all pledged to it, were told that if they voted in its favour they would bring down a government pledged to Home Rule. They voted against, and the bill failed by fourteen votes.

The Liberal Franchise Bill still offered a chance, but Asquith now blocked the already promised amendment on the grounds that the House had rejected its principle. When the Bill came in January of 1913, Grey moved to withdraw the word *Male* from its title, and was told by the Speaker that such a change would make it a different bill. And so that bill was dropped, having now served its purpose, among cries that it had never been intended to do more than burke the Conciliation Bill.

Feeling rose on both sides to a very ugly height.[1] There was undoubtedly, as in all such movements, an element of hysteria among the women, though the Press of the period makes it fairly clear that it was mild to that of their opponents.[2] The suffragettes turned at last to genuine violence—breaking of windows, firing of empty houses, and destruction of the contents of pillar-boxes: and no Cabinet Minister could speak in public without being reminded of the Government's record. Those arrested, as usual, went on hunger-strike: and the Government countered with the 'Cat and Mouse Act,' by which prisoners whose lives were endangered by forcible feeding were released, to be re-arrested as they recovered. 182 came under it in the course of that year, and not one surrendered. Meanwhile, the question was a most active issue. Mass meetings—one of men only, with 342 representatives of Trade Unions—filled the 8,000 seats of the Albert Hall, one raising £10,000 in its 'collection.' Where the deadlock would eventually have ended is difficult to say: but the advent of war in the summer of 1914 caused the militants to call an immediate truce. And very soon the official views on women of the Press and the British Government alike had undergone a remarkable transformation.

The basis of the early Radical movement had been in essence the claim of the labouring man to be recognised as a member of the nation and to have a voice in directing its affairs, which as far as he was concerned were most ill-directed. Alongside it, there had grown a further claim, not for a mere re-balancing of the State, but for a re-fashioning of its principles. This was the movement known as Socialism. It began, psychologically if not logically, from the individualist idealism of the French Revolution, and revolted,

[1] It is fair to point out that the opposition to women's suffrage was not entirely male. There was a Women's National Anti-Woman-Suffrage League, many of whose members were active in elections, informing the male voter how to vote.

[2] The present writer, as a young girl, attended a Cabinet Minister's meeting in Glasgow in 1914, and it gave her nightmares for many months thereafter. As was the usual tactic at that time, a number of women rose and cried their slogan. She recalls one delicate-looking old lady with white hair, whose wrists had been grasped by a couple of powerful stewards, who were pulling hard in opposite directions ; and a girl being carried feet first up a flight of stairs, while a respectable elderly gentleman marched alongside flogging her with a gold-topped umbrella. And though she was too young then to read their meaning, the faces of some of the men have stayed in her mind, and returned again vividly to her memory when she came to deal with the witchcraft prosecutions of the sixteenth and seventeenth centuries. It is fair to add that suffragettes of experience have declared that violent treatment was rare in Scotland, and mild compared with that of England and Wales.

logically if not always psychologically, from the materialist individualism of the great Liberal doctrine of *laisser faire*; and eventually arrived at a position which reversed the principles of '89 and achieved as ideal a collectivism in which the individual as such had no rights at all against the bureaucracy representing the authority of the State.

Definitions of Socialism are very easy, and equally numerous. The trouble with all is that the creed has nearly as many sects as Protestantism, and each claims to be the one true and valid form, the only one which appeals to intelligent men. And even more than among divergent religions, the holders of each regard with contempt and anger those intolerant enough to differ from them on any point they conceive to be important. It is thus impossible even for Socialists to arrive at a definition of their tenets that will not be angrily repudiated, by other Socialists, as incorrect. One can only point out a few general principles which are, in the abstract, generally accepted, and with them a few general characteristics revealed, in the concrete, by the movement's adherents.

Its historic root is in the Religious Orders, in the conception of an organised body in which each man gave up his individual rights to a community working for one purpose, who in turn took charge of and supplied his needs. That the purpose was not of this world is rather forgotten, and that this mode of life was devised for exceptional men, who were carefully tested as to their fitness for it.[1] In the ferment of thought that followed the French Revolution, this method of organisation commended itself to two Frenchmen, François Fourier and Claude Henri, Comte de St-Simon, as providing a means for the reintegration of the society disintegrated by a generation of violent upheaval. Both men were serious-minded idealists,[2] with the tendency of their kind to simplify the remorselessly complex business of human life. There were many such men at the time in all countries of Europe. And in Britain a Welshman, Robert Owen by name, having married a Lanarkshire cotton-spinner's daughter and inherited in due course her father's business, attempted to put these ideas in practice in a manufacturing community, and later in others in Ireland and Indiana. They were not,

[1] The Orders, no doubt, had their roots in the idea of army discipline, which is precisely the same in fundamentals : the army's aim is purely terrestrial, but it also is limited to a single purpose, and if discipline is required, it selects its recruits.

[2] St-Simon gave orders to his valet to wake him each morning with ' Remember, Monsieur le comte, that you have great things to do.'

however, conspicuously successful, and in time the good man—a charming, innocent soul—abandoned them for the preaching of secularism, combined with excursions into spiritualism.

The experiment, none the less, attracted others. Its principles, and those of St-Simon and Fourier themselves, appealed to men of a similar turn of mind, and developed into a theory of the State which from the mid-thirties was labelled Socialism. The theory was vague enough in all conscience: but all the more it was very stimulating, and it see-sawed the common habit of reasoning. Men had been thinking from the man to the State. They began to think instead from the State to the man, which though by itself no less dangerous than the other, is yet needed in conjunction with the other. The conjunction, unhappily, was too often to fail, but the new line of thought brought in an element to the Chartist upheaval, and along with that a sense that what came to be called 'the means of production'—the basic raw materials of human work—belonged in some way to the nation at large, and therefore ought to be administered as national property, for the benefit of the nation as a whole.

As they were, rather flagrantly, being administered for the benefit of a section of the nation, the appeal was instant. To this principle other things became attached, their basis, considered psychologically, being violent emotions derived from a sense of injustice. The emotions were no more than natural, for the injustice was real, gross, and flagrant: they were often sincerely generous and noble, but not unnaturally there mixed with them not only a very understandable hatred, but that sort of one-sided egalitarianism which is often found in such movements for revolt. X feels that he has an equal right with the King or Shakespeare or the nearest millionaire to anything that he happens to desire, but denies that they have a right to the things he desires, and in many cases that anyone has a right to the things he does not happen to desire, from religious freedom to beer at three p.m.

In the mid-century a German Jew, living in bitter poverty in London, proceeded to rationalise these powerful emotions and crystallise them in a definite creed, based on a simplification of human life which at the time was immensely fashionable. Karl Marx (1818-83) drew his blue-print for a collective state on that reduction of human history to the interplay of economic forces one of whose parents was, unwittingly, Adam Smith, while the other was that naïve materialism which the clear but limited thought of the Age of Reason had widely popularised all over Europe. His writings, especially *Das Kapital*, whose first volume appeared in 1867, became before long the Koran of a new faith, which spread almost as rapidly as Islam.

The core of the whole doctrine was a division of mankind into those who did the work and those who took the profits the first had earned, and the reduction of all history to a war between them. Now, the one can be made a real base of division, though the line is difficult to draw in practice, and the other has often been a real factor in the complex processes of history. No philosophy based on a lie ever widely succeeds: nor is any, either, apt to be popular if it insists upon considering the whole of the truth about its subject-matter, for to face the whole truth about any aspect of life is necessarily a difficult business, for which few men have sufficient resolution. Marx took chosen points with immediate appeal, gave them a background of fashionable thought, of doctrines which at the time carried prestige, and rationalised a good deal of strong emotion. And the fact that his expression of his creed had the cloudy and immense verbosity characteristic of Germanic thinking helped also to impress those who were stirred by the driving fervour of his Jewish emotion: for to the semi-thinker verbosity has always an irresistible attraction.

The new body of doctrine—labelled Communism, to distinguish it from the older Socialist creeds—had little direct appeal to Scottish thought: but its 'againstness' did appeal pretty strongly to certain tendencies of Scottish emotion, for the virtue of fervent loyalty to the clan has commonly, throughout our history, made a virtue of the hatred of other clans: and the Marxian virtue of 'class-consciousness' sanctioned, indeed made a binding moral duty, resentment of all that differed from one's own habits. Its general emotional effect, which spread beyond those who adopted its actual creed, thus helped the fissiparous tendency which had already shown in the Chartist movement. In Scotland, too, it had a further result. Marxism ignored the nation. It thought in classes. And in Scotland a tendency to ignore the nation, though for different reasons, was already growing. The Socialist, as distinct from the Communist, outlook was also reinforcing this tendency. The essence of Socialism is State control of all the economic life of the State: but Scotland possessed no State machinery by which economic life could be controlled. Thus all legislation with a Socialist trend tended yet further to give control of affairs to Westminster, or in practice, still more to Whitehall.

The directly shaping effect of these two movements on the mechanism of politics was slow. It was not until the year 1874 that a 'Labour' member arrived in Parliament: and then, though he was a Scot, Alexander MacDonald, he was returned for an English constituency. The Act of 1884, however, gave Scotland about a couple of hundred thousand new working-class voters. Two more Labour members went up, in Scottish seats—a crofter's son, Angus Sutherland, for Sutherland, and a chivalrous young laird, R. B. Cunninghame Graham, for N.W. Lanark. In 1888 the latter, with an able young leader of the Miners' Union, Keir Hardie, formed a Scottish Labour Party as an autonomous political body, the heirs of the old Radicals and Chartists, and with a programme based rather on their tradition than on either Socialism or Communism. Its goal was not abstract reform by revolution, but a number of concrete and practical reforms—Home Rule (though it never paid that more than lip-service), adult suffrage with payment of members of Parliament, the abolition of the House of Lords, a second ballot, disestablishment of the Established Church, free education, free feeding for poor children, the principle that no war should be declared without the formal consent of the House of Commons, an eight-hour day, a minimum wage, State insurance for accidents, sickness, death, or old age, arbitration courts for the settling of labour disputes, local veto on 'liquor,' a land tax, the uncompensated nationalisation of mining royalties, nationalisation of transport and of banks, and a cumulative income-tax, beginning at £300. These aims, if heterogeneous in detail, had the common quality of being positive, concrete, and practicable; and they drew to the party a large body of thoughtful and intelligent working men. The movement was weakened, however, from the start, by a doctrinaire Left Wing, who were less concerned for amelioration of working-class conditions than for securing the triumph of the True Faith, with themselves as its authoritative priesthood, and 'liquidation' for all who refused to bow.[1] In 1893 the Scottish Labour Party was dissolved, and many of its members, led by Keir Hardie, joined a new Independent Labour Party, pledged to Socialism: in the

[1] The very close temperamental affinity of Marxism and Calvinism is often remarked on : and it is interesting that the stronghold of both should, in Scotland, be the Cymric South-western districts.

election of 1895 all its 28 candidates were defeated. In 1901 Trade Union, Co-operative, I.L.P. and other groups formed a Scottish Workers' Parliamentary Election Committee. In 1909 this was merged in the British Labour Party, formed in 1906, which in the general election of that year succeeded in getting 54 members into Parliament.

Dissent regarding principles, aims, and methods continued, and until after the end of the century the Labour Party wielded but little direct political power: but it did make 'Labour's' needs articulate, if at times with rather loudly conflicting voices; and if it could not achieve a government, its programme was backed by the weight of the Trade Unions, which by now were a force to be reckoned with in the State.

Besides these changes, the end of the period saw one in the machine of government. It had long been counted as a fundamental of the English constitution that only the House of Commons had a right to pronounce on questions which concerned taxation. In theory, the House of Lords had a right to reject a money bill, but no power to amend one: and by the end of the nineteenth century, even the right of rejection had in practice fallen in desuetude. In 1909 the House of Lords declared that the Government had inserted in the Budget legislation which came within their rights to reject, and therefore rejected it. And Asquith, then Liberal Premier, went to the country, demanding a mandate to lessen the power of the Lords.

The country, however, was somewhat dubious. He had come in at the previous election with a majority of 220, and he now returned with one of only three. He had therefore to depend on the Labour members (who by this time had increased to forty-one) and the Irish Nationalists. There was a bitter struggle in Parliament. The death of the very popular King Edward, on 6th May 1910, brought a sort of truce. The two parties conferred, but without effective result, and Asquith was forced to have Parliament dissolved.

The second general election of 1910 left matters very much where they had been. Next year, the Government brought in a bill to provide that a money bill might pass into law without the consent of the Lords being necessary, and that any bill which should be passed by the Commons in three successive sessions should be law whether the Lords accepted it or not. Duration of Parliaments also was to be shortened from seven years to five. A rather vague scheme was also put forward now for the creation of a new Second Chamber, which should altogether replace the House of Lords. And by way of sanctions Asquith induced the King to promise the creation of new peers sufficient in number to pass the bill through the Lords. The Second House, at the threat, capitulated: and the Parliament Act of 1911 went through.

For a lifetime now the best of the Liberals had been dogged by a sense that the condition of Ireland was, and had been for many centuries, a very dark blot on the record of Westminster. Unpopular as the principle was in England, they gave consideration, thought, and courage to the question of the revision of those terms under which Ireland was attached to Great Britain, and desired now to obtain for her the power to deal for herself with her own domestic concerns and to tackle the problems which Disraeli described as 'an alien church, a starving peasantry, and an absentee aristocracy.' Gladstone, on his part, made 'Home Rule for Ireland' a real issue from the 'sixties onward; and so immense was his influence in Scotland that in spite of the cry that Home Rule would mean Rome Rule, a great part of his Scottish supporters agreed.

Now, the Whigs' record, like that of their forebears since the fifteen-forties, had been extremely far from nationalistic: but this agitation for Irish self-government now called attention to the case for Scottish. Scotland's national affairs were still in the hands of a man who was appointed, not elected—the Lord Advocate, whose Parliamentary status was extremely uncertain, to say the least of it, and whose power depended on personality: and even so early as 1854 there had been a demand that the system should be altered.

In the early 'seventies, a young Liberal peer, Archibald Primrose, fifth Earl of Rosebery (1847-1929), was beginning to make his mark in politics as a man who thought seriously on Scottish matters, and had courage enough to take his own line in them. In 1872 he had protested against the fact that non-Presbyterians were being forced to pay rates for Presbyterian schools, though the opposition of the Duke of Argyll had prevented the protest from being effectual. He came into more popular prominence two years later, when, being still only twenty-six, he had presided at a great Social Science Congress in Glasgow, and opened it with an impressive speech, which is still worth reading. From that time till the end of the century, his influence in Scottish politics was only a little less than that of Gladstone: it is significant that when he died he had been Rector of each of the four universities in turn. In spite of his very inconvenient habit of thinking for himself in political matters—thinking to some effect, too, very often—he became Foreign Secretary, and a good one, and later was twice Prime Minister of Great Britain.

Now Rosebery had, when still a very young man, begun by accepting the common Liberal belief that the Union of 1707 had given Scotland 'every virtue but that of sobriety,' and still more, every advantage that the country possessed, whether spiritual or material. Even then, however, in the very speech in which he approved the Union, he remarked that 'the English knew as much of Scotland as they did of Boeotia, and what they knew they disliked.' The enlargement of his experience at Westminster made him realise soon that this ignorance was not past, and was doing grave harm to Scottish interests, and that, as he told Edinburgh later, 'When an Englishman conducts the government of a country, he at once concludes that it becomes English.' Yet, as he said again in the same city,

Where there is a vigorous and real and loyal nationality, it is not wise to suppress or to ignore that nationality, and the better policy is to satisfy its just aspirations, for by doing so you will be promoting in the highest and the best sense the efficiency and unity of the Empire at large.

He applied these principles not only to Ireland, not only to the Overseas Dominions, but—though many good Liberals were disconcerted—even to his own country. Others agreed. In 1877 Sir George Campbell, the member for Kirkcaldy, was calling attention to 'the extreme neglect of Scottish business,' and there was a general and growing demand that Scotland should have some definite share of her own in the recognised machine of government, which should take cognisance of her special interests. On the 6th June of 1881, the Earl of Fife [1] brought forward in the Lords a demand for a separate ministry for Scotland. Lord Rosebery supported him with vigour, but the House very easily shrugged the demand aside. Rosebery then proceeded to get himself appointed, in his own phrase, as 'backstairs minister for Scotland'—in other words, he acquired the position of Under-secretary to the Home Department. It was a lowly post for a peer in his thirties with already the name of a brilliant orator, but he sought it on the definite understanding that

[1] Later grandson-in-law of Queen Victoria.

Harcourt, his chief, would leave Scots affairs in his hands: and once they were there, he set about them with vigour. Soon an agitation was stirred up against him: protests were made that a peer could not hold the office, and Rosebery was harried into resigning. There was a real alarm and regret in Scotland. He was given at once the freedom of Edinburgh,[1] and at the presentation he spoke with force of the need not only for a Scottish Local Government Board, but of a special Minister for Scotland. Indeed, a measure providing one had been framed, but as the Government took no interest in it, it was some time before it could be passed. In its first session it was not allowed to be moved until it was too late to be discussed. In its second, it had to be abandoned, as the Government, though always most concerned for the rights of minority groups on the Mainland of Europe, could not find time for it. Feeling in Scotland was rising. In 1884 a great convention was held in Edinburgh, and the bill's immediate passage was demanded. A couple of hundred thousand new Scottish voters had just been added to the electorate, and a Government somewhat shakily in power dared not risk their alienation. So a third introduction of the bill was allowed: and on the day when it came for its second reading, supported by the pertinacious Earl, the Government resigned, and faced an election.

The Conservatives came in, under Salisbury: and by them, in the following year, the bill was passed, not without hot opposition. It provided for a Secretary for Scotland, with under him a separate Scottish department. He himself was to receive £2,000 a year, and for dignity's sake should be Keeper of the Great Seal: and he could appoint himself what staff he chose ... and could induce the Treasury to sanction.

The new institution was very warmly welcomed: but in fact it proved to be far from a success. It provided a national executive: but no national parliament controlled its workings. The Treasury did control them, in effect: and Parliament gave one day in the entire year to discuss the national finances of Scotland. Also, the office had barely been created before an Englishman, Sir George Trevelyan, was appointed to fill it, which, though he was a man both able and upright, suggested that the Whitehall end of it was

[1] The reaction of his numerous biographers to these Scottish matters is often distinctly amusing. One of them is frankly perplexed because in his early career the Scottish Liberal Club gave him a dinner. To be sure, Rosebery 'had been vigilant in looking after Scottish interests at Westminster': but the writer does not find this an adequate reason.

17

likely to subordinate the Scottish. Before very long it had been found as well that the work of heading over a dozen departments was too complex for a man who was further hampered by having above him the authority of a Parliament mainly foreign, increasingly busy, and apt to be more than a little irritated if required to spend time, energy, or money on merely Scottish concerns. After half a century's experience, a famous judge who himself had held the office, Robert Munro, Lord Alness, was to speak of the impossibility of one man's controlling

a number of Boards which are four hundred miles from London, in addition to discharging the ordinary parliamentary and departmental duties,

while men of as different political opinions as Mr Tom Johnston and the Duke of Montrose condemn it, the former as

this Pooh-bah business, this conglomeration of sixteen offices in one person, (which) is an insult to a proud nation,

and the latter observing that the Secretary

is helpless when he faces the Treasury or the Cabinet: Ministers not interested in Scottish affairs easily swamp him with prior claims for help in other directions. The fact is that every Secretary for Scotland is powerless, for no matter how urgently a Scottish industry or social question may require consideration, the Minister cannot stand on his own feet and do what he knows to be right for the Scottish people.

In practice, the Department was from the start the Cinderella of the Government. It was overworked, underpaid, and lacked prestige. To any man who counted on a career, it was a mere stepping-stone to something better, to be got over as quickly as possible, and its Secretaries as a rule were chosen from men who would give the Government no trouble by inconvenient insistence on the unwelcome.

Some of these qualities were soon made plain. Discontent with them crystallised in 1886 in the founding of a Scottish Home Rule Association, with the member for Caithness, Dr G. P. Clark, as its President, and on its committee R. B. Cunninghame Graham, the famous English Liberal Augustine Birrell, then member for West Fife, and Sir John Kinloch of Kinloch, whose forebear had suffered in the cause of 'Reform.' With them were former Provosts of Glasgow and Paisley, bailies of Glasgow again and of Dundee, lawyers, ministers, and a dozen Scottish members of Parliament.

The question was raised in the House in 1889. Out of 279 members present, seventy-nine voted for Home Rule, the Scots vote being nineteen for, twenty-two against. In that year the Conservatives, still in power, passed a Local Government Act, creating for Britain a system of County Councils, elected by rate-payers of both sexes, which were given considerable local powers with regard to such matters as transport and sanitation, with power to levy rates to pay their costs. Most Scots Home Rulers approved in principle of this devolution: but the passing of the Act was a demonstration of their country's Parliamentary position. On no fewer than twelve amendments, a majority of from over two to one to over five to one of Scottish members was defeated, on points of serious Scottish interest, by the majority of a House of Commons of which at no time more than a third was present.[1]

In the February of the succeeding year, Dr Clark brought up the principle again by moving an amendment to the Address in reply to the Queen's Speech—

We humbly submit to your Majesty that the present mode of legislating for the domestic affairs of Scotland is unsatisfactory, that measures affecting the welfare of the Scottish people are not considered, in consequence of the pressure of business of the other parts of the United Kingdom ; that when bills relating to Scotland alone are being dealt with, the decision of the House is often contrary to the wishes of the great majority of the Scottish representatives ; and that it is desirable, while retaining the supremacy of the Imperial Parliament, to devolve upon a Legislature in Scotland the consideration of the domestic affairs of that country.

Donald Crawford, member for N.E. Lanark, proposed to change the last clause, making Scottish affairs devolve on

the members for Scotland sitting in Scotland . . . or to adopt some other means whereby Scottish affairs shall be entrusted to the control of the representatives of the Scottish people.

The remit was thus as general as might be, depending purely on the principle that a majority of the elected representatives of a nation had a right to make its laws, and going no further. None the less, though the proposal exemplified the basic principle of democracy, the (Scottish) Liberal Whip led in opposing, warmly supported by the Lord Advocate, who spoke of Scotland as 'being withdrawn

---

[1] The act worked badly, as might have been expected. Rosebery's Government in 1894 formed a general Local Government Board for Scotland, with the Scottish Secretary at its head.

from darkness' by the Union, and went on to fulsome praise of its benefits.

His remarks were too much for Gladstone's sense of logic. The Grand Old Man stood up and thundered at him:

I never heard a more extravagant statement proceed from the lips of a gentleman representing the Government in this House. . . . I am of opinion that the period between the Act of Union and the Reform Act of 1832 is not a very laudable or very creditable period in the history of Scottish Parliamentary representation. Its condition was wretched, its franchise was a mockery, and its results were unsatisfactory in the highest degree, and stand in disadvantageous, not in advantageous, contrast with the proceedings of many of the Parliaments of the sixteenth and seventeenth centuries.

—notwithstanding which, he had already made clear that he intended to vote against the amendment: and so he did. The result was confusion in followers and opponents. When Clark's amendment was put to the vote next day, nineteen of the Scottish members voted for it, thirty-two against: the remaining twenty-one found it more tactful to absent themselves. Crawford's amendment on Clark's was put forward next day, and it received a little more support. Twenty-seven were for it, and sixteen against. But twenty-nine showed their sense of the importance of the concerns of the country they represented by staying away from the House: and they included not only the Conservative Arthur Balfour, but the leading Liberals Campbell-Bannerman, Augustine Birrell (a member of the Home Rule Association's Committee), the rising young H. H. Asquith, and Gladstone himself, the Patriarch of the Party. It is worth noting that in the House as a whole 326 members were present, and of the 283 non-Scots, 116 voted in Crawford's favour, so that the motion was lost, in all, by forty.

The subsequent Parliamentary history of the movement was continuous, and not without its interest. In 1891, 1892, and 1893 Dr Clark again brought forward motions for Federal Home Rule. On the first occasion the House was 'counted out'—that is, too few members were present to form a quorum. On the second, 128 were present, twenty-four of them Scottish members: the motion was lost by twenty, and fourteen of the Scottish members voted against it. On the third, the voting rose to 318, with fifty-nine Scots, thirty-seven of whom, this time, voted in favour: and the motion was lost by no more than eighteen. In each of the next two years

Sir Henry Dalziel brought up the question once more, being seconded, on the first occasion, by Augustine Birrell, and on the second, by Mr Lloyd George. In 1894, 350 voted, fifty-six of them Scottish members: and this time the motion was carried by ten votes, the Scots majority for it being fourteen. In 1895 the Scots majority was again the same, and that of the House had risen to fourteen.

Still nothing was done. Each party feared that any effective action would deliver Scots politics to their opponents. The Conservatives, to the end of the century, were frankly opposed to Home Rule in principle, though individuals made an exception in favour of it for Scotland. The Liberals, in theory, favoured it: Gladstone expressed approval again and again. Lord Rosebery, Sir Henry Campbell-Bannerman, H. H. Asquith, and Mr Lloyd George, who succeeded Gladstone as leaders of the Party, were equally definite. So, also in theory, was the Labour Party: Keir Hardie, Ramsay MacDonald, and J. R. Clynes spoke again and again in favour of Home Rule; and again and again the Party passed resolutions in support. But none the less, after 1895, no more was heard of Home Rule in Parliament for another thirteen years, during which time an experimental compromise was attempted.

In 1894 the Liberal Government formed a Standing Committee of the Scottish members to deal with Public Bills concerning Scotland; and in 1899 a Conservative Government passed the Private Legislature Procedure (Scotland) Act, which took much Scottish Private Bill legislation from Parliament, and transferred it to the Scottish Office, to be dealt with by Provisional Orders. Neither arrangement worked. In 1907 the Standing Committee was made permanent: but it had no control over administration or expenditure, and in order to even the balance of parties within it to that of the House of Commons in general, some dozen or more non-Scottish members sat there. Also, a minority of the Committee could raise once more, in the full House of Commons, any point on which they were defeated within the Committee, and thus perhaps find an English majority which overruled the decisions of their own.

In 1908, after fourteen years of this, D. V. Pirie introduced a definite bill for Scottish Home Rule: and a House of 359 passed its first reading by 107, the Scots members voting forty-one in favour and nine against: and nothing more was done. The inapplicability to Scots conditions of the 1909 Housing Act served as commentary;

and in 1911 Sir Henry Dalziel brought forward the bill once more, and this time the first reading passed by 172 to seventy-three, with the Scots thirty-one to four: and no more was done. Dr Chapple brought up a motion the next year, and again it was carried, by 226 to 128, with the Scots forty-three to six: and no more was done. In the summer of the same year A. M. Scott introduced a bill: again the first reading was carried by 264 to 212, with the Scots forty-three to seven: and no more was done. Next year again, Sir W. H. Cowan at last got a bill as far as a second reading, which produced a majority in the bill's favour of 204 to 159, with the Scots forty-five to eight: and no more was done. November brought a considerable demonstration in Edinburgh, and in May next year Mr Ian Macpherson brought up the bill again, and this time the second reading was adjourned: and no more, though this time for reasons good enough, was done, or could be done for some years thereafter, for that was the summer of 1914.

Between 1889 and 1914—that is, in a quarter of a century—the subject had been before the House of Commons thirteen times. On the last eight occasions the principle had been accepted by a general majority of the House, and on eleven it had received the support of a majority of Scottish members. And yet no bill had ever been allowed to go as far as the Committee stage. And it is a point not perhaps unworthy of note that in the standard general History of Scotland, a large-scale work, which handles most of this period in some detail, Hume Brown (made Historiographer Royal in 1908) has not a word to say about the movement, except a very incidental mention of the establishment of the Scottish Office: he does not refer to any of these bills. The avoidance of his successor Sir Robert Rait, in an able work intended for higher classes in Scottish schools, is equally marked, and equally complete, although both men were adults when these events were in progress, and could scarcely have missed at least some contact with them.

XXII

HOME POLITICS : II—THE CONTENT

EIGHTY-TWO YEARS: 1832–1914

*The cottage is sure to suffer for every error of the court, the cabinet,
and the camp.*   C. C. COLTON, *Lacon.*

A THING all men admit, and many forget, is that the machinery of
politics is not an end in itself but a means to an end. Therefore, the
core of political history is not the changes of that machinery, but
what it effected, or perhaps failed to effect, in the general process of
the national life.

In Scottish nineteenth-century history, the strife and alternation
of the parties, though it filled much space in the newspapers of the
time, is largely unreal and irrelevant. The most realistic way of
looking at it is to see it not as a strife of opposing creeds (which,
when it is real, is no unimportant matter) but rather as a clash of
temperaments, of attitudes to the business of government. It is not
that the good and generous were of one party, the evil and selfish in
its opposite. Nothing so simple. There were generous and upright
men in each, and in each, too, others whose motive was self-assertion,
through power or possessions or merely a loud noise. We may sum
the main difference, roughly but not untruly, by saying that the
strength of the Conservatives was, in the main, their sense of concrete fact, their weakness the lack of thought-out principles to which
the concrete facts could be related: while the Liberal strength, and
that of the Socialists, was that each possessed a coherent, reasoned,
and attractive creed, and their weakness was that they too often failed
to establish a satisfactory working relation between it and those facts
which refused to fit. And it is, incidentally, not for nothing that
(except, as in the Highlands, for special reasons) the Conservatives
were the laird, farmer, and labourer of the country districts, and the
Liberals and the Socialists, as a rule, were the merchant and the
artisan of the towns, who walked on plainstanes and bought their
bread in shops.

Now the 'content' of politics is always two-fold—the dealings of the nation with other nations, and the dealings of the nation with its own people. The former can be left to later chapters. The latter can be conveniently divided—though the division is a very rough one—into questions of political status, which have been dealt with from another angle, as changes in the machine; questions of mental and spiritual relations, legislation affecting religion and education, which also have been discussed in previous chapters; and questions affecting the people's material welfare, which we describe as social legislation . . . although it is always needful to remember that in life all these intertwine with one another, and their separation is therefore nothing more than an artificial convenience for discussion.

The social legislation of the time consisted mainly of an effort to cope with the forces James Watt and Napoleon had set going—the results of the Industrial Revolution and a quarter-century of foreign war. What these were, we have seen. The state of Great Britain was full of crying evils: and something had to be done to put them right.

We are used to think of the Victorians as a very type of prosperous complacence, of a stability very near stagnation. No doubt many of them saw their own age with content. All was well, all was moving in the right direction, all was balanced as it should be. The mighty *Times*, in 1871, could say happily, in a leading article, 'We can look on the present with undisturbed satisfaction.' (That was the year the Prussians were in Paris.) And many good people heartily agreed.

In fact, this is no more than a single aspect of an age of much complexity and conflict, when religious and political convictions boiled, not without noise and smoke, in the melting-pot. And not all, by any means, were indifferent to the less pleasing by-products of 'progress'—the bairns born in coal-pits, the reek of the closes below the Canongate. The ethical interests of the eighteenth century, the revival of the sense that 'a man's a man,' whether gentle or simple, elect or reprobate, had not gone for nothing. There were men and women who cared for those who were desolate and oppressed, and who fought for them with a steady, magnificent courage: it was that fire which lighted all that was best in Chartism, in the hopes of the Socialists, in the Women's Movement. Nor did it burn only there: there was noble intention and very considerable achievement also to be found among men of the older parties. It is true that some, especially of the Liberals, were chiefly concerned

with abuses in other countries—with negro slavery in the Colonies,
or the oppression of Bulgars and Serbs by Turks, or of Italians by
their Austrian masters: these were more romantic than sweated
sempstresses or children of six in the mines of Lanark or Yorkshire
. . . though we must not forget that, if it looked more romantic, their
oppression was not less real or less painful: and the abolition of
negro slavery, which was enacted in 1833 for British possessions
everywhere in the world, cost the British taxpayer twenty millions
sterling, a huge sum then, which he paid up with good will.

The less romantic problems nearer home were not overlooked,
however, by all the reformers. The war against Napoleon was not
long ended before the condition of the industrial districts began to
rouse a strong uneasiness. These huge agglomerations of ill-paid
workers were very difficult even to feed. Land was already going out
of cultivation, and Scotland, the leader of the world's agriculture,
was becoming swiftly unable to feed herself. So was England.
Foreign corn had to be imported. The farmers cried out for protection, and it was taxed. This was a help to the rural population,
but the raised cost of bread (which then, far more than now, was
the basis of diet, especially in England) fell very heavily upon the
urban. The eighteen-twenties saw various attempts to cope more
or less justly with the situation. None was successful. In 1829
Dr Joseph Hume, the Scottish Radical who did much for repeal of
the Combinations Acts, moved that the Corn Laws should be
repealed altogether. He found only a dozen supporters in the House;
and further attempts, before and after the passing of the Reform
Act, were also defeated. Outside Parliament, there was strong
agitation, however. Its leading figures were two men from the
industrial North of England, a Manchester manufacturer, Richard
Cobden, and a Rochdale mill-owner, John Bright, who in 1838
founded an Anti-Corn-Law League.

There followed a lively campaign of propaganda both in England
and in the Lowlands, greatly helped by the railways and the new
penny post: and there was also vigorous opposition. It was not,
as is commonly said, a conflict of classes, but rather one of the
country and the town. The employers of the towns were strong for
repeal, not only because the cheapening of the loaf was the alternative to a rise in wages, but on the broader ground that the Corn
Law limited their overseas market. Britain was then 'the workshop
of the world,' and agrarian countries wished to pay for her goods in

grain, which the duties prevented her from accepting. Their employees saw in repeal not only cheaper food and therefore a greater purchasing power in wages, but beyond it more trade in British manufactures, and consequently lessened unemployment.

In 1841 Cobden entered Parliament, and next year he and Bright made a tour in Scotland, where *The Scotsman* gave them vigorous support. Cobden received the freedom of six burghs, including Edinburgh, Glasgow, and Dundee, and was greatly impressed by Scotland's intelligence, especially that of the farmers, whom he considered 'a century before our Hants and Sussex chawbacons.' (The Scots farmers, being less dependent upon wheat, were less opposed to Repeal than were the English.) In fact, he told Manchester a little later what an excellent thing the Union was for England, and that if the countries should separate once more the Scots

might have a government wholly popular and intelligent to a degree which I believe does not exist in any other country on the face of the earth.

The leader of the Government at the time was the Tory Peel, who like most of his party leant on the rural interest. He was not unsympathetic to Free Trade, which with British manufactures far ahead of those of all other countries at the time, was clearly an advantage in winning markets. Four-fifths of the general British revenue came from indirect taxation: and he judged that the lowering of duties would mean increased imports and thus, in the long run, more money. He now revised the tariff, reducing the duties on 769 commodities, and covered the change by reviving, for three years, Pitt's 'income-tax,' at sevenpence in the pound. In 1845, although he went on after all with the income-tax, he abolished the duties on 400 altogether, and reduced many more. But he still hesitated to repeal the Corn Laws, lest cheap foreign corn should drive down the native supply, and leave an island dependent on overseas foodstuffs. Distress, however, was steadily forcing his hand. In 1841 he had halved the duties, and tried to work out a plan for a sliding scale to depend on the amount of home production. But the distress was rapidly growing worse, and in 1845 the harvest failed and potato disease smote the whole of Western Europe. In Ireland, potatoes were the staple foodstuff, and the people died right and left of sheer starvation.[1] Late in that autumn,

[1] It is no great testimony to British rule that between 1811 and 1911, while the population of Scotland almost trebled, and England's multiplied by three and a half, that of Ireland *fell* from 5,938,000 to 4,390,000.

the leader of the Liberals, Lord John Russell, appearing in Edinburgh to receive an honorary degree from his Alma Mater, declared that abolition was 'a natural necessity.' Great meetings in Glasgow and in Edinburgh, with the Lord Provosts presiding, backed his opinion. Peel capitulated, and spoke for complete repeal of all duties upon foodstuffs. The Cabinet saw in that ruin for British farming, and he resigned. Lord John then tried to form a Whig government to support repeal. He failed, and in a fortnight Peel was back—to force through repeal, in June 1846, with the help of a coalition of both parties, and in face, as he knew, of his immediate fall, and replacement by the Whigs under Lord John.

The repeal of the Corn Laws served to check the more violent fluctuations of prices, and thus did a certain amount to relieve distress without affecting the employers' pockets. The Liberals, proudly conscious of success, indifferent to its effects on mere backward rustics, and aware that there was no real competition to be feared for the products of British industry, sponsored a policy of lowering home prices by the removal of all import duties, unless on sinful things like wine or tobacco, which had to be imported if people would buy them. Henceforth, one standing issue between the parties was the principle of their fiscal policy. The Conservatives believed in adjusting the tariff in accordance with the changes in circumstance. The Liberals believed, in principle, in the abolition of all import duties: and Gladstone, after 1853, removed a great many which in fact were vexatious, such as that on soap, and reduced others, including that on tea. By 1860 no more than forty-eight articles carried duties, and next year he abolished 'the tax on knowledge,'—that is, the duty on imported paper, thus greatly increasing the power of journalism.

In the 'eighties, this policy began to be doubted more widely than it had been for forty years. Other countries now were making for themselves the things which had been the leading British exports, and were raising tariff walls to keep out their rivals. In the decade after 1876 the British share in world trade was contracted from 23 per cent. to 19 per cent. It went on sinking, and in 1903 a cry was raised for a re-imposition of import duties. The general election three years later was fought, indeed, very largely on that issue, the Conservatives now trying to protect British manufactures, and make the Empire an economic unit. Their rivals, however, by pointing out that this would mean rising prices, succeeded in defeating them at the poll.

In the latter part of the century both parties talked of keeping Pitt's promise to end the income-tax: but in fact it proved so convenient an expedient that it soon was the very basis of revenue, even at its original sevenpence. Late in the century, among piteous cries, it was raised to ninepence, and in 1907 to a whole shilling, whereon the taxpayer, *traendo guai*, saw final ruin staring him in the face. He was not to foresee the range of modern improvements.

Fiscal measures alone, though they raised the value of the employed man's wages, were unable to cope with the tide of poverty swelling under the surface of the national wealth in an age that saw Britain the richest power in the world: in 1831 one in ten of the whole population of England were receiving 'poor-relief,' although that country's treatment of her 'paupers' was notoriously not so much inhumane as inhuman. In Scotland the attitude to the destitute was not that which since the abolition of the monasteries had grown in England: they were still regarded as being human beings, and not even necessarily criminal. But machinery for relief was inadequate. It depended on the Act of 1579: direct relief was in the hands of the Sessions, who had in fact the right to impose a cess, but depended as a rule on voluntary contributions. Their administration of what funds they possessed very often shows a real humanity which may help to balance less pleasing qualities: but in face of the growing accumulation of large masses of very poor, it was not enough: and they now had to deal with the problem of the able-bodied workless.

After the war, an increasing number of them took advantage of the permission to raise a cess: but the majority still refused to do so. In 1840 Dr Alison of Edinburgh demanded an overhauling of the system. Chalmers opposed him—not from any sort of lack of charity, but because he believed in voluntary relief, and mistrusted the imposition of a state system. Dr Alison retorted that Scotland was spending £140,000 yearly on poor relief: at the rate of England, it would be £800,000. He carried his point. A Commission was appointed, and in 1845 Peel's government passed an act establishing a central Board of Supervision above a system of Parochial Boards, and gave permission to build poor-houses, though these were not, as in England, compulsory, for the powerful cohesion of the Scots family was against the virtual imprisonment of the destitute for the crime of poverty.[1] The act provided medical relief, and paid heed to pauper children and the insane: but relief for the able-bodied was, however, thought 'neither necessary nor expedient.' Assessment still was not compulsory, and at first no more than 450 parishes —about half—took advantage of the provision for it, though the number rose steadily. By 1884 it was 827, and by 1911 all but four had a poors'-rate.

The act, however, failed to solve the problem, the more as the Irish Poor Law Guardians were in the habit of solving some of their own by decanting their destitute on to the Clyde and the Mersey: in the four months after November 1847 nearly 43,000 almost penniless Irish arrived in Glasgow, where employment was already inadequate; nor would Westminster do anything to check them. It is not surprising that in the late 'seventies Glasgow had 38,000 names for relief.

The Local Government Act of 1894 handed over the work of the Board of Supervisors to its own Boards, and that of the previous Parochial Boards to the new Parish Councils, but kept the general principles of the old Act, still forbidding any relief to the able-bodied. After the turn of the century, however, certain provisions were made from a new direction, on the principle of preventing the aged or injured from *becoming* destitute, by arranging that they should be insured by the State. The Employers' Liability Act of 1880 had already made an attempt at a provision for injury due to bad conditions of work. The Workmen's Compensation Act of 1906 carried the principle further, and the Labour Exchanges established in 1909 attempted to facilitate employment, while the National Insurance Acts of 1911 and 1914 assessed employer and employee in a scheme of benefits for sickness and unemployment, with free medical attendance in the former, and the Old Age Pensions Acts of 1908 and 1911 gave a small weekly allowance to the aged, which often allowed them still to live with their families. Outside the direct State schemes the Trade Unions and Friendly Societies did much, on a co-operative basis, for their members in sickness, old age, and unemployment. And all these later schemes, whatever might be their practical defects, had at any rate the common, and great,

[1] The English Chartists called their poor-houses bastilles, which is rather a libel on the famous prison. Dickens's picture in *Oliver Twist* is not overdrawn— indeed, he leaves out some of the ugliest features, like the forcible separation of married couples, and the auction of labourers chained to the parish cart.

advantage that the 'relieved' were left to live with their fellow human beings, not segregated into separate prisons.

Attempts were made to improve working conditions, which were by no means beyond the need of it. In 1833 Michael Sadler and Lord Ashley (later Earl of Shaftesbury) [1] procured an act forbidding the employment of children under nine, and limiting hours of work for those under eighteen. It proved ineffective, but the principle of the thing had been admitted, and he fought for, and won, in 1842, another Commission. Its report was ghastly. Children of six dragged heavy weights of coal, deep underground, for fourteen hours a day. Peel used the shock of the Commission's report to pass at once an act forbidding women and boys to work underground, and Lord Ashley continued to fight for shorter hours—for a ten-hour day for workers under fourteen. The Government wished to compromise on twelve, but in 1847 he succeeded in bringing the limit down to ten, though the act was so framed that evasion of it was made easy.

Progress, indeed, was desperately slow, for the sacred orthodoxy of *laisser faire*, which to most Liberals was the Eleventh Commandment, protested that legislation to interfere with the conditions of a man's employment was infringement of the individual's rights. Women and children, having in England no legal entity, were, for that reason, easier to protect: but it was not until 1867 that factories which employed them could be made subject to Government inspection and control.

The Second Reform Act of 1868 largely increased the number of working-class voters, and during the 'seventies, also, the Trade Unions developed more weight in their collective pressure. Disraeli's Government of 1874-80, being Conservative, was not thirled to *laisser faire*, and achieved some protection at last for working men, by providing that all factories and workshops must reach at least a certain minimum standard of space, sanitation, ventilation, and cleanness.

The principle of protection was thus granted, and the pace quickened somewhat. Sweated labour had been attacked in the early 'forties, when the London Scot Tom Hood wrote *The Song of the Shirt*: but none the less, it was not till 1890 that the House of

---

[1] Commemorated by the famous Eros fountain in Piccadilly Circus, so well known to all visitors in London.

Lords appointed a Committee, whose revelations showed terrible conditions. Next year, Salisbury's Conservative Government passed a Factory Act intended to deal with these, which their party amended again in 1906. In 1894 Rosebery's Liberals fixed a limit of hours for male dockers and railwaymen, and in 1908 the same party restricted the day's darg in coal-mines to eight hours. The difference between this and the day of fourteen hours worked by mine-children of six a lifetime before shows a very sizeable change in admitted standards.

Not only working conditions but those of living were, as we have seen, in flagrant need of reform: and there the difficulties were even greater. Yet from the 'thirties doctors, ministers, town councillors, and private citizens strove to awake the conscience of the nation. Lord Ashley again was prominent in England, and in Scotland the leaders were Dr Alison, Makgill-Crichton of Rankeillour, William Chambers the publisher, and the Reverend Dr James Begg of the Free Church. In the late 'forties a society was formed for the purchase of slum property, and another, in conjunction, for re-building. Much hard work was done. Dr Robert Foulis, in 1852, made the valuable experiment of re-conditioning an Edinburgh land, and demonstrating that it could be done at a profit, while Dr Begg endeavoured to set going a co-operative effort by working men themselves. Painfully little was achieved, however, and that rather in the complete destruction of old, substantial, and historic buildings than in their replacement or their restoration: when they were replaced the new houses were apt to be modelled on the flimsy building of the English towns. Begg did, in 1861, succeed in forming a Co-operative Building Society in Edinburgh: but though it begot a successful Danish movement, it had little positive result at home. William Chambers, as Lord Provost of Edinburgh, procured an act in 1867 which enabled the city itself to undertake a municipal scheme of slum clearance. Well over a quarter million was expended, and nearly three thousand houses were demolished: but re-building was left to private enterprise, which unfortunately proved inadequate. In Glasgow, another publisher-Provost, Blackie, attempted the same thing. An act was obtained in 1866 which gave power to the Corporation to 'clear' some ninety acres of the worst slums. Thirty thousand people were dislodged from their dwellings, and most of Glasgow's historic buildings were razed; but the rates went up, and most of the reconstruction was therefore again left to private enterprise. The commercial crisis of the late 'seventies intervened before very much else had been done, and in 1888 thirty per cent. of Glasgow dwelling-houses were one-roomed, and one in four of the people lived in them. The Corporation tried again, but between 1889 and 1901 had achieved no more than 2,400 new dwellings.

In 1911 8·4 per cent. of the country's population—10 per cent. of the urban—were living in one-roomed houses. In Glasgow, somewhere about half a million, or more than half the inhabitants of the city, were living 'overcrowded'—that is, with more than two people to a room. (Four people in two rooms, or six in three, is not considered technical overcrowding.) 8·6 per cent. of that city were more than four to a room—thirteen or more in a two-room-and-kitchen flat. In Dundee, the 'overcrowded' were 50 per cent. The figure for London was 16 per cent., and for Liverpool in the neighbourhood of 8.

In 1905, deciding that the problem was something beyond merely local efforts to deal with, Glasgow appointed a Commission, which spent two years in an investigation: then it laid its results before a further Committee (English and Irish) of the House of Lords, who declined to take action. In 1912 the city tried once more: and this time a Committee of the Commons went to Glasgow, and refused to hear evidence, on the grounds that if any action was needed at all—a point on which the Chairman expressed his doubts—it should be suspended until it was convenient to deal with the question over Britain at large. And many worthy gentlemen still wondered why the people of Glasgow nourished Communist dreams of a red revolution in the happy future.

If the housing problem proved too much for them, the municipal authorities, none the less, were by no means wholly ineffective. In certain directions, there was real progress. Until the mid-'fifties, Glasgow's water-supply was in the hands of private companies. In 1855 the town bought them out, and set going a great scheme to provide the city with Loch Katrine water: between that time and the end of the period the city found, and spent, five million pounds on that one item. It was not until 1869 that Edinburgh followed Glasgow's example, and bought out its companies. Five years later the Town Council spent £400,000 on a new scheme, supplemented in the 'nineties by the great Talla Works, which cost a million.

Glasgow, again, took its lighting into its own hands in 1869, and Edinburgh in 1888—the latter proudly planting its braw new gas-works east of the Waverley Station, in one of the finest prospects of the city, where it remained till 1903. Glasgow's municipal supply of electric light came in 1890,[1] Edinburgh's the next year. The number of Glasgow consumers, by the way, in 1893 was a hundred and eight.

Better light and water—for the smaller towns followed the lead of the greater ones—brought a new standard of cleanliness. Schemes for cleansing grew, and for direct medical supervision of the people's health, especially that of children. These did not do all that needed to be done, for the housing conditions, which were fundamental, remained an obstacle to all Public Health work. Yet much was done. The death-rate of Edinburgh in 1863 was 25·88 per thousand: in 1913 it was 14·39. The reduction is even more marked in the case of children under five, whose rate for Edinburgh fell in that time from the truly appalling figure of 93·29 to 33·6. The figures scarcely gave cause for complacency: the death-rate for Holland in 1937, for instance, was 8·8. And the actual 'infant mortality rate'—that is, the rate for children in their first year—went on growing, the highest figures being reached in the last five years of the nineteenth century, when it was 129·5. After that it began to decline, though still but slowly, reaching 110 in the last year or two of the period. (The New Zealand figure for 1937 was 31.) It is worth remarking that though until 1912 the Scottish rate had always been much lower than the English, which in the last years of the nineteenth century had been something like 156, after that the Scottish rate became the higher, and so has continued till the present day, when the English rate is less than three-quarters of the Scottish one.

It was a good sign when the Town Councils once more began to recall their mediaeval duty of providing for the people's recreation. Physically and spiritually, much of Scotland had been sorely hampered, for long, by lack of anything better than the shebeen . . . though, to be sure, worse places were easy to find. Now, not only did the towns begin to take pride in such needful accessories to education as museums, art galleries, and above all, libraries: provision was made for the playing of golf, bowls, and football, in

[1] A private company had lighted St Enoch Station by electricity so early as 1879, making it one of the leading sights of the city. The first British Post Office to work by electric light was Glasgow Central, in 1884.

decent surroundings and at low cost or none. Later tennis, swimming, and sometimes cheap fishing facilities were added, and parks were provided, and, by the end of the time, playgrounds for children that were not starkly hideous. It became possible for energetic, high-spirited, and not specially intellectual young people to do something outside the workshop and the church besides propping up street corners, getting drunk, and getting into what was known as 'trouble.'

Besides improvement by direct legislation, both parliamentary and municipal, a good deal with regard to working conditions was achieved, so to speak, directly, without new laws, by enlightened employers and public-spirited workmen.

Victorian employers were not all ogres. As the figures given above make clear enough, there were far too many like that notorious firm of the early 'nineties, who were splendid benefactors of the Free Kirk and given to financing 'evangelical tours,' and who worked the greater part of their employees a twelve-hour day in abominable conditions, seven days a week. But many of them also were, in the main, no worse than fairly decent business men, who gave their people what was customary because it was customary, and thought no more. Others did think, and without troubling to wait for legislation, tried to change the conception of what was customary, giving a lead that other men privately, or the law in time, might follow when it had been presented to them. Quite early, even before the First Reform Act, some firms were providing medical and educational services for their people. By 1833 at least fifteen were maintaining schools for their workmen's children, and by 1861 Lanarkshire had fifty-one 'colliery schools,' often better equipped than the run of the parish schools, and giving a sound elementary education for twopence a week. Some at least went beyond the 'elementary' level: David Livingstone testifies that at the Works School at Blantyre those who desired might learn both Greek and Latin. In 1872 Baird's of Gartsherrie were spending some £3,000 a year on their schools, which 4,500 children were attending. And as the customary day's darg shortened, many firms encouraged their employees themselves to improve their education: the great publishing firm of Chambers, for example, gave its young work-people an hour's teaching daily, and provided them also with a library. Other less obvious benefit schemes were formed. By the later part of the time the Border wool mills were organising works, co-operative

societies, building societies, and sickness and benefit schemes, and
had begun to provide recreational centres. And the great Dumbarton shipbuilding firm of Denny's were encouraging their men to
feel that they had an interest in the firm, by a system of awards for
improvement in skill, competitive examinations for promotion, and
conferences of workmen and directors.

A more democratic basis to 'big business' was helped by the
growing power of the Trade Unions, which, if they helped to per-
petuate the evil theory that the interests of employers and employees
were necessarily in opposition, at least brought about a useful recognition of the principle of 'collective bargains' between them, and
formed for the working man a growing defence against the oppression
of unenlightened employers. Long after the Combinations Acts were
repealed, their legal position remained ambiguous, and was worsened
by inequality of the law as regarded the employer and his men. If
the master broke a contract concerning employment, it was a civil
offence: but if the breach was made by the employee, it was criminal,
and he might receive as much as three months imprisonment. It
was not until 1867 that the Master and Servant Act checked this
injustice.

That year brought a test case which was to be important. An
English union prosecuted an official who had embezzled its funds:
and the Lord Chief Justice of England declared that Trade Unions,
though not illegal, had no legal standing, and therefore no legal right
to their property. The injustice was manifest, for the Union funds
represented a great deal of courage and sacrifice by people many of
whom were very poor, and (the more as the franchise was at the
point of extension to a very large number of urban working men) a
Royal Commission was appointed. In 1871 Gladstone's Liberals
formally recognised the Unions as legally constituted organisations,
with the right to hold property, but made strikes equivalent to
criminal conspiracy. There were many protests, but Gladstone
refused to do more, and at the election of 1874 the great new body
of English working-class voters accordingly voted Tory and put him
out. The Tories thereon appointed another Commission, and in
1876 Disraeli's Employers and Workmen Act recognised fully the
right to collective bargaining, with its sanctions, strikes and 'peaceful
picketing.'

Even before this legal recognition the Unions were a power in
industry. In 1872 the English engineers of the North-east had

struck for a nine-hour working day, and got it: and the Clyde men secured a fifty-one hour week without the necessity of 'coming out.' The Scots Unions were already well organised, thanks largely to the leadership of two Glasgow Highlanders, Alexander Campbell of the Carpenters' Union, and Alexander MacDonald, a miner-schoolmaster, who founded in 1863 the Miners' Union. These led, between 1858 and 1867, in the formation of local Trades Councils, which made possible relations between Unions, and were a powerful force in politics: the Master and Servant Act of 1867 was indeed very largely due to a campaign initiated by the Glasgow Council, which also took a very prominent part in the agitation for the Second Reform Bill. MacDonald, returned to Parliament in 1874 (for Stafford, not a Scots seat), was one of the first two Labour members to sit, and did much to procure the Employers and Workmen Act.

Until the end of the 'eighties, trade-unionism had been practically confined to the skilled workers. The unskilled, who needed protection even more (for the huge influx of very cheap Irish labour was a serious handicap), then began to organise, led by John Burns and Keir Hardie, and in England by Tom Mann. While the older Unions were politically of much the same solid democratic creed as the early Radicals, the new ones were fertile soil for the more revolutionary hopes of the Socialists, especially in England, where many looked forward to a world revolution in 1889. The general tendency of the older Unions was by no means revolutionary, however: they worked for a Parliamentary Labour Party, and believed in strictly constitutional action; and though the less intelligent type of Tory was inclined to denounce them as upsetting the State, they were actually a stabilising factor.

By the end of the period over five million British men and women were members of one Union or another, and the movement had spread outside of 'industry,' for teachers, clerks, nurses, and land-workers were adopting the system, much to their advantage; while a greater power and solidarity was achieved by the increasing tendency to form a single union for a whole trade, with skilled and unskilled workers joined together. And the defects of the system began to appear—a tendency to regimentation, to rule by professional committee-men, and (through the junction of some of the powerful unions, including those of the railwaymen and miners, with the parallel organisations existing in England) a tendency also to let the control of Union activities drift as far outside the nation as that of Parliament.

While in the urban districts the period witnessed a marked improvement in working conditions, and a tendency to improvement in those of living, the tale in most of the landward parts of Scotland continues to be very far from cheerful. Lowland farming, till the end of the period, remained fairly prosperous; but the case of the Highlands grew more and more desperate. 1836-37 saw them not far from famine. 1846-47 brought the potato blight, and in many districts the people were, quite literally, starving: the reports sent in by the parish ministers to the Glasgow Relief Board of 1849 are appalling reading. An economic blow increased the distress. The use of kelp for chemical manure had done something to check the effect of the Clearances. The sea-ware proved a profitable crop— and rents of coastwise holdings thereon increased. The remission of import duty on barilla, in 1825, ruined kelp: but the rents stayed up. Many families were forced to live on fish and sorrel, since they lacked money for meal or ground for oats: and there were times when fish was not to be had.

As usual, the only remedy which commended itself to West-minster was emigration. The population of Scotland at its highest— today—is about five million. From this small nation, in the seventy years of one lifetime, a million and a third of the best stock were drained away overseas. In the nine years after 1875, 260,000 left the Clyde, the greater number not for British soil, but as a free gift to the United States. In the first decade of this century, it was well over 342,000. Thousands, as well, and of all social classes, sought work in England, thousands more in the cities. In a century, the whole population of Scotland nearly trebled: but in three of the largest counties in that time it remained the same, and in three more it fell.

And yet the drain was not only unchecked. It was helped. Nor were Parliament, in this, the only culprits. In 1841 an Inverness-shire laird and M.P. of the name of Baillie induced a Parliamentary Committee to report that the West Highlands and the Isles had 'an excess of population of 45,000 to 80,000 souls'—a nice vague figure. Landlords, scared of poor-rates, called on the Government to assist emigration: and the quality of assistance thus supplied sometimes lessened the numbers rather forcibly. In one ship, of four hundred who sailed, fifteen arrived: and in 1848 Labouchere reported in the House of Commons that of 106,000 emigrants who went out, in a single year, from Scotland and Ireland, 6,100 died on the voyage out, 4,100 at the ports of landing, 5,200 in hospitals overseas, and 1,900 on reaching their destination—a really useful reduction of that surplus which the Highland Emigration Fund was removing, with the help of a Colonial Land Commission. And the Scottish Patriotic Society, founded two years earlier, was doing its best in a similar direction, while the Crofters' Commission of 1883 recognised emigration as the great remedy, and Town Councils, Trade Unions, and the Free Church agreed (although they did not put it in those words) that Scotland needed heroes to live in it, and that the heroic thing was to clear out. None the less, in the twenty years after 1862, the rent-roll of the Sutherland Estates rose from £35,000 to £73,000: and many good people were genuinely surprised at the spread of revolutionary doctrines.

We have seen that after the mid-century, evictions for sheep gave way to evictions for sport, as when Mr A. C. Pirie of Aberdeen bought Lochbroom, cleared all the arable and pasture lands, and forbade the people even to keep hens, then turned them out when they could not pay their rent—this in January 1882. And in 1884 1,709,892 acres were deer ground. It is perfectly true, and must not be forgotten, that much of this land was completely uncultivable, even by modern methods: but even by the methods of the time, nearly half a million acres of that area could be cultivated, and most of it had been so.

In 1882 the situation boiled over, on the Braes of Portree, where the sheriff-officers had to burn their summonses and the people fought a large force of police. There was everywhere unrest, and the authorities landed marines in places. It bred some nervousness at Westminster. Oppressed racial minorities in the Balkans might revolt with the blessing of all good Liberals: but if they should do so as near home as this, it might mean a second Ireland. In the 'eighties, one Ireland was emphatically enough: so Gladstone's Government, in the following year, appointed a Commission, which reported that a third of the area then under deer was suitable enough for cultivation. Three years later, the Tories under Salisbury succeeded in passing the Crofters' Holdings Act, which fixed rents (reducing some by seventy per cent.), gave security of tenure, save in Argyll, and compensation at outgoing for improvements, and appointed also a permanent Crofters' Commission, with both executive and judicial functions.

It was a useful step forward, but not enough: and the people were losing faith in Governments. 1887 brought the 'Deer Drive' in Lewis, when ten thousand people turned out with pikes and guns to drive 'the accursed beasts' into the sea. The authorities only dared prosecute a handful; and when they came to trial in Edinburgh, the jury gave them a verdict of Not Guilty and the crowd bore them in triumph down the High Street. Next year there was trouble again, and in Assynt also. Gunboats were sent, and promises were made. In 1892 a new Commission was appointed, and scheduled 1,782,785 acres as land suitable for new holdings of arable with pasture, land to extend grazings, and land suitable for moderate-sized farms with rents over the 'crofter' limit of £80. Five years later a Congested Districts Board was set up for the settlement of this land. It achieved so little that in 1911 its work was passed to the Board of Agriculture, in the hope that it might prove more energetic. By the end of 1912 this new authority had 5,332 applications on its hands: and by August 1914 it had settled 434 of these men on new holdings, and enlarged those of 239. 4,459 were waiting: they had to wait for what proved a rather long time. Also in 1912, the Crofters' Commission, which though it had not got near the root of the matter, or improved the systems of working and marketing, had yet done much to fix rents and enlarge the holdings to economic size, gave place to a new body, called the Land Court. And 1913 brought a new institution of great value, the Highlands and Islands Medical Service Board, founded in terms of actual Highland needs, which soon achieved so remarkable a success that it was copied in several other countries.

Yet for all these things, by 1898 the deer ground had risen to 2,510,625 acres, by 1908 to 2,958,490, and by 1912 to 3,584,966—these figures for the 'crofting counties' only, for in 1908 there were also 195,000 acres in Aberdeenshire, 75,000 in Banff, 199,000 in Perthshire, 60,000 in Angus. And between 1891 and 1901, when the population of the whole of Scotland rose, in round figures, by 446,000, that of the rural districts likewise fell, by something a little under 43,000.

XXIII

HOME POLITICS: III—THE VACANCY

EIGHTY-TWO YEARS: 1832–1914

> In states there are often some obscure and almost latent causes, things which appear at first view of little moment, on which a very great part of their prosperity or adversity must essentially depend.
>
> EDMUND BURKE, *Reflections on the Revolution in France*.
>
> Men have been sometimes led by degrees . . . into things of which, if they could have seen the whole together, they would never have permitted the most remote approach. *Ibid.*

THE last of the conspicuous elements in domestic political history of this time is a sad and strange one, which is rarely faced, but which must be faced if it is to be undone. It is the disappearance of our nation, the disappearance from the world's consciousness (and even, in any true sense, from our own) of what the word *Scotland* had meant for centuries.

It is a curious phenomenon, with no real parallel in history. Scotland, of all the European kingdoms, was the first to discover a true sense of nationhood, of the nation as something to be guarded and honoured, as a thing to which every man owed loyalty. That loyalty was to the nation in its true meaning: it was no mere tribal sense of the kin or the race. The nation could hold men of many races, and transcended race. One can see that, for example, in the steady loyalty of Gaelic clansmen to chiefs of Norman, Flemish, or Anglian stock, who were not regarded as in any way foreign, but accepted as representative of the clan: or in the equal footing at the King's court of Gael, Cymru, Angle, Norse, Norman, and Fleming, all accepted as rightfully part of a Scottish nation, and servants of one 'universall' king, who was master and servant of all six equally.

It is a point of view completely opposed to that of certain Nationalists today, who declare, with a noble disregard for fact, that Gaelic Scotland is all that is truly Scottish, or that Gaelic Scotland is merely an excrescence, and we must all be as Pictish as we know how. The latter view has a real convenience, as the absence of information about the Picts allows its holders a pleasantly ample

260

range of excommunications. But either would have puzzled James the Fourth: and both, and their variants, are historically in absolute opposition to the attitude of the men who fought Bruce's Wars.

One sees that sense of the nation very early, so early indeed as 1176, when the Scottish prelates, the bishops of the Universal Church, in the hands of the formidable Henry II of England, refused at the risk of their lives to do homage to him: or again in the year 1242, when the common folk turned out at the threat of invasion, 'Not fearing death' (so an eye-witness remarks) 'because they were justly to fight for their own country'—*pro patria sua justi dimicaturi*.

That deep sense of the *patria* continued. It endured a three hundred years war against long odds, which is a test of its sincerity. At a time when the odds were as long as they well might be, a hostile ambassador had to warn his master 'there is not so lytle a boy but he will hurle stones . . . the wyves will come out with their distaffes, and the comons unyversally will rather dye' than submit to any attack upon their country. And it was a noble conception of nationhood, that looked with a generous eye on other nations, and was free from aggression, ready for friendliness. There is much in our history calling for contrition, but we do well to remember the glories also: and surely the wise and generous attitude to friends and to beaten foes of David I, of Alexander II and his son, of the great Bruce, of the Jameses, and of the Scots Estates in 1607—a consistent record of nearly five centuries—is not least among these, nor least worth recollection at the present.

Yet, in the nineteenth century, this happened. The country's history was blotted out from the sight and the remembrance of other nations, and even very largely from her own, was distorted in her own sight and falsified. Men will die for a flag: but Scotland lost her flag, so completely that even Scotsmen themselves forgot it, and if they desired to fly a flag that was Scottish, flew that of the Kings, to which they had the same right as John MacDonald has to mark his spoons with the armorial bearings of Buccleuch. What the flag stood for disappeared with the flag. Scotland lost her name and status as a nation. She who had faced, since she had been a nation, continued, almost continuous, assaults, by war and diplomacy, and with all odds against her had beaten them back again and again and again, was regarded by the world (when it saw her at all) as a conquered province of another kingdom, her people bearing in sight of other nations a name that was not hers; while her achievements in the sciences, in industry, in scholarship, in the arts, in war, in colonisation, were credited among the achievements of another nation —of the very nation she had withstood so long, undefeated by bitter centuries of war.

The situation is incredible. Yet by the later nineteenth century the people of Scotland became so accustomed to it that to mention it as a thing remarkable was to invite surprise, not at the strangeness, but at the fact that one should think it strange. It was quite new. It is the product of that century. Europe, and Scotland, round about 1800, still regarded Scotland as a nation in being. How did this obliteration come about, and by what twist or pressure on the mind that was lacking, for instance, in the case of Poland?

The process is a subtle and complex one, involving a score of elements small in themselves, but remorselessly cumulative in effect. It is neither easy nor pleasant to unravel: but it must be unravelled if it is to be undone . . . and if it is not undone there will soon be no Scotland. If the subject were mentioned among the Respectable (where it would certainly not be well received) it would certainly be dismissed as a fuss about words. 'Words' is undoubtedly true, so far as it goes: but the implication, that words, in political matters, are unimportant, is, as perhaps these last years have made clearer, in very exact opposition to the truth. Words that are commonly used in political senses are precisely what we mean by propaganda: and we have seen, in the last year or two, that propaganda, handled successfully, can effect as much as armies, and with more ease. Words carry meaning—what else are they for? If the words are accepted, the ideas which are their meaning are accepted, whether they happen to be true or false. And accepted ideas form the basis of men's conduct, in politics as in other aspects of life. If that ancient truism were better remembered, this sentence would not be typed to a background of gunfire.

Let us face the unpleasant business, and with candour, not attempting to pretend that it does not exist, that it does not matter, that it is not polite, that to mention it shows ungenerous prejudice. (Is care for one's country's survival prejudice? Then those guns have no sort of business to be firing.) And let us squarely face our own share in it. Those who are conscious (their number grows) of the danger are too apt to throw the whole of the blame on England: but Scotland, like other small countries facing aggression, has had her Quislings, and she has them still.

England's share comes first, as historically older: indeed, it goes back for over a thousand years. To begin with, as soon as an English nation was born, it cast its eyes on Scottish territory, as on something desirable. This was hardly surprising, nor indeed blameworthy, for the territorial outlines were fluid still: and in those early days Scotland's record was no better.[1] From that (the process is not peculiar to England) came a sense that this desirable *lebensraum*, with its appurtenances, ought to be England's: and it was a short step thence to enduring conviction that, in some way or other, it was England's, that it was a thing to which she had a right. This frame of mind shows very early indeed, and persisted for century after century. Again and again it led, as we all know, to vigorous attempts at annexation: but few know how often, when these were beaten off, the English Government, in the clearest terms, abandoned all territorial claims in Scotland, to renew the claim on the first opportunity, and with apparently no qualms of conscience.[2] Even in Elizabeth's time the claim was made: even so late as the year 1705, when it was put forward by an eminent lawyer. And after 1707, in spite of the formal admission in the Treaty of Scotland's status as a separate kingdom, we find English members affirming in Parliament that she was nothing more than 'a county of Britain.'

An attitude widely held for a thousand years leaves a print on the mind of the nation which takes it up. Most English people really did believe this: their historians and politicians helped them, because it was the popular line to take. That facts were often, and flagrantly, against them; that they had spent, for centuries, blood and treasure in a vain endeavour to make the belief come true, and had been in that consistently defeated by a nation only a fraction the size of their own, made it a sort of point of national honour to hold to the belief, as their Kings held to the Royal Arms of France, till it was counted as self-evident that Scotland, Scots, and all things done by Scots were rightfully, and therefore truly, English, and to speak of them so was natural and correct. With some few men it

[1] One may, however, point out that when Malcolm II 'lifted' the wealthy provinces of Lothian and the Merse, which remain a part of Scotland to this day, he did so from Cnut, who had no better right to them than himself, and not from one of their lawful sovereigns.

[2] There is a highly significant phrase in Sir Thomas Gray's contemporary record of Edward III's attack on his brother-in-law's kingdom. The attack was made five years after Edward had himself signed the Treaty of Northampton, expressly renouncing and describing as baseless any English claim to sovereignty over Scotland . . . not the first, by many, of such renunciations. But Gray gives as his motive that ' he desired arms *and honour*.'

would be deliberate lying: but with most the belief was as entirely sincere as that of most Germans at the present day that Germany has a similar right to Europe.

Thus, in all joint concerns of the United Kingdom, the official words were *England* and *English* alone. These were used, especially, in all intercourse with the other nations of Europe, who naturally assumed that phrases like 'the English Ambassador,' 'the King of England,' 'the English Army and Navy,' and an 'Anglo-French Treaty' were an expression of fact, and that Scotland's relation with her sister kingdom was very much that of Normandy to France. So was it at home, in all historical and political writing—all writing, indeed, from school-books to the novel. Nor was the procedure confined to things held in common. From James Watt to Lord Lothian, any native of Scotland who achieved anything that was to his credit, from inventing a drug to making a dominion, was officially and currently labelled 'English': indeed, the word was even applied, by the *Times*, to the cities of Glasgow and of Aberdeen. And as English people were eight times as numerous as Scots, and their literature, during the later two-thirds of the nineteenth century, was a good deal more than eight times as voluminous (and it may also be added, a great deal better), the cumulative effect upon the mind of this constant propaganda was sizeable.[1]

It did not work only in England, or overseas. It worked, to a surprising extent, in Scotland. There also the roots of the problem reach far back, to the minority of Alexander III. It constantly happens in small states open to the attacks of larger that those men or those factions who have not power enough to satisfy them seek to win it by alliance with the assailant: we need not give a name to the attitude. From the mid-thirteenth century, in Scotland, there had always been a small pro-English party who were prepared to yield anything to England from which they might themselves win place or profit. And from the mid-thirteenth century England used them, increasingly and with a growing skill: it is doubtful if Hitler's dealings with Dutch Nazis could have taught Elizabeth more than a very little in her handling of Moray and the Scots Reformers. Now

---

[1] It has, indeed, been so powerful that it may be as well to use a hypothetical parallel as illustration. Suppose, at the time of her launching, the *Normandie* had been described in a periodical largely used in German schools as ' a triumph of German shipbuilding ' : and consider the psychological and political implications of the constant reiteration of thousands of similar statements. The *Queen Mary*, in a similar, but actual, English paper, *was* described as ' a triumph of English shipbuilding.'

the Scots Whigs of the seventeenth century were the inheritors of this tradition. To reach power and keep it they had to conciliate England, on this point as on others. They did reach power and keep it: and the power included control of all Scots education for well over a century, and of most till now.

Add to this, as the nineteenth century went on, the social pressure which has already been mentioned in the section on the English public schools, and the element of religious prejudice, which to prove that all good things began with the Reformation was obliged to burke a good deal of our history, not only after that event but before it: and the total pressure becomes considerable. The historians' part in the matter, indeed, was large: academic preferment depended a good deal on making the appropriate omissions; and a spice of false statement, in the right direction, was useful socially and professionally.

This charge, to those who have not gone into the facts, but who have been submitted to the pressure, will certainly appear to be so shocking that it needs concrete examples. These are not easy to give very briefly, for first of all the whole thing was cumulative, and depends on a vast number of small touches, all of them pushing in the same direction; and again, an opinion that has soaked into the mind can be stated in a few phrases, while its rebuttal may need page after page of minutiae, for which there is here no room. The traditional travesty of James the Fourth and the processes leading to the campaign of Flodden, the complete obliteration from popular knowledge of all the splendid achievements of David I and the three Alexanders, or of the less splendid events which led to the Union, are too large to tackle in a paragraph. One may instance, however, the statement of Andrew Lang, that Bruce's War 'was won by Lowland Scots, in origin mainly of English descent.' Now the part of the Lowlands which had been Anglian territory is the South-east. We know who were the hundred and thirty-five landed gentlemen who joined Bruce at his coronation, or soon after: and only fifteen of them are from the South-east, while that part of the country was last to be recovered: so late as the very end of 1312, when all the rest of the country was cleared but two castles, that province was still so firmly in English hands that Bruce failed in his first attempt to recover it. Yet teachers and scholars still repeat Lang's statement. Lang, no doubt, though the facts just quoted above were as freely available to him as to anyone else, made it in all good faith, as the thing that 'naturally' must have happened: it was wishful thinking, that merely ignored the data. It is difficult to say if mere wishful thinking would account for some statements of Sir Herbert Maxwell's in what long has been the standard life of Bruce—a book which for a whole generation affected (whether they happened to have read it or not) the attitude of educated men with regard to the greatest of our national heroes. Since he actually goes so far as to cite, as sole evidence for one of his worst charges, a document which does not refer to Bruce, but merely to Robert Keith (whose surname it gives, though in a paragraph Maxwell does not quote), one may doubt if the lies were all deliberate. But at least they all tend in the same direction, which is never to the credit of the writer's own country. And what is scarcely less remarkable, it does not ever seem to have occurred to intelligent readers that it was surprising that a man of the public record of Maxwell's Bruce should have been able to get men to trust him so far as to risk their lives and all their fortunes by beginning a war against impossible odds, and to carry it through twenty-two hard years, to success.

It is true that such false statements were sometimes contested. Those just mentioned, for instance, were shot full of holes a quarter of a century ago by the scholarly work of Mr E. M. Barron. But the lies had a good start of the contradictions, and the contradictions were unpopular with gentlemen in authoritative places, who might have been forced by them to revise their opinions and take up a line which did not conduce to promotion: so eminent reviewers, *ex cathedra*, dismissed the inconvenient criticisms.[1]

Quite few false statements, when made with authority and given intellectual prestige, or social, or both, have a cumulative effect. Men tend first to believe and then to repeat them, till they are *sincerely*, and widely, taken for granted. This happened in Scotland, as it has done elsewhere. A country's sense of nationhood depends

[1] An amusing example of the methods used was supplied by an eminent Professor of Ecclesiastical History in a review, in a learned periodical, of the present writer's *The Passing of the Stewarts*. Having politely remarked on the book's readability, he pointed out with a grave shake of the head that it made no reference to the use of French troops at the Reformation, or to the Articles of Perth, the obvious implication being that it omitted important facts which the writer found inconvenient. He did not point out, though presumably he knew, that the date of the Reformation was 1560, that the Articles of Perth were passed by the General Assembly in 1618, and that *The Passing of the Stewarts* begins its narrative with 1638 . . . nor that the use of French troops, and the Articles, had been fully described in the author's previous volume, which he himself had reviewed three months before.

above all on its sense of its own history. That of Scotland was gutted of most that made its glories, and then its insignificant remains were thrust into a corner, as only fit for children. The history commonly taught in Scottish schools, above the most junior classes, was that of England, with its strong and consistent anti-Scottish bias. If the Maire of Paris, in a public speech, should chance to refer to 'the France of Frederick the Great' there would, even today, be considerable comment: when the Provost of Edinburgh, in similar case, did refer to 'Elizabethan times' in Scotland, the phrase was accepted as merely natural.

If a nation should be trained, for a century, to believe that her own past, and her present name, and all (except her established form of religion) that marks her out as a nation among nations are either negligible or at the best picturesque survivals, that may be brought out in a mood of condescending sentiment; if you teach her to forget her very flag; if you teach her able men, choosing a career, to take for granted that they must turn from her, and those who set the standard of her manners to send their sons, for their whole education, abroad; if, in addition, her seat of government is some three hundred miles outside her border, and draws to it, as such inevitably do, both the spending of her wealth and the forces that made it; if you leave her for long in other nations' eyes no nation, but a province that has been conquered: then strange and unpleasant things will happen to her, as to a man who loses his memory, and with it a great part of his self-respect.

These things happened, in that century, to Scotland. Not completely: not with uniformity. There was always, at the worst, a faithful remnant, and a lingering tradition among the common people. When in 1901 the new King was proclaimed, in the capital of Scotland, as Edward VII—that is, by a title which flatly contradicted the most glorious phase of Scottish history—there were shouts of protest: but they came from the crowd. The Lord Lyon, whose duty it was to guard such matters, used, and endorsed by his office, the false title. Yet men give their lives for a flag, and are praised for it. If a flag has meaning, then these things have meaning. If they have not, we may as well fly the Swastika.

There are very few things worse for a nation's health than a narrow refusal of foreign ideas as such. This Scotland had always recognised in the past. Her greatest kings had never been afraid to take good new things from any country in Europe, and adapt them to her use and to her profit. There were many things Scotland might well have learned from England: and she did learn good things. It was a very healthy interchange that gave Scotland her first training in agriculture, England the steamship and her system of roads—that gave Scotland the basis of bacteriology, and France aseptic surgery and anaesthetics. There was every need and every valid reason for seeking close and friendly intercourse with a great and in many ways most likeable country with whom, by geography and by dynasty, she was closely connected. In 1800 the way to a sound relation between the two, of much benefit to both, appeared to be opening. It was not attained: and the result was that by 1900 Scotland was only the shadow of a nation. Her apparent prosperity—she still seemed rich—was something with neither the bone of political framework nor the spirit of a sense of nationhood to enable it to stand against heavy stress. She had reached her autumn, and the Martinmas wind was soon to come sweeping in a furious blast before which her brittle structure, drained of sap, was to show a conspicuous lack of that power of resistance which for many centuries had been her glory.

XXIV

BEYOND THE MARCHES: I—THE EMPIRE

EIGHTY-TWO YEARS: 1832–1914

> The existence of Englishmen (sic) like Joseph Thomson ought to reassure any who are dejected by disquisitions on the decadence of the race.
> 'Learned journal' quoted in J. B. Thomson's *Joseph Thomson*.

THE Scotland of the late nineteenth century was in a state of growing decadence. None the less, there is one aspect of national life which, ironic as it seems at the first glance, yet proves, and with a comforting completeness, that sore as the decadence was, and sorer to grow yet, it came from no deep decay in the national stock, but from grave maladjustments in the sett of the nation (using the word in as wide a sense as may be, and including more than the mere political framework), which caused an amazing wastefulness in the use of much vitality and intelligence.

Scotland lacked leadership. She lacked men who could rouse the sense of the nation, who could work to shape and guide and rule a nation, and inspire others to carry on their work. Yet she was producing such men, and in quantity. Only the factory worked for the export trade.

Many of them went no farther abroad than England, where they made themselves careers in her affairs. Several won the headship of her national church. Others played prominent parts in politics, among them the great War Secretary, Lord Haldane, whose service to Britain included the creation not only of the Territorial Army but of the splendid small 'army of mercenaries'

> whose shoulders held the sky suspended

in the terrible autumn of 1914. Half a dozen became Prime Ministers of Britain: between 1850 and 1914 there were Aberdeen, Gladstone, Rosebery, Balfour, Campbell-Bannerman, and the Scots-Canadian Bonar Law. That Scotland should at last receive a share of the great political offices of the joint kingdom was, on any theory, both right and just. In practice, it was apt to work less well. She had,

19   269

on the face of it, more than her fair share: of the last seventeen Prime Ministers, at the time of writing, seven have been Scots and seven Englishmen, the rest being one Welshman, one Irishman, and a Jew: but while this meant that, for a large part of the time, England was not being led by an Englishman, it did not mean that Scotland was led by a Scot, for of these seven, how many gave heed to Scotland's peculiar problems and difficulties? With the exception of Lord Rosebery (Lord Haldane, in lesser office, provides another) they were, like King Charles I, anglicised Scots, alien in blood from the country whose life they lived, alien in life from that whose blood they shared.

For the real achievement of the exported Scot we must look instead to the process of creation of that great federation of free nations, bound in free union by a common Crown, which is popularly known as the British Empire. Since the Union of Crowns, that Empire had steadily grown, though for long, at first, almost wholly by English action. The loss of the American colonies caused a change in British outlook on the Empire. Men came for a while to think of colonies not as 'plantations' of the mother-country, but in the first place as sources of raw material and in the second as useful areas in which to dump such surplus populations as criminals, Radicals, and Highland crofters—conceptions to which the Napoleonic Wars added that of supplying bases for naval power.

During the first half of the century, the Government took small interest in the Empire. Even Disraeli, in his early days, thought the Colonies 'a mill-stone about our necks.' The Liberals wished to get rid of them altogether. Only the Radicals had a use for them, as places where 'the surplus population' could find scope for a fresh start. In 1838 an English Radical peer, the Earl of Durham, produced, in a report on Canada, a point of view which derived to some extent from Edmund Burke. He saw the Colonies as possible nations, who could best be developed in a 'free union' with the Mother Country, possessing responsible government of their own, with rulers not sent out to them from England, but appointed at home by the Colonial voter.[1] The report had no great effect on its own generation, but it gave an inspiration to later men. Another influence was the growing humanitarianism which had caused the abolition of slavery. There was a sincere if sometimes muddled

[1] The report has been assigned to his secretary, Charles Buller, a pupil of Carlyle: but at all events Durham supported its opinions.

desire for the protection of the backward races. At times sheer ignorance caused it to do great harm, with the best intentions, as when, after winding up the East India Company, the Government introduced to India a purely European education, divorced from the rich and ancient native cultures.[1] To them, 'nothing was knowledge that was not taught in England,' and a very ancient native civilisation, brimful of complex and formidable problems, had another, and very serious, one added, and suffered much at the hands of 'Padgett, M.P.,' who often undid the work of the men on the spot. Even with races really uncivilised, the work of devoted, heroic missionaries was sometimes, as in the Pacific, completely deadly, through its failure to consider local conditions.

The 'seventies brought a change. Disraeli, as he matured, began to see the Empire as a whole, and its possibilities: he proposed an Imperial tariff, an Imperial scheme of defence, and a central Imperial Council. At about the same time, the figure of Livingstone profoundly touched the general imagination: and the working-class voter, who had commonly a brother or a cousin or at least a wife's brother-in-law somewhere overseas, responded. Disraeli's bold purchase, in 1875, of a controlling interest in the Suez Canal, was well received; and his stroke two years later in proclaiming the Queen as Empress of India caught the popular mind.

The man in the street had just begun to think about the Empire as something in which to take a personal pride when he suddenly found there were rivals in competition. As result of the Industrial Revolution, other countries were hunting for sources of raw material; and the 'eighties brought not only the first Imperial Conference, in 1887, but a general partitioning of Africa between various, and jealous, European powers. Consciousness grew, much helped by the vivid new writing of a young Anglo-Indian journalist, Rudyard Kipling,[2] who revealed the Empire not only as a possession, but as a great responsibility also. The phrase 'the White Man's Burden' covers much cant: but it corresponds to a reality which was something a good deal finer and larger than cant. Men suddenly knew what it meant to be confronted with, for instance, the relief of an Indian famine, or to steer a crowd through Moharram without bloodshed. By the middle 'nineties even the Liberals were coming

---

[1] A Scot, Lord Macaulay, was largely to blame for this disastrous error.
[2] It is worth noting that Kipling was half a MacDonald, and that both his qualities and his defects have a strong Scots colour.

to see the Empire not as a nuisance but as a privilege which involved many duties: and 'Joe' Chamberlain called it 'an undeveloped estate' which must be developed for the general weal. There was to be later, after 1918, much rather crude highbrow mockery of the conception. Since 1939 there has been less.

Scotland, as such, took of course no direct part in creating the Empire. She supplied many soldiers for its defence and policing. She exported to it large masses of her people, in circumstances which did her no great credit. As a nation she had no voice in its common concerns. But individual Scotsmen did a work quite out of proportion to Scotland's relative size as a part of Great Britain. They had the energy and adaptability which in earlier days had scattered the whole of Europe with Scottish soldiers, merchants, churchmen, and scholars, who remained good Scots while serving many countries. And they had what is a great gift for any man who deals with problems involving different races—the sense of humanity, that 'a man's a man.' They seldom lumped the peoples they ruled as 'natives'; so that, even when stern, their rule could be accepted by free and independent fighting men.

One cannot sum their work in a generalisation. The story is one of many individual achievements by many men, and in brief summary it cannot be more than a swift kaleidoscopic panorama. But none the less it is part of Scotland's story, and therefore an outline of it must be attempted. It will be simplest if we take in turn the various great divisions of the Empire, and run through the share of Scots in building them, noting not only its extent and importance, but its astonishing variety.

Of all the great Dominions, Canada [1] is that which is most essentially Scots in texture. By the latter part of the eighteenth century there were solid masses of Scots in its population, who held firmly to their national tradition; and Gaelic still is a living vernacular. (Quite lately the police of Winnipeg were using it in official communications.) Of the two great Companies which opened up Canadian territory, the Hudson Bay Company was, in origin, English, but soon fell into the hands of a group of Scots, and these never made less than two-thirds of its personnel. And the North-

[1] Rather more than 3¾ million square miles, or slightly less than Europe, and ¼ million square miles larger than the United States. Great Britain is under 89,000, with Scotland something under 30,000.

west Company was from the start under the management of Scots-Canadians, while the amalgamation of the two was achieved by Ellice.

The first shaping of the Dominion was of course French. The Scots followed. The first man to cross Canada from sea to sea was Alexander Mackenzie, of Stornoway, in 1793. Simon Fraser, between 1805 and 1808, reached the river which bears his name, and in 1834 John McLeod reached the Liard, while at much the same time Robert Campbell passed the Klondyke. The fifth Earl of Selkirk, in 1811, laid the foundations of Winnipeg and the province of Manitoba; and Vancouver and British Columbia grew from the work of Dr John McLoughlin and James Douglas, while Ontario owes its existence very largely to the Canada Company, which was founded by the novelist John Galt.

The political building up of these foundations into a nation is largely Scots work also. In 1822 the Government at home contrived to ruffle very seriously the large and important body of French Canadians, the senior settlers, who clung with tenacity to their native traditions and their native speech. The storm nearly blew Canada clean out of the Empire, into the arms of the United States. Lyon Mackenzie, the first Mayor of Toronto, led a clamour for 'responsible government,' which seemed to threaten a War of Independence on the lines of that already fought farther south. In 1847 the young James Bruce, Earl of Elgin, was sent out in the thankless role of Governor-General. As a Scot, he understood and got on with the French: his first speech from the Throne was made in both French and English. In his seven years tenure he not only gained responsible government by his vigorous representations to Westminster, but won the loyal liking of the French, to such an extent that his statue stands today in the *Palais législatif* of Quebec, by those of Cartier, Champlain, Frontenac, and Montcalm. On the foundations he laid, modern Canada was built by the Scots-Canadian Sir John Macdonald, the son of an evicted crofter from Lairg. He would, indeed, have made a Canadian kingdom, but the Home Government feared to rouse prejudice in the United States. He did achieve federation of the provinces in one great Dominion, of which he was the first Prime Minister, and drew within it British Columbia: and he won it that right to control its own economic affairs without which self-government would be but half real. He gave it, indeed, economic unity by threading its enormous territory with the backbone of the Canadian Pacific Railway. He led there, but other Scots supported him, notably Donald Smith, later Lord Strathcona, and his cousin George Stephen, later Lord Mountstephen; while the actual engineering of the railway—three thousand miles in five years, and much of that through uninhabited country—was carried out by another Scot, Sandford Fleming.

The *Times* remarked, in May 1939,

In Canada, the British Empire first learnt the art which is now its special distinction—that of holding people of diverse origin within a single political system, while preserving absolute respect for the individuality of each.

That well describes the work of Lord Elgin and of John Macdonald . . . and that of David I, who was somewhat their senior. But the kingdom of that monarch was not mentioned: and when in that month the same great journal produced a magnificent special number on Canada—thirty-two twenty-five by nineteen inch pages, of seven columns apiece, containing sixty-four articles on every aspect of the Dominion, it gave fully France's part in its creation, but the word *Scots*, or its equivalent, appears just thrice, all three times in one very brief account of the various religious denominations.

Australia's [1] development into a nation came in the early nineteenth century. New South Wales received a constitution in 1842, Victoria, South Australia, and Tasmania in 1850, and Western Australia in 1890, while their federation was mooted in 1856 by the Scot Deas-Thomson. Its general texture is more English than Canada's—in fact, when testing immigrants' acquirements, it refuses to give official recognition to Gaelic as a European language. But its geography and its history are very thickly sprinkled with Scots names. The first of its great explorers, Captain Cook, was himself a 'lost Scot'—and not lost very far, since it was he who christened New Caledonia and the New Hebrides. He was not the last. Captain Currie and Major Ovens discovered the fertile Murrumbidgee country. The distinguished botanist Allan Cunningham did much to open the trackless interior. Hamilton Hume discovered the Murray River, and opened millions of acres of fertile land. John McKinlay first found a route across the huge island, and with Angus McMillan opened South-east Australia: and Major Mitchell con-

---

[1] Nearly 3,000,000 square miles.

ducted the survey of New South Wales. McDouall Stuart was the first white man to reach the centre of Australia (in a heat where horn combs and spoons split into shreds), and he first crossed Australia from south to north. John Forrest, again, was the first man to explore the coast of the Great Australian Bight. And many more names could be added to this list.

New South Wales, when Lachlan Macquarie, in 1809, received its governorship, was no more than a rotting convict settlement, bankrupt and ridden with famine. When his term ended, in 1821, he had made it a self-respecting colony. Sir Thomas Brisbane gave it its legislative council, and Sir Stuart Alexander Donaldson obtained for it responsible government, while its great wool-trade, which now produces a quarter of the world's output, was established by John Macarthur, who is described as the founder of Australian independence: and the meat trade which goes alongside and rivals wool was made possible by James Harrison, who invented the first ice-making machine . . . and the first successful refrigerator ship was the Clyde-built *Strathaven*, launched in 1880.

Western Australia, and its capital Perth, were founded by Stirling and Fraser, Victoria by John Duncan Lang. In the latter colony James Macpherson Grant solved the very difficult problem of the squatters, while it was Syme who obtained for it manhood suffrage. And the federation of the colonies was largely achieved by the work of George Houston Reid, and completed on the first day of 1901 under Lord Hopetoun as Governor-General.[1]

In New Zealand George Rennie led a remarkable and very successful experiment in colonisation, the foundation of the Scots colony of Otago, the old streets of whose capital, Dunedin, bear the names of those of the capital of Scotland. (That city, incidentally, is the site of the first university founded in New Zealand.) Here again the difficult problem of the relations of the incoming whites and the native population was solved, and to the satisfaction of both, by Sir Donald MacLean: while John Mackenzie dealt with that of the squatters, and created a working agricultural economy which brought success to thousands of small farmers. Indeed, it is more than a coincidence that when the war opened in 1939 the Premiers of three of the four chief Dominions—of Canada,

[1] Sir Thomas McIlwraith, Governor of Queensland, annexed British New Guinea, and its first Governor-General was the crofter's son Sir William Mac-Gregor, one of the greatest of British colonial administrators, whose name even today is a legend in the Pacific.

Australia, and New Zealand—should bear the names of as many Highland clans.

Africa too was to see much Scottish work, though there are no such solid blocks of Scots as one can find in Canada and New Zealand. Scots explorers appear as early, indeed, as 1777, when Robert Jacob Gordon and William Paterson, in Dutch service, found and named the Orange River. In that century, the chief British link with Africa was through the Bristol and Liverpool slave-traders, who ran a thriving business with North America. In 1795 Sir James Craig and Admiral Keith Elphinstone annexed the Cape, which was, however, returned to Holland again, to be re-taken in 1806 by Sir David Baird. In early days its connection with Scotland was close, for its first State schools were staffed with Scottish teachers (brought in by an English Governor-General), and Scottish ministers worked in the Dutch Reformed Church, and in fact came near uniting it with their own. Indeed, one can fairly say that the greatest achievements of Scottish Presbyterianism are its work in creating modern South Africa. From 1821 the Glasgow Missionary Society was working from Lovedale, and was happy in recruiting for its service men of genuine greatness of both mind and heart. John Philip, for instance, defended the Hottentots, and succeeded in winning legal recognition for the principle that the African coloured peoples were not to be mere slaves in their own land: and Dr Robert Moffat did splendid work as a teacher alike of white men and of black, while the settling and pacification of Griqualand were largely the work of their colleagues.

The greatest Scottish name in Africa—perhaps the greatest in all its history—is that of a man inspired by Dr Moffat, David Livingstone, whose curt and yet voluminous epitaph is 'Missionary. Explorer. Liberator.' He came from Scotland in 1841, his first journey being through the Kalahari Desert to the Zambesi. On it he saw for himself the dreadful slave-trade, and resolved to end it: it is characteristic that his attitude was not merely negative, for he grasped from the start that it would only end when a legitimate commerce could take its place, and he held it part of his missionary work to open routes to the heart of Africa. In this place it is scarcely possible to give even a bare outline of what he did. He crossed all Africa from west to east, discovering the Victoria Falls, 'the Place of the Sounding Smoke.' Palmerston, seeing the value of what he was doing, backed

him in further journeys on the Zambesi, the Shiré, and Lakes Shirwa
and Nyasa, in the course of which he explored a huge territory that
was to see great colonising and missionary activity, much of it Scots.
The Royal Geographical Society then sent him, with a very small
subsidy, to Lake Tanganyika: and he discovered Lakes Mweru and
Bangweolo. He died in an effort to reach the source of the Nile.
All through his journeys he did an immense amount of missionary
and political work, doing more than any other man of his time to
shatter the slave-trade that was the cancer of Africa, and striving
always to found a native Christianity—no spoon-fed exotic attractive
to 'rice-Christians,' but an integral part of native life.

He is but one of many great Scots explorers. The first European
to cross Africa in the reverse direction from Livingstone's journey
was Lovett Cameron. James Augustus Grant shared with the
Englishman Speke in the great expedition of 1860-63 to discover
the hidden sources of the Nile. Alexander Keith Johnstone, who
died at thirty-seven (when his work was carried on by Joseph
Thomson), did work that includes the opening of the route between
the sea and Victoria Nyanza, through the Masai country. He laid
the foundations of Rhodesia, blazed the trail to Uganda and the
country round Lakes Nyasa and Tanganyika, and did important
scientific work in both geology and botany.

The Continent was so huge, and the Scots so active, it is hard
to systematise their list of achievements. Perhaps the simplest way
is to sketch by districts the work of the men who built on these
foundations. South Africa saw a good deal of it. Sir Henry Loch
worked with a growing success for the peaceful amalgamation of
Dutch and British, and had Rhodes not intervened and attempted
to rush things, might have prevented the costly miseries of the
second Boer War. John Mackenzie again had to suffer from
Rhodes's impulsive interference. Like Livingstone, he was Dr
Moffat's pupil. He had reconciled the Bechuanas to British rule,
and was rapidly turning their fighting-men into good farmers, when
the discovery of gold and diamonds caused their exploitation by the
sharks of the Rand. He fought hard for them, and won appointment
as British Commissioner of Bechuanaland. Rhodes, though he later
worked on Mackenzie's ideas, was jealous of him and ousted him
from his post. Rhodes's own greatest lieutenant was a Scot, the
brilliant, puzzling, Leander Starr Jameson. He is best known by a
failure. Everyone has heard of 'the Jameson Raid'—a *putsch* to

overturn the Dutch Government of the South African Republic. Its leader, however, was let down by the Uitlanders whose cause he was fighting, and repudiated by the Government at home. None the less, he led the Chartered Company of Mashonaland, brought Matabeleland into the Empire, and eventually became Prime Minister of the Cape, though he never would draw his official salary.

East Africa is closely connected with South: and here again were many Scots. The mission stations of the Church of Scotland (Blantyre, founded in 1876) and of the Free Church (Livingstonia, founded in 1875) did a great civilising work, building roads and breaking 'chains and slavery': the African Lakes Company grew out of the latter. Outside the missions, it was Dr John Kirke whose ability to stand up to 'Seyyid Burgash in a tantrum' enabled him, by pure moral suasion, to end the vast and ancient Zanzibar slave-trade. He ranks as one of the main creators of British East Africa, being greatly aided there by Sir William Mackinnon, the founder of the British India Steamship Company, who in 1888 founded also the Imperial British East Africa Company, whose members were mostly Scots. His work was carried on by Sir George Mackenzie. The Company was short of capital, but some of the members were extraordinarily generous with their own money, and they spent £450,000 on the colony. When the Government bought them out (for half that sum) they had saved Uganda from falling to Germany, and had made Kenya.

North Africa shows a string of military names—Gordon, Archibald Hunter, Hector Macdonald, and Sir Reginald Wingate, who having finished the Khalifa in 1899, brought about the political, economic, and social regeneration of the Sudan. But most of the leading British work in Egypt was done by Englishmen, and for anything comparable to the Scots share in South and East Africa, one has to look westward, where the British West African Colonies generally—one of the most truly beneficial of all our colonial schemes —were largely Scots work. The great mysterious Black River, the Niger, seems to have had a strong fascination for Scots. In the later eighteenth century it witnessed the incredible adventures of the handsome young Border surgeon, Mungo Park, the first white man to see, though he did not enter, the legendary city of Timbuktu He died on the river, and so did Peddie and Gray, who followed him. Later, Clapperton, starting from Tripoli, found Lake Chad and working again from Lagos, reached Sokoto: and the first white man to enter Timbuktu was a Scot after all, Alexander Gordon Laing.

Again Scots built on the explorers' foundations. The creation of the West African trading system was the work of Macgregor Laird (who also founded the West Africa Steamship Company) and of William Baikie. The Gold Coast Colony was made by George MacLean, a great pioneer of the 'protectorate' system, and the founder of a scheme of government which has thoroughly proved its value. But the greatest names here are those of the two Scots bacteriologists, Sir Patrick Manson and Sir Ronald Ross, whose work upon the tropical diseases changed 'the White Man's Grave'—and a good many other most dangerous parts of the world—to places where both white and coloured men could exploit in safety enormous natural riches. The most picturesque figure of them all, however, was that of 'the White Queen of Calabar,' a mill-girl from Dundee, turned U.P. missionary, who landed in 1876—the timid Victorian creature—in Old Calabar, then as dangerous a place as there was in the world, and till her death in 1915 was a greater power in the land than the Government. Mary Slessor was fearless, cheerful, and confident, and ruled cannibal chiefs and English Governors-General with a sort of serene high-handed maternalism that is faintly comic to look at: but it worked. A Scots Governor-General, Sir Claude Macdonald, recognising her gifts, took the unprecedented step of making her the head of a native court: and she proved herself one of his best subordinates.

India presented quite different types of problem. Here were neither new white countries to build up, nor a form of symbiosis to be contrived for white settlers and coloured folk of a primitive culture. There was a varied congeries of native states, with their own ancient and complex civilisations, all used, for long centuries, to foreign rule, that was the only chance of peace between them. The history of British India flickers from end to end with Scottish names: only a few of them can be mentioned here, for the purpose of this chapter is not to give a record of them all, but to suggest the various kinds of work that Scots were doing for the Overseas Empire.

So early as 1774 George Boyle was the first white man to penetrate Tibet. Alexander Dalrymple charted the Bay of Bengal, and J. B. Gilchrist the Hindustani language, preparing a grammar and a dictionary which by systematising it made it a *lingua franca* for a vast sub-continent of many tongues. Calcutta was very largely the work of Scots. Its famous and valuable Botanic Gardens were founded by Robert Kyd, and the great jute trade which had created its wealth was in Scots hands for long, while the basis of what was to be an enormous tea trade was laid by William Jameson, the first man to cultivate tea in India.

The most conspicuous names, however, are those of soldiers and administrators. Even in the eighteenth century there were Scots high in the service of the native princes: John Morison commanded the armies of the Great Moghul, and John Stewart was Vizier of Arcot. Later, Kirkpatrick, as British Resident in Hyderabad, brought the Nizam to our help against Tippu Sultan. It was in 1795-1811 that Jonathan Duncan was Governor of Bombay: and even generations after his time the best compliment that a native of the province could pay a white man of tact and sympathy was to describe him as 'Duncan's little brother.' Sir Hector Munro's part has been mentioned already, for his victory of Buxar was the first step to British supremacy in India: and we have spoken too of Sir David Baird, and the douce St Andrews historian Professor Hugh Cleghorn, to whom the British Empire owes Ceylon.

In the generation round about 1800 the great names are those of Thomas Munro, John Malcolm, and Mountstuart Elphinstone. Munro, a fine soldier, administered and pacified Southern India, in such fashion that it came willingly to accept British rule: an eminent Indian who lately received the freedom of Edinburgh declared that he had given the Indian Empire 'imperishable lessons in administration and statecraft.' Malcolm's record in the East is such that in his own day the Shah of Persia created a special order in his honour, and in ours his name is still used as a charm, in Indian amulets, to bring good luck. Elphinstone was the Governor of Bombay, and the pioneer of a system of education including both English and the vernaculars. He was one of the greatest of all Indian statesmen, and his constructive mind looked forward to making an India capable of self-government.

The soldier Ochterlony made the treaty that won for Britain the loyalty of the Gurkhas, the traditional comrades of our own Highland regiments. The first Scots Governor-General of India was Gilbert Elliot, first Earl of Minto, between 1807 and 1813. He was successful in a difficult task, but he yields to a later man, James

Andrew Ramsay, tenth Earl and first Marquis of Dalhousie, made
Governor-General in 1848, at the age of thirty-five. He found himself faced with the Second Sikh War, fought it out, and annexed
the Punjab—a district about as large as the whole of Great Britain—
and so administered it afterwards that the Punjabis became the
Queen's loyal subjects.   In fact, he added much to the Indian
Empire, for he had a genius for attracting huge areas that happened
to lack heirs . . . though he did not take himself too seriously, for
he could write of himself as

The Laird o' Cockpen sitting here and bowling about kings and
kingdoms as if they were curling stones ! But although one does laugh,
it is anxious work, I can tell you.

It was: but it was very fruitful also, for he, more than any man,
fused the huge heterogeneous sub-continent into a whole by giving
it a system of communications—railways, roads, ports, canals,
steamships, and 40,000 miles of telegraph wires. It was he who
founded the Indian railway system, the Grand Trunk Road, the
great Ganges Canal. He worked important constitutional and
social changes, and above all, he showed that he loved India and
understood her, and made her people love him in return.

When the Mutiny came, many Scots played a prominent part.
Charters Macpherson kept Scindia out of it, Cuthbert Davidson the
Nizam, and Lord Elphinstone not only held Bombay in peace, but
made the famous Central India Field Force. Colonel James Neill
saved Benares and Allahabad against huge odds. Delhi rings still
with the great name of Nikhal Seyn, the Irish Scot John Nicholson,
the idol of Indian soldiers ever since. (There is a sect who worship
him as a god.) The Commander-in-Chief who at last broke the
Mutiny and saved India from lapsing into anarchy was Sir Colin
Campbell, later Lord Clyde: the Highland regiments still proudly
remember his famous order in a desperate action, 'Colonel Stuart,
bring on the tartan—let my own lads at them!' The greatest of
his subordinates was perhaps Sir Hope Grant: but beside him on
the roll are Hugh Ross (Lord Strathnairn), Sir George Maxwell,
Sir John Ross, and Lord Napier.

The frontier wars are no less full of Scots. There is Sir Robert
Sandeman's pacification of Baluchistan, Sir George Scott Robertson's
defence of Chitral, Sir John McQueen's Hazara Expedition, and
Sir William Lockhart's Tirah campaign, that saw the great charge
of the Gordons at Dargai, with their piper, shot through both legs,

playing *The Cock of the North*. Indeed, the 'honours' of the Scots Regiments read like a gazetteer of Indian wars: and two of the most famous Indian regiments, Thomas Rattray's Sikhs and Sir Harry Lumsden's Guides, were created and led to victory by Scotsmen.

It would need a book [1] to give a mere impression of the work of Scots in governing provinces, or of the varied missionary achievement. The great Presidency College in Calcutta, the Medical College there—the first in India—are Scots foundations. But these are only specimens of many.

Even this slight hurried sketch of Scots work for the Empire suggests its scope and its variety. One cannot regret that very great achievement. Yet suppose that even a fraction of these men had been able to make careers in their own country, to find a natural place in its national structure? Suppose the Scots political machine had given room for the exercise of their gifts? Suppose it had not been commonly taken for granted that any Scot of energy and talents must look past his own land to make use of them? Might not the man who achieved the establishment of the successful *ryotwari* system have been able to cope with the Highland Clearances? Could not Dalhousie, or even a pupil of his, have given us an adequate plan for transport? And what might have happened had Sir John Macdonald become the Prime Minister of his own country, David Livingstone been M.O.H. for Glasgow, or Mary Slessor a bailie of Dundee?

[1] There is a book which in fact gives a most fascinating survey of the matters so slightly and briefly sketched in this chapter—Professor Andrew Dewar Gibb's *Scottish Empire*: this chapter is greatly in its debt.

XXV

BEYOND THE MARCHES: II—EUROPE

EIGHTY-TWO YEARS: 1832-1914

Anyone who has pottered among *old* Continental works of reference—
historical, geographical, biographical, or the like—will have noticed how
large and respectable a place Scotland, with all her counties, towns,
institutions, and celebrities, holds in them.

J. HILL BURTON, *The Scot Abroad.* (Italics not in original.)

THERE had been a time when the small kingdom of Scotland was the
key to the balance of power in Northern Europe: and even in 1800
she had still been a leader in its intellectual life. By the mid-
nineteenth century, however, Scotland was fading from the sight
of Europe. Scholars, mainly French, recalled that she had been:
but not even the Frenchmen regarded her as being. None the less,
the affairs of Europe affected her—her culture little, her commerce
considerably, and her domestic life a good deal more, for first and
last, they were to cost many Scots lives. We need therefore to give
some slight outline of their course.

The Europe which after the wars of Napoleon was shaped by the
Treaties of Paris and Vienna was patterned rather by dynasties than
by nations: but Napoleon made nations conscious that they were
nations, and most of them had not forgotten the lesson. The results
of this sense of nationality were a major force throughout the century,
and were made also a great deal more complex by the fact that the
ideas of race and nation—two different things—were often identified.[1]

Already, by 1830, events were moving. France had once more
thrown off the elder line of the Bourbons, and replaced Charles X
with a constitutional cousin, Louis Philippe of Orleans, who ascended
the throne as king not of France but of the French: and Belgium
now cut herself away from Holland, and was threatening to unite with
France instead. It might have caused a European war, but a vigorous
nationalist rising in Poland held the attention of Austria, Prussia,
and Russia, and gave Palmerston, then British Foreign Secretary, a
chance to negotiate. He induced Louis Philippe (and Talleyrand,

[1] See Appendix II.

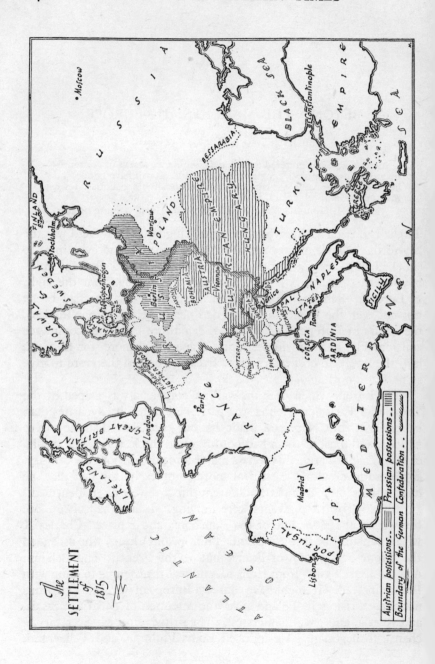

The SETTLEMENT of 1815

who counted for much more) to agree in making Belgium a separate kingdom. Her neutrality was guaranteed by the Powers, and a wise, and pro-British, king was found for her—Queen Victoria's uncle, Leopold of Coburg, whose first wife had been heiress to the British Crown, and whose second was an Orleans Princess of France.

War was avoided, and the early 'forties had a deceptive air of stability. (1839-42, however, saw Britain engaged in inglorious conflict with China, who had forbidden the import of opium, which, from a monetary point of view, was one of India's most valuable products: the war opened China to trade, and gave Britain Hong Kong.) The Czar had crushed the Poles, and in Vienna the wily Metternich still reigned supreme, controlling all Germany and Italy, while in 1840 Britain and Austria had saved Turkey from being overthrown by Mehemet Ali, Vizier of Egypt. The disturbances of the 'thirties seemed to have settled, but none the less trouble was brewing everywhere.

In 1848, 'the year of revolutions,' it boiled over noisily. A quite small dispute between Louis Philippe and the French Liberals,[1] on a franchise question, suddenly flared up into what was to be a third French Revolution. It settled quickly, with France again a republic . . . and Napoleon's nephew as her President: but it touched off masses of piled-up explosives in Germany, Austria, and Italy, all which blazed also in nationalist revolutions, demanding democratic self-government for their tangled races. All Italy was alight, with Piedmont declaring war on Austria, whose garrisons were expelled from Milan and Venice. Austria's hands were full enough without that, for Magyar and Czech were clamouring for Home Rule, and Metternich had to flee for his life from Vienna, in the Falstaffian guise of the week's washing. Germany rang with songs of Liberty. The King of Prussia granted a constitution, and even accepted the revolution flag: the minor princes followed his example, and a German national parliament met at Frankfurt, and made ecstatic speeches upon Progress.

The armies, however, were left: and unlike those of France in 1789, they did not sympathise with the revolutions. And more important than the reserve of the armies was the fact that, while the revolutionaries had been able everywhere to seize the power, they

---

[1] The word *Liberal* is constantly met with in nineteenth-century European politics. It meant anything from desire for the control of legislation by an elected representative assembly to desire for rule by the mob for the mob-leaders.

20

had small idea what to do with it when they had got it. Italy wanted to shake off Austria. Every Italian was agreed in that. But then? Was she to form herself as a monarchy, under the patriotic King of Piedmont? Or should she be a republic, under Mazzini? Most of Germany disliked the old state of affairs. But then? Should she be monarchy or republic, a state or a federation of extant states? Was the monarch, if she should be a monarchy, to be Hapsburg or Hohenzollern, Austrian or Prussian? Was German Austria to find a place there? And suppose Home Rule were granted to the Magyars, were they to rule the great mass of Hungarian Serbs?

Disunited idealists were an easy prey to the canny realists of the *status quo ante*, who still had disciplined and obedient armies. The Austrian nationalisms were soon defeated. In Germany, nothing was left but the memory of a completely futile parliament. In Italy there were tales of heroism, but their courage had, it seemed, been entirely vain—though Cavour proved right when he claimed that out of defeat had sprung what Italy needed, a national flag. And the Second French Republic lasted four years, and then, by overwhelming popular vote, its Prince-President was enthroned in the Tuileries as Napoleon III, the Emperor of the French.[1]

Most British opinion was startled and scandalised. But Victoria, as German as she was, had from the very beginning of her reign made friendship with France a central point of her foreign policy. She was not yet 'the Grandmother of Europe,' but a reign which already had lasted for fifteen years had made her an outstanding personage in the closely linked caste of professional hereditary rulers. She gave a lead by taking the change serenely, even becoming both the guest and the hostess of the Emperor and his lovely Scots-Spanish Empress: and the lead, for the time being, was accepted.

The Queen's policy grew from a real desire for peace. She had thrown herself with passion, the previous year, into her husband's dearly beloved plan for a great international exhibition of the Arts of Peace and had seen it a huge success, in spite of much preliminary foreboding [2]—a success not only at home but throughout the world, from every point of view but the aesthetic.

[1] The Bonapartists reckoned Napoleon I's son, the unhappy young Duke of Reichstadt, as Napoleon II.

[2] The British press prophesied riots, the American massacre and insurrection. Actually, everybody behaved with the greatest politeness, and 'the delicate female whose tempered sway is owned by a hundred millions of men pursued her course among the contributions of all the civilised world' untroubled by anything but the London sparrows.

Public opinion swung happily round again. The Great Exhibition was going to open an era of hope, enterprise, free trade, cheap production, and peace. Unluckily, the year when the Crystal Palace rose among, and even over, the trees of Hyde Park, opened an era not of peace but of wars—a good many of them quite unnecessary. The generation which had seen for itself the huge waste and the economic dislocation brought about by Napoleon's worship of martial glory was dying out. The new one desired to win glory for itself, and Europe was growing militant again, and looking across her fields for shaking landmarks.

There was a tempting one by the Black Sea. Turkey, bolstered up for a time, had grown weak again, and Russia cast eyes upon Constantinople. This was a challenge both to France and to Britain. France's old rivalry with Austria had left her a traditional interest in Turkey. Britain held India, whose rule for centuries had gone to the invader from the North: and with Constantinople in Russian hands, the Black Sea became a gate to the Middle East, to Persia, and the road to the Khyber Pass. Russia refused to be warned, and in 1853 declared war on Turkey. Next year France and Britain came to the latter's aid, joined by Austria. The Russians withdrew from Turkish soil, and the war might thereupon have come to an end had not the British Government considered the great Crimean fortress, Sebastopol, to be a menace still to Constantinople, and accordingly, in time, to India.

The Crimean War was mainly Britain's concern: but Napoleon III took an active part in it for the sake of maintaining a useful friendship with her, and also because fresh military glory might stabilise his uncertain dynasty. There was, in fact, little glory for anyone. The war was won, in time; but the victory was due to Russian weakness, not to Allied strength. Britain has gravely mismanaged many wars, but none of them more spectacularly than this one, which was muddled through at cost of 25,000 British lives, and brought deep discredit on everyone concerned but the common soldiers and Florence Nightingale, an heroic and efficient Englishwoman who in spite of Whitehall revolutionised the whole conception of Army medical work, saving millions of lives of men who were yet unborn.[1]

The results of the Crimean War were unpleasant. Russia was

[1] The 'fifties were to see several ' Imperial ' wars away from Europe—one with Persia in 1856-57, the dangerous outbreak in India, called the Mutiny, in 1857, and the Second Chinese War in 1857-60, which, like the First, was a none too creditable struggle for trade.

indeed for the time kept out of Turkey, and forced to promise to leave the Black Sea neutral. Turkey's uncertain life was prolonged once more. But Britain became both angry and uneasy at the revelation of incompetence, and comforted herself by dislike of France, who was (quite fairly) claiming most of the credit for victory, and whose capital was again the centre of Europe: the papers of the time are very full of contrasts between the arrogance of France and the unvarying modesty of England, and assertions that if the British Lion roared, the Froggies would be sent scuttling for their lives. Franco-British relations became, largely thanks to their Press, acutely strained. In 1858, when an Italian refugee from London tried to murder Napoleon III with a Birmingham bomb, a good deal more than the bomb was threatening explosion: and when next year Britain set about the formation of a Volunteer Force it was frankly aimed at France—and 150,000 rapidly joined it.[1]

Napoleon still desired peace with Britain, however: indeed, it was one of his cardinal beliefs that his uncle had made his most serious mistake in rousing that country's hostility against him. His major interest just then lay not north but south, where Italian patriots were threatening to rise again. His own Italian blood gave him a quite sincere sympathy towards them: and if there should be a new Italian kingdom, it would be a great deal to France's future advantage if she should have acted as its liberator. He held out a hand to the long-headed Piedmontese statesman Cavour, who was as much the brains of Italian nationalism as Mazzini was its soul. He probably thought that he could use Cavour: but Cavour used him, and that most dextrously.

They worked out a complex plan to free Italy; and in 1859 Napoleon opened the first moves of it. He did much, for he freed Lombardy in the north, and made possible the freeing of the rest: but he did not do enough to make Italy feel she had cause for gratitude. Rather she felt he had left her in the lurch, and in Britain, where Garibaldi's heroic exploits had roused a strong romantic sympathy, the tendency always to think the worst of France welcomed the thought that she had betrayed her ally. France herself disapproved of any further effort: Napoleon could not free all Italy without attack on the temporal power of the Pope, who recruited French anti-imperial feeling to aid him, and stirred the devout against

---

[1] The review by the Queen of its Scottish section in 1881 has come down in tradition as ' the Wet Review,' and seems to have deserved the epithet.

Napoleon. And Austria, of course, was antagonised, while Prussia saw France at once too strong for her liking, and entangled in an awkward false position, which she saw her way to exploiting very soon.

Disappointed Italy, half liberated, declared that she would *far da sè*, and did. By 1861 *il Rè galantuomo*—Vittore Emanuele, King of Sardinia—was King of Italy, but an Italy where Venezia was still in Austrian hands, and Rome in those of the stubborn Pius IX—that is, an Italy with two first-class grievances at home, and another against France. This last helped anti-French sentiment in Britain, who, even to the blouses of her women, was enthusiastically pro-Italian, and therefore (this also was to have its importance) both anti-Austrian and anti-French.

Britain was also no less enthusiastic over Prussia. The careful cultivation of anti-French feeling, which in Scotland had gone on, slowly and uphill, since the Reformation, was now bearing fruit—a fruit ripened by the long war against Napoleon. England had never needed to cultivate it: and now the general passion for all things German which had begun with the Romantic Revival rose to its zenith. It is summarised in a vivid passage of G. K. Chesterton, which does not in any way exaggerate it.[1]

The whole English life of the period was overshadowed by Germany. We had now reached . . . the final fulfilment of that gathering influence which began to grow on us in the seventeenth century, which was solidified by the military alliances of the eighteenth century, and which in the nineteenth century had been turned into a philosophy—not to say a mythology. German metaphysics had thinned our theology, so that many a man's most solemn conviction about Good Friday was that it was named after Freya. German history had simply annexed English history, so that it was almost counted the duty of any patriotic Englishman to be proud of being a German.

There was, in fact, very little need of that 'almost.' The immensely popular *Short History of England* of J. R. Green, which widely affected the general thought of the time, set out to prove, to the common satisfaction, that Englishmen were really noble Germans—that England owed her superiority to any other nation whatsoever to the fact that she was 'the one purely German nation that rose on

---

[1] He is actually speaking of the later part of the nineteenth century, but the condition was already well-established before the 'sixties, very largely thanks to the influence of Carlyle. Also, his ' we ' refers to England : but what he says is no less true of at least the greater part of contemporary Scotland.

the wreck of Rome.' Even Scots historians were very busy disparaging 'the Celt' and the old French intimacies, and eagerly claiming that Scotland, in all that mattered, was really Teuton. And it was therefore to be of some importance that 'German,' to the general British mind, meant not the old Catholic culture of the South, represented by Austria as heir to the Empire, but that newly risen in North Germany, with for centre the efficiency of Prussia.

For over a century already, Prussia, thanks to the British support of Frederick the Great, had been a powerful force in politics. She was now, for the next lifetime, to dominate them: and Britain, taking her at her own valuation, accepted her exaltation with delight.

In 1860 Austria was still, in appearance, the leader and senior of the German states, and Prussian influence had somewhat lessened. On the second day of the following year, however, the Prince Regent of Prussia became King Wilhelm I, with behind him the ruthless driving efficiency of his minister Otto, Prince von Bismarck-Schönhausen. Wilhelm, a capable professional soldier, desired to make Prussia a military power. In his case it was very largely art for art's sake. But Bismarck behind him had the further reason of that idolisation of power for the sake of power which has from their beginning been the weakness of the Slav-Teutons of North Germany, and with that the knowledge that the new ideas threatened the domination of his caste; and to bring Germany to depend on the army which that caste led was the way of preventing this.

In 1863 things began to move. The Czar of Russia, Alexander II, emancipated twenty-five million serfs, and showed some signs of freeing Russian Poland, then in revolt. Such action was awkward for Prussia, who was holding down another limb of Poland. She induced the Czar to crush the Poles by force, and formed a convention with Russia, which caused some uneasiness in France and Austria. Then the King of Denmark (which commanded the Baltic) died without near heirs, and left a succession problem, in which was entangled a more complex one, over the duchies of Schleswig and of Holstein, which had made up the southern part of his kingdom, and were largely German in their population.

Bismarck saw far ahead. He was planning to make Prussia a naval power; and to hold the duchies was a long step to commanding the north coast of Europe. He first of all induced Austria to ally herself with Prussia in seizing the duchies. In 1864 the two powers together began a war on Denmark. The small kingdom, encouraged and then abandoned by Britain, and refused help by France, fought gallantly for a while, but was swamped by sheer weight of numbers, and lost the duchies.

The next seven years were crucial for Europe. Bismarck had won the first hand, but the main game was yet to play. He held strong cards. Russia's share with Prussia in dismembered Poland gave her a powerful interest in Prussian friendship. Great Britain, though slightly ruffled over Denmark, as the country of the popular Princess of Wales, saw in Prussia (capably aided by Prussian writers) the splendid apotheosis of all things German—that is, of the noblest type of humanity, the *Herrenvolk*, to which she herself belonged. The new kingdom of Italy was a dubious factor, but could be bought by the gift of Venezia, which would weaken Austria further. And the French Empire, though outwardly it stood tall and prosperous, was shaky, and much of its power was then absorbed in an ill-judged and unsuccessful attempt to bolster a Hapsburg empire in Mexico.

The first step was hegemony in Germany; and in the summer of 1866 Bismarck launched a lightning war on Austria. In six weeks she was beaten, and driven out of the German Confederation. Prussia now, annexing the kingdom of Hanover, formed a new Confederation of the North, from which the southern states—Austria, Bavaria, Baden, and Wurtemburg—were excluded: and by giving to the new Confederation a Parliament with universal suffrage, he won the support of the German Liberals for just so long as he happened to require it.

Austria, thus weakened, was, as he foresaw, at once weakened further. Italy attacked her—without success, but Napoleon, to conciliate that kingdom, contrived the transfer to it of Venezia: and the Magyars were induced to rise again, and to demand a Dual Monarchy, which Austria was in no case to refuse. Napoleon, seeing the Prussians pressing west, tried to strengthen his position by a bid for the control of the Palatinate. Bismarck published the demand, with the swift result that the South German states hostile to Prussia fell into her arms, and demanded her protection against France.

That country now was where he wanted her. And she herself was willing to make war, for united Germany, with a Prussian head, threatened her gravely. She was therefore inclined to tackle the menace before it consolidated: and her optimistic War Ministry assured her that all was ready to the last gaiter button. It was not ready: but Prussia was quite ready. In 1870 affairs in Spain provided a convenient *casus belli*. In July the war began, and swept very rapidly to Bismarck's conclusion. In the next January, Paris was in the hands of the Prussian army, Napoleon was a prisoner and deposed, and France a republic split by violent factions, with her Reds beginning a fierce civil war in Paris, under the very eyes of the invaders: the peace terms included the loss of Alsace and Lorraine—the latter the birth-country of St Joan—and what was meant as a crippling indemnity. And while France was thus split and weakened, her two neighbours were at last effectively consolidated. The French troops who guarded the Pope having been withdrawn, Rome was taken by the Italian nationalists, and became the capital of the Italian kingdom. And in Louis XIV's palace of Versailles, on the 18th January 1871, Wilhelm I of Prussia was proclaimed German Emperor, head of an Empire which included all the German-speaking states with the exception of Hapsburg Austria, who was left with her fringe of Czech, Slav, and Magyar dominions to swing, a diminishing comet, round the new sun.

From 1870 to 1914 the European system turned on Berlin. The new Empire feared a French recovery, and in 1871 she drew together, in the *Dreikaiserbund*, the League of Three Emperors, Austria and Russia, a league to which, two years later, the new kingdom of Italy became attached. France, grimly determined on recovery, recovered with an unexpected speed, paying off her indemnity and training new armies who looked for *la revanche*. In 1875 an anxious Prussia showed signs of trying to strike her down once more before her strength should fully be regained. Queen Victoria intervened, and staved off war by inducing the Czar to put pressure on his ally, who then as now was haunted by the nightmare of having to fight a war on two fronts at once.

From that time till the middle 'eighties, however, British relations with Russia grew more and more strained, for Russia still looked south to India, and her intrigues upon the North-west Frontier brought about the Afghan War of 1878-80. A new focus of trouble was growing in Europe also, in the steady kindling of a national feeling among the various peoples of South-east Europe, who were held down by Turkish or Austrian masters, neither of them remarkably enlightened, and desired to follow the road of Italy.

In 1876 Turkey horrified all Europe by massacres of her restive Bulgarian subjects. The Balkan countries flickered with revolt, and

Russia, as the greatest of Slav powers, declared war on Turkey. Gladstone supported the Bulgarian cause. Disraeli feared that Russia would make use of the general horror at the Turkish methods to establish herself as mistress first of the Balkans, and then of Constantinople and the Straits, neatly outflanking the road to India. He backed the Turks. The Liberals opposed, insisting that Turkey must leave Europe 'bag and baggage.'[1] Turkey and Russia, however, made a peace in the early spring of 1878, much to Russia's territorial advantage. Disraeli insisted that the settlement should be remitted to a Congress of the Powers, which was held at Berlin and determined the map of Europe till the Treaty of Versailles in 1919.

Now Russia, through most of the last generation, had posed as the patroness of the Slav peoples, and had pointed out Austria as their enemy. In 1877 she had sought none the less to win Austria's goodwill by helping her to a protectorate of the Serbs in the Turkish provinces of Bosnia and Herzegovina. This convenient arrangement gave the Serbs a new grievance against Austria: and the Treaty of Berlin did not alter it, but created a new and stormy group of states. Turkey was saved from being driven clean out of Europe, but her power was lopped, for her former territories of Rumania, Serbia, and Montenegro were recognised as independent states. Bulgaria was left with a grievance also, for Russia's treaty with Turkey had arranged that she was to be an autonomous principality (under Russian control) to include Macedonia and Eastern Roumelia. Instead, though she was left autonomous, Roumelia was given back to Turkey, under guarantees of its good government, and parts of what Bulgaria had claimed were given to Serbia and Rumania, while Macedonia, which Greece also had wanted, was left to Turkey. There was a general juggling with the Balkans which, though intended as a compromise from which all the powers concerned might receive some advantage, gave none of them as much as they had hoped, and like most compromises in politics, created rather a general discontent.

Disraeli claimed to have made a peace with honour: but the Peace of Berlin was the most serious failure of his career . . . though it is none the less much easier to criticise what he did than to suggest a better alternative. It cost his party their place as government, for

---

[1] It was in the course of this conflict that Disraeli achieved his famous description of his opponent as 'a sophisticated rhetorician, intoxicated with the exuberance of his own verbosity.'

Gladstone, not having to negotiate it, was strongly placed to point out its defects, including the fact that it had not demolished Turkey; and his whirlwind campaign in Midlothian next year carried the Liberals to power in 1880. And Germany and Austria, far from pleased by the group of new Slav states on the road to the East, formed a secret alliance, offensive and defensive, against Russia, which Italy joined in 1882.

The various European disturbances of the early and middle nineteenth century arose from causes within Europe itself. The 'eighties, however, brought a new source of trouble—the race for colonies. As nation after nation became industrialised, it looked round for supplies of raw material, and for new markets in undeveloped countries. All the great powers joined the scuffle, save Austria, who was busy at home, for in that uneasy Empire eleven million Germans and nine million Magyars were holding down the growing and irritated nationalisms of twenty-seven million Czechs, Slovaks, Serbs, Croats, Slovenes, Poles, Ruthenes, Rumanians, and Italians, and had therefore little leisure to look overseas.

Egypt for many years was a storm-centre. Disraeli had seized the chance, in 1875, of buying her Government's shares in the Suez Canal. This gave Britain a valuable controlling interest in what was now the main route to India: but it also made the stability of Egypt an important factor in Imperial safety. Egypt then was very far from stable, however. Soon after, the Khedive defaulted on large borrowings from France and Britain. They therefore put in the sheriff's officer, and established in Egypt a system of dual control. This was in 1879, and in two years Arabi Pasha headed a nationalist insurrection against it. The French withdrew, but Britain stayed and fought, for the sake of Suez. Next year Arabi was defeated at Tel-el-Kebir, and an unofficial British protectorate was established. The Mahdi, religious leader of the Sudan, proclaimed a Holy War next year again. He was kept out of Egypt proper, where British officers were trying to raise an economically foundered country by the help of a new great irrigation system. The Sudan, in his hands and those of his successor the Khalifa, sank into sheer barbarism, losing three-quarters of its population; and in 1896 Britain decided to reconquer it. This was accomplished at Omdurman in 1898, and her rule pushed south to the borders of Uganda.

There was a clash with France, for a French force coming eastward from the Congo raised the French flag at Fashoda. France, however, withdrew, leaving the Sudan under British administration, and turned to Tunis, annoying Italy, who wanted it. In the 'nineties the latter country tried for Abyssinia, and was bloodily defeated, worsening her relations with France and Britain, and being driven closer to Austria and Germany.

These affairs were but part of the general African scramble. Before the end of the nineteenth century, almost all Africa had been partitioned among the various European powers. Britain had colonies or protectorates in British Somaliland, British East Africa, Uganda, Nyasaland, Rhodesia, Nigeria, Ashanti, the Gold Coast, Sierra Leone, and Gambia. The French were expanding Senegal into French West Africa, and held a large part of the Congo Basin and the great island of Madagascar. The Belgians again had a large colony on the Congo. Portugal had old-standing colonies in west and east. Italy held Libya in the north and Italian Somaliland on the Red Sea: and Germany, who had gone to work rather late, held Togoland, the German Cameroons, German South-west Africa, and German East Africa, and was by no means contented with her share.

Towards the end of the 'eighties the German Empire was once more 'in the news.' In 1887 the Triple Alliance—in effect, the German control of the Central Powers—was made public. Next year, however, Europe breathed more freely, for the Emperor Wilhelm died and was succeeded by his son Frederick, a sympathetic and broad-minded man, with no lust for arms: but he died within a year, and left the headship of the Triple Alliance to his young, arrogant, and restless son, besotted upon military glory, histrionic, and more than a little neurotic also: and Wilhelm II's first act on his accession was to 'drop the pilot'—to get rid of Bismarck, who was, to be sure, entirely unscrupulous, but who did not make wars unless he was sure to win them.

Europe, accordingly, began the 'nineties with a solid Triple Alliance in her midst, controlled by a bellicose and unbalanced young man and surrounded by three isolated Great Powers, then in a state of strong mutual mistrust. And though British admiration for Germany was as strong as ever, it was not reciprocated. Since her formation in 1871, the new German Reich had industrialised herself. Her population, and her apparent wealth, had greatly increased: but the wealth very largely depended on Government loans to her industrialists; and without a constantly expanding trade, the interest on the loans was unpayable. Therefore she must secure expanding markets, expanding sources of raw material. Britain dominated the markets of the world: and Britain also was well in the lead in the race for colonies, which Germany had entered rather late. Thus Germany's 'place in the sun' seemed inadequate, and someone else must be shouldered out to make room. And since Germany possessed the world's finest army, and was rapidly becoming a naval power, her diplomats saw an easy road to success, to hegemony first of all in Europe itself, and then among the great colonial empires. But Britain, being able to keep the balance of power, stood right across the path of this coveted triumph, and already had thwarted Germany more than once. Germany worked herself into a belief that the only alternatives that lay before her were *Weltmacht oder Niedergang*—world-power or downfall: and that the encirclement planned by wicked Britain would achieve the second if the first were not seized.

France and Russia decided, in 1893, to sink their differences, and make an alliance, with an eye to the growing German danger between. Britain, however, was still isolated. She had, to be sure, the most powerful fleet in the world: but her efforts to keep the peace by throwing her weight on one side or the other of the scales of power, and her huge colonial and commercial success (to say nothing of her complacence over it) had not added greatly to Europe's liking of her. 1894 brought considerable tension with France over Siam, and 1896 with Germany over the Jameson Raid in South Africa. When in 1899 Britain went to war with the Dutch Republics in South Africa—a foolish war which might well have been prevented—she had the feeling of all Europe against her. And in the East there was a general friction over trade with China, while Japan was rapidly, and efficiently, westernising not only her industry but her fighting forces.

The South African War dragged on, with small glory for Britain, and came at last to an end in May 1902, sixteen months after the death of Victoria. The peace was better handled than the war: but the war was more in the front of consciousness, and though, in the end, she had won it, by sheer weight, it showed a serious rot in the organisation of her fighting forces: and an alliance with the new power of Japan, in that same year, did nothing to win European friendship.

The Liberal Imperialist, Joseph Chamberlain, grew aware of the dangers of British isolation, and sought help in what seemed to most Englishmen at the time, and to many Scots, the natural direction— an alliance with Germany. He was snubbed, however; and the Scot

Balfour, who by that time led the Conservatives, was aware that Victoria had been right in seeking for Britain a closer and more intimate friendship with France.

At the time she was very far from possessing it: but the new King Edward, who had a very real love for that country, agreed with Balfour, and so, in France, did Delcassé, who was Foreign Minister, and Paul Cambon, then French Ambassador to St James's. In 1903 the King went on an official visit to Paris, and used his charm and his diplomatic skill to such effect that the crowds who had greeted him with *Vivent les Boers!* saw him off when he went away with *Vive notre roi!* The Press and the diplomats helped. The atmosphere changed. Friendly discussions cleared away points of dispute, which were formally dealt with, next year, by a treaty. Although there was as yet no formal alliance, a friendly understanding— *entente cordiale*—had been achieved: and almost immediately it proved its value.

It was growing rapidly clear to every one that the German bid for *Weltmacht* was not far off. The Entente, however, seemed to discourage it. Immediately after it had been concluded, the Kaiser threw out a challenge to France at Tangier. The matter was settled by a Conference of the Powers at Algeciras in 1906: and too many people, among them the Liberal Government in Britain, concluded that the danger had ceased for good . . . though the Scot Lord Haldane, who was War Minister and who very well knew where Germany was tending, set to work to reorganise the British Army, which, unlike those of the great Continental powers, was only a very small professional one; to supplement it with a Territorial force for home defence; and to arrange staff talks between France and Britain. Meanwhile Russia, on the far side of Germany, had been challenged and badly beaten by Japan, and her moral effect, as a brake on German ambitions, largely deflated. Something had to be done to make her effective once more: and in 1907 a fresh rapprochement with France drew her into what was now the Triple Entente.

By 1907 Europe stood in two great camps—the Triple Alliance ringed by the Triple Entente, besides a group of peaceful northern neutrals, and another of far from peaceful Balkan states. And Germany grew exceedingly uneasy. Two generations of steady propaganda had made Prussian hegemony within the Empire a powerful fact: yet still there were threats to it, for in 1912 a third of the German voters were 'Social Democrats.' The power of the

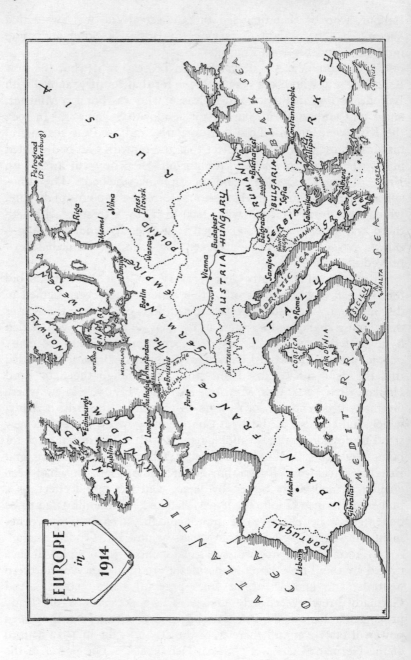

EUROPE in 1914

Prussian junkers who ruled them was shaken: it depended on keeping the prestige of the army, and that on the sense that the army was sole protection against imminent dangers. A popular panic over these was worked up . . . while the army itself grew more and more confident that any war would be a walk-over. Russia's army had been proved a mere façade, and though she was certainly reorganising it, the process would not be complete till 1917. Britain had none to speak of, and was soft with prosperity, while her control of the seas could soon be snatched by the magnificent new German navy, and her colonies would never fight for her. One lightning blow that should knock out France again, and Britain would have to accept the *fait accompli*, and then could be tackled and overwhelmed in turn. And France was an easy prey, for her politics were suffering from the disease of democracies—the free voter's confiding habit of leaving rule in the hands of the professional politicians, who depended on place for status, power, and income, and were determined to hold these at all costs: and her frontier defences did not reach the sea, and could easily be turned by a brief march through neutral and undefended Belgium.

The German officers happily drank to *Der Tag*, when their Jericho should fall at the sound of the trumpets. In 1908 its dawn seemed to be breaking. Austria bitterly suspected Russia, and was constantly worried over the stormy Balkans and their intrigues with her own Slav populations: tension grew, and the Kaiser made a flamboyant speech about backing Austria 'in shining armour.' Russia, however, contrived to adjust the matter, and Germany put *Der Tag* off a little longer.

It had a second false dawn in 1911. Italy quarrelled with Turkey in Tripoli, and induced the Balkan states to threaten her flank, while the Kaiser, fishing in the troubled waters, sent a gunboat to Agadir, to demand a slice of French Congo. Mr Lloyd George, in a vigorous speech, however, recalled the Entente—and France and Britain made a naval agreement which drew it closer.

Next year the Balkans blazed. Bulgaria, Greece, and Serbia made war on Turkey, and overran her European lands. There was a crisis of the first magnitude. Austria and Italy collaborated in keeping Serbia out of Albania, and the original war had soon developed into a contest of Serbia and Greece against Bulgaria, which ended with her defeat in 1913, and Serbia, considerably enlarged, looking northward to the Slavs of Russia.

Next year, the great German Kiel Canal was completed, leaving Germany free to move her navy swiftly from her major Baltic ports to the North Sea. And that summer, on the 28th of June, an Austrian Archduke, Franz Ferdinand, heir to the throne, drove through the Bosnian capital Sarajevo, and was shot and killed by an Austro-Serbian insurgent.

Austria snatched at the excuse for a war that should stifle the danger of a Slav insurrection. There was a passage of angry diplomacy. Russia, the great protectress of the Slavs, used her influence to make Serbia surrender very nearly all that Austria asked of her, and demand that the Tribunal at the Hague (founded fifteen years before for just such cases) should arbitrate on the rest. But Germany saw her chance for *Der Tag* at last, and stiffened Austria, who on the 27th of July sent Serbia a sudden ultimatum, of a kind that left her no choice but to fight.

Northern Europe to this point had looked on calmly. There was always trouble of some kind in the Balkans, and July was a holiday month, and that year a fine one. Now it woke, startled. The diplomats of Russia and Great Britain still tried for a Conference. Austria refused, and Germany supported her refusal. Both had mobilised, as did Russia. On the day after the Austrian ultimatum, Austria declared war on Serbia. Russia and Germany were moving to war—and France was Russia's ally. Germany at the time believed herself to be capable of tackling both France and Russia, but preferred not to have the British Navy as well: she offered, if Britain would undertake to stay neutral, to annex nothing more than the French Empire, not France itself. Britain countered with the question, would France and Germany observe Belgian neutrality (vital to her), which they both had guaranteed? France replied that she would, but Germany gave no answer.

There were four crashing days. On the first of August, Germany declared war on Russia. On the second, Sunday, her troops invaded France, and next day their grey masses poured into neutral Belgium to turn the flank of France before Britain could move. But Belgium refused to give them a free passage: she resisted, and she called for British help. Britain sent Germany an ultimatum, and Germany, sure that three weeks would see her in Paris, left it unheeded. At midnight on the 4th August it expired. The Victorian Age went crashing into smoke, and from the small villages in the Western Isles the men were already pouring to the colours.

IV
WINTER

TWENTY-FIVE YEARS: 1914–39

We do not exist to restore a past, but to create a future which embodies the greatness of that past.

STEPHEN SPENDER, in *New Writing*.

XXVI

MARTINMAS WIND

FOUR YEARS: 1914–18

> . . . Martinmas wind,
> To shake the green leaf off the tree.
> *Lady Douglas's Lament.*

THE war lasted for four years, three months, and a week, and came to involve the greater part of Europe, and before it ended, the greater part of the world, from Japan to Portugal, and round again. And for very nearly four years of that time, France and Britain were upon the losing side. Yet they held out, held out through what seemed disaster, held when it seemed that all that could be saved was death without surrender, and came through—sick, shattered, Scotland and France wounded almost to the death, and England sorely hurt: but they came through. They did not fight alone: there were many allies, but these came late, save Belgium, Russia, and Serbia; and the two latter of these were forced out early. France and Britain bore the weight for all the war—they and their Empires. It had seemed to the world that these loosely-held Empires would dissolve at a touch. Instead, the frail bonds held stronger than iron chains, and the weight those cobwebs drew in was to turn the scale.

The war at its beginning was a contest of the five great powers of Europe and two small ones, one of which was a fighting people, to be sure, but one which had just been through two heavy wars. On land, it was apparently a contest between Germany and Austria, Russia and France, with Italy allied to the former pair, and Great Britain and Serbia fighting beside the latter. Austria and Germany had fewer men than the powers of the Entente taken together: but their seven million were ready, prepared, and united, and holding the inner lines, could strike with massed man-power and formidable machines west, east, or south, against separate and unready antagonists. France and Russia had then some four million men apiece, but they were far apart, and the first blows fell when they were still in confused mobilisation. British military power seemed negligible. True, Britain had a long-service professional army, of high quality: but it was very small—she could put but seventy thousand men in the field. Serbia's was larger, but it had just borne the strain on men and supplies of two severe wars fought largely on Serbian soil. As for Belgium, nobody, then, considered her troops as more than a ceremonial decoration.

There was also a factor which Germany underrated, as Revolutionary France had done—sea-power. The small British Army was backed by the world's best navy, and France had a fine one. But Germany's also was strong, and in the very short war she contemplated there would be small time for sea-power to take effect. Her judgment of sea-power and her judgment of Belgium were her two major mistakes: and they cost her the war.

Germany's plan was to smash France at once, before the cumbrous Russian machine could move, or sea-power take any effect. The French frontier, marching with Germany, was strong: so Germany's scheme was to tear up 'the scrap of paper' that guaranteed the neutrality of Belgium, and pour a million and a half of men, well equipped, finely trained, the best army in the world, round the unguarded flank of the French defences. This would carry the war at once off German soil, would upset the whole of the French plan of defence, and by holding the Channel ports, threaten Britain to stillness. After that, a mere three weeks should see her in Paris, before Britain could fight—if Britain dared to fight. France down, Britain was powerless, and her Empire would fall into Germany's hands like so much ripe fruit.

Now Germany, then as now, understood very well the weaker and baser side of human nature, and founded her plans on it, though with less science than she has since brought to bear on that black art. But then as now, her psychology had a weakness, for she either overlooked or underrated human courage and loyalty and decency. A small peaceful country, bred for a hundred years to take its safe neutrality for granted, stood in her path, and she summoned it to give way. But King Albert called to his people, and they answered: and before the astonished eyes of Europe they stood, resisting, especially, in the forts of Liége. They could not stand long against the avalanche: but they stood just long enough to break the momentum, to disconcert the careful time-table. The hideous retaliation that fell on Belgium is the measure of German anger. That anger had cause: for first of all Belgium had given France priceless hours to get her armies into some kind of position, and secondly, the spirit of her resistance fired all Britain, and sent men crowding to the recruiting centres. And there was one thing more: the British Fleet, just before the war, was united on manœuvres, and Mr Winston Churchill, First Lord of the Admiralty, and Prince Louis of Battenberg, the First Sea Lord, acted swiftly and kept it together, controlling the Narrow Seas. By these two things, the *blitzkrieg* was held a few days, and those few days turned the fortune of the world.

The French plan was an immediate counter-offensive, but they were ill served by their Intelligence, and underestimated alike the force of the magnificent German artillery and the effect of the German attack on Belgium. The counter-offensive was a ghastly failure. It cost France nearly a quarter million in *killed*. By the 23rd August Belgium was swept almost clear, and Von Kluck was facing the tiny British Expeditionary Force at Mons, in Belgium, on the left of the French. He took them for outposts, and their rifle-fire for machine-guns covering a large force; and though he had twice their strength he held his hand, and they slipped out of his envelopment, and fell back in a fighting retreat, still a force in being. Still the retreat went on, through glorious summer. On the 28th August there was at last a good omen. A British squadron under Admiral Beatty sank three German cruisers in Heligoland Bight—and the German Fleet did not come out to face them. But still the grey masses poured on into France. On the 2nd September the Government left Paris for Bordeaux.

Joffre, by then, realised what was happening. He could make mistakes, and he had made some grave ones. But now he saw what was to do, and he took all risks. He drew back his forces, fighting a rear-guard action, 'giving up French territory to save France.' Behind their screen he made new dispositions. On the 4th September, with the Germans across the Marne, he made his arrangements: on the 7th the French counter-attack began, under Manoury. It very nearly failed, but was saved by Gallieni's reinforcements, rushed to the field in the taxi-cabs of Paris. On the 9th the British too were advancing again, and next day Moltke withdrew north of the Marne, and Paris was saved: and meanwhile, farther east, De Castelnau held before Nancy, Sarrail before Verdun, De Cary in the Argonne, and Foch at La Fère. The first thrust had failed. The Germans had played and—not won. But they were far indeed from having lost, and they were to win for nearly four years yet. They dug in on the Aisne, and the next phase of the war is the race to the sea. On the Eastern front very much the same thing had happened. Russia invaded Galicia and East Prussia. In the latter, Hindenburg, on the 28th August, had beaten her heavily at Tannenberg. In Galicia, however, she was succeeding, and Germany had to send reinforcements to Austria, against whom the Serbs too were striking with success. Already, in the East, the war was spreading: two German battleships, the *Goeben* and *Breslau*, had slipped through the British fleet and the Dardanelles, and enabled Germany so to put pressure on Turkey that she came into the war in late October— on the German side, thus gravely hampering Russia.

Meanwhile, the war was thundering in the West. In early October the Germans were in Ypres and took the Belgian ports— Antwerp, Ostend, Zeebrugge: the Allies' swift march barely reached the coast in time to hold them from taking the French Channel ports as well. That month the war in the West ceased till near its end to be the familiar war of manœuvring masses, and became a strange locking of siege and counter-siege, swaying a few miles back and forth in the mud at cost of many thousands of men's lives. On the 13th October the Germans fell back from Ypres, and on the 19th counter-attacked once more, in the month-long struggle called the First Battle of Ypres. Haig made a name then for defensive fighting, and the Scottish regiments did superbly also, stamping themselves on the German imagination, which called them, because of their 'skirts,' the Ladies from Hell.[1]

The circle of the war was still enlarging. When Turkey came in, the British Government seized Cyprus and Egypt, and in Africa Togoland, and attacked the German Cameroons. A Boer rising in South Africa was suppressed, very largely by Boers under Botha, who carried the war into German South-west Africa, while the Germans invaded British East Africa. There was also lively naval activity: on the 1st November, fighting against odds, a British squadron off the cost of Chile was defeated at Coronel by Graf von Spee—to be avenged soon on the 8th December, when Sturdee destroyed Von Spee's force off the Falklands. Many German raiders, on and under sea, attempted a blockade of France and

---

[1] Lord Haldane's Territorials were in the war by this time : the first of their units to go into action was the London Scottish.

Britain: the most famous of these, the *Emden*, was destroyed on the 9th November by H.M.A.S. *Sydney*. British open towns were bombarded from the sea, and Britain and France blockaded Germany.

By the end of the year the conduct of Germany in occupied countries had left the moral issues sufficiently plain. From a military point of view, the contest so far was drawn: but the sea-ways still were open to the Entente, and the French and British Empires had both stood in with all the help they could bring to their mother countries, while Germany had lost most of hers already.

The prospect, in fact, at the opening of 1915 was not disheartening for the Entente. But in their councils there were two schools of thought, and both of these, disastrously, took action. One, seeing rightly enough that the West was the major theatre of the war, was all for concentrating on breaking through there. The other, led by Mr Winston Churchill, grasped, also rightly, that the German wall was too strong to break through by merely frontal attack, and proposed, by beating down Turkey, the weakest part of the Central Alliance, to make touch with Russia, and drive back from the East, forcing Germany to dissipate her strength. Had either plan been whole-heartedly supported, there might have been success. Both, however, were tried, and neither was pushed home, for lack of the forces expended in the other; and both accordingly were costly failures. On the 19th February the British fleet bombarded the Dardanelles, with heartening success: but they failed the next month to take Constantinople. At the same time, the French made a push in Champagne, and advanced—and were held: and on the 10th of March the British took the offensive, at Neuve Chapelle, with the same result. Both actions, unluckily, looked like victories. At the end of April there was another such semblance. A British and French force, with a Scots leader, Sir Ian Hamilton, made a superb attack on Gallipoli. The landing was the greatest feat of arms in the whole course of the war: but it was wasted. The earlier abortive naval attack had warned the Turks, who by now were strongly prepared. Too few men had been sent, and too few guns: and there were no reserves. Hamilton's force fought grandly, but it was held, and in the West the Germans were already counter-thrusting at Ypres, preceded by a terrible new weapon, the clouds of gas which on 22nd April mowed down the French troops on the right of the British line. A Canadian brigade held the gap—God and the souls of their officers know how—till British troops (among them, to their great honour, the Argyll and Sutherlands and Territorials of the Royal Scots) came up to help them. 'Second Ypres' dragged on into the middle of May. Then the Entente made a counter-attack in force, the British at Festubert and the French at Arras: and both failed, for lack of sufficient guns and munitions.

In the East, where the new year had begun with Russian victory, the Germans in May were already driving back the Russian armies, and they continued to do so. None the less, at this time, the Entente received a surprising new accession, which made a great difference in the Mediterranean, and to the completeness of their southern blockade. Italy had been the ally of Germany and Austria, but loved the one little and hated the other much. She had refused to enter the war with them, and now in May she came in—but with the Entente, seeking to free *Italia irredenta*, the Italian lands in Tirol and Istria, still in Austrian hands: and she struck her old foe through the difficult hill country of her march.

Most of that summer passed in a dull stalemate, though Britain at home took off her coat at last, joined her parties in coalition under Asquith, and with Mr Lloyd George in the Ministry of Munitions, was beginning to give her troops the guns they needed. For lack of guns, in that year's spring offensive, the British had lost 100,000 men, and the French a good deal more than twice that number.

In July, General Botha finally completed the conquest of German South-west Africa. It seemed an agreeable omen for the autumn, when the British New Armies could be thrown in at last. They were thrown in, in September. The French attacked in Champagne, the British at Loos. There was splendid valour: the British citizen-soldiers—the 9th Highland and 15th Lowland Divisions among them—took their place worthily by those of France. But though some ground and many prisoners were taken, and the Germans had cause to regret their use of gas, which was now turned back on them in the autumn west winds, the seeming victories were again ineffective. In October, uncertain Bulgaria made up her mind, and joined the Central Powers, while all the Balkans were thrown into unrest. Greece was bound to help her old ally Serbia, and her minister Venizelos would have done so, but her King Constantine (whose Queen was a sister of the German Kaiser) kept neutral, plainly leaning to Germany. Britain and France tried then to take

Greece's place. Venizelos wished them to send 150,000 men to Salonika. They sent 13,000—and from Gallipoli. By the end of November, unhappy Serbia, in spite of a magnificent resistance, was over-run by Germans, Austrians, and Bulgars: and the German route to the East was clear and open, with the result that before the end of the year the Gallipoli campaign had to be abandoned, with enormous loss of life and of prestige, the more as General Townshend's attempt at Baghdad had also been checked: and now Russia stood alone, cut off from the West.

At sea there was growing danger for the Entente, and in the air also. German airships, the great silvery Zeppelins, dropped bombs on London and the East of England, expressly to shatter civilian morale: and ever since February of that year the U-boats, breaking the recognised laws of war, had been sinking at sight the ships of the Entente . . . though in May of this year they came to sink one too many, the great transatlantic liner *Lusitania*, when 1,200 civilians, women and children among them, and many neutral Americans, lost their lives, shocking public opinion in the United States.

The year, in fact, ended in a growing gloom. The German line in the West was unbreakable. The Russian line in the East had been pushed far back, with a loss of three-quarters of a million prisoners; and the 'sideshows' had mostly been spectacular failures. Yet still the great Russian army, for all its losses, was a force in being, and Italy, strung out on a front of 460 miles, was hammering at the south of Austria.

1916 began with the resolution of both sides to make an end, by breaking the opposite line. In February the Germans brought back many troops from the Russian front, and threw them hard against the French salient outside the town of Verdun. They battered it with their full weight all through spring. France lost 179,000 men in killed and missing, 263,000 wounded: but in all her history there is no greater glory than that defence . . . and it was Pétain who led it. The British, through that spring on the Western Front, did no more than hold. In April Townshend surrendered to the Turks: but the Cameroons were taken from Germany, and Botha carried a successful campaign into German East Africa, while in the East, the Russians, with pressure on them somewhat weakened, took Erzerum. In May, there was naval action. On the 31st, Beatty with the Grand Fleet battle-cruisers met the German battle-cruisers off the coast of Jutland. The German High Seas Fleet came out to attack, and Jellicoe brought the Grand Fleet to help Beatty. (King George, as a young naval officer, was in this action.) A fog came down on the battle, and the combatants lost touch, after hard fighting. As a battle it was, at the time, a draw, with the advantage in losses to the Germans: but none the less, it helped to decide the war, for while hostilities lasted, the main German fleet never again came out of its safe harbour, leaving all its work to the U-boats, which still were a menace. And in less than a week after Jutland, Lord Kitchener, British Minister of War, was lost, on his way to Russia, in H.M.S. *Hampshire*.

The tide eddied back in the end of June, however. The attack on Verdun had risen to its crisis in early April, and failed to break through. The Germans continued to pound the salient still, but initiative seemed to have passed to the Entente, the more as in June Russia struck a heavy blow at Austria, and threatened Hungary. On 1st July the French and British counter-attacked on the Somme. (Our last volunteers to enlist, and our first conscripts, went into that battle.) The new munitions were beginning to come, and a new strategy had been devised, of a series of blows. The battle opened with Homeric fighting, the main weight of which was borne by British troops: the Scots regiments are not likely to forget Longueval or Contalmaison or Beaumont-Hamel. But though the southern flank of the attack drove forward on the first day, the northern was held. The battle proved the longest yet in war, for it went on from July until November. The Gordons, the Royal Scots, the 9th and 51st Highland Divisions, the 15th Lowland, recall their share with pride: but there was to be no pride for the Higher Command, and the pride of the regimental officers and the N.C.O.s and the ranks was in gallant death. It cost the British 20,000 officers, and no less than 460,000 men in casualties: and all it seemed to achieve was to hold its ground . . . though in fact its 'attrition' of the German troops was to be by no means wholly without effect.

By the end of August, the Russian thrust in the East and Italian successes on the Austrian front had brought Rumania to side with the Entente: but her war was to be a short one and unhappy, for by Christmas the Germans were in Bucharest, and Rumania's resources in food and oil were at their service. It was a serious blow to the blockade, which so far had seemed to be the Entente's best weapon: and though the Zeppelin attack on England had been

beaten off (they came no more after that winter) France was torn by
a hideous crisis in politics, the result of revelations made at Verdun of
the state of her munitions and defences. When Germany, in December, proposed a peace, there seemed to be every probability that
France, Britain, Russia, and even Italy (who so far had been the most
successful of them) would accept in despair and make the best of it.

Only, they did not despair. If Germany had shown generosity
to any of the countries she occupied, it is possible they would have
fallen into the trap, and yielded on what terms they could secure.
But it was clear already what those would be, and they chose rather
to take the chance and go on.

Go on they did, through 1917, a year that began with a delusive
hope. A great conjoined attack of the outer powers was planned—
of Britain, France, Russia, and Italy. But Germany by now was
using the weapon that twenty years later was to be her strongest—
the weapon England so often in the past had used with such disastrous effect against Scotland, of political cleavages in her opponents.
She worked on the reactionary forces in Russia, first, to take a pro-
German line: then on their rivals, all those who wished for Russia's
internal 'reform'—in a number of different meanings of that word.
As result, in March the Czar had to abdicate. To the Allies the
movement at first had seemed to promise a new zeal in the prosecution of the war: but Russia, amorphous and unintegrated, with no
unified culture, was only held together by her centralised machine
of government, and very largely, in fact, by the place of the Crown
in the common imagination of her peoples: her ill-found armies
were worn out and depressed and growing mistrustful of those who
commanded them, while her politicians were at mortal odds, each
sure that the millennium would be won if he and his little group,
and only they, could control the power. Germany, watching with
a cynical eye, realised she had little more to fear on the East, and
in February disconcerted Western attack by withdrawing her troops
to a new and very strong prepared position, the Hindenburg Line,
which in places was twenty miles behind her old front. It cheered
the civilians of the Entente, but it gave the forthcoming Franco-
British attack a great stretch of devastated No Man's Land to cross,
and dislocated all its plans : and in the preceding month Germany
had begun what she called an unrestricted sea campaign, intended
to dam the flow of reinforcements and munitions from Britain to

France, and of food and supplies from overseas to both. She had already shown her attitude to the international laws governing war by sinking hospital ships, clearly marked as such.

The new violation of the deep-rooted code of the sea was to prove an error, for just as Russia was foundering in the East, its moral effect brought in a new Western ally. President Wilson of the United States broke off diplomatic relations with Germany: and when soon thereafter his country became aware that German diplomats accredited to her were using their position of privilege to stir up a war between her and Mexico, there was a flare of anti-German feeling, already stirred by the methods of the U-boats and the German lack of the decencies of war. America ceased to be 'too proud to fight,' entered the war, in the April of that year, and put in force conscription to raise armies.

It heartened the Entente. But Germany knew that it would be many months before American help could be effective on any but the economic plane, which, if Germany won, would not matter very much. The rest of the year brought disaster after disaster.

The plan for the new joint offensive had been delayed by the German retreat behind the Hindenburg Line and the uncertainty of affairs in Russia. In April, however, it was put into force. On the 9th, a great British attack, in a heavy snowstorm, took Vimy Ridge, near Arras—and there was held. A week later the French struck also, under Nivelle, between Soissons and Reims; and they had the same fortune, a brilliant beginning followed by a halt, and appalling slaughter. Some French troops mutinied. Nivelle lost his command, which then was given to Pétain, who could do no more for the time than hold his ground and work to stop the rot. And in the South-east the same thing was happening. Maude took Kut, and in mid-March Baghdad itself: but a spring campaign in Palestine was a failure.

The British on the Western Front that summer had to take the main weight. In June, they scored at Messines, but again were unable to force a real decision, though the battle was not useless— far from that, for it held the Germans till the French recovered. At the end of July Haig, who by now was the British Commander-in-Chief, began the Third Battle of Ypres, a push to reach the ports of the Belgian coast. It lasted till November, and did not reach them. The long-drawn agony of Passchendaele, whose mud is still the nightmare of those who served there, was part of this 'battle.'

From that huge torment, little seemed to be won, but none the less France had been given her chance to recover, and under Pétain on the 23rd October she struck forward and took the famous Chemin des Dames, 11,000 prisoners, and 200 guns.

The moral effect of the victory was needed, for elsewhere things were going from bad to worse. The collapse of Rumania had repercussions on the Italian front in that October. A great Austro-German attack broke the Italian line at Caporetto, destroying one of the Italian armies and driving the rest back through all the ground they had won since 1915. Venice itself was threatened for a while, and Italy looked like following Serbia. In four weeks she had lost 800,000 men. But Diaz, superseding the beaten Cadorna, pulled his troops together, with Franco-British help, made a stand on the Piave, covering Venice, and held the triumphant enemy advance.

The affair was helped by, but in turn gravely hindered, another great British effort in the West, where on the 20th November Byng struck at Cambrai, the heart of the German line. He tried new tactics: instead of the orthodox 'preparation' by heavy artillery fire, he threw in at once large masses of the new tanks, an arm which had appeared, though on a small scale, in the previous year. The surprise was most effective. It at last achieved a real breach of the German line, to a depth of five miles. Had Byng had reserves to throw through the gap and deploy, he might have won a conclusive victory. But the divisions which should have been his reserve were on the way to the Italian front, and Ludendorff, in front of him, had his ready, and counter-attacked within a couple of days, before the ground won could be consolidated. The splendid fighting of the Guards Division saved the British from what might have been crushing disaster: but nearly all the gains of the battle were lost.

The autumn fighting had cost the British alone 22,000 officers killed, wounded, and missing, and 427,000 men: and to the moral effect of that huge loss and the sickening failure of hope there now was added the final collapse of one of the three great powers of the Entente. The Russian armies, already gravely weakened in morale by the recent political events behind them, had fought badly through this year, greatly adding to the odds against French and British by allowing the Germans to shift large masses of men from the crumbling Russian front for use in the West. Germany helped the political débâcle by returning to Russia the exiled leaders of the extremist

Left, the Bolsheviks. In November they overthrew the weak government of well-meaning Socialist intellectuals under Kerensky; and Russia disintegrated into chaos. The Bolsheviks, seizing the power, made an armistice, and Russia was effectively out of the war. A flicker of success against the Turks came then: in October Allenby in Palestine fell heir to the careful preparations already made by Sir Archibald Murray, and used them brilliantly, sweeping through Gaza and Askelon in November, and on the 11th December—on foot, as became the story of that ground—entering Jerusalem.

It was little to balance the huge loss of Russia and the fact that the Germans now had been released to use all their effectives on the Western Front: and all through that year, though the Zeppelins were gone, the new menace of the bombing aeroplane was striking French and British civilian morale, and the U-boats threatened with increasing danger not only reinforcements and munitions but supplies of food, especially for Britain . . . and retaliation for the air attack had barely begun over Germany by autumn.[1]

The new year of 1918 brought little cheer. The Treaty of Brest-Litovsk in January gave Russia peace—but a peace of the spurred jack-boot. The terms were as humiliating as might be, and took from her great masses of territory, whose people were henceforth to become the serfs of the imminently victorious *Herrenvolk*. But Germany, too, was paying for her war. The blockade was telling hard on civilian morale, and the beginning of the air bombardment, though Berlin was still untouched (it was never bombed), was threatening it further. The armies were very weary, and in spite of the resounding Russian success, were conscious of little gains for their huge losses in a war that had not been the promised walk-over. Now that America was in the war, her fresh troops would be against them in a few months. And the British Navy, by the convoy system and the guerilla valour of the Q-ships, was beginning to slacken the grip of the German blockade. A disconcerting number of submarines stayed overdue when they were expected at Kiel.

It was needful, therefore, to come to a rapid end: and a rapid,

[1] We should consider those air-raids trifling now: the total civilian deaths were about 1,400. But A.R.P. services were negligible, and the terror was new and uncanny, and seemed almost impossible to parry. London, of British cities, suffered most. Scotland received very little air attack: there were a few small raids on Edinburgh, which caused some casualties and a certain amount of damage (One bomb missed the Castle by a matter of feet.) Aberdeen had one raid, which missed the city clean, the bombs falling harmlessly in a field of neips.

and German, end was nearly achieved. Ludendorff learned from the methods of Byng and Nivelle, and put them in practice with terrible effect. In a fog on the morning of the 21st March, he struck with full strength at the weakest of the line, the junction of the French and British forces, close to St Quentin. He meant to take the pivot of Amiens, and then to thrust to the sea at Abbéville, driving a wedge between the French and British that would give him the power to outflank and roll up either. This attack, the Second Battle of the Somme, very nearly brought the war to a conclusion. The British defensive tactics were entangled by a half-thought-out idea of the fluid defensive and a general breakdown of communications: and their reserves were scanty and ill-placed. The line was crushed back and back, losing 90,000 men taken prisoner, 1,200 guns, and all the ground won at such tremendous cost since 1916. But by sheer human valour, the grim dour courage of the common soldier, the tenacity of the battalion officers, the line, somehow, kept cohesion, and kept in touch with the French on its right. It was bent and driven back and back again: but somehow, by miracle, it remained unpierced, and Amiens was saved.

Yet the disaster was more than serious: and it was only to be the first of a sequence. In April Ludendorff shifted the weight of attack to the British left, and in what is called the Battle of the Lys, between the 9th and the 17th of April, he drove for Ypres and the Channel ports. Again the line was forced back, nearly to Calais: and yet again, incredibly, it held, clinging desperately to Hazebrouck and Béthune, whose loss would mean the surrender of all Flanders. Those troops lost, in very little over a week, 15,000 officers and 288,000 men: and yet they held. The news came in May of a German peace with unlucky Rumania, in another jack-boot treaty, of Bucharest. In all Eastern Europe was German victory: and they were now on the verge of it in the West.

There had been one change there, however, that was to count. Haig had grasped, and forced his government to grasp, the handicap of the divided command, and had won permission to put himself and his troops under that of Marshal Foch, who controlled the French armies, and who now could handle the whole great line as one. The Americans, too, realised the situation, and instead of waiting to carry out their full programme, sent over what divisions they had ready, to serve under Entente command: and these, though they were comparatively few, were fresh men, superbly equipped. Also, though it was not known to the Entente yet, the valour shown in the desperate resistance had weakened the German armies very gravely: the battles on the Somme and on the Lys had cost the Germans 40,000 more men than the British, and not far from as many officers. Also, Ludendorff had driven on too far, and he had to halt to consolidate his position, and to reorganise his battered troops.

Foch used the lull. The effect was not seen at first, for on the 27th of May, preceded by intensive use of gas, the Germans struck the weakest of the French line, between Soissons and Reims. It was nearly the finish. In a mere few hours, the French gains in three great offensives and the ground the British had won upon the Aisne in 1914 were in German hands, and the Germans were driving onward to the Marne, over ground that had not seen fighting for more than three years. A French counter-attack held up the German right, but their centre still advanced, taking Soissons and La Fère with their huge dumps of stores, and reached the Marne, threatening Paris once again. All for which thousands of men had given their lives in forty-five months of more than human endurance was gone. Britain and France were reaching the end of their powers, with men of fifty being called up for service. One more such blow would bring German victory.

Again the long forward drive of the German advance brought a halt, however. And Foch made the most of it. With magnificent daring he took the enormous risk of drawing back troops from the line, both French and British, and forming them in three armies to the rear, giving him thus a free 'mass of manœuvre.' It meant commanding his subordinates—Haig, Pétain, Gouraud—to take the first impact of the coming drive with their forces weakened. They obeyed, through the anxious weeks of the high summer, holding the enemy in play and waiting. Then, on the 15th July, the Germans struck. Gouraud, in front of Reims, made a masterly defence, and they failed there. West of Reims, Pétain was driven back from the Marne, grimly resisting. For two days he was pressed back, Ludendorff throwing in everything he had.

The advance, in part checked by Gouraud before Reims, came on unevenly. Part of it came too far, and exposed a flank: and on the 18th July Foch struck that flank, hurling in the reserves he had gathered at such risk, and the new American troops. It was Ludendorff now who had to resist as he stood. And it was Ludendorff who was pushed back. By the 4th of August—the fourth anniversary of the war for Britain—the Second Battle of the Marne was won, and Reims and Paris once more were out of danger.

The August so begun was so to continue. On the 8th, Haig struck with the British, before Amiens. The attack began as an attempt to free the railways, but the sudden thrust ended four days later on with a nine-mile advance on a front of forty-seven, the taking of 40,000 German prisoners and 600 guns, and the German army beaten back again to the very edge of the battlefield of the Somme. All down the line ran the word 'We are going forward': and already Ludendorff, on the 13th, when Haig's force knew their advance was a success, told the Kaiser that the war was as good as lost.

It was not won yet, however, by a good deal, for the Germans fought well almost to the finish. The Entente were not sure yet of victory. So many costly advances had been made, and all their fruit lost: but by the 1st September Haig had broken through on the line Bapaume–Péronne, the British infantry had reached open country, and the evil spell of trench war at last was ended. By the 12th, the new Americans, far to the south, had freed Verdun: and still the advance went on, the French hammering the German left and centre, and the British bending back and back their right. By the 26th these had reached the Hindenburg Line, and now it was the Germans who watched the fruits of great and costly advances disappear. And Foch at last saw his way to a decision. In sole control, he had planned four great offensives—by the Americans against Sedan, by the French against Mézières and the Argonne, by the British against the Hindenburg Line and Cambrai; and the Belgians, who still held a fragment of their country, should go with Allied help through Flanders to Ghent.

They struck, the assault running upward along the line. The southern attack began on the 26th, the British next day, the northmost the next again. The tide turned and went roaring. Places the Germans had held since 1914—Ostend, Lille, Douai, Cambrai, St Quentin, Laon—were retaken, and things were moving too in the East. The Serbs also had pulled together for a great effort, and on 19th September Franchet d'Esperey had struck north from Salonika. Bulgaria was not defeated in the field, but suddenly, at the thunderous news from the West, and this new blow, her morale disintegrated: on the last day of September came the news that she was asking for

22

an armistice. At the same time a great advance from Jerusalem had rolled up the Turks, taken 60,000 prisoners, and on the 1st October entered Damascus.

Already, on the 28th September, the day that saw Foch's offensive fully launched, Hindenburg told the German Foreign Office to propose an armistice. This, then, was done, the new German Chancellor, Prince Max of Baden,[1] offering to accept the 'Fourteen Points' of the terms which had already been outlined by President Wilson. The Entente refused, knowing that if an armistice should be granted, the Germans would then call the war a draw, and so save the regime which had begun it. German territory had not been touched by the war: and the German people had to be taught the lesson that the war was lost, and that the policy which had been their obsession for a lifetime had now brought as much disaster to themselves as to the lesser breeds of the rest of Europe.

The advance pressed on through Flanders, beyond the trenches. On the 30th October, Turkey surrendered, and then on the 3rd November Austria. Till then the German people had still believed that in spite of reverses they were invulnerable. Now they found suddenly that they were not. There was revolt and a cry of 'We are betrayed,' and all the enemies of the regime found a sudden hearing. The climax came when the Fleet was ordered to sea, for a last throw: men and ships had rotted in harbour. Now they mutinied and hoisted the Red Flag. The Kaiser fled to an army that would not receive him. On the 9th he declared that he would abdicate, and next day in fact he went over the border to Holland, leaving a revolution in Berlin, and others in the lesser capitals, that sent kings and princes flying left and right.

Already, on the 8th, Foch had received the surrender of the Germans. The terms given were firm, but one cannot call them unjust. First of all Germany must evacuate the territory she had seized and pillaged—Alsace, Lorraine, Belgium, Rumania—and give back the gold reserves looted from the two last. She must cancel the brutal peace treaties with Russia and Rumania. It was also urgent that she should be prevented from carrying on the war after a halt, so that she must surrender her submarines and large quantities of guns, vehicles, and planes, transfer her High Seas Fleet to Allied ports, and submit to the occupation of the Rhineland (the

[1] Professedly ' Liberal ' and democratic, and therefore, it was hoped, *persona grata* with the Entente.

country lying against the march of France) by troops of the Allies, who should hold the Rhine bridges.

The Germans accepted these terms. On 11th November, as the British troops marched into Mons again, the Armistice was signed at Compiègne: and at eleven o'clock on that winter morning, on the long line that ran from the Alps to the sea, there came a sudden silence. The guns had ceased.

XXVII

AFTER THE STORM

TWENTY YEARS: 1918–1938

The cross-head jammed sideways in the guides, and in addition to putting further pressure on the already broken starboard supporting-column, cracked the port, or left-hand, supporting column in two or three places.   RUDYARD KIPLING, *The Devil and the Deep Sea.*

THE twenty years that followed the Peace of Versailles are one of the strangest times in history, and for most countries, one of the most depressing. For Scotland, however, they were not all depressing. The first fourteen, indeed, were acutely so, and some of their worst elements carried over, and deeply coloured the remaining six. Yet there were other elements showing also, that increasingly brought the promise of a new hope, which, though new storms have seemed to beat it down, may yet bring better life in a happier world.

It was no happy world in 1919. When the first dazed joy of the Armistice was past, men saw, as Field-Marshal Smuts said at the time, that the War had

resulted not only in the defeat of the enemy armies . . . we witness the collapse of the whole economic fabric of Central and Eastern Europe. Unemployment, starvation, anarchy, war, disease, and despair stalk through the land.

Austria had lost 1,132,000 killed. Germany had lost two and a half million, and something like three-quarters of a million civilians, dead as a consequence of the blockade, which had left 80 per cent. of her children with rickets. Her industries had perished, her agriculture was at its last gasp for lack of fertilisers, and her governmental framework was in ruins. Nor were the victors in much better case. France's killed, in the Army alone, were 1,383,000, those of the British Empire 1,060,000, Italy's half a million. France had lost three-quarters of her coal and iron, 80 per cent. of her works and manufactures, and 90 per cent. of her great linen industry: nor was it a mere stoppage of their trade, for the plant of all of these had been destroyed, in battle or by the retreating enemy. Many

320

towns and hundreds of villages had vanished. Britain had still the
plant of her industries, but the war had cost her £40,000 million, the
cost of living had risen by 40 per cent. and was rising still, 25 per
cent. of her shipping had been sunk, most of her export trade had
disappeared, and the overseas countries, once her customers, who
had sent her food and raw materials, were rapidly industrialising
themselves. Even the neutral states had suffered severely. In 1917
the trade of Rotterdam was 10 per cent. of that before the war, and
the Dutch had been forced to rationing of bread, while a month or
two later their cotton mills all closed.

Nor were these material losses, grave as they were, the worst, by
a long way. There were worse wounds in the mind. The worst was
a weary hatred of all effort. It took many forms. One was a hatred
of clear thought, save what would go into an easy formula which
could be used as a substitute for thought. Linked closely with that
was a hatred of definite choice—that is, of self-control, self-discipline,
the holding of a consistent line of action determined by choice and
not by external pressure.[1] And resentment of spoiled lives in a
spoiled world bred a deep and bitter hatred of the past, of tradition,
of values which had been accepted as the fundamental bases of
civilisation. In self-defence, these hates were proclaimed as virtues,
and rapidly became a strong convention. Few ages have been such
abject slaves to convention as those nineteen-twenties which took
such pride in its lack. They did not even invent one for themselves:
it was merely an inversion of past convention—Mrs Grundy with
her frock turned inside out.[2]

The writers and artists did little to change the mood. The novel,
the time's chief literary form, bears witness to it in its choice of subjects. To be the outstandingly interesting figure in an imagined
group—as we say, the hero—it had been taken for granted in the
past that a man had to be in some fashion larger than they. In the
nineteen-twenties, the rule was firmly reversed. No longer might
he lead: he must not even be a reasonably effective follower. That
cowardice, ugliness, and petty baseness were more interesting and
significant than valour, beauty, or nobility was a convention which

---

[1] To this there were two curious exceptions : in matters of sport or of personal
adornment these haters of discipline would undergo an ascesis as rigid as that of
any Trappist.
[2] Cf. the shocked tone of Victorian critics over any novel whose heroine was
not chaste, and the equally scandalised attitude of the 'twenties towards one where
she was.

became so rigid that critics faced with a case of its contravention were quite sincerely and genuinely shocked. If heroic figures were taken, they must be 'debunked,' brought below the level of the giggling writer. The blame, no doubt, does not all lie with the 'twenties: many sham nobilities of the previous age, insincere admirations, had asked for a reaction. But healthier men would have fallen less completely before the temptation to safeguard themselves by concentrating upon what they could look down on.

This *trahison des clercs*, the abandonment of values, was to count: for artists are, as much as priests, the guardians of a civilisation's values. If they sweep these out by a creed of pure negation, they breed a generation without values: and since healthy young minds cannot bear that deprivation, this generation may follow some queer gods, and give honest devotion to the Powers of Hell.

The intellectual disintegration affected most what the 'twenties liked to describe as the intelligentsia. Both these and the simpler folk were affected alike by an unhealthy craving for emotion, not as motive power to action or becoming, but in itself, as an intoxicant. Writers preached the gospel of 'thinking with the blood,' and the general public revealed a widespread passion for the hypnosis of the film, of jazz, of a strange, monotonous and graceless dancing, and of flooding words—words heard without precision, to daze rather than stimulate the mind, and conveniently supplied by the new 'wireless,' which provided them at all hours of the day. The habit of giving to all household life, including conversation, a steady background of streaming radio noise, is significant: it reveals an unhealthy condition of the nerves, alike unstable and insensitive. And no indweller in any modern town can have failed to notice its widespread prevalence.

Where thought was still practised, it met a further depressant, seldom consciously noted, but profoundly felt—the growing lack of easy political hope. The eighteenth century could look happily forward to the replacing of monarchy by republics as a certain means to the Kingdom of Heaven on earth. The nineteenth had discovered that republics could develop most of the vices of monarchies, besides a few others peculiar to themselves: but it still could believe that if the Socialist State, or the Communist State, could only be established, all its members would automatically thrive. The twentieth, before a third of it had gone by, had seen Socialism and Communism in practice: and reluctant as their advocates were to admit that states which adopted them were not Paradise, the un-prejudiced and first-hand student inclined to feel that there might be, in practice, a certain difference. Thus it was far less easy than it had been to believe that a simple change of constitution, a simple change in the economic structure, or a simple anything else could bring the solution of mankind's pressing and painful difficulties. Free education, universal suffrage, Labour governments, the eman-cipation of women, prohibition of alcohol, the League of Nations . . . so many things from which so much was expected had been tried, and had left a world much like the old: if some problems were solved, there were now a number of new ones, and a simple and automatic cure for all ailments had grown increasingly difficult to prescribe. In fact, there seemed nothing for it but hard thinking and a continuous and patient effort: and in the bewildered weariness of the time, those never popular activities were even less attractive than they had been.

These things were true of all Europe, more or less, and did much to determine the course of the next fifty years. The men between thirty and forty in 1919 felt the impact of the economic landslide more, perhaps, than that of the intellectual. Those between twenty and thirty felt the latter: and both underwent a profound emo-tional strain. And it was these men who in 1939 were those forty to sixty—the governing generation. Those born in the war, for whom such fears were expressed, grew up not in the 'twenties but in the 'thirties. Some of them, now, man Hitler's Panzer divisions: but others today are in our own R.A.F. And the general outlook and values of these latter have little in common with those of the nineteen-twenties.

While all these things are true as generalisations, they are, being generalisations, but true in part. Countries reacted in different degrees, and at different paces. Our own suffered very badly. Like England, she had never been invaded, and such air attack as she had undergone was only a fraction of the attack on England, itself but slight compared with modern standards. But even before the begin-ning of the war, Scotland, in spite of her prosperous appearance, was already sick, already disintegrated. There was no sense left of Scot-land as a whole, of the Public Thing that was every man's concern. There was no Government to stand for it, and lead the common effort of all men, or even serve as scaffold for common action.

Certain 'scaffolds,' organisations within the whole, were still in existence, however. The churches and the educational system both carried on movements begun before the war. The churches suffered, of course, in the mood just described, for there was a general falling away from 'religion.' A great deal of it called itself a hatred of dogma, without any very clear notion of what the word meant. Examined, what the phrase amounted to was often a terror of committing one-self to definite responsibilities. Some part was due to a more respect-able reason. Men had been presented with 'Christianity' in a form which intellectual honesty or their instinctive sense of decent conduct forbade them to respect, and were ignorant that there were other, different, versions. Much also was due to the changes in con-vention. It had been the proper thing to go to church: with the inversion of previous conventions, it became the proper thing to stay away. And *toleration*, while very widely praised, had in practice a noticeable limitation: it applied to those whose beliefs were less strict than one's own, but those whose beliefs were more strict were *ipso facto* intolerant, and need not be tolerated.

By the end of the decade a fifth of the population professed no religious allegiance of any kind, and though there was a marked growth in superstition (often attached to what was thought to be science) the actual membership of the various churches was reduced to those who were on the one hand either too stupid or too isolated to feel the pressure of the time's atmosphere, or, on the other, had the wit and strength to see it for what it was and to resist it.

In formal ecclesiastical history, the chief single event is reversal of the Disruption. Since the beginning of the century, the United Free Church and the Establishment had been moving steadily nearer to one another. The Church of Scotland Act of 1921 was so framed as to facilitate their re-union. The process went slowly forward through the 'twenties, and in 1929 the final reports were presented to the Assemblies of both communions and accepted by these, and the way lay clear at last. The Assemblies met separately in October, then joined at a great service in St Giles's, and proceeded thence as a united body, who thereon elected as their Moderator Dr John White of the Barony Kirk of Glasgow, who had taken a leading part in negotiations.[1]

The re-united Church has much in common with the Moderates

---

[1] The Union left some problems to be solved concerning the endowments of the Churches, and these were settled by successive Acts of 1925, 1932, and 1933.

of the eighteenth century, and shares their interest in social problems. The movement already in being before the war, for a greater beauty and dignity in worship, has continued: and though the sermon is still the centre of worship, certain ministers are now inclined to lay a greater emphasis on the Sacraments than has been common in Presbyterian thought.

The Union was not quite unanimous. Some eighty ministers of the United Free Church judged that the body formed in 1929 'would still be a church by law established and endowed from public sources' and that the Union therefore 'did violence to the fundamental principles and testimony of the United Free Church of Scotland on religious equality, spiritual freedom, and the voluntary support of the Gospel ordinances.' They remained as the United Free Church (Continuing), and an amicable settlement was made with regard to their share in property and endowments.

The largest religious body after the Establishment was, as before the war, the Church of Rome, though, as before, the majority of its members were Irish by either birth or near descent. They in this time were relieved of an injustice. Since the Education Act of 1872, they had paid rates for Presbyterian schools, besides supporting sufficient of their own to teach one in seven of the school population. The Act of 1918 had at last recognised the principle of separate schools. These were now brought within the national system, their distinctive religious teaching being guaranteed, while their educational efficiency was controlled by inspection, as in other State schools.

In the third largest body, the Episcopal Church, 1929 was to witness the publication of a revised Scottish Prayer-book, greatly enriched, and a fine piece of liturgical scholarship. The concordat of the Reformed Episcopal Churches and the Orthodox Communions of Eastern Europe (proposed first in the eighteenth century by Arsenius, Metropolitan of Thebais, to Bishop Archibald Campbell of Aberdeen) was accomplished at last at the opening of the 'thirties, to the comfort, in the near future, of many exiles.

The Presbyterian Dissenting bodies continued to retain their traditional temper. Even in 1933 the Seceder Provost of a northern burgh was excommunicated for permitting children to dance at a party in his house: and the proposal to build a village hall where young people could find decent recreation was denounced in print that year by one of the godly, who described the hall (which had not yet been built) as 'a destructive and mischievous den of Satan.' These bodies, however, were steadily decreasing. The Free Church still has some hundred ministers, and a good deal of influence in parts of the Highlands. At the present day the members and adherents of the five Dissenting Presbyterian communions—the Reformed Presbyterians, United Original Seceders, Free Church, Free Presbyterians, and United Free Church—represent between them less than one per cent. of the total population, while those of the Establishment now number just on forty-three per cent.

A growing tolerance and friendliness between at any rate the authorities of at any rate the greater religious bodies had already come into being before the war, and, strengthened during it by joint social work, continued; and a pleasant custom grew of mutual courtesies on each other's 'occasions.'[1] The attitude was not, to be sure, universal: even so late as 1935 a Eucharistic Congress in Edinburgh—an affair which purely concerned the Roman Church— was the scene of very ugly disturbances, when bus-loads of children were stoned and women kicked. None the less, these demonstrations were reprobated, not only by the leading newspapers,[2] but also by general public opinion, led in emphatic terms by so prominent a Presbyterian churchman as Dr W. M. Macgregor, Principal of Trinity College, Glasgow, and a former Moderator of the United Free Church.

The Education Act of 1918 has already been mentioned. It set up new Education Authorities in each of the counties and in the four chief cities, permitted grants to poor children for books and food, and established new bursaries for those who wished to go on to the universities. It sought also to raise the school age to fifteen: but as England was not yet ready for such a change, this was deferred for more than twenty years.

---

[1] For instance, in a Tweedside village in 1936, an Episcopalian sisterhood produced a Nativity Play, acted by the children of their own communion. The choir of the Parish Church supplied the music, and the Parish and Episcopal ministers shared between them the reading of the Scripture lections. Even twenty years earlier, such a function would have been impossible: as it was, it was received with such enthusiasm that it had to be repeated a week later, to enable people from other villages—and of several denominations—to attend.

[2] The worthy Bailie who had led the fray made an angry attack upon the *Glasgow Herald*: and the *Herald* neatly and gaily revenged itself by printing his letter exactly as received, without amending its spelling or punctuation.

The Local Government Act of 1929 abolished the *ad hoc* Authorities, vesting their power in the various County Councils and the Town Councils of the four chief cities, controlled by the Scottish Education Department. The system, like those before it, was handicapped by a cumbrous division of organisation: in 1932 the Education Department had 96 of its staff in Edinburgh, and 68 at the far end of England.

The excellence of Scottish education had long, and quite justly, been a national boast. Even before the war there had, however, been doubts as to whether the boast were still justified. In 1929 it was observed that 60 per cent. of the children in the schools failed to pass the Qualifying Examination at the age of twelve, when they were supposed to do so. So disquieting, indeed, was the general situation that in 1932 the Council for Research in Education applied a scientific 'intelligence test' to all school-children born in 1921—87,498 of them. The test was very carefully thought out, and exhaustive analysis of its results gave a remarkably interesting conclusion. The average figure for the whole was normal: but less than half of the individual children had an individual figure that was normal. There proved to be a surprisingly large number well above or below the established norm for their age, and the range between the lowest and the highest was very much greater than had been expected. In fact, our national tendency to extremes seems to hold in the field of intelligence as in others.

The increasing number of subjects where research and even the ordinary teaching of students demanded up-to-date and expensive equipment was a handicap to the universities, who like every other national institution were sorely hit by the post-war poverty. Leaving out the colleges of Oxford and Cambridge, whose separate figures are difficult to arrive at, the income of English universities for the last academic year of the 'twenties works out, not counting grants from Government, at £87, 11s. for each whole-time student, while that of the Scots was a little less than half this—£43, 5s. The Government recognised the difference by granting to the Scots universities just under two-thirds per head of the English amount—£29, 14s. as against £45. The total English income per student, therefore, was £132, 11s., the total Scots £72, 19s.

Various other national cultural institutions were dealt with very much in the same spirit, of a comparative economy. It was not all a matter of population. The people of Wales number half of those of

Scotland, or rather less: in the last five years of the 'twenties, the National Library of Wales received £80,666 in Government grants, while the grant to that of Scotland was £13,212: and in the first year of the 'thirties, the grant to the Welsh was £25,000, to the Scots £2,600. In the next year again, the Scots had £1,200, while two minor, though very delightful, London museums received well over £10,000 for one and a little under £6,000 for the other. And while in the past a Scots Prime Minister had obtained a grant for the important work of compiling an English Dialect Dictionary, none was forthcoming for its Scottish sister. As for the condition of the National Records, it was said in 1932 in Parliament that 'great numbers of valuable uncodified records are lying about in garrets and cellars . . . many in a state of hopeless decay': and the late Lord Tweedsmuir, then member for the Scots Universities, endorsed the statement:

The public records are in a deplorable condition, and there is great danger that they may be destroyed altogether. . . . [The Record Office] is hopelessly understaffed. There is not enough money for the mere business of physical preservation, not to mention the reorganisation of the Department to make it properly accessible.

Yet records are the basis of history: and what his memory is to a man, so is its history to any country. They can live without them: but not with either fullness or dignity.

To be sure, it was inherent in Whig tradition—we need not seek to analyse here the reasons—that the past of Scotland was insignificant, and its study no more than an antiquary's hobby. That tradition was weakening its hold, but it was not dead, for even so late as 1938 we find a Scots knight and member of Parliament, Sir Murdoch Macdonald, declaring that Gaelic teaching in Highland schools was 'fantastic and undesirable,' whereas the English language was

a new lever to help in the amelioration of life—to permit some *to wander forth from their native glens . . . and take their place in the world.*

The statement, though the italics are not his, is one which will bear a little thinking over, as the revelation of a point of view.

If the framework of older conceptions of education was ill-supported, there was no lack of support for certain new mechanisms, then beginning. The dominants of popular ideas, the determinants of popular ideals, were the film and after 1922 the radio. These had their benefits. The film can be of the greatest help in teaching, and there its importance soon was recognised. Indeed, by the end of the 'thirties, 20 per cent. of British school projectors were in Scotland, and their work was much helped by the Carnegie Trust, which gave £5,000 for a Central Film Library. The film as an art too can do certain things which no other medium handles so adequately: and its qualities there were recognised and exploited, with fine results, by a Scots producer, John Grierson. But the film as a cheap and popular entertainment—and it was by far the most popular of the time—was exploited to a very different end by a wealthy and powerful American industry, and the popular mind was steadily bombarded not only by a quite amazing range of historical and social inaccuracies but by an inculcation of false values, not only aesthetic but ethical as well, whose grip was confirmed by the strong hypnotic effect that is characteristic of the cinema.

The radio was, on the surface, far less pernicious. It became, before long, as popular as the film: in 1936 there were nearly $7\frac{1}{2}$ million sets in Britain. The warning of the film was not thrown away, and when 'broadcasting' became practicable in Britain, it was not left to commercial exploitation, but placed in the hands of a national company pledged to achieve a certain decent standard. This pledge, indeed, was honourably fulfilled, and the radio had, in many ways, high value. But it was none the less, by its very nature, a powerful standardising influence, like the film before it. And, though it made a sincere and honest endeavour to cater for all tastes, and in music did so, its verbal part naturally played for safety by taking as greatest common denominator the outlook of average educated London. Scottish stations were in time established, however. These did very useful work for Scottish music, and the volume of abuse which has been levelled at their non-musical work contradicts itself sufficiently to make it fairly clear that they have at least made a reasonable attempt to present the public with differing points of view.

A radio for the eye as well as the ear—television—was worked out by the early 'thirties, a Scot, John Logie Baird, playing a prominent part in its evolution. The British Broadcasting Corporation began in 1936 to broadcast for it, but though the method has been proved practicable, it is still at a tentative stage of development.

With conveyance of minds we may take conveyance of bodies, for the new changes in the transport system were scarcely less important in those decades than were those of the preceding century. On the negative side there were two, of great importance. Scots shipping, wrecked by the war, appeared in the 'twenties to be moribund; and the Scottish railways passed into English control. On the positive side, in Scotland as in most countries the motor revolutionised road transport. Not only did private cars very greatly increase, becoming a kind of domestic furniture as common, very nearly, as a bath: a system of public services was set up, running hither and yond whenever there were roads. The Scottish Motor Traction Company,[1] Messrs Alexander, and a score of others [2] developed a complex and admirable system linking the country and the town together—on the whole, very much to the benefit of both. Women who no more than twenty years ago used to walk sixteen miles to the nearest town perhaps twice a year, go now, for a shilling, in comfort, in half an hour. It is not all gain. Miss Aphasia Vandeleur in *Purple and Passion* is poor exchange for the ceilidh, and mass-produced cakes from London for Scots baking: but having seen her film and bought her cake she does go home, and to less loneliness than has driven the wife of many a countryman to urge her husband towards a job in town. And the Sports and Dramatic Clubs and the Rural Institutes find a very difficult problem solved for them, while the lad from a country home working in town is not wholly cut off by planestanes from the earth now. There is, to be sure, another side to the motor. Its transport is often to another world. It was characteristic of that muddled age that irresponsible lads not out of their teens could fling masses of metal, at the speed of a train, over public highways. In the one year of 1935, 7,343 people in Britain were killed upon the roads, and much over a quarter of a million wounded, which would have been thought a fairly high butcher's bill for a sizeable war of the nineteenth century.[3]

Air-services also grew, bringing both the Northern and the Western Isles into closer touch with the Mainland. Aberdeen established in 1928 an Allied Airways Service across the North Sea,

---

[1] It is wholly in keeping with one of the pleasantest sides of our time and country that this Company should have issued a magazine for those who love Scots roads, and that this venture should meet with so much approval as to grow into a handsome and flourishing monthly whose contributors include some of our best writers. One recalls the library of the S.S. *Comet*.

[2] In 1938 the Highland Transport Company put on the road an anthracite bus which ran 20,000 miles, with only minor repairs, at three miles a penny.

[3] The British killed in the Crimean War numbered 2,755—though, to be sure, 16,323 died of disease and wounds in hospital.

although it was refused the subsidy which the British and Imperial Airways Service received for Continental routes. And the introduction of the radio-telephone brought a boon to isles which had often been isolated by the damaging of their cables in winter storms.

Underlying all these changes, affecting most, and strangling much in them that might have been beneficial, was the shattering economic collapse of Scotland. We have seen, at the beginning of this chapter, what was the general effect of the war on Europe. Of all the countries on the winning side, Scotland was slowest in recovery. She lost gravely in men, first of all: she had recruited about the same proportion as England, and rather more in proportion—between a fifth and a sixth of them—were killed. (The Royal Scots, for instance, in four years, lost 583 officers and 10,630 of other ranks killed.) Nor was this loss all. There were many cripples also, and many wounded in mind and in morale. And the old and evil tradition of emigration as the natural remedy for all Scotland's ailments continued to bleed away many more of the best. In the 'twenties, alone of the countries of Western Europe, Scotland showed an actual shrinkage of population, from 4,882,497 to 4,842,980. That is, in ten years, she lost nearly 40,000, while England increased by over a couple of million—nearly 33,000 of whom, by the way, were Scots, in addition to those already in that country.[1] As for the overseas figures, in the fifty years after 1861, 735,000 had emigrated: a good deal from a country of four and three-quarter million. The *twenty* years after 1911, however, added to these 630,000. In the *ten* years after 1921, 8 per cent. of the people of Scotland emigrated—more than left Belgium, Holland, Sweden, Denmark, Finland, and Switzerland all put together, though these nations, of comparable size with ours, have between them much more than seven times our people. The percentage for England during that same decade was, by the way, a half of one per cent. And by way of commentary on these figures, a leading Scottish sociologist, Dr J. A. Bowie, Principal of the Dundee School of Economics, has said,

Emigration tends to take the young and healthy, the enterprising, the courageous, the adaptable, precisely those people of whom Scotland to-

---

[1] One in four of Scottish graduates are said to be resident in England nowadays. The record of Fellows and Scholars of the Carnegie Trust published in 1935 shows that, of some 205 physicists and chemists awarded Scholarships and Fellowships between 1905 and 1933, 105 hold Government research posts in England, the Empire, and the U.S.A. and 25 hold university appointments out of Scotland.

day has need. There is no scientific evidence that Scotland is over-
populated, and still less evidence that emigration will cure her persistent
unemployment.[1]

Moreover, the population which remained was growing not only
urbanised but older. The birth-rate, in one lifetime, had been
halved. In 1901-5 it was still 29·2. In the early 'twenties, it was
23. In the early 'thirties, it was 18·2. In 1937 it was 17·6. That is,
in thirty years, it went down by a third. To be sure, a greater proportion of babies lived. The infant mortality rate for 1870 had been,
in Scotland, 126. (The English one was 156.) In 1937 it was 80.
But that was almost a third as much again as the rate in England,
and more than twice that of Holland: suppose the Scots rate were
even no worse than England's, this would mean in practice that 1,800
babies who died in Scotland in that year would have lived.

It is true that there was, in spite of the poverty, a quite real
improvement in general physical welfare. In 1910-14, 9 per cent. of
Scots children were affected more or less by rickets: in 1937 it was
1·5. Certain epidemic diseases had almost vanished. In Glasgow
in the first three years of the 'thirties, only one death from typhus
was recorded (cp. p. 172). But in 1936-37, of 205,206 school-
children, over 56 per cent. had defective teeth. As for adults, the
death-rate in 1934—12·9—was the lowest ever recorded in our
country. But the amount of general ill-health, as distinct from fatal
disease, was spectacular still. The amount of incapacitating sickness
among those insured, in 1937, was higher than it had been at any
time. It was estimated, towards the end of the 'thirties, that something like half the population of Scotland were in what could not be
described as good health : and in Glasgow seven school-children in
eight were in need of some kind of medical attention. And the
proportion over forty-five increased year by year, while that under
fifteen fell steadily.

While the population grew older, it also grew urban. By 1931
four-fifths of Scottish people lived in towns, and most in large towns.
During the 'twenties, while the general population markedly fell, the
four great towns increased by 4 per cent.—not by natural growth
but by influx from the country. In 1931 no less than a fifth of the
people of Edinburgh, Glasgow, and Dundee were country-born,
while the figure for Aberdeen was not far from a third.

[1] From *The Future of Scotland* (1939), a book which no Scot who regards his
country's welfare can afford to leave unread. It is, by the way, in spite of its grave
warnings, both constructive and stimulating in its outlook.

As for the living conditions of these people, 'overcrowding' in Scotland in the middle 'thirties was more than six times as bad as it was in England. More precisely, a quarter of the Scottish nation lived in houses with less than one room for two people. (More than a third of the houses, so late as that, had no bath.) Over seven per cent. were in dwellings of one room only. In 1917 a Royal Commission said that 260,000 new houses were needed: and in 1937 the Secretary for Scotland could still speak of a shortage of 250,000.

Scotland once led the industry of the world. Here are some figures for the last twenty years, with the comparative ones for her neighbour country, who had fought the same war, was hit by the same slump, and was governed by the same legislative body. After the war, it could only be expected that general production should be lowered. But it did not rise with the return of peace. It was lower, so late as 1929, than in 1913. Then all the industrial world was heavily stricken by an economic blizzard from New York. Certain countries recovered somewhat in a few years. But the general amount of Scottish production was lower even in 1935, when that of England was showing a well-marked rise, than in 1930. In 1932, just after the slump, England closed 130 factories: but she opened 626 as well—a total gain of 496. Scotland closed 36 and opened 20— a loss of 16. Next year, England closed 380, but opened 449—a gain of 69. Scotland opened 14, but closed 29, which left her with another loss of 15. In 1937, England had 648 more factories than in 1932: Scotland had nine less.

Scotland's strength had lain in the 'heavy' industries, coal, iron, steel, engineering, and shipbuilding, in the two last of which she had led the world. All of these, of course, had been needed in the war, and in the first reconstruction after the war. The peak output, indeed, of Scots steel was in 1920—2,074,000 tons. The greatest since has been in 1936, and then it was but 1,643,000. In 1932, out of 77 blast furnaces remaining, no more than seven were working at a time—at some times in that year it was only one. Engineering had gone into a deadly decline. As for ships, Scotland had made the world's first steamships in time, and had kept on making the first in quality. A quarter of British tonnage was sunk in the war: but while England had in 1937 61,000 tons more than in 1913, Scotland had still a million and a half less. The Clyde took to ship-*breaking* to keep going, while the ships she had built lay rotting in the Gareloch. In 1938 the Clyde received no mercantile shipping order of

23

any importance between July and November, and none of any kind throughout September. And in all these great industries, world-famous firms, with the highest technical standards in all Europe, were vanishing like the smoke of their own stacks. The financial control of the impoverished country was rapidly passing into English hands: and the cry in England was 'rationalisation.' The word had indeed an admirable sound, as of a duty for all men of sense: the thing was the purchasing of Scottish firms and their closing down to prevent their competition. Among them was the historic Beardmore shipyard, known all over the world, which had during the war built the Government 68 million pounds worth of ships, and in 1918 had 42,000 men upon its pay-roll.

Farming suffered rather less spectacularly. It went down by a slow decline, less steep than in England. None the less, Scottish employment on the land was in 1921 127,000 workers, in 1929 118,000, and in 1938 104,300—this in a country world-famous for its farming. The Government offered some protection to wheat, the English main crop, but not to meat, which in the middle 'twenties represented nearly 80 per cent. of Scots sales. By 1936 the acreage of Scotland under crop was smaller than it had been for sixty years.

As for fisheries, in the year 1914 Scotland stood with Norway at the head of Europe. She had 20,500 men at sea, in 3,121 boats: and the world bred no better coastwise sailors. By 1930 there were well under 10,000 men, and the boats had gone down in value and in number by over a third. Soon thereafter a Commission (mainly English) investigated the fishing industry, and declared that

the chief necessity of the Scottish industry is to succeed in adapting itself little by little to the contraction of the demand. Any action, therefore, which would tend to delay or even to reverse this process would be injurious to the prospects of the individual.

It recommended also that British trawlers should be forbidden to fish the Moray Firth, though foreign ones were permitted so to do. The 'contraction of the demand' was shown by the fact that during the period between the wars, the fisheries of Denmark, Norway, and Sweden all showed increases. In 1937 those of Russia exported £1,300,000 worth of fish *to Britain*. Japan also sent a couple of million pounds worth. When fresh herring were unobtainable in Devon, or if to be had were selling at sixpence a pound, they were being thrown back in the sea off the Ayrshire coast, where the market was glutted with them at eight a penny. In April 1938 the

Fishery Board declared that the total number of Scottish vessels was going down by no less than five a week. In a year, the number of men fell by over 2,000, and the value of boats and gear by £183,034. Yet the industry is the nursery of seamen: and when the Fleet Mobilisation Orders went out, in a town where 110 boats were still in use, no more than three could put to sea next day.

Nor were these losses all. By the middle of the 'thirties Scotland had ceased to be economically autonomous. Such industry as was left was falling more and more into English hands, and being 'rationalised' in the same way as the shipyards. Half the Scottish banks had been assimilated to London houses. The Scottish railways were all of them managed from London, and in London interests: their workshops were most of them closed, their repairs and their construction work done in England. Small businesses were being closed in every town by the invasion of English multiple shops, selling English products. The financial grasp of London grew and tightened till it was as close as the political.

The effect of these changes on the finances of Scotland can be briefly shown. At the beginning of the century, the average Scot was as wealthy as the average Englishman. By 1929, before the slump, he had 13s. for the Englishman's £1. By 1937-38, it was 10s. The revenue of both countries fell in the 'twenties—England's by 20 per cent., Scotland's by 43 per cent. In 1900, Scottish customs revenue was 10 per cent. of that for the entire United Kingdom. In 1926 it was 5·9. Scotland, at the beginning of the century, had contributed 12½ per cent. to the total revenues of the United Kingdom. In 1931 it was 8½ per cent., though still that was something like £67,000,000—greater than that of Belgium, Holland, or Denmark, or of Norway and Sweden together, though these countries, of comparable size with our own, had the highest standard of living in all Europe.[1]

So much for finance. As for the effect on employment, the Scottish craftsman yields to none in the world in energy and skill: yet since 1923 there has never been less than 10 per cent. of the insured population unemployed. In 1931-33—the years after the

---

[1] It has to be recalled that £8,000,000 of the amount was spent on by no means unrequired defence. This is a much larger proportion than in any of these five countries. (It is also worth recalling that nearly every penny of it was spent furth of Scotland, instead of again going into circulation.) But none of the five had a revenue conspicuously greater than our remaining £59,000,000.

slump—the total figure for Great Britain varied from 21·9 to 19·8: that for Scotland alone from 26·1 to 27·7—the latter meaning that 400,000 were idle, unwillingly. This truly appalling figure was the worst: yet in the summer of 1937, while the English figure was worse by 25 per cent. than that of 1929 had been, the Scottish was worse by twice that—by 50 per cent., although it had fallen. In 1938, the 400,000 had shrunk: but there still were a quarter of a million, and the figure at the beginning of that year was in comparison with the English one as 166·5 to 100. In the spring of that year, there were still in Scotland 20,909 men who had not done paid work for three years and more—11,064 of them for five years and more. These men were not superannuated workers. Nearly half of them were under forty-five. In the previous year more than a quarter of men who were unemployed were between twenty-five and thirty-four—the age for setting up homes and supporting young children. Nearly an eighth were in the early twenties, come to manhood, their boy's training over, to find no work. And these figures are more than economic data. They bear on the state of a nation's soul and mind. The deepest need of any vigorous life is impact of some kind on its surroundings. Denial of work thwarts this: the thwarting is poison, and this not only to the man who suffers. What a large mass of unemployment means is that a mass of the national organism is in danger of atrophy, which means of gangrene. And those medical phrases are more than a figure of speech.

As for the economic side of the question, Mr John Torrence has recently observed

In the last seventeen years (1922-38) the incidence of unemployment has been heavier in Scotland than in England by an average annual figure of 73,000. The aggregate result is that Scotland has lost 1,253,000 man-years over and above what the total would have been if unemployment had been at the English rate. Sir Gwilym Gibbon has told the Royal Statistical Society that if a million men were put to work, the national wealth would increase by £200,000,000 a year. On that calculation, Scotland has suffered, over seventeen years, a loss of £250,000,000 for which there was no corresponding loss in England.

In the December of 1934 the National Government set up Special Commissioners for the Distressed Areas. Those areas, in Scotland, were found to include a quarter of the country's population. But in March 1935 a Scottish member, Mr C. Milne, told the House that all Scotland was a Distressed Area. From several points of view, he was not far wrong.

XXVIII

HOME POLITICS

TWENTY YEARS: 1918–38

It is pointed out in London today—
The B.B.C.

THE broadening franchise, the growing power of Labour, the growing scope of 'social legislation' which had marked the period before the war continued to distinguish this one also: and to them in this twenty years were added decrease of Parliament's power and importance and a steady extension of autonomy among the components of the British Empire.

In the beginning of 1914, a prominent issue in British politics was the question of Women's Suffrage. The struggle reached a climax in that year, but the outbreak of war brought an immediate truce. Women everywhere turned to give service to the State. A well-known Scottish doctor, Elsie Inglis, approached the War Office at once with an offer of fully staffed hospitals, and was curtly told to 'go home and keep quiet,' 'they could not be troubled with hysterical women.' So the famous Scottish Women's Hospitals won their brilliant reputation with the Allies. They raised £500,000, staffed fourteen units, and served with the Belgian, French, Russian, and Serbian Armies, sharing the terrible retreat of the last. Dr Inglis, whose devotion cost her her life, ranks as one of Serbia's national heroines.

Before long, however, the Government changed their tune: even the War Office, in 1915, was to put a Scots and an English woman doctor—Dr Flora Murray and Dr Louisa Garrett Anderson—in charge of a military hospital. 10,000 British women were Army nurses, with 8,000 more in the Territorial Service and 10,000 again as 'V.A.D.s'—a body created by a Scotswoman, Elizabeth Haldane of Cloan, in 1909. By 1917 women were being officially recruited to serve in collaboration with the Forces, the Women's Army Auxiliary Corps (in a carefully unbecoming uniform) being followed by the Women's Royal Naval Service and the Women's Royal Air

337

Force. 150,000 were enlisted. 162,000 entered other Government service of one kind or other; and in spite of complex trouble with the Trade Unions, some half a million turned to making munitions, while thousands more took men's places in civil life, from shepherds and sweeps and porters to grave-diggers.

By 1916 their work was being greeted with a chorus of praise: and the new addition to the nation's man-power was too valuable to be longer snubbed. Asquith gave up opposing 'Votes for Women.' In February of 1918, when the Representation of the People Act gave the vote to, in practice, all men over twenty-one, women (over thirty) at last received it also, and were eligible to sit in Parliament . . . although at the Khaki Election of that November, the one elected, Countess Markievicz, stood for Sinn Fein, and refused to take her place in Parliament, and it was not until the following year that Viscountess Astor (who was American born) entered the Commons. By 1923 she had seven companions, and one Labour and one Conservative woman member were in the Government, the latter being a Scotswoman, the Duchess of Atholl. The last step was taken when in 1928 the Conservative Government, by 387 votes to 10, reduced the voting age to twenty-one, and gave equal franchise to both men and women.

It did not end the ugly conflict between them, for men returning home after the war found the wage-earning world full of women in men's former jobs: and the women, knowing their chances of marriage decreased, knew that many must thenceforth be self-supporting, or else a drag on brothers who wished to marry. Hence grew bitter resentments, for both sides had a case: and the breakdown of the moral code in the 'twenties brought often another, unpleasing, complication. The position greatly stabilised in the 'thirties: but even today a woman of any sort of outstanding achievement may run at times against a surprising rancour, even in men of normally generous outlook.

The familiar machine of party government continued nominally to exist: but it changed. One marked change was the replacement of Liberalism by Labour as one of the two major parties. It was a more real change than is sometimes thought, for though the Labour Party twice refused (in 1923 and 1936) affiliation with the Communists, and their general temper was very similar to that of the old Victorian Radicals, they stood for collective action by organised bodies, the State or the Trade Unions within the State, and cared little for what to the old-fashioned Liberal was fundamental—individual freedom. In fact, those two parties had opposite weaknesses, the Liberal making a fetish of that freedom, while Labour was not concerned enough to guard it.

The parties swung in and out in the old fashion, with earthshaking noises and much ceremony, though in fact the old oppositions tended in practice to be merged in a series of coalitions. The Labour Party achieved a Government in 1924, under Ramsay MacDonald, held it for some months, and returned again in 1929, to hold office then for nearly two years and a half, and share it thereafter, in 1931 and '35, as a portion of a 'National Government.' For Scotland, it was all very much a sham fight—an opinion to be endorsed, in 1941, by the Government's cynically frank admission that it does not matter to his constituents whether the holder of a Scottish seat is in Canada, in Westminster, or in gaol.

Democracy everywhere during this period was being seriously weakened by three factors. The selection of representatives had passed to small semi-official bodies, tightly closed, with the result that voting was purely for parties, not for men: and it matters a good deal in practice what men are chosen. The representatives themselves suffered badly from the prevailing tendency of the time, always to take the line of least resistance. And everywhere, very markedly in Britain, the real government tended more and more to pass from the nominal legislative body into the hands of the executive. Whatever the nominal form of it might be, a European state in the nineteen-thirties was essentially ruled by a bureaucracy—by its permanent civil service, who not only assumed a growing power to interpret the laws which it was their duty to administer, but won that of adding to them of their own accord.

In practice, these tendencies mattered little to Scotland, who had for long been governed, in theory, by a majority not elected by her in what was her primary legislative assembly (528 to 74)[1] and by now was generally in practice ruled from an increasing number of government bureaux, of which the Scottish Office was but one. Thus the Railway Act of 1922 gave the control of the Scottish rail-

---

[1] Thus the Licensing Act of 1921 was carried, for Scotland, against a majority of Scottish members. Much Scottish Parliamentary legislation consists of 'legislation by appendix'—by application clauses pinned on at the end of a bill designed in the first place to meet the needs of another country with different conditions. Even this modification may not be made.

way system to the London Ministry of Transport, the London Wages Board, and the London Rates Tribunal, who might, or might not, know or care for Scottish conditions. Under the Road Traffic Act of 1930 appeals lay to the Minister of Transport. Those under the Unemployment Insurance Act must be heard by an Umpire in London. Even in matters of local administration, a town wishing powers to make any sort of change in its water, gas, or electricity needs a Provisional Order, and must call in a London Parliamentary Agent. Into the 'thirties a Town Council could not put in a new boiler or move a cab-stand without consulting London. As more and more 'social service' acts were passed,[1] dealing with unemployment, public health, housing, slum clearances, and other such domestic matters, so more and more of the citizen's affairs were regulated by Government departments: and these were all in the long run controlled from London, although the Scots taxes were the same as in England.

As an instance of what ensued, a Royal Commission for Court of Session reform reported in the year 1927 for important improvements in the supreme Civil Court: but five years later nothing had been done. Again, in 1875 the English Supreme Court ruled that Scottish Departments could be sued in England for contracts made in England. The rule was, however, after much protest, amended. None the less, in 1920 it was promulgated once more, and supported by an English Court of Appeal. Protests were made by the Faculty of Advocates, the Society of Writers to the Signet, the Society of Solicitors of the Supreme Court, the Faculties of all the four great cities, the Incorporated Society of Law Agents, the Society of Accountants, the Convention of Royal Burghs, and the leading Chambers of Commerce. These pointed out that the rule was an infringement not only of general international law, but of the 19th clause of the Treaty of Union. The rule remained.

In fact, the position of the Kingdom of Scotland was that of a Crown Colony. She possessed a partial executive of her own, but it was appointed from outside the country, and was not controlled by a nationally elected assembly, while such powers as it actually did possess were constantly crossed by those of foreign Departments. Incidentally, that part of revenue which is spent on defences and administration, though raised in the country, is only in small part

---

[1] The cost of 'social services' in 1910 was £8,000,000 of the taxpayers' money, in 1920, £35,000,000, and in 1930, £60,000,000.

spent there, and does not therefore circulate in Scotland as do such costs in almost all other countries.

During the nineteen-twenties the principle described as 'national self-determination' or 'national autonomy' played a great part in the politics of the Empire and of Europe. The Peace Treaty indeed professed to be based on it, and its manifestations within the British Empire were extremely active through the whole of the time.

In Ireland they led to a bitter civil war. A Home Rule Act, passed at last in 1914, had promised to suspend the long sore struggle, with its memories of secular oppression. It split Ireland, the Northern Counties from the main body, and threatened a war between Ulster and the rest, for the North, fully colonised by England and Scotland, desired to preserve the union as it stood. European war suspended the Act, however . . . and then brought another division. The Irish Constitutional Nationalists, who wished for Irish freedom within the Empire, supported the Empire, and fought most gallantly. But the long delay in assuaging long oppression had given time for the growth of another party, who desired an Irish Republic, outside the Empire. Civil war between these broke out in 1916. In 1920 the 1914 Act was superseded by the Government of Ireland (Partition) Act, which separated the six Ulster Counties. The Civil War continued bitterly—a guerilla war, with ugly incident on both sides. In six months of 1921 Dublin alone saw 147 fights in her streets: and no man knew at night when he went to his bed whether he would be alive in it at dawn. In December 1921 the Treaty of London made twenty-six counties into the Irish Free State, as a self-governing part of the British Empire, in coronary union with the rest. War continued, however, between the party which had signed the Treaty and the Irish Republicans. Even to this day, the relations between the two, and of Ireland and Britain, are very far from satisfactory.[1] No doubt Christian charity demands that Ireland should forgive and forget: but eight centuries of consistent severe oppression, even punctuated

[1] The fact puzzles many honest Scots and English. They would do well to read Mr Stephen Gwynn's brilliantly written *Short History of Ireland*; and after a canto or two of Spenser's *Faerie Queene*, with its noble and generous outlook a life and ethics, and then the *Veue of the Present State of Ireland*, with its morseless doctrine of savage suppression, and recall that these two were written the same man . . . who held an administrative post in Ireland. The exercise a grim enlightenment on one side of political psychology.

by frequent grim revolts, are more easily forgotten by the oppressors than by those who suffered under their regime.

India's road to self-government, if less troubled than Ireland's, has been complex enough, owing, in part, to economic factors, but much more to a conflict of religions, and the difficulty of forming a regime in which Hindus and Moslems will collaborate without considering that either's rights have been infringed by the other. The problem was a leading one through the time, and underground intervention from other states (not lacking even in Ireland now and then) never tended greatly to simplify a solution which had not, at the end of the 'thirties, been discovered.

The various Crown Colonies almost all moved in some degree towards self-government. The most satisfactory developments were however in the status of the Dominions, where what had not been done in 1770 was done, and with the fortunate result that what was done in 1776 was made very easy—and highly improbable. By the beginning of the century, the great Dominions were distinctive nations, and their relations as such with the Home Countries were therefore somewhat difficult at times. These difficulties were faced in the early 'twenties. In 1926 the Imperial Conference adopted a report which stated, truly, that the British Empire

considered as a whole, defies classification, and bears no real resemblance to any other political organisation which now exists or has yet been tried.

That extremely important truth having once been grasped, it was possible to go on to declare that the Dominions, no less than Great Britain,

are autonomous communities within the British Empire, equal in status in no way subordinate one to another in any aspect of their domestic or external affairs, though united by a common allegiance to the Crown and freely associated as members of the British Commonwealth of nations.[1]

This declaration of sisterly independence was literally true, if not wholly in spirit, since within the unit which was described as Great Britain a sub-unit, not a colony grown to a nation but a much older nation sunk to a province, held a position which somewhat contravened it. The Dominions had their due and accepted places in the Assembly of the League of Nations, at times on its Council and Canada at least was sending her own accredited diplomats to

[1] The formula is that of A. J. Balfour,

those countries with whom she was in close relations. In 1931 the Statute of Westminster sought to define the relations expressed in the Balfour Formula, and to remove the restrictions which still remained upon the national freedom of the Dominions. Many, at home and abroad, considered that the Statute was lunacy. Were not many men living in South Africa—some barely fifty—who had fought against Britain in a long hard war? Was not Australia at the Antipodes? The Statute, however, was to be ratified, with some emphasis, in 1939, in a manner which proves that for free men, free union is likely to be the most enduring bond.

In Scotland the movement towards the restoration of self-government continued, and grew, in spite of handicaps. England regarded it as the Government in the nineteenth century did Women's Suffrage—as an unnatural and offensive joke. With most Scots, two centuries of Whig propaganda caused the country's position after 1707 to be taken as much as a part of the nature of things as a Roman citizen in the year 400 took the existence of the Roman Empire. If, like the weather, it could at times be a nuisance, one merely cursed it and hung one's clothes to dry. Men bred from their earliest schooldays to take for granted that the Union, as Mr W. H. Marwick puts it, 'gave Scotland all virtues but that of sobriety,' had been too thoroughly conditioned to it to consider that any change was feasible: and the general temper of the nincteen-twenties discouraged all forms of effort except in sport. There were Nationalists who encouraged this apathy. A sprinkling of romantics lived in a past which had no link of reason with the present, and gave those unwilling to think out the issues an excuse to put them aside as sentimental. Others, noisy out of proportion to their number, belonged to a type that is always to be found on the fringe of any movement which opposes an extant regime—that type whose inward 'inferiority-complex' seeks safety and comfort in an aggressive 'againstness.' These Habakkuk Mucklewraths repelled by their shrillness and their parochial notion of a nation, and gave still more excuse to those who were unwilling to face the exertion required to tackle facts or withstand the social and often domestic pressure which in all ages has been bent on those rebellious against the *status quo*.

None the less, the serious and stable elements continued patiently, in the manner of the Victorian Suffragists, to work for a more satisfactory relation between the component countries of Great Britain, and to secure for this old and unconquered kingdom that autonomy which the various Colonies and the conquered land of Ireland were in process of achieving, not wholly by peaceful means, for themselves.

Their experience was that of the Suffragists. Their case, stated temperately, and firmly based on a mass of concrete facts, was unanswerable, the more as all parties were vocally professing belief in 'national self-determination' not only for Poles but for Slovaks, Czechs, and Letts—indeed, any racial group that might be mentioned. The Conservative Party, as such, made no pronouncement, but not only the Duke of Montrose and Sir Gideon Murray but the English leaders Austen Chamberlain, Walter Long, and Lord Selborne professed, in 1919, their approval, as did the Liberal leader Mr Lloyd George. In 1920 Mr Robert Munro (later Lord Alness) was given the Scottish Office in spite of his belief in 'Home Rule for Scotland.' The Scottish Labour Party and I.L.P. and the Scottish Trade Union Council, from 1920, passed a number of resolutions in support, as they had already done before the war.

In the late summer of 1918 the Young Scots Society held a meeting in Glasgow—without their President, who had been killed in action. It was proposed there to initiate a non-party National Movement, and a new Scottish Home Rule Association was formed: six years later it had sixty-nine local branches. In the May of 1919 a bill was brought forward in Parliament by Sir W. H. Cowan: on its second reading, the House was counted out. A few weeks later Major Wood produced a motion for Devolution, strongly supported by Austen Chamberlain. It passed by 187 to 34, the Scottish votes being 35 to one. It is worth noting that of 116 Unionists voting, 84 were in favour. The 36 Scots who voted were made up of 14 Coalition Unionists (including the one Scot who opposed the motion), 12 Coalition Liberals, 5 Independent Liberals, and 5 Labour men. No more was then done, but in the following April, of 1920, Mr Joseph Johnstone brought in a definite bill. This time 38 Scots members were for it, 9 against: but in a House where a very bare quorum was present, the closure was carried by a dozen votes. Mr J. A. Murray MacDonald, twelve days later, brought in a Parliamentary Relief Bill, 'to provide for relief of the Parliament of the United Kingdom by establishing subordinate Parliaments in England, Scotland, and Wales': but it failed to get as far as a second reading. In the same year, a Conference on Devolution was held,

with the Speaker in the Chair. Its proposals were an awkward compromise for a five years experiment in which the English, Scottish,
and Welsh M.P.s were to sit separately every autumn, and meet
together for the rest of the year. No one, as possibly had been
intended, admired the idea, and it was dropped at once.

Meanwhile, the Scottish National League had been founded, by
the Hon. Ruaraidh Erskine of Marr, for 'the resumption of Scottish
National Independence, in conjunction with the establishment of
Scottish democratic institutions.' The impact of the movement
still was lessened by the dissension between two schools of thought.
The little group of Wee Free doctrinaires clamoured for wholly
isolated freedom, breaking all connection with England and the
Empire. The rest, no less desiring autonomy, pointed out that
geography and history made such isolation, if possible, unwise, since
Scotland's interest in the British Empire, which Scots in the past
had done so much to create, and her intimate connection with the
Dominions, made severance from the Empire unjustified, while at
the same time the position in Europe of an isolated small nation
between great powers was (as 1940 was to demonstrate) precarious,
to say the least of it. And opponents were presented with the chance
of answering the first group, which they could easily do, and thus
avoiding argument with the second, while preserving an appearance
of candid discussion. Yet discussion, at time acrimonious, increased, and frequently recalled, *mutatis mutandis*, our past ecclesiastical history: by the mid-twenties the issues were widely debated,
and many had been forced to consider them.

In the spring of 1924 another bill, backed by large and vigorous
demonstrations in Scotland, was brought up by Mr George Buchanan
(Labour) in a Parliament where his party were in office under the
Premiership of Ramsay MacDonald. The bill had been carefully
drafted. It proposed that two members for each of the then constituencies should meet as a Constituent Assembly—that is, one
which should work out a new Scots Constitution. Scotland should
control her own Treasury, Judicature, Land Tenure, Education,
Agriculture and Afforestation, Fisheries, Labour, Local Government,
Police, Public Health, Housing, Transport, Trade, Customs, Excise,
and Income-tax, Coastal Lights, Ports, and Civil Navigation, and
Ecclesiastical matters. The Post Office, Army, Navy, Air Force,
and Foreign Office should rank as joint concerns of Scotland and
England, and be paid for jointly. The bill reached its second

reading, when it was discussed in detail for seven hours—to be talked out in the end by Mr Leng Sturrock. The Scottish members approached the Prime Minister, and requested facilities for further debate. He professed his own approval, but declared that the majority of the Cabinet considered it inopportune. Several days, just after, were given to a London Traffic Bill.

On the 9th and 10th of the following October, with Parliament in the act of dissolution, the Scottish Liberal Federation at Stirling passed a resolution embodying another scheme, demanding a single-chamber Scots Parliament (with due safeguards against hasty legislation) to authorise all taxes levied in Scotland and to deal with all such matters of Scottish interest as were not reserved to the Imperial Parliament—on which, of course, Scotland would still be represented. The subjects so reserved were the Crown, Peace and War, the Armed Forces, Foreign Affairs, the Dominions, Colonies, and Overseas Possessions, Dignities and Titles, Submarine Cables, Aerial Navigation, Currency, Trade Marks, Patents and Copyrights, Customs and Excise. Scotland's Imperial contribution should be debated by both Parliaments. The membership of the first revived Scots Parliament should be as in Mr George Buchanan's Bill.

In that year too the Conservative Duke of Montrose sponsored a third scheme, remitting Imperial Finance to a joint Treasury Committee with England—a less cumbrous arrangement than that of the Stirling Plan: for the rest, the two were in substantial accord.

That year, indeed, was one of active discussion. During the General Election in its October, the Home Rule Association asked all Scots candidates if they would agree to a National Convention, to discuss the establishment of a Scots Parliament. Most agreed. A Convention representing Members of Parliament, Town Councils, County Councils, Parish Councils, Education Authorities, Trade Unions, the Scottish Home Rule Association, the Scottish National Movement, and other various Nationalist bodies, met in November, in the City Hall, Glasgow, and set up a widely representative Committee to draft a bill.[1] After two years work, the Convention met again, and accepted the proposals of the Committee. The bill was brought before the House in spring, and public meetings in all the chief Scottish towns supported it. It passed its first reading, and

---

[1] The *Scots Independent* made its first appearance at this time, Messrs W. Gillies and T. H. Gibson being editors.

on the 13th May 1927 came up for its second. After three-quarters of an hour's debate, it was talked out, by Sir P. J. Ford.

It was the ninth occasion in eight years on which the question had come before the House—the twenty-first since 1889. On all these occasions, except the first in 1889, there had been a Scottish majority in favour. On almost all since 1893, there had been a majority in the House in favour: but none of all these bills had been permitted to go any farther than its second reading.

There was considerable indignation. The National Convention met again. It was suggested that previous efforts had failed because their conduct was left to existing parties, whose point of view put the party before the nation. (In fact, the attitude of many people recalled that of earlier opponents of Women's Suffrage, who objected to it on the alternate grounds that all women were naturally Conservatives and that all women would vote Liberal.) The formation of a National Party, therefore, which should put the establishment of a Government before the question of who was going to lead it, was proposed: and the proposal split the Convention. That section of it which backed the new proposal was joined by various other organisations, and on the 24th March 1928 the National Party of Scotland was established, R. B. Cunninghame Graham becoming its President, Mr R. E. Muirhead its Chairman, Mr J. M. MacCormick its Secretary, and Mr D. C. MacKechnie its Treasurer: its aims were set forth as being to secure 'Self-government for Scotland with absolute national status within the British group of nations, together with the reconstruction of Scottish national life.' Scotland should co-operate with the other units of the Commonwealth, but have separate representation on the Imperial Conference and on the League of Nations, and separate trade—and where needful diplomatic —representatives abroad, while Scottish credit, motive power, and transport were to be nationally controlled.

Alongside it there shortly took shape a Scottish Party, which favoured the principles of the Duke of Montrose: its leaders were the Duke, Sir D. M. Stevenson, and Sir Alexander MacEwen. The two were united in 1934, and became the present Scottish National Party, which demands a Scots Parliament with final authority on all Scots affairs, Scotland's future relations with England to be based on equality of status and real partnership in such joint concerns as Defence, Foreign Policy, Customs, and the Empire. The new party has several times put forward candidates for Parliament. None so far has been returned, though Mr R. E. Muirhead could remark in 1938 that in the first ten years of its existence the Scottish Labour Party had contested 19 seats and won 14,457 votes, while the National Party in that time could claim 27 contests and 98,610 votes. Much other work of various kinds has been done, including leadership of a vigorous protest against the deportation of young Scots, and in that re-starting of work on the *Queen Mary* which signalised the beginning of revival.

While changes were sought in Scottish government, certain other changes were actually made. The Local Government Act of 1929 brought a far-reaching reorganisation. Before it there had been nine Local Government authorities—Town Councils, County Councils, District Committees, Standing Joint Committees, Commissioners of Supply, Parish Councils, Education Authorities, District Boards of Control, and District Committees. After the Act, the first three alone remained, the 869 Parish Councils being abolished and their work handed over to the large County Councils, which might meet as seldom as three times a year. The Town Councils lost control of public health, housing, roads, police, education, and poor relief, and the Royal Burghs were more or less wiped from the administrative map. County Councils are largely appointed by indirect election, the members for the small burghs being chosen by the Town Councils from their own number. In the larger counties the time and expense required by membership make it unwelcome.[1] The Small Burghs Committee produced a report in 1935 which declared that

The general consensus of opinion provides ample evidence that the Act has not . . . effected material improvement in the administration of Local Government in Scotland : on the contrary, local administration is in many ways less efficient than before, and the Act has led to increased expenditure in practically every department of municipal activity.

Nineteenth century self-government agitation had led to the granting of a Scottish Office as a placebo. That of the twentieth transferred the Office from Whitehall to Edinburgh. On the report of Sir John Gilmour's Committee the decision was made in 1938 that the administrative staff of the Office should be moved to the country with which its work was concerned, leaving only a liaison

---

[1] Lewis members of the Ross-shire County Council must cross seventy miles of rough sea and the breadth of Scotland to attend a meeting. They represent a population of 30,000, with distinct and difficult problems of its own.

staff in Whitehall. In 1939 the move was achieved, to a comely new building on the Calton Hill.

As had been intended, the change was widely received as an agreeable compromise with Home Rule. In fact, the flitting of Scotland's administration was less complete than appeared at the first glance. The Departments of Health, Education, and Agriculture were indeed now housed in the capital of the country, and a new Home Department there took over the Boards of Fisheries, Pensions, and Control. But though the Ministries of Home Security, Information, Labour, Transport, Building, Food, Pensions, War, and Air, the Admiralty, the Board of Trade, the Forestry Commission, the Post Office, and the British Broadcasting Corporation each has a 'regional branch' in Edinburgh, these are none the less directly controlled from Whitehall by a Minister chiefly concerned with English affairs; while the power that controls them all, and the Scottish Office, is the London Treasury. This final control is increasingly realised, the more as Scots national expenditure receives for its discussion in Parliament no more than a couple of days in the course of a year [1] and is often determined, not by Scots requirements, but by those of England: thus, for education, Scotland's estimate is automatically eleven-eightieths of whatever sum England decides she requires for her own needs. Many people who had received St Andrew's House with joy as a real national government soon came, in fact, to agree with Sir William Goodchild, the Secretary of the Scottish Economic Committee (and incidentally an Englishman) in describing the new arrangement as a makeshift.

[1] When Mr Tom Johnston and Mr Henderson Stewart suggested reform of the Scottish Grand Committee in order to secure a proper debate on the Scots Estimates, they were heavily snubbed by the Secretary for Scotland, Mr Walter Elliot . . . who on another occasion had remarked, ' As Secretary for Scotland I look round for persons who can carry out some great task. I think of the ideal man, and he is at the end of the earth, or in a very good post in London, and cannot be got.'

XXIX

NOISES OFF

TWENTY YEARS: 1918–38

A big blooming buzzing confusion.
    WILLIAM JAMES, *The Principles of Psychology*.
Saying, ' Peace, Peace '—   Jeremiah, vi. 14.

IT is nearly a century since Stratford Canning remarked in a despatch, 'The extreme desire for peace, if care be not taken, may bring on the danger of war.' It is longer since the prophet Jeremiah spoke of those who say 'Peace, Peace,' when beyond their borders

a great nation . . . lay hold on bow and spear . . . they are cruel and have no mercy : their voice roareth like the sea.

That 'extreme desire' and its grim corollary are the dominants of the politics of Europe throughout the twenty years between two great wars. There were others. One recognised major element was the importance of nationality. Another, unhappily less well recognised, was that this sounding word was used for two different things, as opposite to each other as God and Satan. The huge error involved in this failure of recognition springs from another mark of that restless time—its overwhelming flood of words, words, words, and the habit they bred of thinking in words, not things. This last is not new. All ages have suffered from it more or less; but it has grown much since the invention of printing, and the addition of the radio has immensely multiplied its sinister power of drawing a veil between man and the world he lives in. Words, like fire, are excellent servants, but ill masters. By the late 'thirties, they were the masters of Europe.

At such times, there is always a captain word, which draws round it robes of a vague and veiling glory. In the sixteenth century it had been Truth. In the late eighteenth and the nineteenth, it was Freedom. Now it was Peace. Peace, freedom, truth, are among the greatest *things*. Their names are among the most subtle enchantments of Hell.

After the Armistice, all the world looked for peace. Its possible terms had been discussed already. Early in 1918 Mr Lloyd George had demanded restoration of the sanctity of treaties, territorial resettlement on a basis of 'national self-determination,' evacuation of all occupied lands, and the future limitation of armaments; he disclaimed desire for Germany's destruction or for the changing of her constitution. President Wilson's famous Fourteen Points added to these aims the conduct of diplomacy in public, removal of economic barriers, impartial adjustment of colonial claims as should be best for the Colonies' own interests, guarantees for general disarmament, and the freedom of the High Seas. He undoubtedly meant well.

When the Armistice came, the most immediate need was to settle the Central European chaos. Blockade was still considered necessary to keep Germany from resumption of the war: and this was probably a first-class blunder, for the new German Government really craved peace, and the continued hardships of the blockade gave many people bitter personal reason for enmity to the powers that still enforced it. None the less, more was done than was later recalled to help enemy civilians in Middle Europe. Great Britain alone gave £12 million for free relief, and private organisations fed four million children.

In Britain, a General Election was due at once, and the most important matter, for all politicians, was to make such appeal to the Free and Enlightened Voter as should ensure their return to Westminster. They began by speaking of 'just and lasting peace,' in terms of a conspicuous moderation. Before November was at an end, however, Mr Barnes (Labour) had raised the cry 'Hang the Kaiser,' and the scared and bellicose civilian voter, or some of him, answered with a howl of joy. The bidding rose. One month after the Armistice, the Government's policy was re-formulated as the trial of the Kaiser, punishment for 'atrocities,' full indemnities from Germany, 'Britain for the British,' rehabilitation of those broken by war, and radical reform of land, health, housing, and conditions of labour.

Some of these things were feasible enough, and it proved an attractive programme for the civilian. Only a third of the fighting forces voted, but the Coalition Government which had framed it came in with a majority of 262. The Kingdom of Heaven did not

appear on earth. The 1919 Budget did, however, with a vast deficit
—which Germany must pay. As the rest of the Allies were in the
same case, or worse, and as Germany was in still worse case than
they were, this simple thesis was easier to state than to translate
into effective action.

Then four considerable errors were made. One was over-
lenient. There were Victory Parades in Paris and London, but
none in Berlin; the Germans were given no ocular demonstration
of a conclusive military defeat. One was over-severe. The new
German government had not made the war—had in fact overthrown
that which had made the war; but it was not admitted to peace
negotiations. The third was short-sighted. The dynasties of the
smaller German states had never loved Berlin: now they were
ignored, and the Treaty made Germany's formal unity into something real, by considering only Berlin. The fourth was sentimental.
Negotiations were not conducted by professionals in a privacy where
mistakes could be made and altered: seventy plenipotentiaries,
1,037 delegates, and secretaries beyond all computation pranced and
clattered beneath the reporters' magnesium flares, in an atmosphere
of headlines and future votes. Moreover, the Peace was indissolubly
linked with the forming of an ambitious League of Nations, from
which Germany was excluded, and of whom her suspicions were
very soon aroused by the plebiscite in Upper Silesia, when—though
62 per cent. of votes were for Germany—the League gave five-
sixths of the colliery districts to Poland.[1] In conclusion, a Germany
with a sense of grievance, some points of reality on which to hang
it, and no real conviction that she had been beaten, was left bordered
by a chain of new small states, whose safety depended on external
support.

Such as it was, the Treaty of Versailles was signed on the 28th
June 1919. (Negotiations with Germany's allies dragged on:
Turkey's Peace was not signed till 1923, and then with a regime
on the point of collapse.) The power of words as weapons, known
in all ages, but never used so skilfully as in ours, has been directed
for nearly twenty years at convincing the world that the Treaty
was unjust. In assessing the point, one fairly may consider the
conception of just peace that Germany had shown not only at

[1] In fairness to the League, one has to recall that the German majority was
greatly helped by the fact that the German Government worked hard to import
into Silesia, for the occasion, all Germans who had been born there and now lived
elsewhere.

Frankfurt in 1871, but in March of 1918 at Brest-Litovsk and in May of 1918 at Bucharest.[1] Versailles was far less severe: but it was handled with grave lack of skill, with an eye less on the future than on votes. Inevitable under democracy? It depends a good deal whether one considers that the role of a democratic electorate is to fidget continually round its servants, or to choose servants it can trust, and trust them. A lively family debate behind the surgeon (with a good deal said about rival practitioners) does not always produce the best results for the patient.

For the greater part of the next twenty years the kaleidoscope that was Europe's politics shows three patterns of activity superposed. One recalls the children's game with a box of letters—a scuffle, increasingly tearful and ill-tempered, to pick out of the possible unions and oppositions the five magic letters which, arranged, should spell PEACE. The second was also a game with boxes of papers, where the loudest shouter got most of those marked X. It scrambled over and through and about the others, and shook the table at the most difficult moments. The third layer was a most unholy blend of sham fights and fights that were intensely real. One was the class war which Communism believed in, between those who had and those others who had not: and this fight was both real and fictitious. There was another, which Communism fought, but did not believe in, with those who saw that the Russian Revolution had meant not only that after eleven years of absolute power the government of a great wheat-producing country, with the world's richest natural resources, was faced by recurrent and enormous famines, but that Russia was under the iron autocratic rule, over men's minds and souls as well as bodies, of a minority of bureaucrats—an oligarchy of the post-office clerk, with as much power and as little security as any mediaeval Italian despot.

The opponents of Communism in the first fight borrowed its structure from it in order to fight it: they established what was in effect the same regime, but as the Red Flag was international, they set up the National Flag to be worshipped instead. The opponents of Communism in the second—those who still believed in the

---

[1] By the former, Russia lost 6,000 million marks, 56 million people, territory equal to Austria-Hungary plus Turkey-in-Europe, a third of her railways, 73 per cent. of her iron, 89 per cent. of her coal, and 5,000 factories. By the latter, Rumania lost the whole Dobrudja, her frontier districts and control of her passes, her oil-fields and forests, and the first claim on her foodstuffs, and had to pay the costs of a German Army of Occupation of 90,000 men.

freedom of thought and speech—found themselves fighting, for one and the same reason, not only Communism but its opponents.

That, however, in 1919, was still to come. The first issue, that year, was to guarantee the Peace. There was trouble at once. France and Britain, of the Allies, had borne the main weight of the war: and further peace depended on a good understanding between them. Now Britain, in international politics, meant in practice England. England and France find it hard to work together, and the men who had to ensure that they should do so were Lord Curzon, Mr Lloyd George, and Raymond Poincaré. One could not have chosen a trio less likely to mix well. France's major idea was that two German wars, in a lifetime, were enough for any country: *il fallait en finir*. Accordingly, she wanted the Saar in her hands, and a Rhineland buffer state on her eastern march. The doctrine of racial self-determination, to which everyone was pledged, forbade this, however. America and Britain offered instead to guarantee her, with military support, against any German aggression. She accepted; and all three signed a Treaty of Triple Guarantee on the same day as the Treaty of Versailles.

It was a wise move, that might have saved all Europe. But the Senators of the United States, in their anxiety to be rid of Wilson, repudiated it, and refused the League. Britain declared that the Treaty was dissolved, and France, thus calmly abandoned by her allies, turned resentfully eastward. It was the beginning of sorrows.

The nineteen-twenties present a dissolving view of a procession of statesmen—so to call them—in Conferences volubly advertised and dominated by France's uneasiness over the danger on her eastward march, and Britain's annoyed incomprehension of it. In 1920 a Communist *putsch* in the Ruhr brought German troops into the zone of territory demilitarised by the Peace of Versailles. France insisted on occupying further towns, and pointed out that Germany had not disarmed. Nor was she paying the agreed reparations. Germany promised that she would soon do both; but did not. In 1921, indeed, she received an actual ultimatum; while Franco-British friction steadily grew, Mr Lloyd George being so much disliked in France that the mere suspicion of a friendship with him brought down the French Premier Aristide Briand. Poincaré then succeeded to his place, and had just one point in common with Lord Curzon—that neither knew how to handle a committee.

As result, a Conference at Geneva failed, since neither France nor the United States would attend it. Also, the Government of Germany—for the most part well-meaning middle-class intellectuals—made a treaty of alliance with Bolshevik Russia, who was looking forward to world revolution. In the Near East, Turkey, under Mustapha Kemal, was becoming an efficient dictatorship, and was at war with Greece over Smyrna, which in 1917 had been promised by the Allies to Italy, and given by them to Greece the following year. France and Italy backed Kemal, Britain Greece. And Egypt demanded self-determination, which was first refused, then after violent revolts, conceded, demonstrating that violence paid.

By the end of 1922 there was revolution or the threat of it almost everywhere east of the Rhine and south of the Meuse, with Ireland as an outflung sideshow westward: and to the Communist totalitarianism was opposed a new and anti-Communist brand, newly exemplified in Italy, where Mussolini, at the end of October, had marched on Rome, smashed a far from satisfactory Parliament, and obliterated King Victor Emmanuel.

A Conference met at Lausanne, and was a failure. Germany declared that she could not pay any further reparations, as her currency had collapsed. France affirmed that the collapse was her own fault, and occupied the Ruhr, producing there a condition like that of Ireland in those years. The German government deliberately debased the currency further and further, till the mark, by October 1923, was worth 19,000 million to the pound sterling: a pre-war fortune, equivalent to a million in British money, would leave 2¾d. change on a threepenny bit. In this way it paid off its own internal debts, but it wholly ruined its own middle class, by far the most stable element in the country. The Dawes Loan—£40 million from the United States—saved German finance. But the damage had been done, and the German people were delivered, mentally, to the waiting Nazis, who were ready to preach national awakening and delivery from the ruinous Socialists, and to comfort Germany's sense of defeat and disaster by assuring Germans that they were the *Herrenvolk*, betrayed by their Government and tricked by the world, but able, if they submitted to the right men, and made sacrifices which were little more than what they had been forced to suffer already, to march forward to future supremacy and vengeance.

1924 promised better things for a while. Baldwin and Curzon were replaced by Ramsay MacDonald as both Premier and Foreign Secretary: and with all his faults, he knew the importance of France, while there Poincaré and the *Bloc national* were replaced by Herriot and the *Cartel des gauches*. Herriot and MacDonald worked well together, attempting to find a substitute for the Treaty of Triple Guarantee. It seemed to be secured in the Geneva Protocol, intended 'to secure the solidarity of the members of an international community against aggression on any one of them.' The Protocol sought to forward disarmament by substituting for war the arbitration of a Court of International Justice. The League approved. So did most of the Continent. Britain and the Dominions disliked it, however; and before it could be carried into effect, Ramsay MacDonald's government had fallen. He had however done much to improve relations not only with France, but with Italy as well, who was smarting under a well-based sense of grievance.[1]

Austen Chamberlain then became Foreign Secretary. He had the accomplishment, rare among politicians, of a working knowledge of past history, and knew France and her supreme importance in Europe, and to Britain. 'Pray God they stand together,' he said of the two, 'or our common cause will perish.' But the country had disarmed too far to fight, and was happily sure it would never be called on to do so. Yet to accept the alternative, arbitration, as a general and binding principle was against the constitutional English habit of arrangement *ad hoc*: the Dominions too saw in it an infringement of their new sovereignty; and both were alarmed for a naval dominance which was then, in fact, rather rapidly declining. In spite of the urgings of Briand and Dr Benes, the Protocol was refused, and the Government instead proposed a renewed Franco-British Alliance. France wanted it to include a guarantee for the states on Germany's eastern frontier also. Germany was harrowed: there was talk of *lebensraum* and encirclement. Britain refused. And the German Foreign Minister, Stresemann, contrived to set Britain and France again by the ears, while a casual remark of Briand's, that it would not much matter if Austria joined the Reich, was considered ominous in Italy.

After a deal of haggling and intrigue, the famous Pact of Locarno

---

[1] The broken promise of Smyrna was not all: another, of the cession of Jubaland, had also been broken. It was later redeemed, but not until after the breach had given rise to doubts of British good faith.

was arrived at, towards the end of 1925. It consisted of a group of intricate treaties, the most important being a mutual guarantee of Germany, Belgium, France, Britain, and Italy, the first three pledging themselves to settle all disputes by peaceful means, while Great Britain and Italy promised aid to any which should be attacked by any of the rest. Arbitration treaties also were included between Germany and France and Germany and Belgium, while a corresponding Eastern Pact included material guarantees between France and Poland and France and Czecho-Slovakia, and arbitration treaties between Germany and Poland, Germany and Czecho-Slovakia. The whole arrangement seemed to give promise of peace. There was hopeful talk of the Locarno Spirit: and few people out of Germany were reading a wordy book by an Austrian house-painter, unsuccessful leader of National Socialists, that sketched turgid dreams, and plans, of world domination to be won by manipulation of men's minds.

Locarno does indeed mark the end of a phase, and an end that gave justification for high hopes. Three lessons had been learned— the third, unhappily, learned but not accepted. Armaments, being the result of fear, would not be abolished till there was security. Security could only be obtained if the use of force in the settlement of disputes could be made unsafe. And it could not be made unsafe until there should be some higher authority than the individual claims of any nation . . . which meant a sacrifice of some sovereignty. On that the Locarno Pact, in the end, was to founder: but at the time it made a real attempt to achieve security, while bringing Germany back to a place in Europe. She entered the League now, and should have had a seat upon its Council: but (to her well-exploited indignation) a number of the smaller powers objected, and this dignity had for a time to be postponed.

Time went on. Europe seemed at last to be stabilising. But the psychological imprint of the 'twenties had not worn off yet. Much of Europe grew down—if that is the reverse of growing up. There was a retrogression of mental age. The predominant temper of the Middle Ages, in spite of their naïvety over science, is adult: so is that of the Renaissance. But the Age of Reason, that of Sentiment, and the Romantic Revival which followed them, are coloured by a sort of adolescence—its clear and narrow security of judgment, its bewilderment when its beliefs are a little chipped, its generous and desperate revolts, its black despair and excited

NORWAY

GREAT BRITAIN

North
Ireland
IRISH
FREE
STATE
(from 1922)

Edinburgh

NORTH
SEA

DENMARK *Cop*

Belfast

Dublin

London

Amsterdam
The Hague

HOLLAND

Berli

GERMA

BELGIUM

Brussels

ATLANTIC

OCEAN

Versailles *Paris*

FRANCE

Geneva SWITZERLAND

USTE

Tr

Lisbon

PORTUGAL

Madrid

SPAIN

CORSICA

Rome!

ADR

Gibraltar

BALEARIC
ISLANDS

SARDINIA

ITALY

MEDIT

SICILY

ER

M

THE SETTLEMENT
of
1919

Former German Empire... ▥ | Former Austria Hungary... ▤

optimism. It may have been that idolisation of Youth which was part of the 'twenties' revolt against tradition: at least, through much of the population of Europe and a great part of the United States, there was growing a mood which cast back before adolescence, to the mentality of twelve years old, the age of the gang and of all that that implies. Germany had it worst: the perfect Nazi has a twelve-year-old brain with the body and powers of a man. But all nations were touched by it to some extent—the Low Countries, Scandinavia, and Britain much the least, but even they in some sections of them.[1]

The next step, it seemed, must be disarmament. Unfortunately, this was by no means simple. At Geneva in June 1927, Britain, Japan, and the United States held a Naval Conference. It achieved no more than to make bad blood between them and reveal some unpleasant details of the conduct of paid agents of great American armament firms. 1928, on American instance, however, brought the Kellogg Pact, otherwise the Pact of Paris. The United States were still violently prosperous, with an attitude, towards the complications of Europe, of a superior and detached aloofness. But there was much good American money in Europe, and its owners desired the outlawry of war. All nations, therefore, were asked to sign a repudiation of war; and sixty did. If the Pact did not end war, it did put an end to the decent old convention by which formal declaration preceded attack: and it did convince the bulk of the British public that there would be no more war, and that expenditure for the Services was a waste of money that might be more pleasantly spent. Britain and France, the same year, attempted a conference on naval disarmament, whose chief effect was to frighten Mussolini

[1] On the night on which I had written the above, I cast round my shelves for some light literature, and came on a copy of John Buchan's *Three Hostages*, bought on a journey a good many years ago. Before I had read many pages, I came on this, *written before mid-1924* :
'All the old sanctities had become weakened, and men had grown too well accustomed to death and pain. This meant that the criminal had far greater resources at his command. . . . The moral imbecile . . . had been more or less of a sport before the War ; now he was a terribly common product. . . . Cruel, humourless, hard, utterly wanting in sense of proportion, but often full of a perverted poetry and drunk with rhetoric—a hideous, untameable breed had been engendered. . . . All this desperate degenerate stuff is being used by a few clever men who are not degenerates or anything of the sort, but only evil. There has never been such a chance for a rogue since the world began.'
Later : 'He said that the great offensives of the future would be psychological, and he thought the Governments should get busy about it, and prepare their defence . . . the most deadly weapon in the world was the power of mass persuasion.'

by a rumour of secret partition of 'his' sea. And a distant commentary was supplied by Chinese seizure of British concessions in Hankow and a threat to Shanghai, which between them made clear that Britain, nowadays, could not protect her nationals from attack.

Meanwhile, in the lands between Russia and Germany, there was in progress a constant bickering, with flickers of war, and a constant invocation of the principle of national boundaries . . . in which 'national,' when equated with 'racial,' could mean, in that part of the world, what the strongest chose, since centuries of shifting frontiers had left a broad mosaic of tongues and peoples inconceivable to the average Western voter, who thought of frontiers as something fixed by nature. And also, by this time, the average Western voter, at any rate of the class which read the papers (and that, by now, included most of him), had discovered that in foreign politics he could find the counters of an entrancing game, which could be played with passion: and he played it, not only with passion but with the ballot-box, though very unluckily without more knowledge than went into a few simple formulae. And the gentlemen who desired his suffrages found that the formulae made first-rate red-herrings to draw over inconvenient domestic trails.

June 1929 brought Labour back again to power in Britain. Ramsay MacDonald was Premier once more, but this time handed over the Foreign Office to Mr Arthur Henderson, who already was sufficiently occupied with Transport House. Labour, by this time, was generally pro-German. Thus there was friction once again with France, Philip Snowden, as Chancellor of the Exchequer, in fact entertaining a Conference held at the Hague, to discuss the question of German reparations, by an undignified row with his French colleague. The reparations, none the less, were dealt with. Germany, so far, had contrived to pay them, with the help of transfusions of foreign capital. In this year they were scaled down by the Young Committee, and a scheme agreed on by which their future payment should be spread out until 1987. The next year brought a stormy Naval Conference, held at London, between the Great Powers. Its real issue was the Italian claim to naval parity with France. It ended with a measure of agreement between Britain, Japan, and the United States, and with France and Italy in evil tempers. But by then a new and distracting force had emerged.

That year of 1929 had begun in hope. Its end brought the

crash of a starting avalanche of new disasters—economic more than political at first, but with political issues of huge importance. For some years, the world as a whole had been growing richer. It is estimated that between 1913 and 1925 the world population had risen by 5 per cent., its food production by 10 per cent., its production of raw materials by 25 per cent., and the general volume of trade by 7 per cent. In that twelve years, however, thanks to the war, Europe's share in the rise had been a great deal less. Her population was up by 1 per cent., her food production by twice that, but her trade had dropped 9 per cent. In the next four years, however, European figures rose, and very steeply: while the world's population rose 4 per cent., its food 5 per cent., its raw materials 20 per cent., and its general trade 19 per cent., the figures for Europe, from 1925 to 1929, are 5 per cent., 10 per cent., 31 per cent., and 22 per cent.: by the end of that time the wealth per head of the world's population was the highest economists have yet recorded.[1]

The world's pre-war economic stability had turned, however, largely on that of Britain, and more especially on that of London. The war had shaken London's badly, however, and the centre had seemed to pass, for a time, to New York. Now America's economic policy demanded the keeping out of foreign goods, and insisted on payment for her own in gold, of which she had plenty. Also, political instability all over the world discouraged long-term loans, and produced a constant shifting of investments. American credit depended on American politics, and they were narrow, hysterical, and corrupt.[2] The general uncertainty of the credit system produced a general fall in the 'price level' and—it seemed—an immense and boastful prosperity. It also produced a good deal of reckless gambling. Then in October of 1929, the American economic system collapsed. American banks were breaking by the hundred, and eight million people were suddenly out of work.

In June 1930 the last Allied soldiers had left German soil—more than four years before the date fixed at Versailles: and Germany's emotions had bent her already to the sounding creed, of her supreme racial right and of work for resurgence, that was preached by the Nazis as a new religion. At the September election of that year, 107 Nazis were returned. (The British Foreign Office expected

[1] Cf. the figures given for Scotland in Chapter XXVII.
[2] The enormous social and moral damage caused by the experiment of 'Prohibition,' and the famous Dayton Case of 1925 are unfortunately typical of the time.

thirty.) And trouble over a customs agreement with Austria brought down the Government and played into Nazi hands.

In the midst of this, the slump crossed the Atlantic. By 1931 the finances of Central Europe, and especially of Germany, were chaos, and everywhere governments (and parliaments, as a means of government) were discredited. Britain went off gold, causing a further shock—emotional rather than economic, perhaps; but emotion can very strongly affect economics. A somewhat hysterical General Election, in the October of 1931, returned a so-called National Government, with a huge majority. There was, in the next few years, much talk in London about 'planning': in fact, upon the talk, there ensued an extension of Government control over the actions of individuals greater than Labour Governments had ventured. From the Scottish point of view, it might also be noticed that the boasted planning was seen all in English or Imperial terms.

The core of British foreign policy was still, at this time, support of the League of Nations. Now, the League had undoubtedly effected some good, in the direction of 'social hygiene.' It had done valuable work, for instance, against the drug traffic which was so great a danger in those neurotic years. Even in politics it had more than once staved off a war between the lesser powers. Its basic weakness was two-fold. The League could not compel obedience. Mussolini had successfully defied it so early, indeed, as 1923: his example was followed, and on every occasion the prestige which was the League's sole strength was weakened. And the League did not always keep its promises, which lowered prestige again. It played for peace, not justice. By 1930 it was a pompous façade, and little more.

By the latter part of 1931, when Sir John Simon went to the Foreign Office, Japan was threatening an attack on China, Spain had driven out her King, and Germany was re-arming, and had launched the famous pocket-battleship *Deutschland*. At Westminster the signs were not much noticed. The Conservatives were obsessed with India. Labour was terrified of 'Imperialism,' and refused to help pay for the country's armed protection, though it clamoured continually for 'vigorous action' of a kind an armed country alone could carry out. Politicians followed 'my party, right or wrong.' The public were sure there would never be war again. And the Nazis were strengthening in Germany, and preaching the doctrine that war meant salvation.

The Disarmament Conference of 1932 was highly popular, and effected nothing. By the 30th of the succeeding January, the Nazi leader, Adolf Hitler, had become Chancellor of Germany, with old Marshal Hindenburg as figure-head: and Hitler thoroughly understood his people. He was indeed to prove, in the next decade, an outstanding practical psychologist. Few men in history have better grasped the basic weaknesses of human nature, while he had enough understanding of its virtues to enlist those long enough to build his power. He called, at first, to generous impulses as well as evil, and appealed, with a marvellous gift of dramatic production, to the emotions of a despairing people. They gave him control of the state. He used it at once to cut away from them their mental defences, and anaesthetised them, during the operation, by rousing their fear and their hate, and focussing these. The Reichstag fire came in that February—a deft move, for the campaign against Communism gave Germany something on which to sharpen her teeth, with the general benediction of most of Europe, and enlisted for him, so long as he required them, those Germans able to finance his movement.

No sooner were German emotions in his control than Hitler began his programme of expansion. Austria had been marked out as the first victim. 1918 had left her in very evil case. Vienna had once been the pivot of Eastern Europe. Now it was nothing: and that was unfortunate, for South Germany has always been more civilised than North, and had Vienna rather than Berlin been the focus of German unity, much might be different. The religious wars of the seventeenth century had fatally weakened Austria, however, and 1866 drove her out of the rising Empire. 1918 had left her in nominal independence, but cut off from her natural customers, her sources of supply—a peasant state with a fourth of her population in a huge city whose trade was stricken with death. Her Socialist rulers were well-meaning theorists, who did all they could to stamp out patriotism. Her middle class, with no future in their own country, were attracted by Nazism; and Hitler's 'racial' creed appeared to give them hope of a place within it. When the Chancellor, Dollfuss, became awake to the danger and tried to rouse Austrian national feeling again, it was too late: the old core of it, the dynasty, was gone, and no time was left for another to develop, while the Nazi penetration of Austrian minds was increasing rapidly. On the 25th July of 1934 Dollfuss was murdered, with a brutality that was eloquent of the nature of the new forces. Hitler, however, had this time struck too soon. Italy massed her troops on the Austrian border, and Hitler had to make a journey to Venice, to an interview with the Italian Duce which he has not forgotten. It tamed him for the time, and he held his hand. Just then Hindenburg died: and Hitler became in name as well as in fact ruler of Germany.

By 1935 it was growing clear that the basis of antagonisms in Europe was not the old rivalry of state and state—though that was present too as a strong complication—nor even the opposition of Communism and society based on personal possession. It was something deeper—the difference between what was called totalitarianism and what was loosely labelled democracy. The ideal of the former is a state in which a privileged minority have absolute and irresponsible power over not only the action but the thought of all the rest—and *ought* to have that power. The ideal of the latter was based on the doctrine that man, as man, has his own dignity, has the right to free thought, free speech, and free action, so long as he does not infringe the rights of his neighbours. More briefly, one can sum the opposition as between a state in which men exist for the state, and one in which the state exists for men. And the former, making the state an absolute value, has no room in it for any other god.

The 'duty' of complete mental submission and the power of forcing it, first by persecution and then by the barring out of all counter-ideas, give totalitarianism an enormous strength: and it has its rewards. The dutiful may not win freedom for themselves, but they may win the power of controlling others: and it is a part of the system of control to train them to desire this above all. In fact, the totalitarian fundamental, that supreme good is the power not to be but to force, is the antithesis of Christianity. That inversion pervades it, even in its details. The word *Antichrist* has been used often, and loosely, for any great evil power, through history. It was not until the twentieth century that it could be used with complete and detailed precision, for something in actual objective existence.[1]

This new doctrine spread first by peaceful penetration. Its missionaries were skilled psychologists, and its seed-bed was prepared by the time's mood and the *trahison des clercs* which had cut

---

[1] Cf. the Totalitarian Beatitudes as contained in the official teachings of Nazism—blessed are the unmerciful, blessed are the arrogant, blessed are those who despise righteousness, blessed are the war-makers.

away the framework of old values. The Russian brand appealed to the town 'workers' by its promise that it was they who should have the power: the Italo-German to the wealthier, for the same reason: and both, for the same reason, to the lower middle class, who in fact, when the regime had once been established, supplied its executive bureaucracy. Both, too, appealed to a class which advanced them further, being vocal, the rootless 'intellectuals' who pullulated in Europe at the time, and were besotted with psychology and totally ignorant of human nature: it gave them that for which they unconsciously craved, a clear creed in a time of mental deliquescence, and it gave them that for which they craved consciously, an ideal labelled 'new,' 'advanced,' 'of the future.' Being profoundly ignorant of history, they failed to grasp that its general principles were not only as old as man, but a good deal older.

Their equation with goodness, however, was so novel that many, everywhere, failed to grasp the danger. They had been used to think in words, not things; and a thing which did not go into their formulae was something they could not evaluate. There was growing, however, a sense that danger was present. Mr Winston Churchill was one of those who saw it. In March 1934 he forced from Baldwin a promise that the R.A.F. in future should

no longer be in a position inferior to any country within striking distance of our shores.

It shocked many. Was not Germany forbidden by her Treaties to build an Air Force? Mr Baldwin, in spite of his promise, was with the many. In November Mr Churchill pointed out that Germany had a secret Air Force already, nearly equal to Britain's, and soon to be much larger. Mr Baldwin denied the statement: and in March, Hitler brought in conscription in Germany and announced that Germany had in fact built an Air Force, and that it was already equal to Britain's. Mr Baldwin in May produced another promise, of an Air Force 'not inferior to any country's within striking distance.' But Hitler had declared that he was 'not creating an offensive military instrument, but only and exclusively an instrument of defence,' and in October 1935, with an Election pending, Baldwin felt—as he himself was later to say in the House—

Supposing I had gone to the country and said 'Germany is re-arming. We must re-arm.' Does anyone think that this pacific democracy of ours would have rallied to that cry?

So he had told it, just before the Election, 'I give you my word there will be no great armaments.'

The League scolded Hitler, but could do nothing more. In April, Mussolini, Ramsay MacDonald, and M. Flandin, for France, forgathered at Stresa, and talked of 'collective maintenance of peace,' and the sin of unilateral breach of treaties. And at the end of that month, in Germany, Christianity was declared to be 'a danger.' Russia already professed the same opinion, and had done all she could to make it effective. In May France signed a Mutual Assistance Pact with Russia. In June Britain made a Naval Agreement with Germany—over France's head. In July Mussolini threatened Abyssinia.

Abyssinia, as a member of the League, appealed for protection: but the League could do nothing. And what Mussolini wanted, by this time, was not redress of Italian grievances, but a war to increase the prestige of his regime—a safe easy war. He was therefore much annoyed when the League proposed to apply 'economic sanctions'— a check to his supply of material. This could only be inconvenient, not effective. It broke the tenuous friendliness of Stresa, but did nothing else. One main reason was a British General Election in the November of 1935: Mr Baldwin dared not say that sanctions were useless, in case the Opposition should accuse him of too much sympathy with Fascism (which was still regarded, by all the Leftward parties, as the antithesis to Socialism), and he could not enforce them, for the simple reason that Britain had not the arms to risk a war. At the same time Labour was damning the Government for its 'vast and expensive programme of armaments'—without mentioning Germany's, over the North Sea—and in the same breath condemning its supineness in doing nothing in face of Japan's aggression in Manchukuo. That election, by the way, returned the Commons who were still in place in 1939.

A totalitarian state had defied the League, succeeded, and thoroughly discredited Britain . . . and had also stolen Hitler's coveted thunder. Already Goebbels was telling the German people 'We can do without butter: we cannot do without guns.' On the 7th March of 1936, before Italy could reach Addis Ababa (for her war did not prove so easy after all), Hitler denounced the Treaty of Locarno and marched into the Rhineland: it was just a year since he had declared that he could keep that Treaty, because it had been freely negotiated, and described the demilitarised zone of the Rhineland as a great contribution to the peace of Europe. Now he gave as the reason for his changed opinion the Franco-Soviet Pact. The occupation should lead to a New Order, with security for all. He desired no further territory in Europe . . . and almost in the same breath he professed his friendship with Poland and his understanding of her need to have an outlet to the sea.

If France had marched, the German troops would have been forced to withdraw, and the Nazi government might well have fallen. But France had an election on her hands: and in Britain most people were of the opinion that the poor dear Germans had only regained their own, and if France was insulted . . . well, it served her right. The Czechs would have moved, but were called off by France and Britain. And Hitler now had a base for the Siegfried Line, and for much else. He had stated his plans already, in a book that all Germany was compelled to read: but no one, outside Germany, believed them. It was simpler to believe what he said at the time. And his missionaries worked quietly everywhere.

In July a civil war broke out in Spain, whose Red government was attacked by General Franco. The three totalitarian powers joined in, Russia hoping to bring France with her. France refused, Léon Blum declaring for non-intervention, and probably holding off European war. British members of the various Services took their holidays that year on the end of a wire. The war, however, was confined to Spain, Britain professing a strict neutrality but showing official sympathy with the Reds, so that Franco, when in time he came to power, was anti-British.

1937 brought at its beginning a British-Italian naval 'understanding,' the two powers agreeing to respect each other's interests in the Mediterranean. In May of that year Baldwin passed from office, and was succeeded by Neville Chamberlain, a man with a very real desire for peace, but with very little knowledge of human nature. Chamberlain sought for friendship with Italy. Russia spoked that wheel: and Chamberlain held Britain from making a third in the Pact between France and Russia.

1938 then opened very darkly. Germany and Italy had drawn together and had trained their troops and tested their tanks and planes on the same side of the Spanish Civil War. There was restlessness and violence everywhere; and everywhere, also, in the democracies, in the men who were in position to be leaders, and in the general masses of the people, a blind intense desire to stave off war. Hitler knew that his time had come. If he attacked one of the small weak countries with which Versailles had surrounded him, the others would not dare join and come to her help, nor would the Great Powers. He chose Austria first: it was the ripest fruit, and the easiest, for it was full by now of his racial doctrines: and the union of Germans and Germans—what was that but the doctrine of 'racial self-determination' which all Europe had been so lustily proclaiming, with so little attention to the facts of its map?

He moved, in March of 1938, into Austria; and the country collapsed at once, not before force, but before the threat of force. And neither Britain nor France would intervene. Italy did not like the situation, and in April made an agreement with Great Britain, which upset the British Left very badly indeed: they had been converted to re-armament, but were strongly opposed to any sort of rapprochement with any European state but Russia.

And in Czecho-Slovakia, on the German march, there was not, as in the Rhineland, a territory which had been part of the pre-war German Reich; there was not, as in Austria, a German nation: but there were some three million German people. Hitler and France, in the month when Austria fell, both promised Czecho-Slovakia their support; and Hitler set his machinery moving there.

XXX

BRAIRD

NINE YEARS: 1930–39

Meaning to have spring again.
JANE AUSTEN, *Persuasion*.

WE have seen that the nineteen-twenties had bred by the 'thirties the monstrous growth of the Totalitarian State, with which the 'forties are now in process of coping. Other things, however, grew beside that upas, and reaction against the deliquescent 'twenties was not all so ill-guided as in Germany.

In Scotland the end of the 'twenties had brought to ruin the structure which, two hundred years before, had risen valiantly out of ruin. Men looked upon a growing desolation, where the hard-won fields were turning again to muir and the emigrant ships were sailing down the Clyde between empty yards. The silent skeleton of the huge Cunarder, that was to have been the greatest ship in the world, loomed over Glasgow, gigantically mocking the thousands on thousands of the world's best craftsmen who hung about street corners, waiting the dole, their manhood and their craftsmen's pride degraded in a country which had no place nor use for them. And those more fortunate cried that all was well, or if not, that there was nothing they could do: it was the Government's business—not their concern.

Indeed, it was a sick Scotland in 1930. But Scotland, more than once in her history, has been sick to death—has been laid in her very coffin. What had she been in the year 1305, when she was a country conquered from end to end, after nine years of heavy and losing war, with Wallace's blind eyes staring at the Thames? What had she been in the years when Bruce was gone, when the enemy she had forced to beg for peace tore up the Treaty and swamped a leaderless country? And in the dark generations after Flodden? And the hopeless beggary of 1720? To any rational onlooker, dead and damned.

Yet, each time, there was that in her which would not die: and by 1930 that life was stirring again, like the first green braird of corn across a field that is muddy and desolate with long barren winter.

The life sprang as the braird springs, here and there. There was no leader: as in the seventeen-twenties, and the thirteen-thirties, men fought where they stood. The varied directions of their activity were determined by circumstance and their own gifts.

One very significant phenomenon which appeared very early—indeed, well before the 'thirties—was a sudden widespread passion for the drama. From one point of view, it is a natural art for Scotland to practise: we have always had, since our history began, an instinctive sense of the dramatic gesture. From another, even leaving out a tradition which had damned the drama beyond any other art, we have not the talent of our next-door neighbours for that co-operation in such gesture which gives the English people so striking a gift for significant and coloured ceremony. That Scotland should suddenly turn with a growing fervour to this most co-operative of the arts was a sign of something more than a shift of fashion. The Scottish National Players were founded so early as 1921, by Andrew P. Wilson. Then a wave of amateur drama swept the country. Excellent work was done in villages and in the grimmest of the industrial towns. Societies with no money but much resource sprang up hither and yond. They multiplied slowly at first: in 1927 there were no more than 35 teams competing in a Community Drama Festival, but by 1931 it was 260, by 1938 349; and Scotland was producing dramatists whose work could be taken seriously, and was, not only in Scotland but abroad—the brilliant James Bridie, Gordon Daviot, Robins Millan, Joe Corrie, Andrew P. Wilson, Neil Grant, Hal D. Stewart, John Brandane, Cormac Simpson, J. A. Ferguson, Robert McLellan: a varied assortment, but all with life in them. A professional theatre was growing also, sponsored by such groups as the Glasgow Curtain Theatre, the very successful Repertory Theatre at Perth, the People's Theatre at Dumbarton, the Byre Theatre at St Andrews, the Little Theatre at Inverness—note the scattering of place: and the Scottish Theatre Society looked forward to a National Theatre on the most modern lines, to be built in Glasgow.[1]

[1] This new feeling for co-operative creation shows very strikingly in some other places. The Scottish War Memorial is an almost startling instance of something scarcely seen anywhere in Europe since the Middle Ages—a piece of work that is a unity, carried out by a score of individual artists, working together. On a smaller scale one can see the same thing again in the wonderful series of little carved and painted wooden figures in the Scottish Military Museum, designed, to be sure, by Mr Pilkington Jackson, but carried out by a whole team of carvers. They are far more than mannequins to show uniforms : each is a vigorous and living piece of sculpture, individual but in unity with the rest, and as Scots as the Riding Ballads which they recall.

This braird of life shows in the other arts: indeed, as in drama, it soon grew to more than braird. Painting, before the war, had been less desolate than the rest, for a generation. Of the brilliant Glasgow Group, George Henry, Macaulay Stevenson, Sir James Guthrie, and Roche, still survived, and Sir D. Y. Cameron, Sir Muirhead Bone, and James McBey, perhaps the most distinguished painter-etchers of their time. John Duncan and Douglas Strachan are yet with us: and largely through the latter's inspiration, much fine new work was done in 'applied art'—not only in glass but in textiles, iron, and furniture. In 'pure' painting, new names began to emerge in the 'twenties—A. A. McGlashan, Sirell, James Cowie, Lamont, W. J. Crozier, William MacTaggart, W. G. Gillies, MacLauchlan Milne, and D. M. Sutherland, and a group of women—Katherine Cameron, Cecile Walton, Mary Armour, Mrs Harwell Miller, and the mural painter Phoebe Traquair. There was also some very notable black-and-white work, conspicuous among it that of James and Stephen Bone, Keith Henderson, and the brilliant comic artist, George Whitelaw: we might add also the 'lost Scot,' Clare Leighton. Most of these younger artists show a kinship to the 'post-impressionists' of France and elsewhere: but their work as a rule is definitely Scottish, not so much by choice of subject as in temper: the breadth of feeling and quality of light derive, even in 'still life' and decorative painting, from Scottish landscape and the Scottish weather.

In sculpture there was less: but the fine work of Pilkington Jackson would stand out anywhere. The animal sculpture of Phyllis Bone is worthy of her distinguished family tradition, while William Lamb, Thomas Whalen, and Messrs McGillivray, Carrick, and Reid Dick are outstanding names: it is worthy of note that almost all of these show that strong sense of their art's close intimacy with architecture which is found in Greek and mediaeval work.

The old major Scots art of architecture revived too (there was much need of revival) and brilliantly. There were two schools: one followed Charles Rennie Mackintosh, whose own life lasted almost through the 'twenties, for he did not die till 1928. Sir John James Burnett made frank use of new methods of construction and was a pioneer in design for ferro-concrete: much of his work, as with Gibbs and the Adam brothers, was done out of Scotland. Thomas Tait, his junior partner, stands at the head of Scots work in the new tradition: his bold gay use of colour and simple proportion showed not only in the Glasgow Exhibition but in more permanent work

such as Paisley Hospital, while the stately St Andrew's House, which
grows so finely against its setting of the Calton Hill, links him to the
other group, led by Robert Hurd, whose ancestor is less Mackintosh
than Lorimer: their ideal is that which has had such noble results
in our time in Sweden, of building frankly modern yet frankly sprung
from the historic national tradition.[1] The two strains show in varying proportions in James Miller and Leslie G. Thomson. The
results of the modernist ideal are not always happy: St Andrew's
Square, Edinburgh, has been gravely injured by the new building
at the corner of George Street, which, good enough in its mode as
design by itself, is a piece of blatant discourtesy to its neighbours.[2]
One very hopeful sign of the new life (it was not peculiar to Scotland,
but she shared it) was the attention very widely given to design in
the more workaday kinds of building—the bridges of F. C. Mears,
the excellent pit-head baths at Cardowan in Lanark, factories, shops,
railway stations, and small houses, such as Joseph Weekes's at Milton,
Dumbarton, John A. W. Grant's at Westquarter, Stirlingshire, or
Messrs Johnson and Baxter's at Alyth. Their standard, unhappily,
was not universal. There is hideous testimony to that effect at, of
all places, the foot of Arthur's Seat—a litter of paltry mass-produced
concrete boxes, designed in the first place for English climate and
landscape, and far from happily designed for those: there is probably,
in fact, a special hell for the inventor of red asbestos roofing. But
the standard was there: it gave a canon of judgment, brought back
an old lost sense of dignity to the surroundings of common life and
work, and began to create a most wholesome discontent.[3]

Of music there was less, but there was keen interest. The
Glasgow Orpheus Choir was famous through Europe, and the
Scottish Orchestra did splendid work. There were new com-
posers—Francis George Scott, Erik Chisholm, Cedric Thorpe Davie,

[1] An important by-product of their work is that new appreciation of our
smaller domestic building—the harled stone house with its characteristic ' storm
windows,' and such matters—to which Mr Hurd has greatly contributed.
[2] A good deal of trouble has been caused, not only in Scotland, by a rapturous
acceptance of the phrase that a house is ' a machine to live in.' Words again!
A house is not a machine : a house is clothes, and the canons by which the two
are to be judged belong to two different universes of thought.
[3] One cannot pass without mention the large amount of sound restoration.
Some, of course, was a purely antiquarian preservation of museum pieces, which
in its place is right and necessary. But the sense of tradition as something still
alive shows for instance in Robert Hurd's work at Acheson House, where a seventeenth-century building sunk to a slum is frankly made habitable by modern
people, without loss of its fundamental character.

and W. B. Moonie. Mrs Kennedy Fraser's work on Gaelic song was
well carried on by Duncan Morison.

Scots writing, before the war, had seemed nearly dead. Mr
William Power describes it pithily:

> The idea of Scotland had shrunk till it comprised little but Kirk news,
> mediocre bourgeois sentiment, and babblings about Burns and Scott,
> bens and glens and heroes.

Now an almost fierce outburst of creative writing sprang up, as
various as it was vital. It recalls the sudden renaissance of creation
in the Scandinavian countries earlier, and like it had a strongly
national colour, and often a nationalist temper also. Indeed, some
of the finest sprang from deliberate effort to re-create Scots as a
literary speech that could cope with more than a narrow range of
subjects. Lewis Spence had already made experiments: these were
carried on in the volcanic work of Hugh MacDiarmaid and the
chiselled weighty terseness of William Soutar. Some was harmed,
to be sure, by the angry self-consciousness that often mars experimental writing: but there is nothing of that in William Soutar, and
all three are poets of a quality we have not seen, save in Gaelic, for
long enough. (Deliberate experimental work in the suppling and
enrichment of the Scots language was also done by two most accomplished translators, Professor Alexander Gray and Margaret Wine-
fride Simpson.[1]) In English Edwin Muir stands among the leaders:
and there are others—William Jeffrey, William Montgomerie, and
more, in both Scots and English, from the intricate intellectual
emotion of Nan Shepherd to the fragile and delicate religious verse
of Marion Lochhead. The old tradition of genre-verse in Scots was
still alive too, and in Marion Angus drew back to it some of the
qualities of the ballad.

The novel, the chief creative form of the age in most countries,
was prominent also—indeed, so variously and in such numbers that
even a bare catalogue of names is more than there is room for in this
place. There was, as elsewhere, a good deal of bogus and very noisy
work, based—with or without a choice of Scottish subjects—on
fashions just going out in Bloomsbury. But there was much very
genuine creation, intensely Scots, not always in subject or setting,
but in temper and technique: it was indeed a very wholesome sign

---

[1] Translation was not confined to Scots: Edwin and Willa Muir and C. K.
Scott-Moncrieff also won deserved fame in a difficult art; and their medium was
English.

that the subjects were not limited to Scotland, and Scots literature claimed the right which belonged to all others, of taking its subject-matter where it chose. The old genre-tradition, going back through Burns and one aspect of Walter Scott, continues enriched and still with a lively vigour, in Frederick Nivcn, Jean White, Nan Shepherd, Willa Muir, and one may find a more 'modernistic' form in the short stories of Ronald MacDonald Douglas. The most interesting and significant sign, however, is what amounts to a genuine re-naissance, in a wholly new form, of the spirit of the Makaris—very often with a strong kinship to their technique, its clear line, bright colour, fantastic or decorative realism. It begins, perhaps, with the sardonic work of Norman Douglas and is prominent in Eric Linklater, whose *Juan in America* is nearer Dunbar than anything since Flodden. One sees a good deal of it, naturally enough, in the historical novels of Julian Duguid, Naomi Mitchison, Jane Oliver, Christine Orr—recognisably kin, yet each vividly first-hand and original. One can trace it again, in a quite different key, in such work as N. Brysson Morrison's delicate *Gowk Storm*, which is not 'historical' but set back in time to detach its subject a little from normal perception, as does verse. All these have a quality of imagination which is close to the poet's: and one sees that very markedly again in Ian Macpherson, Margot Robert Adamson, and Neil Gunn, whose very beautiful *Highland River* is perhaps the finest Scots novel of this time . . . and one has it even in the substantial Dutch-master realism of George Blake, which throws back to the Makaris by another road, with a look-in at Ellisland by the way.

Two of the world's supreme biographies had come earlier from Scotland: their tradition continued in John Buchan's noble quar-tette, in a lovely prose; in the brilliant *John Knox* of Edwin Muir, and in the delicate little medallion portraits of George Malcolm Thomson. As might be expected, there was a crop of various historical research, with upsetting results to academic tradition. A. O. Anderson's monumental collection of source-material for our early history appeared in 1922, and roused new interest in the neglected Scottish Middle Ages, expressed by, for instance, Dr Annie Cameron and Dr Marguerite Wood, while Mr G. Black Scott, Mr A. Boyd Smith and Dr Douglas Simpson did valuable work on the Dark Ages. Indeed, there was so much sound and solid work that even a list is impossible to give here, though one cannot omit Dr G. Pratt Insh's on the Darien Scheme: the bibliographies at the end of these volumes suggest the range of the new interest. One characteristic must be remarked on, however—a new sharp sense of the national past of Scotland, not as the board for an antiquary's game or a pageant of the romantic and picturesque, but as something real, and important to the present.

The literary revival was somewhat hampered, in its early years, by the unfortunate lack of either critics, publishers, or public who were ready for it. The reviewers, sensing revival in the air, often felt for it a genuine sympathy, but did it also a great deal of harm by an ancient and widespread habit of reviewers, of judging creative work solely on its subject, and that with most arbitrary limitations. The publishers, even those flourishing with huge outputs, were as heartily terrified of Scottish books as Constable was of the *Annals of the Parish*. (Messrs Oliver and Boyd, Mr Æneas Mackay, and the Moray Press may be mentioned, however, as honourable exceptions: and Messrs Chambers's imprint is on this book.) The public's palate had been spoilt with sugar, while those who rejected Crockett and Ian Maclaren were convinced that Scotland could breed no novelist . . . the more as the leaders of literary fashion were still, in the nineteen-twenties, in Edinburgh, while the writers came, for the most part, from anywhere else—conspicuously from Glasgow and Aberdeen. Most new writers, indeed, received their first recognition, and often very generously, from London: one, with cause to believe the experience not uncommon, had books reviewed in French, American, and Swedish papers before she saw one on sale in Princes Street. The Saltire Society, founded in 1936, has already, however, done much for 'the preservation *and development* of the Scottish tradition in the arts,' as well as for its various other objects, among which stand the study and teaching of history and the publication of out-of-print Scottish classics.

By the 'thirties, the mind of Scotland was rousing again. With the rousing came a new perception of Scotland. The perception of her past roused a quickening doubt of the dead and deadening perversion of her story which had weighed on her for over a century. Men turned to fill in the astonishing omissions, re-discovered lost glories, and overset some idols. They ceased to see Scotland as something attached to England, and conceived her again as a nation, part of Europe. And they looked at her as she stood in their own time, and were filled with horror and generous, angry fear.

There was a spate of books, articles, and pamphlets on Scotland's evil condition. A phrase used long ago in reviewing one of the first —'This is Cassandra sane, and primed with Bluebooks'—comes to the memory.[1] It describes the best. Some were over-passionate with a startled horror. A few, too clearly, were written by men delighted to find a good excuse for scolding the world. Between them, they warned the water. The sense of peril—and it was a peril increasingly huge and real—stirred men and women once again to face it, as their fathers had done when the beacons lit on the hills.

Precisely as happened in the seventeen-twenties, the courageous and clear-sighted set to work to discover what needed doing, and to do it, in a hundred directions. A good deal of solid historical research had the driving power of this spirit under it. It was specially notable in one direction. The economic history of Scotland had been gravely neglected: in the early 'thirties, however, almost together, Miss I. F. Grant, Mr W. H. Marwick, Dr Henry Hamilton, and Mr A. Birnie produced important work. The sense of Scotland and of Scotland's danger partly coloured, partly was in turn inspired by, much of the lively new flood of creative letters. Various groups went to work. The Saltire Society, which has been mentioned already, organised exhibitions for Scottish artists, concerts for Scottish musicians, enlarged a public for history and letters. The National Trust set about the restoration of old buildings which, being occupied, could not be dealt with by the Office of Works: the Marquis of Bute, at his personal expense, was responsible for Acheson House in Edinburgh, the north side of the magnificent Charlotte Square, Loudoun Hall in Ayrshire and Lamb's House in Leith, which last is designed to house a Scottish Maritime Museum.

In 1938 it was proposed to set up in Canna an institute for the vocational and cultural training of men and women of eighteen to thirty: it was modelled on the Danish Folk-schools by which the genius of Bishop Grundtvig roused Denmark from collapse after 1864.[2] The Carnegie Trust and the Education Authority promised support: but An Comunn Gaidhealach disliked the site, and the plan fell through, though Sir Daniel and Lady Hamilton of Balma-

---

[1] It was used in 1928 of Mr George Malcolm Thomson's *Rediscovery of Scotland*, a book which probably had a good deal to do in forcing the writing of this *History* when a daring publisher afforded the chance.

[2] Denmark, with two-thirds of our population, had sixty of such schools before the war, with something like 6,000 students a year. They virtually created Danish agriculture, and they certainly re-created Danish literature.

cara had offered Duncraig Castle for a second school. The Marquis of Lothian's gift of Newbattle Abbey for a Workers' College is part of the same movement, which affected also an institution already venerable, and valuable, the Workers' Educational Association. Even the Education Department's new draft Code, of February 1938, showed a new interest in music and the arts: and individual teachers everywhere turned with zest to Scottish history, past, present, and future, while new school-books, often scholarly and lively, were being written to help them. The study of Gaelic and its literature received a new stimulus, and that of Scots now came alongside it, even in the schools.

The new vision of needs and possibilities, the new desire for knowledge as basis for action, were by no means confined to what is known as 'culture.' The equivalents of the old Board of Manufactures and of the Agricultural Society, which had played such a part in the great eighteenth-century revival, appeared again. Magnificent work is being done for agriculture by the Rowett Institute at Bucksburn, near Aberdeen. It was established in 1919, with funds partly from Government, largely from private donors, especially the late John Quiller Rowett: its work, and its benefits, stretch far from Scotland, for under the leadership of Sir John Orr it has won a world-wide fame for its researches in animal nutrition first of all, then as its work developed, in dietetics and 'the marriage of agriculture to public health.' Within a decade the Institute at Bucksburn had enlarged itself into an Imperial Bureau, supported by the Governments of the Empire. Its Reid Library was added in 1923—a gift from Dr Walter Reid, Aberdeen. In 1925 they were joined by the Duthie Experimental Farm, which commemorates John Duthie of Collynie, one of the greatest of Scottish cattle-breeders: in seven years it had become self-supporting, with a turnover of some £10,000 a year. In 1927 Lord Strathcona offered £5,000 towards a Residence, which soon housed students from all parts of the world.

While the Rowett Institute is perhaps the most famous, it was far from being the sole venture of its kind: and the others showed an equal resolution in coming to grips with fundamental problems. Its sister and complement is the younger Macaulay Institute, founded in 1930 by Mr T. B. Macaulay of Montreal, a Lewisman born. The Soil Research Institute at Craigiebuckler is a branch of it, but its main work is for the Highlands. Its stations at Carnwath and at

Stornoway deal with problems concerning peat soil, and the use of peat for commercial purposes.[1] The results so far have been most encouraging. At a cost of £2 to £5 an acre, peat land which before had fed a dozen sheep has been made capable of bearing ten times as many, with 35 cattle, 2 pigs, and 200 poultry. Private foresight and generosity show again in the Hannah Research Station at Kirkhill in Ayrshire, which was founded there in 1931 to study milk-production in all its aspects.[2] The older Agricultural Colleges have by no means stood still. They are working actively, and that of the North of Scotland has begun the only school in Britain for farm-women, while its county organisers and dairy and poultry instructresses carry on active missionary work in all the counties of its area.[3] Some private experiment has been done as well. In Ardnamurchan, on the estate of an English laird, Lord Trent, hundreds of acres have been reconditioned and sown, and are bearing crops. The National Trust has attempted the same thing in Mull, and the principles of the English scientist Sir George Stapledon, with regard to the use of formerly barren land, are exciting great interest. The development of silage fodder also appears to promise important results, for a Renfrew farmer, broadcasting during this war, was able to say that he had not bought, in a year, an ounce of imported food-stuff, and yet his beasts were in better condition than they had ever been.

Till this time, experiment in rural life had confined itself to work and possibly housing. The immense importance of rural *social* problems is however coming to be recognised, and a quiet but very valuable movement, which might go far to finding their solution, was set going so early as 1916 by a Lothian farmer's wife, Mrs Catherine Blair. The original model came from Canada, where it goes back to 1897. In the war, it was copied in England. Mrs Blair, realising that much of the townward drift from the country was due to the lonely lives led by country women, approached the newly formed Council of Agriculture, which resolved, in 1917, to back her. The first Women's Rural Institute was formed that June at Longniddry, its aim being to improve the general conditions of

[1] Scotland was the only country in Europe where no commercial use was made of peat. Sweden in 1936 exported 270,000 tons for fuel. The immense reclamation work done in Denmark during the nineteenth century was the foundation of her great dairying industry, now so brutally wrecked.
[2] It is interesting to note that the fat-content of Scots milk has been deliberately reduced by legislation, to bring it level with that of the English product.
[3] Orkney now leads all Britain in poultry-farming.

rural life by providing centres for social and educational intercourse, to study domestic science and child welfare, housing and problems of national education, to increase home food supply, encourage home and local industries, help to preserve the beauties of rural Scotland, and work for peace and the country's recovery. These aims revolted many of the pious: one lady announced 'No, I can't come to your meeting—I'm on the Lord's side,' while a Northern minister preached fierily against 'the serpent which has come into our midst, with W.R.I. branded on its tail.' A well-intentioned Board of Agriculture helped to defeat an important part of its purpose, the training of women voters in citizenship, by insisting on organising it from above, and strangling it in red tape leading-strings. But it grew, none the less, and has now a full thousand branches; and more and more its members are using their power to speak in the name of feminine public opinion to the Local and Education Authorities and the Board of Health, while an enormous amount of quiet work is being done for domestic science and child welfare, amenities, and healthy recreation, including some lively production of amateur drama.

The question of re-settlement on the land has lagged badly behind the rest. It is very slow. The Department of Agriculture owns 110 properties, and in twenty-five years had settled 7,515 applicants: but in 1937, for example, 98 were settled, while 675 had applied. The Carnegie Trust has spent, in England, £68,000 on co-operative land settlement schemes, but no parallel has been attempted in Scotland, for lack of an organisation through which it can work. Co-operative schemes were indeed beginning, in an attempt to solve the small-holding problem. Crofters' Associations were being formed, and Mrs MacLeod of MacLeod has endeavoured, in Skye, to work out arrangements for co-operative sale and purchase. As in everything to do with the Highlands, however, all is handicapped by the enormous costs of transport.

These also hamper re-afforestation, which would solve a good many serious Highland problems, and afford a base for much useful light industry. The State has indeed been building up reserves at the rate of 20,000 acres a year: but Britain still imports £50,000,000 worth of timber every year, and Lord Mansfield has declared that it is cheaper to bring pitprops to Fife from Archangel than from Angus.

None the less, in Scots agriculture, by the late nineteen-thirties, the position was not so much that of the seventeen-twenties, but already that of the seventeen-sixties at least. There was, indeed, an immense amount to be done: the figures given in Chapter XXVII attest that amply. But the first great steps had been taken—and they were long strides.

In fisheries, the conditions were even graver. But again the same spirit was in operation, and tools were being forged for re-building. In 1920 the Marine Laboratory at Torry, Aberdeen, was opened, under the wing of the University. It has grown from a very small start to a large and important institution, partly afloat, since it owns a steamer for research at sea. The Torry Research Station, added nine years later, deals with the use of the fish when it is landed —as food, as a source of oil and fertilisers, and in the provision of an important drug: it has set going the commercial production of the valuable halibut liver oil. (In 1932 the city of Aberdeen backed its hopes in the new work by the expenditure of £180,000 on its quays and a new Fish Market.) The Marine Biology Station at Millport in Cumbrae began an extension scheme in 1937, and the next year again brought the establishment, at Leith, of a station for North Sea research.

The condition of industry after the war, and after the war plus the slump, has been suggested. In the early 'thirties our greatest industrial city, one of the world's great centres of industry, was a grey purgatory of despair. And yet again, as in the seventeen-twenties, men set to work, and the braird began to show. It was further from the full ear than in agriculture, for the problems were even larger and more complex: but men by themselves or in little private groups, and soon in larger quasi-official groups, were at work; and again new organisations for research were being founded, hither and yond throughout the country—for Glasgow by this time was changing her role. Once Edinburgh had led Scots thought and art, and Glasgow was the country's industrial centre. Now the centre of intellectual life is Glasgow, and the eastern towns have shown more vigour and enterprise than the western in guiding the new move-ments in industry.

One may mention first, since it deals with fundamental prin-ciples, the Dundee School of Economics and Commerce, founded in 1931 by Mr George Bonar (whose firm built a great mill in the worst of the depression) and happy in its Principal, Dr Bowie. The Heriot-Watt College continued its technical work, and in 1935 was largely extended: it had 2,800 students that year. In the worst

26

time of the depression again, the Convention of Royal Burghs and the Association of County Councils sponsored the National Development Council, 'to assist the promotion and development of industry, agriculture, fisheries, mining, transport, and the commercial and economic interests of the people of Scotland generally,' and 'to examine in detail the disabilities, if any, under which Scotland operates, and to endeavour to arrive at a solution of those problems, either by action on the part of the industry concerned or by other means; and when necessary by obtaining from Parliament such legislation as is required.' It recognised as immediate problems calling for solution the drift to the South, the inequitable incidence of rating and taxation, the need for light industries, the need to use Scotland's resources for electric power, the need for Scottish Houses in London and in selected centres abroad, to enable Scottish interests to exhibit and distribute their products, the need for advertisement to encourage export, and the need to mobilise financial resources and develop existing industries in Scotland, to frame an agricultural policy and set up groups of rural industries, to reorganise the Scottish transport system, and to re-inspire Scots with a belief in their country.

The Council was very seriously hampered by the general and prevailing apathy, which made men readier to criticise, as an excuse for continued inertia, than to share in projects demanding initiative. (Even so late as 1938 there were fewer Scots exhibits at the British Industries Fair than were sent up to it by the town of High Wycombe, which is roughly the same size as Inverness.) The Council has laid very useful foundations, however, by carrying out important investigations of Scottish agriculture and industry, and by setting Mr C. A. Oakley to work at a stimulating general survey of new movements; while its lively quarterly *Scotland*, under its Editor Mr Norman Bruce, fought gallantly the atmosphere of despair. An important practical 'sideshow' of its work was Scottish Industrial Estates, Ltd. —a non-profit-making company which has established four factory estates on good modern lines. That at Hillingdon, in two years, carried eighty new factories, with work, under first-rate conditions, for 2,000 people: it expected soon, in 1938, to double these figures, while another factory, employing 10,000, proposed to come there. Lord Elgin established the Financial Trust Company, to deal with the financing of new ventures. It proposed to issue £4 debentures, to a maximum, in the first place, of £100,000, and to co-operate with other institutions, especially the banks. Again, the Scottish Economic Committee set to work to survey schemes of public utility, that should lessen the great army of unemployed. Sir John Orr proposed to it the enlistment of labour battalions of unemployed for a war on bracken, which is a most dangerous enemy to Scotland: but the Trade Unions objected, and the plan failed.

In the Highlands again, in 1936 the Highland Development League began to work on the framing of a long-term policy, though it again was hampered by refusal to *begin*, or to recognise possibility of beginning, until the whole campaign could move at once. All these groups attempting to work on the national scale were hindered because, on the one side, they had no authority, on the other because political opposition—sometimes apathy or envy under its name—destroyed co-operation. They therefore met more success in diagnosis than in treatment: but diagnosis was needed as a first step; and the favourite complaint of their many critics, that they had not recovered Scotland in twelve months work, shows, besides perhaps less engaging qualities, a rather inadequate grasp of history.

Other smaller groups met more positive success. In the long run, action on a national scale requires a Government to handle it. A Development Council or other similar body may recommend or even inspire such action: but it has not itself the power or the machine to carry it out. For speedy results, legislation is required: failing that, little more positive can be done than a slow conversion of individuals. Groups which deal with a smaller geographical unit, or a single trade, can work through the organisation of that trade, or through the machine of local government: national government may hamper them—as markedly in the case of fisheries—but at least they have much less need of its assistance. The Ayrshire Development Council, for example, founded in 1934, with offices in the beautiful County Buildings, has done much for the planned development of its area, and already has been remarkably successful in setting off lively new activities. The older trade institutions were reinforced, as by the addition, to the old Woollen Technical College, of Hawick Technical Institute, the gift to the town in 1928 of a local private citizen. And unpretentious but useful work was being done on a small scale, as at Beith Academy, which supported the new local industry, furniture-making, with classes in fine wood-work and design, that look forward to training future artist-craftsmen on a level with those of contemporary Sweden, or of our own old printers and fine weavers.[1]

As in the eighteenth century, however, much direct work in industrial revival was done by a number of individual firms, who 'fought where they stood.' This means, in some ways, danger: but it also means the short-circuiting of committees, which, in emergencies, can have its value. Indeed, by the last years of the nineteen-thirties, an amazing amount of new industry was rising: very few people seem to realise how much already, quietly, has been achieved of the things they declare someone really ought to begin. It is widely, and probably very truly, held that one reason why Scotland had collapsed so badly was concentration on 'heavy' industries.[2] We have heard much of the need for 'light' industries, accompanied sometimes by much explanation of the many and various reasons for their absence. But in the late 'thirties, they were far from absent: they were widely present already, and flourishing.

Not all were new: but the old ones flourished also. One great firm, well known the world over for its thread, had 10,000 employees. Another, which has made 2,500 kinds of sewing-machines, had 5,000. In the old Edinburgh printing trade, employment, between 1921 and 1931, went up 19 per cent.; and Glasgow's now includes both the largest printing firm in Britain and the largest book-producing plant in the world, with an output of three million volumes a year. Another publisher, in 1929, was building a great new model factory; and for 'fine' printing on the commercial scale, Scotland has still no rival. In dyeing again, one firm handled 200 miles of material daily, 95 per cent. of it sent up from England. Fine Scots fabrics were going to Paris and New York, the highest qualities of shirtings among them,

[1] None the less, Dr A. B. D. Cassie could point out, in 1941, that ' the location of British industry reflects its dependence on centres of scientific thought,' and that ' the seven Government Research Stations wholly financed by the Department of Scientific and Industrial Research are in London. Of the eighteen research associations financed partly by the Department of Scientific and Industrial Research and partly by industry, thirteen are in London, four are elsewhere in England, one is in Northern Ireland, and none is in Scotland. Scotland contributes to the Department of Scientific and Industrial Research in taxes, and her industries contribute directly to the research associations; in return she gets nothing, or less than nothing, for she finances centres of science that are at the elbow of English industry. . . . It is no good trying to run a modern industry a thousand or even a hundred miles from a centre where scientific research is done on a large scale.'

[2] Towns of mixed industries came off best in the slump. Glasgow, which lived by the heavy industries, had 8·3 per cent. out of work in 1937 : Dundee, which lived mainly by jute, had 9·3. But Aberdeen, whose activities ranged from tombstones to tinned carrots, by way of bacon, hosiery, and paper, had 4·4.

their lowest price higher than the top price of English. Certain materials, indeed, went farther abroad, for Scotland now sent muslins to the East, Irak being the chief market of one firm.

As for the new, it is not possible here to do much more than suggest their vigour and variety: and unluckily, though the names of firms deserve mention, *honoris causa*, it is unwise to give them at the moment, or even to speak of some important ventures. Old firms turned to new branches of their trade. One East Coast shipyard, as old as 1790 (it built the very first ship for the Japanese Navy), turned in 1924 from drifters and tramp steamers to tugs and dredgers, and in ten years was at the head of British makers. In 1935, only 45 of 112 distilleries were open, for whisky was paying four times the excise duty of foreign wine with equivalent alcohol: by the end of the next year, there were 100 working, on industrial alcohol and motor fuel. A firm which had lost its locomotive repairs turned to welding-machines, and in 1937 received a huge order from the London Passenger Transport Board, which had before that bought them from Germany. Wool and linen firms turned to tapestry and silk, another from fountain pens to celluloid fittings—and it captured 80 per cent. of the home market. A weaving firm founded in 1649 added dyeworks and a laundry to its plant. A light engineering works made new machines for handling anything from cakes to tombstones. A hard-hit oil-shale firm, which had employed 10,000 men in the war and been virtually ruined by the slump, developed a new method of making bricks from its own bings of waste, and in two years time was working double shifts. A wire-rope firm adopted stainless steel, a brewer took to producing yeast vitamins. A tobacco importer's, founded in 1809, gave up its wholesale trade, and branded and marketed its own production: in 1937 it was forced to double its works. An engineer's, founded in 1882, and the first in the world to make, in 1917, a new type of high-pressure boiler, developed a new form of electric welding, and very soon was called on to supply 83 per cent. of the boilers for 'the Grid.' A cooper's turned to tin boxes and tin printing, and now makes containers for most of the trades in Scotland. A rope-yard founded in 1736, which supplied the launching ropes, in 1812, for the *Comet* and in 1934 for the *Queen Mary*, made waterproof cloth, and when 'hiking' brought a new market, had to enlarge. And that is not the whole list, by any means.

There were also quite new trades—new in Scotland at least. There was artificial silk, which by the 'thirties was the stuff of half the average woman's clothing and at least a third of the 'soft furniture' of her house. There was chemical glass-ware, of which one firm is already the chief producer in the British Empire. There was sugar beet: one firm handles the crop from 1,500 farms, to which the pulp goes back as feeding-stuff. There was bitumen for roads, electric lamps, rubber flooring, power transmitters, furniture polish, bakelite, safety-razors, auto-gyros, cellular blankets, typewriters, disinfectants, casein, spring mattresses, air-conditioning plant, domestic electrical gear of every kind: and there was most promising enterprise in foodstuffs, in canning our fine fruit and vegetables, meat and fish. One old canning firm, founded in 1883, can handle half a million herring a day. The superb Scots tradition of baking was freshly exploited: one bakery in a small North-eastern town sent out three tons of biscuits every week, and a sweet-firm had 210 retail branches in Britain, another 180. And all these trades required machinery, fuel, and raw material, while the wages paid to their increasing number of employees enlarged national spending power and the demand for domestic commodities.

It was not enough? Of course it was not enough, for the unemployment figures were still enormous. In the late 'thirties Scottish industry and Scottish agriculture and fisheries were still in very grave and imminent danger. But the danger was being recognised and tackled, as it had been in the eighteenth century. There were heavy weights of ignorance, inertia, and despair to be shifted yet: but the braird was pushing through them.

The spirit stirred everywhere on the face of the field, bringing new vision, a new sense of Scotland, as more and more men recognised that the different problems had perforce to be seen in terms of a national whole, of a whole which involved past and future as well as present. An increasing sense of the lack of a government to frame and guide that whole as a unity was naturally one of its manifestations. Indeed nationalism (with upper and lower-case Ns) was spreading with so vigorous a growth that certain worthy people, who regarded the political *status quo* with as much admiration as did the General Assembly of 1780, were alarmed, and published in 1932 a solemn and handsomely printed manifesto, which proclaims, in effect, that neither they nor any other Scots are capable of governing their own country: its signatories include a number of peers, with the Duke of Argyll in the lead, a string of knights that (on paper at least) recalls a page of Froissart, and some prominent ministers of the Establishment.[1] It added to the gaiety of nations, and the records of the Order of the Thistle, but as a counter to nationalist feeling it was probably less effective than the behaviour of the small number of Wee Free Nationalists, who were less concerned with being Scots than with being non-English. By the later 'thirties, on a conservative estimate, there were probably more than a quarter-million voters who were prepared to put Scots self-government before their ordinary party allegiance.[2] The number who wished for it but preferred to secure it through the party to which they were affiliated is not likely to be less: and a number more who were nationalists, so to speak, with a small n, formed a penumbra difficult to assess, but certainly considerable and increasing.

The new spirit began to colour public life, and even its official machinery. It showed in a changing relation to the Crown. George V, who had a sailor's sense of duty and a sailor's eye for the concrete facts before him, recognised, as his nine predecessors had not done, that it is a part of the duty of a King to spend some time in the capital of his kingdom, not as a transient guest, but as a citizen and a resident. Save for a shooting-lodge in the Deeside Highlands, the royal palaces were derelict. He had Holyrood made habitable again, under the wise supervision of Queen Mary: and there was a court in Edinburgh once more, if only at intervals and in undress. The reign of his brilliant, wayward, and popular son was brief and had very little connection with Scotland. He resigned his throne at the end of 1936 to a brother who had much in him of their father and had married a Scotswoman of an ancient house: and it was recalled that at her marriage to the son of the King she had claimed for the Primus of her Scottish Church a share beside the English Archbishops. The new sovereigns, certainly, made it clear from the start that they knew they were King and Queen of more than one kingdom: it may seem a trifling matter of millinery that ladies should make their curtsey to their sovereign in trains and plumes instead of their best hats, but in fact it marks a change in attitude, a distinction between the capital of a kingdom and a provincial city like any other. And the attitude was maintained in other things, as in the

[1] Few of those signatories to be found in the reference books appear to have been educated in Scotland, and there is a rather notable scarcity of names prominent in intellectual life.

[2] A little under 100,000, in a little over a third of the constituencies, had already done so, at all events.

Queen's share, in such anxious circumstance, in Glasgow's gesture of launching the great Cunarder that bears her name, and the human contact of both King and Queen with all ranks of their subjects—a thing which Scotland had lost for three hundred years.

The attitude of the sovereigns was reflected, if not so easily or so willingly, in that of officialdom and the Government. The significant northward move of the Scottish Office was accompanied, for instance, by more care in the general use of national adjectives and of such signs as flags and coats of arms [1]: and the almost forgotten flag of the Scottish people began to be seen on our public buildings again. All these things, doubtless, are trifles in themselves: but they indicate, *and create*, a frame of mind. Robert Bruce and the present Führer of Germany, who both knew a good deal of psychology, both laid great emphasis on such: and with effect.

1938 brought a vigorous national gesture—the British Empire Exhibition in Glasgow. It was hampered by apathy and the unwillingness of those who played for safety by disapproval of any sort of new activity; and the weather of a most inclement summer dealt with it harshly. But planned and carried out handsomely and boldly, it bore an air of gaiety and chic, in colour and grace of proportion and festal lights. The dowdiness which had sodden two generations of Scottish national life was drying out, and the moribund country was cocking her bonnet again—an important step on the road to recovery.

Yet, if the sun flashed through, there were heavy clouds, on the horizon and sailing overhead. The Nazis, to hold their power, needed constant triumphs, and even before his march into Vienna, Hitler was cannily planning his next advance. Czecho-Slovakia was to be the victim, and already had done much to play into his hands by opposing that restoration of the Hapsburgs which might have stiffened Austria against him. And her three millions of Sudeten Germans allowed him to invoke, as we have seen, the principles of 'self-determination' and of 'racial unification.' His campaign, on lines that were to become familiar, began in February 1938. France was pledged to support the Czechs, and a speech of Chamberlain's was construed by these to mean Britain would do so. Hitler

---

[1] This improvement in courtesy, though perceptible, is not yet universal. Since this chapter was written an English M.P. has asked indignantly in Parliament : ' Is not Scotland England ? '

believed she could not; and already, by May, there was tension in
Europe and the threat of war.

The situation grew worse and worse all summer. Neville
Chamberlain sent Lord Runciman to Prague to mediate between the
Czech Government and the Sudetens. Still tension grew: and
German popular feeling, alike in the Reich and in the Sudetenland,
was whipped up again by incessant press and radio propaganda. By
early September the danger loomed close at hand. The British
Government, by way of the *Times*, suggested that German-speaking
Sudetenland should be handed to the Reich, as a compromise, since
Hitler declared that he had no other purpose than to free fellow-
Germans from foreign domination. The Czechs refused, for their
country's whole possibilities of defence depended on the possession
of these districts. By the 14th, Germany was on the point of
invasion: and France and Britain, both of them half-armed, were
confronted with a threat of general war.

Neville Chamberlain flew then to Berchtesgaden, and talked to
Hitler, who skilfully limited his claims, for the time, to areas with a
German majority. It cut the moral ground from under refusal.
France and Britain forced the Czech Government to consent . . .
and Chamberlain, returning to Hitler at Godesberg, found the terms
had risen. Hitler was now demanding more than these areas, and
within a fortnight: and he sent an ultimatum to the Czechs which
gave them a choice between immediate invasion and surrender of
all their defence. France was pledged to their aid: Britain promised
to stand by France, and the Navy was mobilised.

Then, as the hand ticked upward to the twelfth hour, Mussolini
and Neville Chamberlain once more contrived a conference of four
powers at Munich—Germany, France, Britain, and Italy, but not
Czecho-Slovakia. And Chamberlain returned to a cheering London
with what he called 'Peace in our time—peace with honour.' It was
not magnificent, but it was not war. Hitler had won the Sudetenland, as he had Austria, without a fight: and he had promised to
make no more territorial claims on Europe. Mr Churchill described
the incident bluntly enough as 'a total and unmitigated defeat':
others in Parliament agreed with him. A nation that was in no case
to fight a war settled thankfully, if uneasily, to peace, thought as
little further as possible of the Czechs, and believed that Hitler's
pledges would be fulfilled.

1939 began with optimism: the Government's speakers were

radiating hope, and pessimists were being damned as 'jitterbugs.'
Neville Chamberlain promised 'a more tranquil year,' and went with
Lord Halifax on a visit to Rome, where the Italians, who had no wish
for war, received him with cheers as the Saviour of Europe. This
was in January.

In March, Hitler seized what was left of the Czech Republic. In
April—he chose Good Friday for the attack—Mussolini did as much
for Albania. The British Government were on holiday, the British
Fleet scattered. Nothing could be done. Britain and France
accepted the *faits accomplis*. So far, Hitler had used no force but
the threat of force. France and Britain decided at last that the only
counter was a show of opposite force. The next victim, it was clear,
was going to be Poland, whose fall would uncover the Balkans, with
their great riches of oil, the food of war, and beyond them the road
to Suez and India. Poland therefore was added to the list of countries
Britain was pledged to defend: they now were France and Belgium
(by Locarno), Irak and Egypt; and to these in summer were added
also Rumania and Greece. And a glance at two things—the Army
strength and the map—was eloquent comment. In April the people,
rather than Parliament, forced a Conscription Act. In May, before
the new Armies could form threes, Hitler and Mussolini joined their
forces and made a military and political pact, and the Nazi propaganda machine was fuelled, and turned on Poland. But British and
French strength, it appeared, was growing. France had fortified her
eastern frontier, and no one appeared to be conscious of the fact that
the fortifications stopped at the Belgian march, which was guarded
only by Germany's guarantee. An agreement with Turkey strengthened British hands, and negotiations with Russia were in progress:
when on June 7th Neville Chamberlain declared that in fact an
agreement had been reached between Britain, France, and Russia,
for mutual help, his qualification, that some points relating to the
Baltic States had not yet been cleared up, seemed to matter little;
and it was very generally thought that the Balance of Power had, in
practice, been restored, and the prospect of war had, as result,
gone by.

The countries turned again to their own concerns. This final
lull before the storm was brief, but it lasted long enough to permit
to Scotland a rather interesting demonstration of the general attitude
of her governing body to her efforts for national recovery.

The new life, so far, had barely touched the Highlands: but their desperate condition was recognised, and the Economic Committee had set to work at a detailed investigation of their needs. After two years of close study, mainly by experts, their Commission reported, in spring 1939. It painted a grim picture of the Highlands —no grimmer than was warranted by the facts: but it was by no means uncheerful in its conclusion, for after very careful considerations it believed that this great area of Scotland, now derelict, could be set upon its feet at the cost of an annual grant, for the next ten years, of half a million pounds, or less, for the whole decade, than the cost of one of the smaller battleships.

In the midsummer of 1939, when the threat of war appeared to have been lifted, Parliamentary discussion was demanded in order to procure such legislation as might put these proposals into effect, or alternatively show cause for refusing constructive proposals by a group of experts who had given long study to a most serious problem. All the Highland County Councils, and such bodies as the Highland Development League and the Crofters' Association were backing the demand of the Committee, who themselves were men of influence and position: and a very general feeling was summed up by the County Convener for Ross and Cromarty, Major Stirling of Fairburn, who said publicly

This report must either be the beginning of a new phase in the Highlands, or the end of the Highlands themselves.

The Secretary for Scotland assured them all that their claim to debate the matter was recognised, and that the question would not be pigeon-holed. There was, none the less, a certain anxiety, for such assurances had become familiar: but on the 26th July the *Glasgow Herald* affirmed that

Scottish members interested in the problem (sic) do anticipate that the statement will indicate in a variety of ways the practical sympathy of the Government.

Debate was delayed, for the members of Parliament had the question of possible pensions for themselves to deal with: this matter, being of such vital importance, was given the full discussion it deserved. It was not, in fact, until the 1st of August, which was very nearly the eve of the recess, that time could be found to mention the Highland Report. However, on that day, five Scots members won places on the Question List. Unluckily, but an hour was allotted to questions: and by its end there had been no opportunity for any of the Scottish members to speak. The Secretary for Scotland, Mr Colville, began, however, to read a list of proposals based on the Report. (These, by the way, had cut down the proposed half million for ten years to £65,000 for five.) He was halfway through when an English member shouted ' Take it as read.' Mr Colville pointed out that for a long time there had been many questions on the subject, and that the Report was the fruit of two years detailed investigation, and dealt with urgent matters. Debate began. Scots members wished to speak. A great Scottish newspaper briefly records the scene.

The turmoil for a time was such that they had no opportunity of making their voices heard, and the Speaker had to intervene. He secured comparative quiet, but again the English members became restless, and finally the Speaker had to insist on going on to other business. The Scots members pleaded that one of their usual days had been taken from them by the Government, and that they would have no real opportunity for discussing what was to them an important question. One English member told them that they should demand Home Rule, and then they would be satisfied. The House, or rather the English part of it, very evidently did not want further questions of Mr Colville to occupy its time.

Permission, however, was won for debate to re-open on the 4th of August, the last day of the Session, and a full five-hour day was promised. The day came, and passed: when an hour of it was left, the debate was reached. Two members then spoke for twenty minutes apiece, and carefully avoided the points at issue. Mr Colville summed up then for eight minutes more, and the Speaker adjourned the House for the recess. Someone asked if a discussion could be arranged when the House re-assembled. He received no answer.

Parliament met again unexpectedly soon. On the 22nd August Russia announced that besides her negotiations with France and Britain, she had also, unknown to these countries, conducted others, with Germany and what now was its junior partner, Italy: and that it was these whom she had chosen as allies. And the German press and radio campaign against Poland blazed up with renewed intensity. The issues were plain now. Hitler's word was worthless. War was terrible, but it had now grown clear that there were some things worse even than war, to which war might be the sole alternative.

France and Britain, therefore, declared that they would fight if
Hitler invaded Poland. Suspense was brief. At dawn on the
1st September 1939, without sending any previous declaration, his
troops marched over the frontier of Poland, and his Luftwaffe fell
on Polish aerodromes. Britain and France presented a disregarded
ultimatum. As the church-bells fell silent on the 3rd September,
in golden autumn weather, we were at war.

That war, for Scotland as for the whole of the world, is still the
prime fact. It must end in victory, or civilisation and Christianity,
for Scotland in common with the whole of Europe, will end with it:
and victory will cost dear. Nor will mere victory save us when it
is won. In the last ten years our country has painfully struggled to
her feet. When the war ends, she will face that struggle once more,
and against worse odds than she faced in 1930.

Yet . . . the war will be the death of many Scots and the destruction of many Scottish homes. It will wreck the gallant new factories,
starve the fields. But it cannot wreck the novels of Neil Gunn, the
discoveries of the Rowett Institute. And it need not wreck the spirit
which in Scotland eight hundred years ago built a Scottish nation
from five chaotic and hostile little states; which faced overwhelming
foreign domination in 1306, overwhelming foreign attack in 1333,
1542, and 1547, or economic collapse in 1720. That ancient spirit,
in the nineteen-thirties, was rousing again: nor is it likely to perish,
so long as only a hundred of us stand. The danger, now, is grave
and terrible, and after the war it will be no less grave. But when
has Scotland ever been out of danger? And when, once they were
conscious of the danger, have her sons and daughters failed to rouse
and face it? If we act, in the confusions of our time, with the old
resolute and clear-sighted faith that long ago moved David I and
Robert Bruce, we can save our country in this crisis also. If we do
not so act, there will soon be no Scotland to save. The old choice
is offered again, to our fathers' children: and surely they will
answer, as did our fathers, with the old great battle-cry of

SCOTLAND YET

APPENDIX I

BATTLE HONOURS OF THE SCOTTISH REGIMENTS
BEFORE 1939

These 'official' Honours are not, of course, intended to give a complete account of any regiment's record. The War Office acknowledges, for instance, the claim of the Royal Scots to have taken part in no less than 230 battles and sieges.

CAVALRY
Royal Scots Greys.

Blenheim. Ramillies. Oudenarde. Malplaquet. Dettingen. Warburg. Willems. Waterloo. Balaclava. Sevastopol. Relief of Kimberley. Paardeberg. South Africa, 1899-1902. Retreat from Mons. Marne, 1914. Aisne, 1914. Ypres, 1914, 1915. Arras, 1917. Amiens. Somme, 1918. Hindenburg Line. Pursuit to Mons. France and Flanders, 1914-18.

INFANTRY
Scots Guards.

Namur, 1695. Dettingen. Lincelles. Talavera. Barrosa. Fuentes d'Onoro. Nive. Peninsula. Waterloo. Alma. Inkerman. Sevastopol. Tel el Kebir. Egypt, 1882. Suakin, 1885. Modder River. South Africa, 1899-1902. Retreat from Mons. Marne, 1914. Aisne, 1914. Ypres, 1914, 1917. Festubert, 1915. Loos. Somme, 1916, 1918. Cambrai, 1917, 1918. Hindenburg Line. France and Flanders, 1914-18.

Royal Scots.

Tangier, 1680. Namur, 1695. Blenheim. Ramillies. Oudenarde. Malplaquet. Louisburg. Havannah. Egmont op Zee. St Lucia, 1803. Corunna. Busaco. Salamanca. Vittoria. St Sebastian. Nive. Peninsula. Niagara. Waterloo. Nagpore. Maheidpore. Ava. Alma. Inkerman. Sevastopol. Taku Forts. Pekin, 1860. South Africa, 1899-1902. Le Câteau. Marne, 1915, 1918. Ypres, 1915, 1917, 1918. Loos. Somme, 1916, 1918. Arras, 1917, 1918. Lys. Struma. Gallipoli, 1915-16. Palestine, 1917, 1918.

Royal Scots Fusiliers.

Blenheim. Ramillies. Oudenarde. Malplaquet. Dettingen. Martinique, 1794. Bladensburg. Alma. Inkerman. Sevastopol. South Africa, 1879. Burma, 1885-87. Tirah. Relief of Ladysmith. South

Africa, 1899-1902. Mons. Marne, 1914. Ypres, 1914, 1917, 1918. Somme, 1916, 1918. Arras, 1917, 1918. Lys. Hindenburg Line. Doiran, 1917, 1918. Gallipoli, 1915-16. Palestine, 1917-18.

King's Own Scottish Borderers.

Namur, 1695. Minden. Egmont op Zee. Martinique, 1809. Afghanistan, 1878-80. Chitral. Tirah. Paardeberg. South Africa, 1899-1902. Mons. Aisne, 1914. Ypres, 1914, 1915, 1917, 1918. Loos. Somme, 1916, 1918. Arras, 1917, 1918. Soissons. Ourcq. Hindenburg Line. Gallipoli, 1915-16. Gaza.

Cameronians (Scottish Rifles).

Blenheim. Ramillies. Oudenarde. Malplaquet. Mandora. Corunna. Martinique, 1809. Guadeloupe, 1810. South Africa, 1846-7. Sevastopol. Lucknow. Abyssinia. South Africa, 1877-8-9. Relief of Ladysmith. South Africa, 1899-1902. Mons. Marne, 1914, 1918. Neuve Chapelle. Somme, 1916, 1918. Ypres, 1917, 1918. Hindenburg Line. Macedonia, 1915-18. Gallipoli, 1915-16. Palestine, 1917-18.

Black Watch.

Guadeloupe, 1759. Martinique, 1762. Havannah. North America, 1763-4. Mangalore, Mysore. Seringapatam. Corunna. Busaco. Fuentes d'Onoro. Pyrenees. Nivelle. Nive. Orthes. Toulouse. Peninsula. Waterloo. South Africa, 1846-7, 1851-2-3. Alma. Sevastopol. Lucknow. Ashantee, 1873-4. Tel el Kebir. Egypt, 1882-4. Kirbekan. Nile, 1884-5. Paardeberg. South Africa, 1899-1902. Marne, 1914, 1918. Ypres, 1914, 1917, 1918. Loos. Somme, 1916-18. Arras, 1917-18. Lys. Hindenburg Line. Doiran, 1917. Megiddo. Kut el Amara, 1917.

Argyll and Sutherland Highlanders.

Cape of Good Hope, 1806. Roliça. Vimiera. Corunna. Pyrenees. Nivelle. Nive. Orthes. Toulouse. Peninsula. South Africa, 1846-7, 1851-2-3. Alma. Balaclava.[1] Sevastopol. Lucknow. South Africa, 1879. Modder River. Paardeberg. South Africa, 1899-1902. Mons. Le Câteau. Marne, 1914, 1918. Ypres, 1915, 1917, 1918. Loos. Somme, 1916, 1918. Arras, 1917, 1918. Cambrai, 1917, 1918. Doiran, 1917, 1918. Gaza.

Seaforth Highlanders.

Carnatic. Hindoostan. Mysore. Cape of Good Hope, 1806. Maida. Java. South Africa, 1835. Sevastopol. Koosh-ab. Persia. Lucknow. Central India. Peiwar Kotal. Charasiah. Kabul, 1879. Kandahar,

---

[1] The only infantry regiment to bear this honour.

1880. Afghanistan, 1879-80. Tel el Kebir. Egypt, 1882. Chitral. Atbara. Khartoum. Paardeberg. South Africa, 1899-1902. Marne, 1914, 1918. Ypres, 1915, 1917, 1918. Loos. Somme, 1916, 1918. Arras, 1917, 1918. Vimy, 1917. Cambrai, 1917, 1918. Valenciennes. Palestine, 1918. Baghdad.

Gordon Highlanders.

Mysore. Seringapatam. Egmont op Zee. Mandora. Corunna. Fuentes d'Onoro. Almaraz. Vittoria. Pyrenees. Nive. Orthes. Peninsula. Waterloo. South Africa, 1835. Delhi, 1857. Lucknow. Charasieh. Kabul, 1879. Kandahar, 1880. Afghanistan, 1879-80. Tel el Kebir. Egypt, 1882-4. Nile, 1884-5. Chitral. Tirah. Ladysmith. Paardeberg. South Africa, 1899-1902. Mons. Le Câteau. Marne, 1914, 1918. Ypres, 1914, 1915, 1917. Loos. Somme, 1916, 1918. Ancre, 1916. Arras, 1917, 1918. Cambrai, 1917, 1918. Vittorio Veneto.

Queen's Own Cameron Highlanders.

Egmont op Zee. Corunna. Busaco. Fuentes d'Onoro. Salamanca. Pyrenees. Nivelle. Nive. Toulouse. Peninsula. Waterloo. Alma. Sevastopol. Lucknow. Tel el Kebir. Egypt, 1882. Nile, 1884-5. Atbara. Khartoum. South Africa, 1899-1902. Marne, 1914, 1918. Aisne, 1914. Ypres, 1914, 1915, 1917, 1918. Neuve Chapelle. Loos. Somme, 1916, 1917. Delville Wood. Arras, 1917, 1918. Sambre. Macedonia, 1915-18.

Highland Light Infantry.

Carnatic. Hindoostan. Sholinghur. Mysore. Seringapatam. Cape of Good Hope, 1806. Roliça. Vimiera. Corunna. Busaco. Fuentes d'Onoro. Ciudad Rodrigo. Badajoz. Almaraz. Salamanca. Vittoria. Pyrenees. Nivelle. Nive. Orthes. Toulouse. Peninsula. Waterloo. South Africa, 1851-2-3. Sevastopol. Central India. Tel el Kebir. Egypt, 1882. Modder River. South Africa, 1899-1902. Mons. Ypres, 1914, 1915, 1917, 1918. Somme, 1916, 1918. Arras, 1917, 1918. Hindenburg Line. Gallipoli, 1915-16. Palestine, 1917-18. Mesopotamia, 1916-18. Archangel, 1919.

Scotsmen have served with honour in all branches of the Artillery, in the Royal Engineers, the Royal Tank Corps, the Machine-gun Corps, the Royal Army Medical Corps, the Royal Army Service Corps, the Royal Navy, and the Royal Air Force : but there are no Scottish regular units of these.

APPENDIX II

RACIALISM AND NATIONALISM

As many Nationalists, in Scotland as elsewhere, agree with Herr Hitler in confusing these, and as such confusion is a potent danger, it is perhaps wise to consider the concrete facts, by examining a typical case in detail.

To prevent offence, I will take that of myself. Like many Highlanders, I can trace my descent for a distance long enough to provide good data—that is, for a matter of thirty-nine generations, to a man who was pretty certainly a Gael. But each of these thirty-nine generations married, and their thirty-nine wives had all descents of their own, and no less than their husbands they transmitted their blood to all the descendants who came after them. Admittedly the wives of the first generations are impossible to trace, with one exception : and she, being a daughter of Rollo of Normandy, was certainly more Norse than anything else. From the middle thirteenth century, however, to my own mother, all of them are known : and as until the later seventeenth they were wives of chiefs, their various pedigrees are easy to trace in reasonable detail, and often for a considerable distance, which includes those of their ancestors' wives as well. The data so provided make it clear that to the original Gaelic-Celtic stock was added in time a various infusion of Pict, Brython-Celtic, Angle, Dane, Frank, and Norse, Scoto-Norman, Anglo-Norman, Picard, Fleming, English, Northern and Southern French, High German, Spanish, Hungarian, and Russian—not to mention three saints, a deity, and the Devil. I cannot be sure of the two last-mentioned lines, though there is some evidence as regards the last in the conduct of his alleged immediate descendants : his ethnological character, however, would not be a simple matter to establish.

Nor is mine. The briefest description would seem to be ' tartan.' Assuredly, I am a Highland Scot, born, bred, and descended, if anybody is. But seventeen peoples at least have gone to make me. And this shocking lack of racial purity is not confined to members of my own clan. Indeed, we are probably nearer to ' the Celt ' than many other Highlanders today : the direct male line of our descent, at least, does run back to a man one can call a Gael. A MacLeod, MacAulay, MacDonald, MacDougall, or Fraser who can trace a descent from the line

27   397

of the chiefs of his clan is surely to be called a Highland Scot : yet the origin of the first two lines is Norse, and the second two derive from Somerled, who may have been either a Norseman or a Gael, but most probably was a mixture of the two, while the ancestral Fraser was a Fleming.

To be sure, a descent from the former chiefs of one's clan may be held—is held by an ancient Highland convention—to bring one within the limits of ' the gentry ' : and by those brought up on the pure milk of Marx, the place of these in a nation is contested. But I fear the conscientious proletarian is not racially in much superior case. He may be pure Gael, pure German, or pure What-have-you : one certainly cannot prove that he is not. Nor, however, can he himself prove that he is : and in view of the possibilities involved in the incessant invasions and settlements which make up so great a part of the history of Europe in the fifth, sixth, seventh, eighth, ninth, tenth, and eleventh centuries (without counting those of pre-historic times) there seem to be rather sizeable odds against it.

What is true of Scotland is true of all the world. Certain black tribes of Central Africa are no doubt purer than any race in Europe. But if, on the whole surface of the globe, there is such a thing as a pure race today, it is the Australian Aborigines, the expression to whom of Herr Hitler's profound respect has somehow or other not yet been forthcoming. Still, if Herr Hitler, or anybody else, should be moved in time to require armorial bearings for a Racial Purity Society, there could be no symbol more appropriate than the characteristic weapon of these people—say two Aryans rampant holding a boomerang proper.

BIBLIOGRAPHY

Only a small selection of books on European and general British political history has been given, but those marked * contain full and excellent bibliographies of their subject. Books on Scottish political and ecclesiastical history, 1720-1748, will be found in the bibliography attached to the Author's *The Passing of the Stewarts*.

The Cambridge Modern History, Volumes VI-XII.
J. A. R. Marriott. *A History of Europe : 1815-1923*.
Winston Spencer Churchill. *World Crisis*.
Arthur Bryant. *Unfinished Victory*.
John Macintosh. *The Paths that led to War*.
*Stephen King-Hall. *Our Own Times : 1913-1938*.
J. A. Spender. *Great Britain : Empire and Commonwealth. 1886-1935*.
P. Hume Brown. *A History of Scotland*. Vol. III.
*Basil Williams. *The Establishment of the Hanoverians : 1714-60*.
*G. S. Veitch. *The Reign of George III : 1760-1815*.
*E. L. Woodward. *The Age of Reform : 1815-70*.
*R. C. K. Ensor. *England : 1870-1914*.
D. W. Brogan. *The Development of Modern France : 1870-1939*.
Sir Alexander MacEwen. *Towards Freedom*.
Journals of the House of Commons.
Journals of the House of Lords.
T. C. Hansard. *Parliamentary Debates*.
Sir John Sinclair. *A Statistical Account of Scotland*. (1791-99.)
A New Statistical Account of Scotland. (1845.)
James Mackinnon. *The Union of England and Scotland*.
P. Hume Brown. *The Legislative Union of England and Scotland*.
H. W. Meikle. *Scotland and the French Revolution*.
H. Grey Graham. *Social Life in Scotland in the 18th Century*.
R. Pococke. *Tours in Scotland. 1747-1750-1760*.
T. Pennant. *Tours in Scotland. 1769-1772*.
E. Topham. *Letters from Edinburgh. 1774-5*.
W. Cobbett. *A Tour in Scotland. 1832*.
Sir John Clerk. *Memoirs. 1676-1755*.
George Lockhart. *The Lockhart Papers*.
John Ramsay of Ochtertyre. *Scotland and Scotsmen in the 18th Century*.
Dean Ramsay. *Reminiscences of Scottish Life and Character*.
Lord Cockburn. *Memorials of His Time. 1778-1850*.
   Journal. 1831-54.
W. C. Mackenzie. *Andrew Fletcher of Saltoun*.

George Menary. *Life and Letters of Duncan Forbes of Culloden.*
W. R. Scott. *Francis Hutcheson.*
J. Hill Burton. *Life and Correspondence of David Hume.*
B. M. Laing. *David Hume.*
Hector Macpherson. *Adam Smith.*
J. A. Lovat Fraser. *John Stewart Earl of Bute.*
Oliphant Smeaton. *Allan Ramsay.*
J. A. Lovat Fraser. *Henry Dundas, Viscount Melville.*
A. Fergusson. *The Hon. Henry Erskine.*
Harold W. Thompson. *A Scottish Man of Feeling : some account of Henry Mackenzie . . .*
Keith Henderson. *Burns—by Himself.*
A. F. Tytler. *Memoirs of the Hon. Henry Home of Kames.*
J. G. Lockhart. *Life of Scott.*
Stephen Gwynn. *The Life of Sir Walter Scott.*
John Buchan. *Sir Walter Scott.*
Stephen Gwynn. *Mungo Park.*
W. Knight. *Lord Monboddo.*
Elsie Swann. *Christopher North.*
Jennie W. Aberdein. *John Galt.*
J. P. Muirhead. *James Watt.*
H. W. Dickinson. *James Watt.*
Andrew Lang. *Life and Letters of J. G. Lockhart.*
James Ferguson. *Letters of George Dempster to Sir Adam Ferguson.*
Sir Alexander Gibb. *The Story of Telford.*
W. G. Blackie. *Thomas Chalmers.*
Eve B. Simpson. *Sir J. Y. Simpson.*
H. Grey Graham. *Scottish Men of Letters of the 18th Century.*
Sir James Caw. *Scottish Portraits.*
C. R. L. Fletcher and Emery Walker. *Historical Portraits : 1700-1850.*
Martin Martin. *Description of the Western Islands.*
James Boswell. *Journal of a Tour to the Highlands.*
Samuel Johnson. *A Journey to the Western Islands.*
Mrs Grant of Laggan. *Memoirs and Correspondence. 1755-1838.*
Elizabeth Grant of Rothiemurchus. *Memoirs of a Highland Lady : 1792-1830.*
David Stewart. *Sketches of the Highlanders. 1822.*
Osgood Mackenzie. *A Hundred Years in the Highlands.*
Frank Adam. *The Clans, Septs, and Regiments of the Scottish Highlands.*
W. C. Mackenzie. *The Highlands and Islands of Scotland.*
I. F. Grant. *Everyday Life on an old Highland Farm : 1769-1782.*
Alexander Mackenzie. *A History of the Highland Clearances.*
J. P. Maclean. *An Historical Account of the Settlement of Scotch Highlanders in America prior to . . . 1783.*
D. F. Macdonald. *Scotland's Shifting Population : 1770-1850.*
J. Hill Burton. *The Scot Abroad.*
A. Dewar Gibb. *Scottish Empire.*
A. Bellesheim. *A History of the Catholic Church in Scotland.*

BIBLIOGRAPHY

401

J. Cunningham. *The Church History of Scotland.*
George Grub. *The Ecclesiastical History of Scotland.*
A. J. Campbell. *Two Centuries of the Church of Scotland : 1707-1929.*
Anthony Mitchell. *Scotland's Church.*
T. Brown. *Annals of the Disruption.*
J. Kerr. *Scottish Education, School and University, to 1908.*
J. Mason. *A History of Scottish Experiments in Rural Education.*
J. Strong. *A History of Secondary Education in Scotland.*
J. H. Millar. *A Literary History of Scotland.*
Magnus Maclean. *The Literature of the Highlands.*
Alexander Carmichael. *Introduction to Carmina Gadhelica.*
John Tonge. *The Arts of Scotland.*
Sir James Caw. *Scottish Painting Past and Present.*
W. D. Mackay. *The Scottish School of Painting.*
A. T. Bolton. *The Architecture of Robert and James Adam.*
Sir John Stirling Maxwell. *Shrines and Homes of Scotland.*
James MacLehose. *The Glasgow University Press.*
James Mackinnon. *Social and Industrial History of Scotland.*
I. F. Grant. *The Economic History of Scotland.*
W. H. Marwick. *The Economic Development of Scotland.*
    Economic Developments in Victorian Scotland.
Henry Hamilton. *The Industrial Revolution in Scotland.*
    The Economic Evolution of Scotland.
A. Birnie. *An Economic History of the British Isles.*
Thomas Johnston. *A History of the Working Classes in Scotland.*
A. W. Kerr. *A History of Banking in Scotland.*
Neil Munro. *A History of the Royal Bank of Scotland.*
R. S. Rait. *A History of the Union Bank of Scotland.*
A. A. Cormack. *Poor Relief in Scotland.*
J. D. Mackie and G. S. Pryde. *Local Government in Scotland.*
Sir William Whyte. *Local Government in Scotland.*
R. D. McEwan. *Old Glasgow Weavers.*
Sir J. B. Marwick. *Glasgow : the Water Supply and various Developments . . . to 1900.*
Sir D. M. Stevenson (introd.). *Municipal Glasgow.*
George Blake. *Down to the Sea.*
John Buchan and J. Stewart. *The 15th (Scottish) Division.*
F. W. Bewsher. *A History of the 51st Division.*
R. R. Thompson. *The 52nd Lowland Division. 1914-18.*
Wilfrid Ewart. *The Scots Guards in the Great War.*
John Ewing. *The Royal Scots. 1914 18.*
John Buchan. *A History of the Royal Scots Fusiliers. 1678-1918.*
A. G. Wauchope. *A History of the Black Watch in the Great War.*
A. E. J. Cavendish. *The 93rd Highlanders. 1797-1927.*
J. M. Finlay. *With the 8th Scottish Rifles.*
M. M. Haldane. *A History of the 4th Seaforths.*
J. H. Lindsay. *The London Scottish in the Great War.*
I. Elmslie Hutton. *With a Women's Unit in Serbia and Salonika.*

Eva S. Maclaren. *A History of the Scottish Women's Hospitals.*
Edwin Muir. *Scottish Journey.*
Moray Maclaren. *Return to Scotland.*
G. Malcolm Thomson. *The Re-discovery of Scotland.*
Cicely Hamilton. *Modern Scotland.*
Colin Walkinshaw. *The Scots Tragedy.*
G. Malcolm Thomson. *Scotland, That Distressed Area.*
A. Dewar Gibb. *Scotland in Eclipse.*
R. M. Finlay. *Scotland at the Cross-roads.*
John Torrence. *Scotland's Dilemma.*
Glasgow Sunday Post. Scotland : Some Facts and Figures.
William Power. *Scotland and the Scots.*
Sir Alexander MacEwen. *The Thistle and the Rose.*
H.M. Stationery Office. *Report of the Committee on Scottish Administration.*
C. de B. Murray. *How Scotland is Governed.*
W. O. Brown. *Scotland and Westminister.*
A. Dewar Gibb. *The Shadow on Parliament House.*
Scottish National Party. *Self-government in Practice.*
Sir Alexander MacEwen. *Scotland at School.*
P.E.P. *The State of the Highlands.*
Scottish Economic Committee. *The Highlands and Islands of Scotland.*
J. P. Day. *Public Administration in the Highlands and Islands of Scotland.*
H.M. Stationery Office. *Report of the Committee on Scottish Health Services, 1936.*
Pilgrim Trust. *Men without Work.*
Sir George Newman. *The Building of a Nation's Health.*
C. A. Oakley. *Scottish Industries Today.*
P.E.P. *Report on Internal Trade.*
H.M. Stationery Office. *Report of the Committee for Special Areas in Scotland.*
Scottish Economic Committee. *Light Industries in Scotland.*
Scotland's Industrial Future.
Scottish Development Council. *Reports : Economic Series.*
Clydesdale Bank. *Annual Surveys of Economic Conditions.*
Peter F. Anson. *The Sea Fisheries of Scotland.*
H.M. Stationery Office. *Reports of the Department of Agriculture for Scotland.*
Reports on the Profitableness of Farming in Scotland.
Report of the Committee on Agricultural Co-operation.
P.E.P. *Report on Agricultural Research in Great Britain.*
Sir R. G. Stapledon. *The Land, Now and Tomorrow.*
The Hill Lands of Britain.
P.E.P. *Report on the Location of Industries in Britain.*
Board of Trade. *Survey of Industrial Developments.*
A. Plummer. *New British Industries in the 20th Century.*

Julian Huxley. *Scientific Research and Social Needs.*
J. D. Bernal. *The Social Function of Science.*
W. A. Robson. *Public Enterprises.*
Catherine Blair. *Rural Journey.*
Alan Reiach and Robert Hurd. *Building Scotland.*
C. R. M. F. Cruttwell. *A History of Peaceful Change in the Modern
    World.*
Scottish Liberal Federation. *A Policy for Scotland.*
Sir Alexander MacEwen and J. Lorne Campbell. *Act Now for the High-
    lands and Islands.*
Lachlan Grant. *A New Deal for the Highlands.*
Hugh Quigley. *A Plan for the Highlands.*
Thomas Burns. *Plan for Scotland.*
Alexander MacLehose. *The Scotland of our Sons.*
J. A. Bowie. *The Future of Scotland.*
Colin Walkinshaw. *Prospect for Scotland.*
*The Northern Countries in World Economy—Denmark, Finland, Iceland,
    Norway, and Sweden.*
M. Cole and C. Smith, ed. *Democratic Sweden.*
Bjarne Braatov. *The New Sweden.*
Marquis W. Childe. *Sweden, The Middle Way.*
Karl Fischer. *Norway Today.*
Agnes Rothery. *Denmark.*
Harold Westergaard. *Economic Developments in Denmark.*
The Danish Year Book.
Files of *The Scotsman, The Glasgow Herald, Scotland, The Modern Scot,
    Outlook, The Scots Magazine, The S.M.T. Magazine, The Scottish
    Standard, The Scots Independent,* and *The Sea Leaguer.*

INDEX

Abercrombie, Sir R., 130
Aberdeen, 31, 36, 50, 103, 181, 332
Aboukir, 127, 130
Abyssinia, 367
Adam, R., 36, 64, 210
Adamson, M. R., 375
Africa, 271, 276, 294, 306
Agnew, Major, 131
Agricultural Holdings Act, 159
Agricultural Society, 10
Agriculture, 9, 98, 157, 257, 334, 378
Agriculture, Board of, 98, 259
Aikman, W., 37
Airdrie, 145
Aitken, J., 199
Aiton, W., 13
Aix la Chapelle, Peace of, 59
Albert, Prince, 214
Alison, Dr, 248, 251
Alison, Sir A., 53, 200
Alness, Lord, 238
America, 5, 20, 50, 59 seq., 67 seq., 103, 137, 312, 317, 354
Amiens, Peace of, 131
Anaesthetics, 198
Anderson, A. O., 201, 375
Anderson, J., 45
Anderson, Sir R., 211
Angus, M., 374
Anti-Burghers, 49, 92
Archer, W., 202
Architecture, 36, 86, 210, 372
Ardnamurchan, 379
Argyll, Dukes of, 12, 43, 56, 386
Argyll and Sutherland Highlanders, 308, 395
Armour, M., 372
Arts, 32, 83, 203, 371
Ashley, Lord, 250, 251
Asquith, H. H., 227, 234, 240, 241, 308
Assaye, 134
Assembly, General, see Church
Associate Synod, 48, 92
Assynt, 259
Atheism, 47
Atholl, Duchess of, 338
Auchmuty, General, 136
Auld Lichts, 92
Australia, 274
Austria, 58 seq., 70, 128 seq., 139 seq., 285 seq., 364, 369
Aviation, see Flying
Ayr, 7, 14
Ayrshire Development Council, 383
Aytoun, W. E., 204

Baillie, J., 84
Bain, A., 200
Baird, Sir D., 127, 136, 276

Baird, J. L., 329
Baldwin, Earl, 356, 366
Balfour, A. J., 200, 240, 269, 297
Balfour, Earl of, see Balfour, A. J.
Balkan Wars, 299
Banks, 16, 19, 97, 156, 335
Bannatyne Club, 83
Baptist Church, 93
Barclay de Tolly, Prince, 141
Barrie, Sir J. M., 204, 206
Barron, E. M., 201, 266
Beatty, Admiral, 305, 309
Begg, Rev. J., 220, 251
Belgium, 149, 150, 283, 304 seq.
Belhaven, Lord, 10
Bell, A. G., 169
Bell, H., 104
Bell, T., 21
Benes, Dr, 356
Berlin Decrees, 137
Berlin, Peace of, 293
Berry, W., 36
Béthune, 315
Bicycle, 168
Billings, R. W., 210
Birnie, A., 377
Birrell, A., 238, 240, 241
Black, J., 22, 26, 32, 81, 168
Black Watch, The, 123, 395
Blackie, Lord Provost, 251
Blackwood, W., 84
Blackwood's Magazine, 84
Blaikie, T., 13
Blair, C., 379
Blairs College, 184
Blake, G., 375
Blantyre, 278
Boer War, 296
Bonaparte, see Napoleon
Bonar, G., 381
Bone, J., 372
Bone, Sir M., 210
Bone, P., 372
Bone, S., 372
Bonnymuir, 146
Boswell, J., 82
Botha, General, 306, 308, 309
Bough, S., 209
Boulton, M., 26
Bowie, J. A., 331, 381
Boyle, G., 279
Braid, J., 199
Brandane, J., 371
Braxfield, Lord, 120
Brest-Litovsk, Treaty of, 314, 353
Brewster, Sir D., 199
Brewster, Rev. P., 217
Briand, A., 354, 356
Bridie, J., 371

Bright, J., 245
Brisbane, Sir T., 275
British Broadcasting Corporation, 329
Brown, G. D., 206
Brown, P. Hume, 200, 220, 242
Browning, Professor C. H., 199
Bruce, N., 382
Bruce, Sir W., 36
Bryce, D., 211
Buchan, J., 375
Buchanan, D., 33
Buchanan, G., 345
Bucharest, Treaty of, 315, 353
Bulgaria, 292, 308, 317
Burdett, Sir F., 144
Burghers, 49, 92
Burke, E., 65, 68
Burn, W., 87
Burnett, Sir J. J., 372
Burns, J., 256
Burns, R., 33, 83
Burton, J. H., 200
Bute, Earl of, 62, 63, 64
Bute, Marquis of, 377

Cadell, F. C. B., 210
Caird, Principal, 186
Calder, Sir R., 135
Cameron, A., 375
Cameron, D., 43
Cameron, Sir D. Y., 210
Cameron, K., 372
Cameron, L., 277
Campbell, Principal, 93
Campbell, A., 97, 217, 256
Campbell, Sir C., 281
Campbell, C., 36
Campbell, Sir G., 236
Campbell, Rev. J., 113
Campbell, R., 273
Campbell, T., 82, 88
Campbell, T., 210
Campbell-Bannerman, Sir H., 226, 240,
    241, 269
Camperdown, 127
Camperdown, Viscount, see Duncan
Canada, 62, 63, 69, 71, 272
Canals, 24, 105, 165
Canning, G., 138
Cape of Good Hope, 136, 149, 276
Cape St Vincent, 126
Caporetto, 313
Carlyle, T., 201
Carmichael, A., 207
Carnegie Trust, 192, 329, 331
Carron Ironworks, 22, 26, 102
Cassie, A. B. D., 384
Cat and Mouse Act, 229
Catholic Church, Roman, see Church of
    Rome
Central Film Library, 329
Ceylon, 131, 149
Chalmers, Rev. T., 177, 248
Chamberlain, A., 344, 356
Chamberlain, J., 296
Chamberlain, N., 389
Chambers of Commerce, 21
Chambers, Messrs, 84, 376
Chambers, R., 84, 185

Chambers, W., 84, 251
Chambers, Sir W., 36
Chanda, 186
Chapple, Dr, 242
Charles Edward, Prince, 49
Charter, People's, 217
Chartists, 217
Chemical industry, 22, 160
Chesterton, G. K., 289
Children, 113, 172, 250, 253, 332; see also
    Education
China, 285, 361
Chisholm, E., 373
Christison, Sir R., 199
Church of America, Episcopal, 50
Church of England, 50, 93, 94, 182
Church of Rome, 50, 93, 95, 184, 188, 190,
    325
Church of Scotland, Episcopal, 49, 93, 181,
    186, 188, 190, 325
Church of Scotland, Established, 47, 88,
    90, 177, 188, 190, 324
Churchill, W. S., 228, 305, 307, 366, 389
Cinematograph, 328
Clapperton, H., 278
Clark, G. P., 238, 239
Clearances, 43, 111, 173, 258
Cleghorn, H., 131
Clerk, J., 12
Clyde, Lord, 281
Clynes, J. R., 241
Coal, 7, 22, 102, 160
Cobden, R., 245
Cochrane, Admiral, 140
Cockburn, A., 10
Cockburn, J., 10
Cockburn, Lord, 144, 147, 217
Code of Canons, 95
Coigeach, 112
Colville, Mr, 392
Combinations Acts, 144, 147
Communications, see Canal, Post, Rail-
    ways, Shipping, Telegraph
Communism, 232
Communities, Religious, 183, 184, 185
Comte, A., 30
Congested Districts Board, 259
Congregationalism, 93
Connell, Sir I., 158
Conservatives, 113, 225, 237, 241, 243,
    338; see also Tories
Constable, A., 84
Constitutional Associate Presbytery, 92
Constitutional Society, 120
Consultative Church Council, 184
Convention of Cintra, 139
Convention of Royal Burghs, 16, 220, 340
Cook, Captain, 274
Co-operative Societies, 97
Coote, Sir E., 70
Corn Laws, 245
Coronel, 306
Corrie, J., 371
Coruña, 139
Cotton, 20, 100, 160
Courier, The, 113
Cowan, Sir W. H., 242, 344
Cowie, J., 372
Craig, Sir J., 276

Craigie, Sir W. A., 202
Crawford, D., 239
Crimean War, 287
Crofters' Associations, 380, 391
Crofters' Commission, 258, 259
Crofters' Holdings Act, 258
Crozier, W. J., 372
Cullen, W., 32
Cumberland, Duke of, 44, 61, 66
Cunningham, A., 274
Cunningham, J., 201
Currie, Captain, 274
Curzon, Comte A. de, 117
Curzon, Marquis, 354
Czecho-Slovakia, 369, 388

Daer, Lord, 120
Dalhousie, Marquis of, 281
Dalrymple, A., 279
Dalrymple, Colonel, 120
Dalrymple, Sir H., 138
Dalziel, Sir H., 241, 242
Danton, G. J., 118
Darwin, C. R., 185
Davidson, C., 281
Davidson, J., 204
Davie, C. T., 373
Daviot, G., 371
Dawes Loan, 355
Deas-Thomson, E., 274
Death-rate, 253 ; see also Children
Declaration of (American) Independence, 69
Deer Drive, 259
Deer Forests, 174, 259
Deism, 47
Dempster, G., 45, 110
Denmark, 70, 129, 130, 138, 149
Denny, Messrs, 104, 255
Dewar, Sir J., 199
Disarmament Conference, 364
Disraeli, B., 221, 224, 250, 255, 270, 271, 293
Disruption, 177
Donaldson, Sir S. A., 275
Douglas, Lord A., 204
Douglas, J., 273
Douglas, Sir J., 63
Douglas, N., 375
Drama, 33, 48, 204, 371
Dudley, D., 22
Duguid, J., 375
Duncan, Admiral, 126, 127
Duncan, John, 210
Duncan, Jonathan, 280
Dundas, H., 45, 46, 57, 76
Dundee, 100, 107, 159, 183, 192, 246, 252, 332, 381
Dundee Advertiser, The, 128
Durham, Earl of, 270
Duthie Experimental Farm, 378
Dyce, A., 202
Dyce, W., 86

Economic History, see Banks, Finance, Trade
Economics, Dundee School of, 381
Edinburgh, 14, 21, 32, 36, 81, 87, 107, 160, 171, 227, 246, 251, 332, 348, 381

Edinburgh Review, The, 84
Education, 28, 31, 88, 187, 254, 325, 326, 349
Education Department, 189, 190, 327
Edward I and VII, 215, 234, 267, 297
Edward II and VIII, 387
Eglinton, Earl of, 12
Egypt, 127, 130, 294, 306, 355
Electricity, 167, 253
Elgin, Earls of, 273, 382
Eliott, General, 70
Elizabeth, Queen, 387
Ellice, R., 151, 273
Elliot, A., 87
Elliot, J., 33
Elliot, W., 349
Elphinstone, Admiral, 276
Elphinstone, M., 280
Emigration, 43, 44, 111, 173, 257, 269, 331
Empire, British, 5, 59, 63, 67, 71, 131, 269, 294, 342 ; see also Emigration
Employers and Workmen Act, 255, 256
Employers' Liability Act, 249
Encyclopaedia Britannica, 181, 185
Engineering, 22, 24, 25, 103, 105, 161, 333, 385
England, 5, 13, 18, 20, 22, 27, 35, 36, 49, 50, 54, 63, 82, 93, 95, 97, 98, 99, 101, 104, 106, 114, 115, 116, 122, 130, 144, 145, 147, 151, 156, 161, 169, 172, 173, 174, 182, 187, 189, 193, 212, 217, 222, 223, 234, 236, 245, 248, 253, 255, 263, 269, 278, 323, 331, 332, 333, 335, 340, 349, 376, 388, 392
Erskine, Hon. H., 124
Erskine, Hon. R., 345
Ewen, J., 75
Exhibition, Glasgow, 373, 388

Factory legislation, 113, 250, 251
Falkland Isles, 306
Fenwick, 97
Ferguson, J. A., 371
Fergusson, R., 33
Ferrier, S., 84
Fettes College, 195
Fiction, see Literature
Fife, Earl of, 236
Finance, 4, 13, 16, 96, 155, 335, 382 ; see also Banks
Financial Trust Co., 382
Findlater, Earl of, 12
Finlay, G., 200
Fisheries, 7, 45, 99, 334, 381
Fitch, J., 103
Flag, Scottish, 261, 267, 388
Fleming, S., 274
Fletcher, A., 10, 11
Flying, 168, 330
Foch, Marshal, 315
Folk-schools, 377
Forbes, Bishop A. P., 183, 186
Forbes, D., 15, 43
Forestry, 12, 380
Forrest, J., 275
Forsyth, W., 13
Foulis, R. and A., 21
Foulis, Dr R., 251
Fox, C. J., 76, 125, 134

France, 25, 30, 31, 34, 37, 41, 58 *seq.*, 72 *seq.*, 116, 125 *seq.*, 148 *seq.*, 168, 273, 283 *seq.*, 303 *seq.*, 320, 354 *seq.*, 388 *seq.*
Franchise, 74, 144, 150, 215, 337
Fraser, Mrs Kennedy, 208
Fraser, J., 217
Fraser, S., 273
Frazer, Sir J. G., 200
Frederick II, 58, 201
Free Church, 179, 186, 188, 190, 326
Free Presbyterians, 326
Friends of the People, 120, 122

Gaelic, *see* Languages *and* Literature
Galashiels, 160
Gallipoli, 307
Galloway, 12
Galt, J., 84, 273
Gardens, 13
Gas, 161
Geddes, A., 86
Geddes, Sir P., 199
Geikie, Sir A., 199
General Associate Synod, 92
Geneva, Conference of, 360
Geneva Protocol, 356
Geology, 32
George II, 56
George III, 49, 62, 63
George IV, 146, 148, 213
George V, 215, 387
George VI, 310, 387
George, D. Lloyd, 228, 241, 299, 308, 344, 351, 354
Germany, 58 *seq.*, 118, 121, 136 *seq.*, 283, 285 *seq.*, 303 *seq.*, 320, 351 *seq.*, 388, 392
Gerrald, T., 122
Gibb, Professor A. D., 282
Gibbs, J., 36
Gibraltar, 69, 70
Gillespie, T., 47
Gillies, W. G., 372
Gladstone, W. E., 183, 221, 222, 225, 240, 241, 255, 269, 293, 294
Glasgow, 11, 14, 20, 21, 24, 28, 32, 100, 103, 107, 145, 150, 162, 167, 171, 198, 209, 217, 246, 251, 252, 332, 344, 381
Glasgow Herald, The, 391
Glasgow Missionary Society, 276
Glasgow Orpheus Choir, 373
Glasgow Trades Council, 97
Gleig, Bishop, 181
Glenalmond, 183, 195
Golbourne, M., 25
Goodchild, Sir W., 349
Gordon, Duke of, 12
Gordon Highlanders, 310, 396
Graham, G., 87
Graham, R. B. Cunninghame, 206, 233, 238, 347
Graham, Sir T., 142
Grant, Sir H., 281
Grant, I. F., 377
Grant, J. A., 277
Grant, J. A. W., 373
Grant, J. M., 275
Grant, N., 371
Grant, P., 86
Greece, 293, 308, 355

Green, J. R., 289
Greig, Admiral, 141
Grenville, G., 67
Grey, Sir E., 226, 228
Grierson, Sir H., 183, 202
Grierson, J., 329
Gunn, N., 375
Guthrie, Dr, 186
Gwynn, S., 341

Haddington, Earl of, 10, 11
Haig, Earl, 306, 312, 315
Hailes, Lord, 35
Haldane, J. and R., 93
Haldane, J. S., 200
Haldane, Viscount, 200, 269, 297
Hamilton, Lord A., 146, 147
Hamilton, Sir D., 86
Hamilton, D., 86
Hamilton, G., 37
Hamilton, H., 377
Hamilton, Sir I., 307
Hamilton, T., 86
Hannah Research Station, 379
Hardie, K., 233, 241
Hawick, 160, 171
Hawick Technical Institute, 383
Hazebrouck, 315
Heligoland Bight, 305
Henderson, A., 361
Henderson, K., 372
Henry Benedict, Prince, 49, 93
Henry, G., 210, 372
Highland Development League, 383, 391
Highland Light Infantry, 134, 396
Highland Society, 45, 158
Highlands, 18, 39, 57, 110, 188, 257, 378, 380, 383, 391; *see* Language *and* Literature
Hill, R., 169
Hillingdon, 382
History, *see* Literature
Hitler, A., 364, 388, 392
Holland, 5, 70, 126, 128, 137, 149, 283, 321
Home Rule, Irish, *see* Ireland
Home Rule, Scottish, *see* Nationalism
Home Rule Association, 238, 344
Hong Kong, 285
Hope-Scott, J., 183
Hopetoun, Earl of, 275
Hornel, E. A., 210
Housing, 171, 251, 333
Howe, J., 86
Howe, Lord, 70
Hume, D., 29, 68, 81
Hume, Lady G., 33
Hume, H., 274
Hume, J., 147, 245
Hunt, Dr, 35
Hunter, General A., 278
Hunter, L., 201
Hunter, W. and J., 32
Hurd, R., 373
Hutcheson, F., 28
Hutton, J., 32, 81
Hymnary, The Church, 181

Illegitimacy, 173
Income-tax, 246, 248

India, 59, 62, 70, 127, 132, 271, 279, 287, 342
Industry, 15, 100, 159, 333, 335, 381
Infant Mortality, see Children
Infant School Society, 89
Inglis, Captain, 127
Insh, G. P., 375
Irish, 125, 128, 130, 147, 171, 235, 246, 249, 341
Iron, 22, 26, 102, 160
Italy, 31, 127, 149, 285, 288, 291, 292, 308, 313, 355, 357, 361, 368, 389, 392

Jackson, P., 371, 372
Jacobites, 8
Jameson, L., 277
Jameson, W., 280
Jamieson, J., 83
Japan, 296, 297
Jebb, Sir R., 202
Jeffrey, F., 81, 83, 150
Jeffrey, W., 374
Johnson, S., 11, 40
Johnston, A. K., 277
Johnston, T., 238, 349
Johnstone, J., 344
Jolly, Bishop, 94
Jones, P., 70
Justice, J., 13
Jute, 100, 159
Jutland, 310

Kames, Lord, 12
Kant, I., 30
Kellett, E. E., 204
Kelvin, Lord, 199
Ker, W. P., 202
Kew, 13
Kipling, R., 271
Kirkcaldy, 160
Kirke, J., 278
Kirkpatrick, A., 280
Kyd, R., 280

Labour Exchanges, 249
Labour Party, 233, 241, 256, 338, 344, 361
Laing, A. G., 279
Laird, M., 279
Lamb, M., 372
Land Court, 259
Lang, A., 200, 202, 265
Lang, J. D., 275
Languages, 34, 40, 41, 81, 83, 208, 272, 274, 328, 374
Lauderdale, Earl of, 117
Lausanne, Conference of, 355
Lavery, Sir J., 209
Law, A. Bonar, 269
Law de Lauriston, General, 139
League of Nations, 352 seq.
Leaving Certificate, 190
Lewis, 208, 259, 348
Liberal Federation, 346
Liberal Party, 113, 159, 219, 221, 228, 234, 241, 243, 245, 247, 270 ; see also Whigs and names of leaders
Licensing Act, 339
Light Industries, 21, 384
Lighting, 161, 253

Lindesay, P., 15, 18
Linen, 7, 15, 18, 100, 159
Linklater, E., 375
Lister, Lord, 198
Literature, 32, 83, 200, 374
Liturgy, English, 94
Liturgy, Presbyterian, 181
Liturgy, Scottish, 50, 94
Livingstone, D., 276
Livingstone, W., 207
Livingstonia, 278
Local Government Acts, 239, 249, 327, 348
Local Government Board, 237, 239
Locarno, Pact of, 356
Loch, D., 20
Loch, Sir H., 277
Lochhead, M. C., 374
Lockhart, G., 7
Lockhart, J. G., 84
Lockhart, Sir W., 281
London, Conference of, 361
London Corresponding Society, 120
London, Treaty of, 341
Long, W., 344
Loos, 308
Loretto School, 195
Lorimer, Sir R., 211
Lothian, Marquis of, 378
Loudoun, Earl of, 12
Lyon King of Arms, 267
Lys, 315

McAdam, J. L., 105
Macarthur, J., 275
Macaulay Institute, 378
Macaulay, Lord, 200, 204, 271
Macaulay, T. B., 378
McBey, J., 372
MacColl, E., 207
MacCormick, J. M., 347
McCrie, Rev. T., 91, 92
McCulloch, H., 209
McCulloch, J. R., 147
MacCunn, H., 208
MacDiarmaid, H., 374
Macdonald, A., 207
MacDonald, A., 221, 233, 256
Macdonald, Sir C., 279
Macdonald, G., 205
Macdonald, Sir G., 200
Macdonald, Sir H., 278
Macdonald, Sir J., 273
Macdonald, J. A. M., 344
MacDonald, J. R., 241, 339, 345, 356, 367
Macdonald, Sir M., 328
MacDougall, W., 199
MacEwen, Sir A., 347
MacEwen, Sir W., 198
Macfie, R. C., 204
MacGibbon, D., 210
MacGillivray, P., 210
McGlashan, A. A., 372
MacGregor, J., 86
MacGregor, T., 75, 76
MacGregor, Sir W., 275
MacGregor, Rev. W. M., 326
Macgregor, W. Y., 210
MacGrigor, Sir J., 88
McIlwraith, Sir T., 275

Macintosh, C., 20
Macintosh, C. R., 211
Macintosh, Sir J., 117
Macintyre, D. Bàn, 33
Mackay, Æ., 376
Mackay, R. Donn, 33
Mackechnie, D. C., 347
Mackellar, M., 207
Mackenzie, A., 273
Mackenzie, Sir A., 208
Mackenzie, C., 206
Mackenzie, Sir G., 278
Mackenzie, H., 34, 45, 82, 117
Mackenzie, Sir J., 199
Mackenzie, J. (New Zealand), 275
Mackenzie, J. (Africa), 277
Mackenzie, L., 273
Mackenzie, M., 211
Mackenzie, W., 104
Mackenzie, W. C., 40, 43, 201
McKinlay, J., 274
Mackinnon, Sir W., 278
MacLachlan, E., 86
MacLachlan, J., 207
M'Laren, Mrs, 225
M'Laren, D., 220
Maclaren, I., 206
Maclaurin, C., 31
MacLean, Sir D., 275
Maclean, D., 11
Maclean, J., 86
McLellan, R., 371
Macleod, F., 207
McLeod, J., 273
Macleod, Rev. N., 185
McLoughlin, J., 273
MacMhaighstir Alasdair, A., 33
McMillan, A., 274
Macphail, D., 207
Macpherson, C., 281
Macpherson, I., 242
Macpherson, I., 375
Macpherson, J., 34
Macquarie, L., 275
McQueen, Sir J., 281
McTaggart, J. S., 200
McTaggart, W., 210
MacTaggart, W., 372
MacWhirter, J., 209
Maida, 136
Mair, Miss, 225
Maitland Club, 83
Malcolm, J., 280
Malta, 127, 132, 149
Mann, T., 256
Mansfield, Earl of, 64
Manson, Sir P., 199, 279
Margarot, M, 122
Marine Biology Station, 381
Marne, 305, 316
Martin, M., 39
Marwick, W. H., 343, 377
Marx, K., 231
Master and Servant Act, 255
Maxwell, Sir G., 281
Maxwell, Sir H., 266
Maxwell, Sir J., 113, 217
Maxwell, Sir J. C., 199
Mealmaker, G., 126, 128

Mears, F. C., 373
Medical Service Board, 259
Medicine, 32, 198
Meikle, A., 11
Melville, Viscount, see Dundas
Merchiston Castle School, 195
Messines, 312
Methodism, 51, 93
Militia, 56, 126
Mill, J. S., 200, 224
Millar, Professor J. H., 84
Millar, R., 371
Miller, G., 217
Miller, Mrs H., 372
Miller, J., 373
Miller, P., 103
Milne, MacL., 372
Minto, Earl of, 280
Missions, 186, 276, 278
Mitchell, Major, 274
Mitchison, N., 375
Moffat, Rev. R., 276
Monarchy, 65, 212, 387
Monboddo, Lord, 32
Moncrieff, C. K. S., 374
Monro, H., 204
Monroe, A., 32
Mons, 305
Montgomerie, W., 374
Montrose, Duke of, 344, 346, 347
Moonie, W. B., 374
Moore, Sir J., 130, 139
Moray Press, 376
More, J., 37
Morison, D., 374
Morison, J., 280
Morrison, J., 86
Morrison, N. B., 375
Motor car, 168, 330
Mountstephen, Lord, 274
Muir, E., 374
Muir, J., 202
Muir, Sir R., 199
Muir, T., 120
Muir, W., 374, 375
Muirhead, R. E., 347
Municipal Reform, 76, 146, 147, 151
Munich, 389
Munro, H. H., 206
Munro, J., 207
Munro, N., 206
Munro, T., 280
Murray, General, 62, 63
Murray, C., 207
Murray, Sir G., 344
Murray, Sir J., 202
Muschet, D., 103
Music, 35, 87, 208, 373
Mussolini, B., 355, 389 seq.

Napier, D., 104
Napier, J., 104
Napier, Lord, 281
Napier, R., 104
Napoleon, 122, 124, 127 seq.
Nasmyth, A., 37
Nasmyth, J., 161
National Conventions, 237, 347
National Development Council, 382

National Library, 328
National Party, 347
National Trust, 377
Nationalism, 235, 260, 285, 288, 292, 343, 361, 377, 387, 397
Neill and Co., 21
Neill, Colonel, 281
Neilson, J., 103
Neilston, 145
Nelson, Lord, 126, 135, 136
Neuve Chapelle, 307
New English Dictionary, 202
New Zealand, 226, 275
Nicholson, J., 281
Nightingale, F., 287
Niven, F., 375
Normal Colleges, 89, 190
North, C., 84
North, Lord, 68
Norway, 70, 129, 149
Nutrition, 9, 378

Oakley, C. A., 382
Ochterlony, Sir D., 280
O'Connell, D., 217
O'Connor, D., 217
Ogston, Sir A., 199
Old Age Pensions Act, 249
Old Lights, see Burghers
Oliphant, Mrs, 205
Oliver, J., 375
Oliver and Boyd, Messrs, 21, 376
Orchardson, Sir W. Q., 209
Original Associate Synod, 92, 180
Original Secession, 92, 180
Orr, C., 375
Orr, Sir J., 378, 383
Orthodox Churches, 325
Ossian, 34
Ovens, Major, 274
Owen, R., 230
Oxford Movement, 182

Pagan, T., 83
Painting, 36, 86, 209, 372
Paisley, 19, 20, 101, 171
Palmerston, Viscount, 52, 150, 276, 283
Pankhurst, Mrs, 226
Paris, Peace of, 63
Paris, Treaty of, 142
Parish Councils, 249
Park, M., 278
Parliament Act, 235
Parliament, Scots, 53, 65, 240
Parliament, Westminster, 7, 44, 55, 68, 71, 74, 75, 95, 99, 113, 117, 120, 122, 125, 144, 147, 150, 156, 159, 174, 178, 189, 190, 191, 215, 222, 233, 234, 235, 243, 324, 326, 327, 333, 334, 338, 341, 343, 351, 366, 367, 391
Passchendaele, 312
Pasteur, L., 198
Paterson, W., 276
Peel, Sir R., 113, 246, 248, 250
Penal Laws, 49, 50, 93, 95, 183
People's Leagues, 219
Peploe, S. J., 210
Philip, J., 276
Phillip, J., 209

Pilcher, P. S., 168
Pirie, D. V., 241
Pitt, W. (elder), 61, 68
Pitt, W. (younger), 72, 119, 125, 131, 132, 134, 136
Place, F., 147
Playfair, W. H., 86
Poetry, see Literature
Poincaré, R., 354
Poland, 290, 390, 393
Poor relief, 115, 248
Population, 15, 107, 110, 253, 257, 259, 331 ; see also Emigration
Portree, 258
Portugal, 138
Postal system, 168
Pottery, 21
Power, W., 374
Prayer-book, Scottish, 184, 325
Pringle-Pattison, A. S., 200
Printing, 21, 160, 384
Private Legislation Procedure Act, 241
Prussia, see Germany
Psalm tunes, 181
Public Health, 172, 332
Public Schools, English, 193
Public Schools, Scottish, 195
Publishing, 84, 376

Quarterly Review, The, 84

Race and nation, 260, 289, 361, 397
Radicals, 145, 217, 221, 270
Radio, 328
Raeburn, Sir H., 86
Railway, 23, 106, 162, 166, 335, 339
Railway Act, 339
Rait, Sir R., 242
Ramsay, A. (elder), 33
Ramsay, A. (younger), 37
Ramsay, Sir J., 200
Ramsay, Sir W., 199
Ramsay, Sir W. M., 200
Rankine, W. J. M., 199
Rattray, T., 282
Recreation, 173, 253
Reform, see Franchise
Reform Acts, 151, 221, 222, 338
Reformed Presbyterians, 48, 92, 180, 326
Reid, G. H., 275
Reid, T., 30, 31, 117
Relief Synod, 49, 180
Rennie, G., 275
Rennie, J., 103
Representation of the People Act, 338
Representative Church Council, 184
Roads, 23, 105, 166
Roberts, D., 209
Robertson, E. W., 201
Robertson, Sir G. S., 281
Robertson, J. L., 207
Robertson, Principal, 35, 81, 93, 117
Rockingham, Marquis of, 68
Rodney, Lord, 70
Roebuck, J., 22, 26
Rorie, Dr, 207
Rosebery, Earl of, 201, 235, 269
Ross, H., 281

Ross, Sir J., 281
Ross, Sir R., 199, 279
Ross, T., 210
Rothes, Earl of, 12
Rousseau, J. J., 30, 34, 73
Rowett Institute, 378
Royal Army Medical Corps, 88
Royal Scots, 308, 310, 331, 394
Rumania, 293, 310, 353
Runciman, A., 37
Ruskin, J., 201, 210
Russell, Lord J., 82, 150, 219, 247, 250
Russia, 61, 85, 128, 129, 130, 137, 140,
    287, 290, 291, 293, 297, 299, 303 seq.,
    353, 390, 392
Rutherford, Lord, 199

Saintsbury, G., 34, 183
Salisbury, Marquis of, 258
Salters, Bound, 57
Saltire Society, 376, 377
Sandeman, Sir R., 281
San Sebastian, 142
School Boards, 189
Schools, see Education
Science, 21, 25, 31, 87, 198, 378, 381, 384
Scotland, 382
Scotsman, The, 145, 246
Scott, A. M., 242
Scott, D., 86
Scott, F. G., 373
Scott, G. B., 375
Scott, Sir W., 81, 85, 97, 146
Scott, W. B., 204
Scottish Art Review, 210
Scottish Dialect Dictionary, 328
Scottish Economic Committee, 383, 391
Scottish Industrial Estates, 382
Scottish Motor Traction Co., 330
Scottish National Party, 347
Scottish Office, 237, 241, 339, 348
Scottish Orchestra, 373
Scottish Party, 347
Scottish Patriotic Society, 258
Scottish Theatre Society, 371
Scougall, J., 37
Sculpture, 36, 86, 210, 372
Seabury, Bishop, 50
Seaforth Highlanders, 134, 395
Seceders, 48, 92, 180, 326
Secretary for Scotland, 56, 237
Selkirk, Earl of, 273
Sempill, Lord, 117
Separated Congregations, 94
Serbia, 293, 304 seq.
Seth, A., 200
Seven Years War, 61
Shepherd, N., 374, 375
Sheridan, R. B., 76
Shiels, E., 171
Shipping, 24, 103, 162, 333
Sidgwick, Mrs H., 225
Silk, 19
Simon, Sir J., 363
Simpson, D., 375
Simpson, Sir J. Y., 198
Simpson, M. W., 374
Simson, R., 31

Simson, W., 209
Sinclair, Sir J., 98, 99
Skene, W. F., 207
Skinner, Dean, 33, 49
Skinner, J., 183
Skirving, A., 33
Skye, 112
Slavery, 6, 245, 276, 277
Slessor, M., 279
Small Burghs Committee, 348
Small, J., 11
Smeaton, J., 24
Smith, A., 29, 68, 75
Smith, A. B., 375
Smith, B. L., 224
Smith, J., 157
Smith, W. R., 185
Smollett, T., 34
Snowden, Viscount, 361
Social Democratic Federation, 234
Socialism, 229, 243
Socialist Labour Party, 234
Society for the Propagation of Christian
    Knowledge, 188
Society of Scottish Artists, 209
Soil Research Institute, 378
Somme, 310, 315
Sorley, Professor, 29
Sorley, W. R., 200
Soudanese War, 294
Soutar, W., 374
South of Scotland Technical College, 160
Spain, 69, 85, 138, 368
Spence, L., 374
Spenser, E., 341
Stafford, Marquis of, 111
Standing Committee, 241
Steam-power, 22, 25, 101
Steel, 23, 161, 333
Stephenson, G., 106
Stevenson, Sir D. M., 347
Stevenson, F., 225
Stevenson, M., 372
Stevenson, R. L., 205
Stewart, B., 199
Stewart, D., 82, 117, 124
Stewart, General, 112
Stewart, Mr Henderson, 349
Stewart, H. D., 371
Stewart, J., 280
Stirling, 346
Stirling, J. H., 200
Stirling, Major, 391
Stockings, 19
Stowe, D., 89
Stowe, Mrs H. B., 111
Strachan, D., 211
Strachan, Sir R., 136, 140
Strange, R., 37, 64
Strathcona, Lord, 274
Stuart, McD., 275
Sturdee, Admiral, 306
Suffrage, see Franchise
Surgery, see Medicine
Sutherland, A., 233
Sutherland, D. M., 372
Sweden, 70, 129, 137, 140, 149
Syme, D., 275
Symington, W., 103

Tait, T., 372
Tariffs, 246
Tassie, J., 36
Taylor, J., 217
Taylor, R. A., 205
Tea, 280
Telegraph, 169
Telephone, 169
Television, 329
Telford, T., 105
Terry, C. S., 183
Texel, 126, 128
Textiles, 7, 15, 18, 100, 159, 383, 384
Thermos flask, 199
Thompson, H., 33
Thomson, Sir A., 199
Thomson, G. M., 375, 377
Thomson, James (elder), 34
Thomson, James (younger), 204
Thomson, John, 209
Thomson, Joseph, 277
Thomson, L. G., 373
Tibet, 279
Tilsit, Treaty of, 137
Timber, 7, 12 ; see also Forestry
Times, The, 112, 274
Tobacco, 14, 20
Tories, 65, 113, 148, 221 ; see Conservatives
    and names of leaders
Torry Marine Laboratory, 381
Torry Research Station, 381
Toulouse, 142
Trade, see Finance and Industry
Trade Unions, 144, 147, 249, 255, 344
Trades Councils, 256
Trafalgar, 136
Training Centres, 190
Trams, 167
Tranent, 126
Transport, Ministry of, 340
Traquair, P., 372
Treasury, 57, 237, 349
Trent, Lord, 379
Triple Guarantee, Treaty of, 354
Turkey, 285, 306, 352
Tweeddale, Marquis of, 12
Tyre, Pneumatic, 168
Tytler, P. F., 83

Unemployment, see Industry
Union, Treaty of, 4, 5, 16, 94, 146, 147,
    240, 343
United Free Church, 180, 324
United Original Seceders, 92, 180, 325, 326
United Presbyterians, 180
United Scotsmen, 126, 128
United Secession Church, 180
Universities, 183, 190, 191, 192, 327, 381

Verdun, 309
Versailles, Treaty of, 352

Veterinary College, 158
Victoria, 213, 286
Vienna, Congress of, 142, 148
Vimiera, 138
Vimy, 312
Vitoria, 142
Voltaire, F. M. A. de, 30, 72
Volunteers, 124, 134
Vote, see Franchise

Wade, General, 23
Wages Board, 340
Walcheren, 140
Wallace, R., 169
Walpole, H., 63
Walton, C., 372
Wasborough, M., 26
Waterloo, 142
Water-supply, 172, 252
Watson, J., 33
Watson, Sheriff, 113
Watt, J., 23, 25
Watt, R., 123
Wee Frees, 180 ; see Free Church
Weekes, J., 373
Welfare Schemes, 255
Wellesley, see Wellington
Wellington, Duke of, 138, 142, 148
Welsh, Rev. D., 179
Wesley, J., 51
Westminster Confession, 89, 91, 92
Westminster, Statute of, 343
Whalen, T., 372
Whigs, 52, 65, 72, 84, 148, 150, 216 ; see
    also Liberals
White, Rev. J., 324
Whyte, J., 375
Wick, 99
Wilkes, J., 66
Wilkie, Sir D., 86, 209
William III and IV, 148, 151, 213
Wilson, A. P., 371
Wilson, J., 84
Wilson, J., 209
Wingate, Sir R., 278
Wintour, J. C., 209
Witches, 10
Wollstonecraft, M., 223
Women's Movement, 222, 337
Women's Rural Institutes, 379
Wood, Major, 344
Wood, M., 375
Wool, 99, 102, 160
Workmen's Compensation Act, 249
Works Schools, 255

Yorktown, 70
Young Scots Society, 344
Ypres, 306, 308, 312